WORSHIP
IN ANCIENT ISRAEL

Its Forms and Meaning

10
09

SPCK Large Paperbacks

WORSHIP
IN ANCIENT ISRAEL

Its Forms and Meaning

H. H. ROWLEY

Edward Cadbury Lectures
delivered in the University of
Birmingham

LONDON

S·P·C·K

First published in 1967
First paperback edition 1976
Fifth impression 1981
SPCK
Holy Trinity Church, Marylebone Road
London NW1 4DU

Made and printed in Great Britain at
The Camelot Press Ltd, Southampton

ISBN 0 281 02956 3

TO
ARTUR WEISER
IN FRIENDSHIP AND ESTEEM
THIS VOLUME IS
INSCRIBED

Contents

Acknowledgements

Thanks are due to the following for permission to quote from copyright sources:

The Clarendon Press, Oxford: an article by H. Wheeler Robinson in *The Psalmists*, edited by D. C. Simpson; an article by H. Wheeler Robinson in the *Journal of Theological Studies XLIII* (1942); *The Psalter*, by A. C. Welch; *Sacrifice in the Old Testament*, by G. B. Gray.

Darton, Longman & Todd Ltd and McGraw-Hill Book Company: *Ancient Israel: Its Life and Institutions*, by R. de Vaux.

Hodder & Stoughton Ltd: *Introduction to the Old Testament*, by E. Sellin.

Oxford University Press and Harvard University Press: *Judaism in the First Centuries of the Christian Era*, by G. F. Moore.

S.C.M. Press Ltd and Fortress Press: *The Faith of the Psalmists*, by H. Ringgren.

University of Wales Press: *Sacral Kingship in Ancient Israel*, by A. R. Johnson.

Preface

It is my pleasant duty first to express my thanks to Birmingham University for the honour of the invitation to deliver the Edward Cadbury Lectures in the Spring term of 1965 and to Professor J. G. Davies and other members of the staff for all the kindness I received at their hands during my weekly visits.

The text of my lectures as delivered and as here published is almost unchanged, but in the footnotes I have shared with my readers some of the material on which the lectures were based. I can claim to have read only a small part of the literature relevant to my subject, but I have tried to acquaint myself with the views of other scholars before forming my own, though I have tried to bring an independent judgement to the material and at a number of points have reached conclusions which many of my colleagues would reject. Where there is so much variety of opinion among scholars it is impossible to agree with everyone, and I am often compelled to disagree with colleagues whose learning I greatly admire and from whom I have learned more than I can ever adequately acknowledge. While in the text of the lectures I have expressed my own views on the questions examined and the reasons which have led me to them, I have not attempted to conceal from the reader who is sufficiently interested to study the footnotes that there are other views, often supported by weighty names. It is my hope that I may have stimulated interest in an aspect of Old Testament study which has been for too long neglected, and which is to-day commanding the increasing attention of scholars, but which is still but little noticed by the wider circle of students of the Bible.

To the patience of my wife, who for several months endured the disarray of her drawing room, to which I transferred some hundreds of books during the preparation of this work, I would pay tribute. I would also express warm thanks to my former secretary, Mrs Ann Kelly, who typed the work for the printer. Her skill in deciphering my writing and in following the snakes and ladders that filled the pages of the footnotes, developed during the years I spent in Manchester, is undiminished, and is a source of wonder even to me.

Stroud, Glos.   H. H. ROWLEY
17 November 1965

Abbreviations

A.A.S.O.R. Annual of the American Schools of Oriental Research
  A.f.O. Archiv für Orientforschung
    A.I. R. de Vaux, *Ancient Israel: its Life and Institutions*, E. Tr. by J. McHugh, 1961
 A.J.S.L. American Journal of Semitic Languages and Literatures
  A.J.Th. American Journal of Theology
 A.N.E.T. Ancient Near Eastern Texts relating to the Old Testament, ed. by J. B. Pritchard, 2nd edn, 1955
   Ant. Josephus, *Antiquitates Judaicae*
  A.R.I. W. F. Albright, *Archaeology and the Religion of Israel*, 3rd edn, 1953
 A.R.W. Archiv für Religionswissenschaft
 A.S.T.I. Annual of the Swedish Theological Institute
 A.T.D. Das Alte Testament Deutsch
  A.V. Authorized Version
  B.A. Biblical Archaeologist
B.A.S.O.R. Bulletin of the American Schools of Oriental Research
  B.C. The Beginnings of Christianity, ed. by F. J. Foakes-Jackson and K. Lake, 5 vols., 1920–33 (vol. i, 1942 printing)
 B.D.B. Brown, Driver, and Briggs, *Hebrew and English Lexicon*, 1906
 B.D.E. H. H. Rowley, *The Biblical Doctrine of Election*, 1950
 Bi.Or. Bibliotheca Orientalis
  B.J. Josephus, *De Bello Judaico*
B.J.R.L. Bulletin of the John Rylands Library
  B.L. Book List of the Society for Old Testament Study
  B.Q. Baptist Quarterly
 B.R.L. K. Galling, *Biblisches Reallexikon*, 1937

B.Z.	*Biblische Zeitschrift*
B.Z.A.W.	Beihefte zur *Zeitschrift für die alttestamentliche Wissenschaft*
C.A.H.	*Cambridge Ancient History*, ed. by J. B. Bury, S. A. Cook, F. E. Adcock, 12 vols., 1923–39
C.B.Q.	*Catholic Biblical Quarterly*
C.R.A.I.	*Comptes rendus de l'Académie des Inscriptions et Belles Lettres*
D.A.C.	*Dictionary of the Apostolic Church*, ed. by J. Hastings, 2 vols., 1915–18
D.B.	*Dictionary of the Bible*, or *Dictionnaire de la Bible*
D.C.G.	*Dictionary of Christ and the Gospels*, ed. by J. Hastings, 2 vols., 1906–8
D.O.T.T.	*Documents from Old Testament Times*, ed. by D. Winton Thomas, 1958
E.B.	*Encyclopaedia Biblica*, ed. by T. K. Cheyne and J. S. Black, 4 vols., 1899–1903
E.Brit.	*Encyclopaedia Britannica*
E.G.T.	*Expositor's Greek Testament*, ed. by W. Robertson Nicoll, 5 vols., 1897–1910
Echt.B.	*Echter Bibel, Altes Testament*, ed. by F. Nötscher, 5 vols., 1955–60
E.R.E.	*Encyclopaedia of Religion and Ethics*, ed. by J. Hastings, 13 vols., 1908–26
Est. Bib.	*Estudios Bíblicos*
E.T.	*Expository Times*
E.Th.L.	*Ephemerides Theologicae Lovanienses*
E.Th.R.	*Études Théologiques et Religieuses*
E. Tr.	English translation
Exp.	*Expositor*
F.S.A.C.	W. F. Albright, *From the Stone Age to Christianity*, 2nd edn, 1946
G.J.V.	E. Schürer, *Geschichte des jüdischen Volkes im Zeitalter Jesu Christi*, 4th edn, 4 vols., 1901–11
G.S.A.I.	*Giornale della Società Asiatica Italiana*
G.V.I.	*Geschichte des Volkes Israel*
H.E.	Sozomen, *Historia Ecclesiastica*
H.J.P.	E. Schürer, *History of the Jewish People*, E. Tr. by J. Macpherson, S. Taylor, and P. Christie, 6 vols., 1890–8

H.T.R.	*Harvard Theological Review*
H.U.C.A.	*Hebrew Union College Annual*
I.B.	*Interpreter's Bible*, 12 vols., 1952–7
I.D.B.	*Interpreter's Bible Dictionary*, 4 vols., 1962
I.E.J.	*Israel Exploration Journal*
I.M.W.	H. H. Rowley, *Israel's Mission to the World*, 1939
J.A.O.S.	*Journal of the American Oriental Society*
J.B.L.	*Journal of Biblical Literature*
J.B.R.	*Journal of Bible and Religion*
J.E.	*Jewish Encyclopedia*, ed. by I. Singer, 12 vols., 1907 edn
J.E.O.L.	*Jaarbericht Ex Oriente Lux*
J.J.	H. H. Rowley, *From Joseph to Joshua*, 1950
J.M.U.E.O.S.	*Journal of the Manchester University Egyptian and Oriental Society*
J.N.E.S.	*Journal of Near Eastern Studies*
J.P.O.S.	*Journal of the Palestine Oriental Society*
J.Q.R.	*Jewish Quarterly Review*
J.R.	*Journal of Religion*
J.R.A.S.	*Journal of the Royal Asiatic Society*
J.S.S.	*Journal of Semitic Studies*
J.T.S.	*Journal of Theological Studies*
K.A.T.	E. Schrader, *Die Keilinschriften und das Alte Testament*, 3rd edn, ed. by H. Zimmern and H. Winckler, 1903
K.B.	L. Koehler and W. Baumgartner, *Lexicon in Veteris Testamenti libros*, 1953
L.O.T.	S. R. Driver, *Introduction to the Literature of the Old Testament*, 9th edn, 1913
L.Th.K.	*Lexikon für Theologie und Kirche*, 10 vols., 1957–65
LXX	Septuagint Version
M.G.	H. H. Rowley, *Men of God*, 1963
M.G.W.J.	*Monatsschrift für Geschichte und Wissenschaft des Judenthums*
M.M.O.T.	H. H. Rowley, *The Missionary Message of the Old Testament*, 1945
M.Q.	H. H. Rowley, *From Moses to Qumran*, 1963
M.T.	Masoretic Text
M.U.S.J.	*Mélanges de l'Université de Saint-Joseph*
N.B.D.	*New Bible Dictionary*, ed. by J. D. Douglas, 1962

Ned. T.T.	*Nederlands Theologisch Tijdschrift*
N.F.	Neue Folge
N.S.	New Series
Nor. T.T.	*Norsk Teologisk Tidsskrift*
N.R.Th.	*Nouvelle Revue Théologique*
N.S.I.	G. A. Cooke, *Textbook of North Semitic Inscriptions*, 1903
N.T.T.	*Nieuw Theologisch Tijdschrift*
O.L.Z.	*Orientalistische Literaturzeitung*
O.T.J.C.	W. Robertson Smith, *The Old Testament in the Jewish Church*, 1907 edn
O.T.M.S.	*The Old Testament and Modern Study*, ed. by H. H. Rowley, 1951
O.T.S.	*Oudtestamentische Studiën*
P.A.A.J.R.	*Proceedings of the American Academy for Jewish Research*
P.E.F.Q.S.	*Quarterly Statement of the Palestine Exploration Fund*
P.E.Q.	*Palestine Exploration Quarterly*
P.R.E.	*Realencyklopädie für protestantische Theologie und Kirche*, 2nd edn, ed. by J. J. Herzog and G. L. Plitt, 18 vols., 1877–88; 3rd edn, ed. by A. Hauck, 24 vols., 1896–1913
P.S.B.A.	*Proceedings of the Society of Biblical Archaeology*
R.Ass.	*Revue d'Assyriologie et d'Archéologie orientale*
R.B.	*Revue Biblique*
R.E.	*Realencyklopädie der classischen Altertumswissenschaft*, ed. by A. Pauly, G. Wissowa, W. Kroll, 1894– (in progress)
Rel.B.	H. H. Rowley, *The Relevance of the Bible*, 1942
R.G.G.	*Die Religion in Geschichte und Gegenwart*, ed. by F. M. Schiele and L. Zscharnack, 5 vols., 1909–13; 2nd edn, ed. by H. Gunkel and L. Zscharnack, 6 vols., 1927–32; 3rd edn, ed. by K. Galling, 7 vols., 1957–65
R.H.P.R.	*Revue d'Histoire et de Philosophie religieuses*
R.H.R.	*Revue de l'Histoire des Religions*
R.o.B.	*Religion och Bibel*
R.O.T.	H. H. Rowley, *The Rediscovery of the Old Testament*, 1946

R.S.V.	Revised Standard Version
R.Th.Ph.	Revue de Théologie et de Philosophie
R.V.	Revised Version
S.B.U.	Svenskt Bibliskt Uppslagsverk, ed. by I. Engnell and A. Fridrichsen, 2 vols., 1948–52
S.D.B.	Supplément au Dictionnaire de la Bible, ed. by L. Pirot, A. Robert, H. Cazelles, A. Feuillet, 1928– (in progress, vol. vii, 1966)
S.E.Å.	Svensk Exegetisk Årsbok
S.L.	H. H. Rowley, The Servant of the Lord, 2nd edn, 1965
St.Th.	Studia Theologica
S.T.U.	Schweizerische Theologische Umschau
S.V.T.	Supplements to Vetus Testamentum
Syr.	Syriac Version
T.B.	Babylonian Talmud
T.G.U.O.S.	Transactions of the Glasgow University Oriental Society
Th.L.Z.	Theologische Literaturzeitung
Th.R.	Theologische Rundschau
Th.W.B.	Theologisches Wörterbuch zum Neuen Testament, ed. by G. Kittel and G. Friedrich, 1932– (in progress, vol. vii, 1964, 4th Lieferung of vol. viii, 1966); E. Tr. by G. W. Bromiley, 1964– (in progress, vol. iii, 1966)
Th.Z.	Theologische Zeitschrift
T.S.K.	Theologische Studien und Kritiken
U.B.	H. H. Rowley, The Unity of the Bible, 1953
U.J.E.	Universal Jewish Encyclopedia, ed. by I. Landman, 10 vols., 1939–43
V.T.	Vetus Testamentum
W.O.	Die Welt des Orients
Z.A.W.	Zeitschrift für die alttestamentliche Wissenschaft
Z.D.M.G.	Zeitschrift der deutschen morgenländischen Gesellschaft
Z.D.P.V.	Zeitschrift des deutschen Palästinavereins
Z.S.T.	Zeitschrift für systematische Theologie
Z.Th.K.	Zeitschrift für Theologie und Kirche
Z.W.Th.	Zeitschrift für wissenschaftliche Theologie

1

Worship in the Patriarchal Age

In choosing my subject for the Edward Cadbury lectures I thought it well to name one which would help me to clarify my own thought on a question which has increasingly claimed the attention of scholars in recent years. In some of the older works on the religion and theology of Israel relatively little was said on the cultus. So recently as in 1946 Millar Burrows wrote in his *Outline of Biblical Theology*: "Large areas of Hebrew religion, such as animal sacrifice or the veneration of sacred places, require relatively little attention, because they ceased to be important for the religion of the New Testament."[1] I am not persuaded that the sacrifices of the Old Testament are of slight importance for the understanding of the New Testament. Certainly they are of considerable importance for the understanding of the Epistle to the Hebrews, and it is undeniable that they figure largely in the Old Testament, so that any work dealing with the Bible as a whole must take account of them. Still more must any survey of the religion of the Old Testament take account of them.

The comparative neglect of the cultus was due to the exaltation of the prophets as anti-cultic[2] and the belief that the emphasis

---

[1] P. 5.

[2] Cf. J. P. Hyatt, *Prophetic Religion*, 1947, p. 127: "The opposition of the prophets to the whole sacrificial and ritualistic system and practices of their day seems to have been absolute, and they thought it should be abolished as an offence against the God of Israel." Cf. also E. Kautzsch, *Biblische Theologie*, 1911, p. 236; Oesterley and Robinson, *Hebrew Religion*, 2nd edn, 1937, p. 232; I. G. Matthews, *The Religious Pilgrimage of Israel*, 1947, p. 128. R. H. Pfeiffer (*Religion in the Old Testament*, 1961, p. 191) describes the cult as "the heathen element of the religion of Israel, derived from the religion of Canaan and attacked by the prophets". (In *Introduction to the Old Testament*, 1941, p. 582, however, Pfeiffer says: "Amos, however, did not, as has been maintained, advocate the abolition

on the cultus in the post-exilic religion represented a declension from the heights of pre-exilic religion. This attitude is well expressed by Volz, who wrote: "Old Testament religion, the religion of the prophets, is the religion of the Word, and hence the Old Testament religion of the prophets stands in the sharpest contrast to the religion of the priests, cult religion."[1] It will be observed that here Old Testament religion is equated with the non-cultic religion,[2] as though the other type of religion did not belong to the Old Testament religion at all.

A marked feature of much recent study is the new attention to the cultus, not only in the post-exilic period or as it is reflected in the Priestly Code, but in the pre-exilic period.[3] Sometimes, as

of sacrifices: he did not oppose the institution but its misuse, and did not introduce a new order of service. He moralized religion but did not substitute morality for religion.") J. Skinner (*Prophecy and Religion*, 1922, p. 182 n) says the prophets held up to their contemporaries the ideal of a religion wholly based on moral fellowship between God and man, in which sacrificial worship was at best an irrelevance, and at worst an offence. E. Balla (*Die Botschaft der Propheten*, 1958, p. 91) describes the teaching of Amos as: "Gott verlangt überhaupt keinen Kult, sondern einzig und allein das *Halten seiner sittlichen Gebote.*"

[1] *Prophetengestalten des Alten Testaments*, 1938, p. 19. Cf. also his paper "Die radikale Ablehnung der Kultreligion durch die alttestamentlichen Propheten", in *Z.S.T.* xiv, 1937, pp. 63ff. Against this cf. G. von Rad, *Old Testament Theology*, E. Tr. by D. M. G. Stalker, ii, 1965, p. 4: "We have abandoned the whole idea of a 'religion of the prophets' as a religion of the spirit diametrically opposed to the 'cultic religion of the priests'."

[2] Cf. S. Mowinckel, *The Psalms in Israel's Worship*, E. Tr. by D. R. Ap-Thomas, ii, 1962, p. 21: "All talk of a 'deliverance from the cult' and of a 'cult-free religion' rests on a misjudgment of the nature of religion as well as of cult." Cf. also R. Martin-Achard, in *Vocabulary of the Bible*, ed. by J. J. von Allmen, E. Tr., 1958, p. 473b: "The prophets in particular and Scripture as a whole do not envisage the substitution of a code of ethical rules for a system of religious practices; that would be risking a rapid fall into moralism and legalism."

[3] N. H. Snaith (*E.T.* lviii, 1946–7, p. 152a) says the reason for this is perhaps to be found in a renewed interest in liturgies and rituals. How far the views of others may have been influenced by their inclination for or against liturgies and rituals I do not know, and I should hesitate to impugn their scholarly integrity in this way. I can say that the Church to which I belong is one of the least liturgical and ritualistic of all the Churches, and that I am and remain of its least liturgical and ritualistic side. Yet for many years I have shared this interest in the Israelite cultus, though I once (cf. *B.Q.* vi, 1932–3, p. 12) accepted the view that the prophets condemned absolutely the entire cultus. My conversion from

Vriezen observes, "this tendency has led to a boom which again threatens to bring the cult into disrepute".[1] The over-pressing of a new emphasis is not unusual, and should not lead us to ignore the enrichment of the study of the Old Testament which the new insight has brought. Needless to say, more is involved than the ritual of sacrifice. For sacrifice was not the only element of the cultus. I should add that neither is the cultus the whole of worship. When Jeremiah was debarred from access to the Temple,[2] he was not shut out from God.

It will be observed that I have defined my subject as "The Forms and Meaning of Worship in Ancient Israel". For it is quite insufficient to pay attention to the forms alone. The quality of worship is to be found in the spirit even more than in the forms, for worship belongs to the heart rather than to the act. Here I may again quote Millar Burrows, this time with more substantial agreement: "For biblical theology the final interpretation is much more important than the origin of a rite."[3] For my purpose I would prefer to say: For worship the interpretation is more important than the origin or the form of a rite. For I am not so much concerned with the *final* interpretation a rite came to be given as with its meaning for the worshipper at the time of his worship. The Old Testament covers a very long period, and neither the forms nor the spirit remained unchanged throughout the period. Nor can we assume a steady and unwavering progress from the lower to the higher in all the development. The mere routine performance of a ritual act may well be a very arid form of worship, as the Old Testament prophets realized, and it is not confined to a single age or to a single point in the development of religion.

My theme is worship in Ancient Israel, and since Jacob is represented as the progenitor of the tribes of Israel, it may seem odd that I should go back in the present chapter to Abraham. I must leave aside the question of how far all the tribes may be thought

this view has been the result of study of the evidence, and not born of a desire to conform the prophets to myself. It is of interest, perhaps, to note that A. R. Johnson, who has played no mean part in the renewed attention to the cultus, belongs to the same Church, as did H. Wheeler Robinson, who shared some aspects of our insight into Old Testament religion, without showing any signs of becoming a ritualist.

[1] *An Outline of Old Testament Theology*, E. Tr. by S. Neuijen, 1958, p. 277. Cf. J. Muilenburg, in *The Bible in Modern Scholarship*, ed. by J. P. Hyatt, 1965, p. 77.　　[2] Jer. 36.5.　　[3] Op. cit., p. 265.

to have sprung from Jacob, or how far they should be thought of as tribes of diverse origin that came into a single confederation. In the Bible we see them only as they recognized common bonds and belonged more or less closely to one another. There are scholars who would begin their study of ancient Israel with Moses or even later, and who find little of substantial historical worth in the older traditions.[1] Yet in their collections of traditions the Israelites cherished stories not only of Jacob, but of Abraham and Isaac, and also of Joseph, and we cannot ignore these stories.

There was a time when the patriarchs were dismissed as merely legendary persons,[2] or personifications of tribes.[3] To-day a large

[1] Cf. M. Noth, *History of Israel*, E. Tr., 2nd edn, 1960, p. 123: "We have no evidence beyond what has been said already for making any definite historical assertions about the time and place, pre-suppositions and circumstances of the lives of the patriarchs as human beings"; p. 125: "The theme of the patriarchs was evolved from the point of view of the promise that was ultimately fulfilled in the occupation of the land by the Israelite tribes." Cf., however, *Oxford Congress Volume* (S.V.T. vii), 1960, pp. 262ff, for modifications of Noth's positions. On Noth's approach cf. J. Bright, *Early Israel in Recent History Writing*, 1956. L. Rost (*Oxford Congress Volume* (S.V.T. vii), 1960, p. 359) says: "Keine der Pentateuchquellen gibt uns die nötigen Unterlagen an die Hand, um ein geschichtlich wahrscheinliches Bild der Gottesverehrung der Väterzeit zu zeichnen, sondern jede hat für ihre Zeit ein Idealbild entworfen." Cf. H. Ringgren, *Israelitische Religion*, 1963, pp. 16f. On the historical value of the patriarchal traditions cf. G. E. Wright, *E.T.* lxxi, 1959–60, pp. 292ff, and G. von Rad's reply, ibid., lxxii, 1960–1, pp. 213ff. E. Meyer (*Die Israeliten und ihre Nachbarstämme*, 1906) begins with the call of Moses at the Burning Bush.

[2] Cf. R. L. Ottley, *Short History of the Hebrews*, 1924 edn, pp. 23f. A. Lods (*Israel*, E. Tr. by S. H. Hooke, 1932, pp. 160f) classes the patriarchal narratives as folklore. Cf. H. Gunkel, *Genesis*, 5th edn, 1922, pp. xiiiff. G. A. Danell (*Studies in the Name Israel in the Old Testament*, 1946, pp. 34f) thinks Abraham was originally a cult-hero and cult-founder belonging to Hebron, who was included in the Israelite genealogical system in the time of David or Solomon, and that Isaac was a similar cult-hero and cult-founder belonging to Beersheba, and Jacob one belonging to Bethel.

[3] Cf. E. Reuss, *L'Histoire sainte et la loi*, i, 1879, pp. 98ff; B. Stade, *G.V.I.* i, 2nd edn, 1889, pp. 28ff; J. Wellhausen, *Prolegomena to the History of Israel*, E. Tr. by J. S. Black and A. Menzies, 1885, pp. 318ff (where, however, Abraham is allowed not to be a personification of a tribe, but is held to be "a free creation of unconscious art"). On this approach cf. S. R. Driver, *The Book of Genesis*, 1904, pp. lvff; J. Skinner, *Genesis*, 1910, pp. xixff.

number of scholars would reject so light a dismissal of them.[1]
Archaeological discovery has shown that much in the story of the
patriarchs remarkably reflects the customs and conditions of the
age in which the patriarchs are set.[2] A modern historical novelist

[1] S. R. Driver, (op. cit., p. lvii) held that it is "difficult to believe that
some foundation of actual personal history does not underlie the patriar-
chal narratives". Cf. T. K. Cheyne, in E.B. i, 1899, col. 26: "Since
Abraham may be a genuine personal name, it cannot be unreasonable to
hold that there is a kernel of tradition in the narratives" (cf. also H. E.
Ryle, in Hastings' D.B. i, 1898, p. 16a). Going beyond this cf. J. Bright,
History of Israel, 1960, p. 82: "We can assert with full confidence that
Abraham, Isaac, and Jacob were actual historical individuals"; W. F.
Albright, The Biblical Period from Abraham to Ezra, 1963, p. 5: "As a
whole, the picture of Genesis is historical, and there is no reason to doubt
the general accuracy of the biographical details and the sketches of
personality which make the Patriarchs come alive with a vividness unknown to a single extrabiblical character in the whole vast literature of the
ancient Near East"; M. L. Newman, The People of the Covenant, 1965,
pp. 18f: "One important result of modern biblical archaeology has been
to increase respect for the general reliability of the Old Testament
historical traditions. . . . Archaeology leads the student of the Old Testament to approach its historical books with great respect, but this does not
mean that all the traditions are to be accepted immediately as providing
unbiased history at every point." On the historicity of Abraham and his
importance in religious history, cf. E. König, Exp., 7th series, x, 1910,
pp. 192ff, 8th series, xxi, 1921, pp. 81ff. C. A. Simpson (The Early
Traditions of Israel, 1948, p. 455) thinks that before the Conquest
Abraham was "venerated as the local numen, the weli, the patron saint of
the shrine, the father of the community, and that owing to the tenacity of
ancient tradition he had retained this rôle when the place and its sanctuary
passed into Jahvist hands".
[2] Cf. S. H. Hooke, in Record and Revelation, ed. by H. W. Robinson,
1938, p. 372: "It is safe to say that the general effect of the discoveries of
the last decade has been to confirm the substantial accuracy of the picture
of life in Canaan in the second millennium B.C., as described in the
patriarchal narratives of Genesis"; H. G. May, J.B.L. lx, 1941, p. 113:
"Absolute scepticism towards the patriarchal narratives as historical records
is difficult to maintain today in the light of the materials contemporary
with the patriarchal period made available as a result of archaeological
research." On the patriarchal age in the light of present knowledge
cf. H. H. Rowley, "Recent Discovery and the Patriarchal Age" in S.L.,
2nd edn, 1965, pp. 283ff; R. de Vaux, "Les Patriarches hébreux et les
découvertes modernes", R.B. liii, 1946, pp. 321ff, lv, 1948, pp. 321ff,
lvi, 1949, pp. 5ff (German Tr. by E. Büsing and M. Wilhelmsen, Die
hebräischen Patriarchen und die modernen Entdeckungen, 1959), "Les
Patriarches Hébreux et l'Histoire", in Studii Biblici Franciscani Liber

may by the thorough study of materials open to him in great libraries present a purely imaginative story in a setting which preserves the conditions of the times in which the story is set. But we cannot ascribe to ancient writers the research and technique of a modern writer, and it is antecedently likely that if a story accurately reflects the conditions of an age long past at the time when it was written down, the story itself has come down from that age.[1] John Bright well observes: "While archaeological discoveries have cast only indirect light on the patriarchal narratives and have not proved them true in any detail, they have shown that they reflect authentically the situation of the first half of the second millennium B.C. and not that of any later period. We must assume, therefore, that the documents as we read them rest on an unbroken stream of tradition reaching back to the age of Israel's origins."[2] While, then, we cannot regard the stories as scientific history,[3] we may accept the probability that they preserve accurate historical memories.[4]

Annuus xiii, 1962–3, pp. 287ff, "The Hebrew Patriarchs and History", *Theology Digest*, xii, 1964, pp. 227ff, and "Les Patriarches hébreux et l'histoire", *R.B.* lxxii, 1965, pp. 5ff. Cf. also H. Cazelles, "Patriarches", in *S.D.B.*, vii, 1966, cols. 81ff. A valuable article on "Abraham dans le cadre de l'histoire" by E. Dhorme appeared in *R.B.* xxxvii, 1928, pp. 367ff, 481ff, xl, 1931, pp. 364ff, 503ff (reprinted in *Recueil Édouard Dhorme*, 1951, pp. 191ff, with additions, pp. 762ff). Cf. also W. F. Albright, *B.A.S.O.R.*, No. 163, Oct. 1961, pp. 36ff.

[1] Cf. S. H. Hooke, *In the Beginning*, 1947, p. 62: "The sagas of Genesis, while they throw light on the religious ideas of the writers who were using this material, also reflect in many ways the customs and social conditions of an age so far removed in time from that of the Hebrew historian who recorded them that he did not always understand what he was recording; so that we may believe him to have faithfully preserved much of the ancient tradition of his people in its early form." Cf. also B. Gemser, *Vragen rondom de Patriarchenreligie*, 1958.

[2] Hastings' one volume *D.B.*, revised edn, ed. by F. C. Grant and H. H. Rowley, 1963, p. 6b.

[3] Cf. Driver, op. cit., p. xliv: "Wᵉ can never indeed regard them as historical authorities in the strictest sense of the word: but that, be it observed, is a claim they never make themselves; they nowhere *claim*, even indirectly, to be the work of eye-witnesses; . . . their contents are nevertheless *substantially* authentic."

[4] With this may be contrasted Wellhausen, *Prolegomena to the History of Israel*, E. Tr. by J. S. Black and A. Menzies, 1885, pp. 318f: "We attain to no historical knowledge of the patriarchs, but only of the time when the stories about them arose in the Israelite people; this later age is here

If the stories were purely fictitious creations of a later age, we should not expect Jacob, the immediate ancestor of the Israelite tribes in the present form of the story, to be presented in so much less attractive a light than Abraham, the remoter ancestor of a wider group of tribes, or Isaac to be represented as so much more colourless a person than either of these. For we cannot suppose that Jacob's cunning was more admired by the later Israelites than the character of Abraham. Abraham is presented as a man who journeyed from Mesopotamia to Canaan in response to a divine urge,[1] whereas when Jacob made the same journey in the reverse direction it was to flee from the consequences of his own deceit.[2] It is quite impossible to imagine that those who told the story or those who preserved it exalted deceit above response to the call of God. Abraham's magnanimity toward Lot[3] cannot have been thought of as something inferior to Jacob's selfishness,[4] or the consequences would have been differently worked out in a fictitious account. Jacob becomes himself the victim of deceit,[5] whereas Abraham is more blessed than Lot as the result of his generosity.

It would seem reasonable, then, to find in these stories reflections of actual persons of the remote past, exemplifying particular qualities of character and religious life. Under the conditions of semi-nomadic life, such as those of the patriarchs, when tribes moved from place to place and lived in tents, personal incidents might be expected to be remembered and told and retold. But even if the stories are held to be fictitious, they are still of great significance. The oldest corpus of stories, contained in the J document of the Pentateuch, is commonly believed to have been collected in the period of David and Solomon.[6] But no one imagines the compiler of J invented them. He collected traditions unconsciously projected, in its inner and its outward features, into hoar antiquity, and is reflected there like a glorified mirage." Cf. H. Gunkel, *Genesis*, 5th edn, 1922, p. lxxix: "Die 'Religion Abrahams' ist in Wirklichkeit die Religion der Sagenerzähler, die sie Abraham zuschreiben." Similarly L. Wallis, *The Bible is Human*, 1942, p. 146: "The patriarchal figures reflect the sociology and ideology which became standard in the central highlands during the epochs covered by the books of Judges, Samuel, and Kings." How far from the truth this is will become apparent as we proceed.

[1] Gen. 12.1ff. [2] Gen. 27.42ff. [3] Gen. 13.8ff.
[4] Gen. 25.29ff. [5] Gen. 29.23ff.
[6] This is not to say that the J document was written at that time, but that it was probably during the early monarchy that the bringing together

already ancient, whether they were true stories of the patriarchs or not.[1] They would therefore at the least reflect the religious and ethical ideas of their creators in the pre-Settlement period. For our records of the post-Settlement period would hardly encourage the idea that that period saw their creation. They would therefore still be of importance as testimony to a surprising spiritual maturity in their creators, if not in the persons depicted.

It is improbable that the patriarchs worshipped Yahweh. It is unnecessary for me here to discuss the two traditions in the Bible, one of which attributes the introduction of the worship of Yahweh in Israel to Moses and denies that the patriarchs knew God by that name,[2] and the other of which traces the worship of Yahweh back to the beginnings of the human race[3] and freely brings Yahweh into association with the patriarchs.[4] Of these two traditions the former is the more likely to be correct.[5] For it is more likely that some Israelites ascribed to their ancestors the worship of the God who had become their God from the time of Moses, than that others denied to those ancestors the worship of this God if they had actually worshipped him. It is true that by syncre-

of traditions of all the tribes took place. Until then Judah had been largely isolated from the northern tribes, but in the reigns of David and Solomon, when the twelve tribes formed a united kingdom, conditions were more favourable than at any other time for bringing northern and southern traditions together, and both J and E contained edited versions of the united traditions. The traditions themselves, in that case, were still older.

[1] Cf. the view of M. Noth (*Überlieferungsgeschichte des Pentateuch*, 1948, pp. 40ff) that J and E depend on an earlier *Grundlage*, either oral or written.

[2] Ex. 6.2.   [3] Gen. 4.1, 26.

[4] Gen. 12.1; 13.4; 15.2; 18.1, etc. Especially significant are the passages in which God is represented as saying to the patriarchs "I am Yahweh" (Gen. 15.7; 28.13) or where the name Yahweh is used by angelic visitors in addressing Abraham (Gen. 18.14), or in which Abraham is said to have called on the name of Yahweh (Gen. 13.4), in direct contradiction of Ex. 6.2, which says that God was not known to the patriarchs by this name.

[5] S. D. Goitein (*V.T.* vi, 1956, pp. 1ff) holds that "Moses was the discoverer of the name YHWH or at least was regarded as such in Israel". This offers no explanation of the ascription of the knowledge of the name in pre-Mosaic days to the patriarchs in the J traditions. The view which I have presented (cf. below, p. 43, n. 1) offers an explanation of both traditions.

tism the gods whose names figure in the patriarchal stories are
identified with Yahweh;[1] but there would have been no point in
so identifying them if they had not figured in the ancient
traditions. Among the gods mentioned in Genesis we find the ancient
Semitic deity El,[2] whose name occurs in non-Biblical texts from
many sources, including the Ras Shamra texts.[3] Sometimes we
find the name in combination with other divine names, El-
Shaddai[4] or El-Bethel.[5] Elsewhere in the Bible we find the name
Shaddai standing alone,[6] and it is probable that Bethel was also
an independent divine name.[7] The same is true of 'Elyon[8] which

[1] Ex. 6.3, where he is identified with El Shaddai, and Gen. 14.22,
where he is identified with Melchizedek's God, El 'Elyon.

[2] Gen. 35.1; 49.25.

[3] Cf. O. Eissfeldt, *El im ugaritischen Pantheon*, 1951; M. H. Pope, *El
in the Ugaritic Texts*, 1955.

[4] Gen. 17.1; 28.3; 35.11; 43.14; 48.3; Ex. 6.3. O. Eissfeldt (*J.S.S.* i,
1956, p. 36 n) conjectures that El Shaddai originally had his seat at
Hebron. O. Procksch (*Theologie des Alten Testaments*, 1950, p. 50)
thought that the name Shaddai was known to Abraham before he
migrated to Canaan. J. M. Holt (*The Patriarchs of Israel*, 1964, p. 151)
says El Shaddai had no shrine, but was with the patriarchs as they moved
along. Cf. H. G. May, *J.B.L.* lx, 1941, p. 121.

[5] Gen. 31.13; 35.7. The former of these texts reads differently in LXX,
and Kittel (*J.B.L.* xliv, 1925, pp. 140ff) emends on the basis of LXX to
secure the sense "I am the God who appeared unto thee in Bethel". So
also E. A. Speiser, *Genesis*, 1964, pp. 241, 244. H. G. May (*J.B.L.* lx,
1941, p. 121), however, thinks the reading of LXX may be interpretative.

[6] Gen. 49.25; Num. 24.4, 16; Ruth 1.20, 21; Ps. 68.14 (M.T. 15),
91.1; Isa. 13.6; Ezek. 1.24; Joel 1.15; and frequently in Job. W. F.
Albright (*J.B.L.* liv, 1935, p. 180) conjectures that Shaddai is an older
form than El Shaddai.

[7] Cf. Jer. 48.13, where the reference may be to the deity rather than to
the shrine. On Bethel as a divine name cf. R. Kittel, *J.B.L.* xliv, 1925,
pp. 123ff; O. Eissfeldt, *A.R.W.* xxviii, 1930, pp. 1ff (reprinted in *Kleine
Schriften*, i, 1962, pp. 206ff); A. Vincent, *La Religion des Judéo-araméens
d'Éléphantine*, 1937, pp. 563ff; J. P. Hyatt, *J.A.O.S.* lix, 1939, pp. 81ff,
and in *I.D.B.* i, 1962, pp. 390f; R. Dussaud, *Les Origins cananéennes du
sacrifice israélite*, 2nd edn, 1941, pp. 231ff; W. F. Albright, *A.R.I.*, 3rd
edn, 1953, pp. 168ff. R. E. Clements (*God and Temple*, 1965, p. 12 n) says
there is no doubt that Bethel was the name of an old pre-Israelite god of
Canaan. On the other hand P. A. H. de Boer (*Ned. T.T.* i, 1946–7, p.
162 n) is not convinced that there was a god Bethel.

[8] Num. 24.16; Deut. 32.8; Ps. 9.2 (M.T. 3); 18.13 (M.T. 14); and
frequently; Isa. 14.14; Lam. 3.35, 38. On 'Elyon cf. R. Lack, *C.B.Q.*
xxiv, 1962, pp. 44ff.

stands combined with El as El-'Elyon.[1] El is found also in other combinations, such as El-'Olam[2] and El-Roi.[3] In texts which deny to the patriarchs the knowledge of the name Yahweh we frequently find the word Elohim used for God. That here we have the names of gods who were once thought of as distinct cannot be gainsaid;[4] but this is quite irrelevant for our purpose.

It is sometimes suggested that here we have evidence that the patriarchs were polytheists,[5] who shared the worship of the people

[1] Gen. 14.18–20, 22; Ps. 78.35. Other combinations are Yahweh 'Elyon, Ps. 7.17 (M.T. 18); 47.2 (M.T. 3); Elohim 'Elyon, Ps. 57.2 (M.T. 3); 78.56. G. Levi della Vida (*J.B.L.* lxiii, 1944, pp. 1ff), basing himself on an Aramaic inscription of the eighth century B.C. which names El and 'Elyon as two deities (cf. S. Ronzevalle, *M.U.S.J.* xv, 1931, pp. 237ff; text in *Z.A.W.* l, 1932, pp. 178ff; translation in *A.N.E.T.*, p. 504), argued that El 'Elyon is a combination of these (cf. H. S. Nyberg, *A.R.W.* xxxv, 1938, p. 336; R. Dussaud, *Les Découvertes de Ras Shamra et l'Ancien Testament*, 2nd edn, 1941, pp. 155f, 170; J. Morgenstern, *J.B.L.* lxiv, 1945, pp. 15ff; M. H. Pope, *El in the Ugaritic Texts* (S.V.T. ii), 1955, pp. 15 n, 52; A. R. Johnson, *Sacral Kingship in Ancient Israel*, 1955, p. 44). This view is rejected by O. Eissfeldt (*J.S.S.* i, 1956, p. 28 n), who maintains that El and 'Elyon are identical (cf. also R. Lack, *C.B.Q.* xxiv, 1962, pp. 56ff; L. R. Fisher, *J.B.L.* lxxxi, 1962, p. 266).

[2] Gen. 21.33; cf. Isa. 40.28: Elohê 'Olam. On El 'Olam cf. O. Eissfeldt, *Forschungen und Fortschritte*, xxxix, 1965, p. 300.

[3] Gen. 16.13.

[4] Cf. O. Eissfeldt, *Z.D.M.G.* lxxxviii, 1934, p. 179: "Die vom A.T. gebrauchten Appellativa für 'Gott' El und Elim, Eloah und Elohim sowie die in ihm erwähnten Götternamen Baal und Aschera-Astarte, Dagon und Milkom und viele andere kommen in den Jahrhunderte älteren Ras Schamra-Texten vor, und viele der hier genannten Götter werden auch ihrem Wesen nach genauer charakterisiert." Cf. also Eissfeldt, *J.S.S.* i, 1956, pp. 25ff; H. G. May, *J.B.L.* lx, 1941, pp. 113ff. On the divine names cf. E. Dhorme, *La Religion des Hébreux nomades*, 1937, pp. 333ff; E. Jacob, *Theology of the Old Testament*, E. Tr. by A. W. Heathcote and P. J. Allcock, 1958, pp. 43ff; W. Eichrodt, *Theology of the Old Testament*, E. Tr. by J. A. Baker, i, 1961, pp. 178ff; B. W. Anderson, "God, names of" in *I.D.B.* ii, 1962, pp. 407ff.

[5] Cf. H. P. Smith, *The Religion of Israel*, 1914, p. 14; Oesterley and Robinson, *Hebrew Religion*, pp. 52ff. Cf. T. J. Meek, *J.B.L.* lxi, 1942, p. 21: "No modern scholar of any standing today believes that the Hebrews of the Patriarchal Period were anything but polytheistic." J. M. Holt (*The Patriarchs of Israel*, 1966, p. 141) says: "The patriarchs may have been on the way to monotheism, but they were practical, if not systematic, polytheists." That there was polytheism amongst the Israelites in the pre-Mosaic period is made clear by the story of the burial of gods at Shechem (Gen. 35.2ff). Moreover, it is improbable that all the

among whom they moved. Toussaint held that they worshipped the gods of Haran, whom they brought with them, and added to these the local gods of Canaan.[1] It seems to me, as I shall say later, that it is very improbable that they worshipped the gods of Haran, and the evidence is strongly against the idea that they entered into the Canaanite worship. Of Canaanite religion in the second millennium B.C. we have much fuller knowledge since the discovery of the Ras Shamra texts;[2] but here we move in a very

tribes formed a single group in the pre-Settlement period or shared a common religious experience (cf. *J.J.*, 1950). Cf. R. Kittel, *The Religion of the people of Israel*, E. Tr. by R. C. Micklem, 1925, p. 43: "If from time to time we find references to other gods, the meaning is simply that individuals within the patriarchal circle and its immediate vicinity still paid homage to other gods."

[1] *Les Origines de la religion d'Israël: l'ancien Yahvisme*, 1931, pp. 202ff.
[2] Of the enormous literature on the Ras Shamra texts the following may be mentioned: H. Bauer, "Die Gottheiten von Ras Schamra", *Z.A.W.* li, 1933, pp. 81ff, lii, 1935, pp. 54ff; S. H. Hooke, *The Origins of Early Semitic Ritual*, 1938; F. F. Hvidberg, *Graad og Latter i det Gamle Testamente*, 1938 (E. Tr. *Weeping and Laughter in the Old Testament*, 1962); A. Bea, "Archäologisches und Religionsgeschichtliches aus Ugarit-Ras Schamra", *Biblica*, xx, 1939, pp. 436ff; I. Engnell, *Studies in Divine Kingship in the Ancient Near East*, 1943, pp. 97ff; T. H. Gaster, "A Canaanite Ritual Drama", *J.A.O.S.* lvi, 1946, pp. 48ff, and *Thespis*, 1950, pp. 115ff; D. M. L. Urie, "Officials of the Cult at Ugarit", *P.E.Q.* lxxx, 1948, pp. 42ff; C. H. Gordon, *Ugaritic Literature*, 1949; H. L. Ginsberg, "Ugaritic Myths and Legends", *A.N.E.T.*, 1950, pp. 129ff; A. S. Kapelrud, *Baal in the Ras Shamra Texts*, 1952; G. R. Driver, *Canaanite Myths and Legends*, 1956; J. Gray, *The Legacy of Canaan* (S.V.T. v), 1957; J. Aistleitner, *Die mythologischen und kultischen Texte aus Ras Schamra*, 1959. On the significance of the Ras Shamra texts for Old Testament study, cf. J. W. Jack, *The Ras Shamra Tablets: their bearing on the Old Testament*, 1935; J. de Groot, "Rās Šamra en het Oude Palestina", *J.E.O.L.*, No. 3, 1935, pp. 97ff; A. Jirku, "Die Keilschrifttexte von Ras Šamra und das Alte Testament", *Z.D.M.G.* lxxxix, 1935, pp. 372ff; D. Nielsen, *Ras Šamra Mythologie und Biblische Theologie*, 1936; R. de Vaux, "Les textes de Ras Shamra et l'Ancien Testament", *R.B.* xlvi, 1937, pp. 526ff; R. Dussaud, *Les Découvertes des Ras Shamra (Ugarit) et l'Ancien Testament*, 1937, 2nd edn, revised and enlarged, 1941; A. Bea, "Ras Šamra und das Alte Testament", *Biblica*, xix, 1938, pp. 435ff; R. de Langhe, *Les Textes de Ras Shamra-Ugarit et leurs apports à l'histoire des origines israélites*, 1939, and *Les Textes de Ras Shamra-Ugarit et leurs rapports avec le milieu biblique de l'Ancien Testament*, 2 vols., 1945; S. Mowinckel, "Rās Sjamrā og det Gamle Testament", *Nor.T.T.* xl, 1939, pp. 16ff; W. Baumgartner, "Ras Schamra und das Alte Testament", *Th.R.*, N.F. xii, 1940, pp. 163ff, xiii, 1941, pp. 1ff,

different atmosphere from that of the patriarchal narratives. Writing of the Canaanites Albright speaks of "the extremely low level of Canaanite religion, which inherited a relatively primitive mythology and had adopted some of the most demoralizing cultic practices then existing in the Near East. Among these practices were human sacrifice, long given up by the Egyptians and the Babylonians, sacred prostitution of both sexes, apparently not known in native Egyptian religion, though widely disseminated through Mesopotamia and Asia Minor, the vogue of eunuch priests, who were much less popular in Mesopotamia and were not found in Egypt, serpent worship to an extent unknown in other lands of antiquity. The brutality of Canaanite mythology passes belief."[1] It is hard to think of this as characterizing patriarchal religion, which belongs to a quite different order.

It is true that El was the high god of the Ugaritic pantheon,[2]

85ff, 157ff, and "Ugaritische Probleme und ihre Tragweite für das Alte Testament", *Th.Z.* iii, 1947, pp. 81ff; H. L. Ginsberg, "Ugaritic Studies and the Bible", *B.A.* viii, 1945, pp. 21ff; W. F. Albright, "The Old Testament and the Canaanite Language and Literature", *C.B.Q.* vii, 1945, pp. 5ff; E. Jacob, "Les Textes de Ras Shamra-Ugarit et l'Ancien Testament", *R.H.P.R.* xxvii, 1947, pp. 242ff, and *Ras Shamra et l'Ancien Testament*, 1960; G. R. Driver, "Ugaritic and Hebrew Problems", *Archiv Orientální*, xvii (Hrozný Festschrift), Pars Prima, 1949, pp. 153ff; J. Gray, "Cultic Affinities between Israel and Ras Shamra", *Z.A.W.* lxii, 1950, pp. 207ff; A. S. Kapelrud, *Ras Sjamra-funnene og det Gamle Testament*, 1953 (E. Tr. by G. W. Anderson, *The Ras Shamra Discoveries and the Old Testament*, 1965); W. Schmidt, *Königtum Gottes in Ugarit und Israel*, 1961; C. F. Pfeiffer, *Ras Shamra and the Bible*, 1962. For a more general study cf. J. Gray, *The Canaanites*, 1964.

[1] *Studies in the History of Culture* (Waldo Leland Volume), 1942, pp. 28f (reprinted in *The Bible and the Ancient Near East*, ed. by G. E. Wright, 1961, p. 338).

[2] Cf. O. Eissfeldt, *El im ugaritischen Pantheon*, 1951; M. H. Pope, *El in the Ugaritic texts*, 1955. Pope says (p. 104): "The El of the patriarchs was the god at the height of his power and prestige and this was the god with whom YHWH was identified." On El cf. also M. J. Lagrange, *Études sur les religions sémitiques*, 1903, pp. 70ff. In a valuable paper ("El and Yahweh", *J.S.S.* i, 1956, pp. 25ff) Eissfeldt notes that all the encounters of the patriarchs with El take place on Canaanite soil, and holds that El was the special contribution of Canaan to the world (so F. Løkkegaard in *Studia Orientalia Ioanni Pedersen dicata*, 1953, pp. 219ff, esp. p. 232), and finds traces in the Bible that El was once thought of as superior to Yahweh, but that Yahweh appropriated his authority and took his place. A Ras Shamra text names Yw as the son of El, and

but alongside him were many gods who do not figure in the book of Genesis.[1] In particular, the patriarchs never invoke Baal, who figures very largely in the Ras Shamra texts[2] and whose widespread worship in Canaan is made abundantly clear in Biblical narratives of later times, when Israelites are freely admitted to have shared in Canaanite religious practices. Moreover, goddesses figure in the Ras Shamra pantheon as well as in Canaanite religion as it is attested in the Bible. None of this do we find in the patriarchal narratives, and as little of the practices of the fertility cult which was characteristic of Canaanite religion. We should therefore be careful before we equate the deities of the patriarchs with those of their neighbours.[3] And if it be thought that later scrupulosity has removed the traces of worship which was offensive to a later generation, it may be replied that it would have been just as easy to remove all these other divine names. Their retention is evidence of the fidelity of tradition, and the tradition is as much to be trusted in what it does not say as in what it does.

Yw has been frequently identified with Yahweh (cf. R. Dussaud, *R.H.R.* cv, 1932, p. 247, and *Syria*, xxxiv, 1957, pp. 232ff; H. Bauer, *Z.A.W.* li, 1933, pp. 92ff; O. Eissfeldt, *J.P.O.S.* xiv, 1934, pp. 298f; A. Vincent, *La religion des Judéo-Araméens d'Éléphantine*, 1937, pp. 27f; C. Virolleaud, *La déesse 'Anat*, 1938, p. 98; A. Dupont-Sommer, *C.R.A.I.*, 1947, p. 177), but this is contested by others (cf. R. de Vaux, *R.B.* xlvi, 1937, pp. 552f; A. Bea, *Biblica*, xx, 1939, pp. 440f; C. H. Gordon, *Ugaritic Grammar*, 1940, p. 100 (but cf. *Ugaritic Manual*, 1955, p. 272); W. Baumgartner, *Th.R.*, N.F. xiii, 1941, pp. 159f; R. de Langhe, *Un dieu Yahweh à Ras Shamra?*, 1942; W. F. Albright, *F.S.A.C.*, 2nd edn, 1946, pp. 197, 328; T. J. Meek, *Hebrew Origins*, 2nd edn, 1950, p. 105 n; J. Gray, *The Legacy of Canaan*, 1957, pp. 133f (cf. *J.N.E.S.* xii, 1953, pp. 278ff); G. R. Driver, *Canaanite Myths and Legends*, 1956, p. 12 n; E. Jacob, *Ras Shamra et l'Ancien Testament*, 1960, pp. 107f; M. H. Pope, *Wörterbuch der Mythologie*, 1962, p. 291).

[1] N. H. Snaith (in Manson's *Companion to the Bible*, 2nd edn, ed. by H. H. Rowley, 1963, p. 525) holds that in patriarchal religion there was a High God and low gods; so also J. M. Holt, *The Patriarchs of Israel*, 1964, p. 151.

[2] Cf. A. S. Kapelrud, *Baal in the Ras Shamra Texts*, 1952; G. R. Driver, *Canaanite Myths and Legends*, 1956, pp. 10ff, 72ff; J. Gray, "Baal", in *I.D.B.* i, 1962, pp. 328f.

[3] N. H. Snaith (in Manson's *Companion to the Bible*, 2nd edn, p. 526) says: "To what extent the wandering patriarchs were influenced by the gods and cults of Canaan, it is impossible to say. There is no evidence." V. Maag (*S.T.U.*, xxviii, 1958, pp. 9f) holds that the patriarchal gods were tribal or clan gods.

Jacob refers to "the God of my father, the God of Abraham and the Fear of Isaac",[1] and also to "the Mighty One of Jacob".[2] Many years ago in an important study Alt[3] argued that Abraham's special deity was "the God of Abraham", while Isaac's was "the Fear of Isaac", and Jacob's "the Mighty One of Jacob", so that each of these patriarchs had his own tutelary deity.[4] Elmer Leslie suggested that the name of Abraham's God was "the Shield of Abraham",[5] and Albright that the name of Isaac's was "the Kinsman of Isaac".[6] This approach would give to the religion of the patriarchs a character quite distinct from that of Canaanite religion,[7] and de Vaux maintains that the patriarchs were monotheists.[8] A similar claim had been made earlier by

---

[1] Gen. 31.42; cf. verse 53.

[2] Gen. 49.24; cf. Ps. 132.2, 5; Isa. 49.26; 60.16. C. H. Gordon (*J.B.R.* xxi, 1953, p. 239) renders "the Bull of Jacob", and connects this with the Ras Shamra text Keret, line 41, where Keret is called the Bull of his father (where the word for Bull, however, is a different one).

[3] *Der Gott der Väter*, 1929 (reprinted in *Kleine Schriften*, i, 1953, pp. 1ff). Cf. H. G. May, *J.B.R.* ix, 1941, pp. 155ff, 199f; J. P. Hyatt, *V.T.* v, 1955, pp. 130ff; K. T. Andersen, *St. Th.* xvi, 1962, pp. 170ff. A. Lods (*R.H.P.R.* xii, 1932, pp. 249ff and in *Record and Revelation*, ed. by H. W. Robinson, 1938, p. 201) is doubtful of Alt's view. B. Gemser (*O.T.S.* xii, 1958, p. 21) says Alt distinguishes too sharply between the type of the "God of the father" and the Elim of Genesis. Cf. also M. Haran, *A.S.T.I.*, iv, 1965, pp. 51f. On the religion of the patriarchs cf. also V. Maag, *S.T.U.* xxviii, 1958, pp. 2ff; Haran, loc. cit., pp. 30f.

[4] Alt thought the gods of the patriarchs were all later identified with Yahweh, but C. Steuernagel (in *Festschrift Georg Beer*, 1935, pp. 62ff) finds some Biblical evidence that Yahweh stands over against the Gods of the patriarchs.

[5] *Old Testament Religion*, 1936, pp. 67f; cf. Gen. 15.1.

[6] *F.S.A.C.*, 2nd edn, 1946, pp. 188f, 327. This is accepted by O. Eissfeldt, *J.S.S.* i, 1956, p. 32 n.

[7] Eissfeldt (*Th.L.Z.* lxxxviii, 1963, cols. 481ff) argues that the Israelites at Kadesh identified Yahweh with the God of their fathers, and that he was also identified with the Canaanite El. On the worship of the patriarchs cf. also L. Rost, *Oxford Congress Volume* (S.V.T. vii), 1960, pp. 346ff.

[8] *Initiation Biblique*, ed. by A. Robert and A. Tricot, 3rd edn, 1954, pp. 888f. De Vaux argues that Isaac worshipped the God of his father (Gen. 26.23f), as also did Jacob (Gen. 31.5, 42, 53). Eissfeldt (*J.S.S.* i, 1956, pp. 31ff), on the other hand, distinguishes between El and the gods of the fathers. C. H. Gordon (*J.B.R.* xxi, 1953, pp. 238ff, and *J.N.E.S.* xiii, 1954, pp. 56ff) maintains that the patriarchs were monotheists and thinks this stems from the monotheistic background of the Amarna age, in which he sets the patriarchs. On the chronological problems of the

Renan[1] and Lagrange.[2] I am doubtful if we should go so far as this, since there is no evidence of any speculative denial of the existence of more than one God on the part of the patriarchs, and we should not disregard the references to a plurality of gods who were once distinct. Yet those references do not seem to me to establish that the patriarchs were polytheists, or to show that they worshipped the local deities. Can it be supposed that it was the local deity of Shechem who first promised Abraham that his descendants should possess the land,[3] and later the local deity of Bethel made him a similar promise,[4] and yet later the local deity of Mamre renewed the promise,[5] and so on? It would be bewildering for so many gods to show so little originality, and surprising for local deities to claim so wide a sway.[6]

It has sometimes been suggested that the patriarchs were animists.[7] Animism is variously defined, and we need not stay to examine the term,[8] but may look at the evidence which is adduced in this connection. Oesterley reviewed the evidence concerning sacred trees and springs and stones to support the view that animism has left its mark on the Old Testament,[9] while Kautzsch preferred to call this polydemonism.[10] We read that Abraham came to the "place" of Shechem,[11] by which it is probable that the shrine

patriarchal age cf. *J.J.*, 1950, pp. 57ff. V. Maag (*S.T.U.*, xxviii, 1958, pp. 17ff) describes the patriarchal religion as monolatry.

[1] *Histoire du peuple d'Israël*, 7th edn, i, 1887, pp. 45ff.
[2] *Études sur les religions sémitiques*, 1903, pp. 7αff.
[3] Gen. 12.6ff.   [4] Gen. 13.14ff.   [5] Gen. 15.18ff.
[6] R. de Vaux (*A.I.*, p. 294) holds that for the patriarchs El Bethel, El 'Olam, and El Shaddai were not local deities, but manifestations of the supreme God El, and this seems to me most probable. So also T. C. Vriezen, *Vragen rondom de Patriarchenreligie*, 1958, pp. 18ff. Cf. H. G. May, *J.B.L.* lx, 1941, pp. 114f; J. Muilenburg, *I.B.* i, 1952, p. 296b; A. S. Kapelrud, in *The Bible in Modern Scholarship*, ed. by J. P. Hyatt, 1965, p. 46.
[7] So, for example, I. G. Matthews, *The Religious Pilgrimage of Israel*, 1947, pp. 29ff; R. H. Pfeiffer, *Religion in the Old Testament*, 1961, p. 21. G. E. Wright (in *The Study of the Bible Today and Tomorrow*, ed. by H. R. Willoughby, 1947, p. 90) says: "We can assert with confidence that by the time of the patriarchs the religion of all parts of the Near East was a long distance removed from the animistic stage."
[8] Cf. G. d'Alviella, "Animism", in *E.R.E.* i, 1908, pp. 535ff.
[9] In Oesterley and Robinson, *Hebrew Religion*, 2nd edn, 1937, pp. 33.
[10] In Hastings' *D.B.*, Extra Vol., 1909, p. 616. Cf. K. Marti, *The Religion of the Old Testament*, E. Tr. by G. A. Bienemann, 1914, pp. 50ff.
[11] Gen. 12.6.

of Shechem is meant, and that he received a theophany by the oak or terebinth of Moreh,[1] which may equally well be rendered "the soothsayer's oak".[2] It is possible that the same tree is referred to in connection with Jacob's burying of idols.[3] At Mamre again Abraham dwelt beside the oaks[4] (for which some would read "the oak"),[5] while at Beersheba he planted a tamarisk,[6] and at Bethel Rebecca's nurse was buried under an oak.[7] At Beersheba Abraham dug a well,[8] which was secured to him by a covenant with Abimelech,[9] while the well known as Beer-lahai-roi receives its name from a theophany to Hagar.[10] At Bethel Jacob sets up a stone to mark the site of a theophany which he experienced in his dream.[11] On the basis of this Kautzsch says: "Real worship was rendered by Israel in the pre-Mosaic period to the many numina, which were believed to be the inhabitants and possessors of certain places, and which were venerated as such. These make their appearance most frequently in connection with trees, stones, and springs, which thereby assume a sacred character."[12] This seems to me to be without evidence.[13] We do not find the patriarchs worshipping the material objects or the spirits which might be supposed to reside in them. In the theophanies the deity invariably appears in human form, and there is no suggestion that the deity is identified with the spirit of the tree or spring or stone. These objects mark sacred spots and are nowhere venerated for themselves, and the fact that the deity invariably takes human form would seem to carry the religion of the patriarchs far from animism or polydemonism. Moreover, the ethical and spiritual quality of

[1] Gen. 12.6; cf. Deut. 11.30. On the concept of theophany in the Old Testament cf. J. Barr, in *Oxford Congress Volume* (S.V.T. vii), 1960, pp. 31ff.
[2] Cf. S. R. Driver, *Genesis*, 1904, p. 146; H. E. Ryle, *Genesis*, 1914, p. 157; L. Aubert, in *La Bible du Centenaire*, i, 1941, p. 14. Cf. also Judges 9.37, "the Diviners' oak" (R.S.V.). H. G. May (*J.B.L.* lx, 1941, pp. 118f) renders "the terebinth of the lawgiver" in Gen. 12.6.
[3] Gen. 35.2ff.   [4] Gen. 13.18; 14.13.
[5] So LXX and Syr., followed in *La Bible du Centenaire*, p. 15. E. A. Speiser (*Genesis*, 1964, p. 97) retains the plural and renders "the terebinth grove", and E. Dhorme (in *La Bible de la Pléiade*: *l'Ancien Testament*, i, 1956, p. 42) renders "la chênaie".
[6] Gen. 21.33.   [7] Gen. 35.8.   [8] Gen. 21.25ff; cf. 26.31.
[9] Gen. 21.31ff.   [10] Gen. 16.7ff.   [11] Gen. 28.18.
[12] In Hastings' *D.B.*, Extra Vol., 1904, pp. 615f. Cf. H. P. Smith, *The Religion of Israel*, 1914, p. 23.
[13] Cf. R. de Vaux, *A.I.*, pp. 278f.

the religion we find in the patriarchal narratives is far removed from that of animism. Animism does not prompt a man to migrate to another land or to act unselfishly, or induce such intercession as Abraham's for Sodom.[1] I therefore agree with Professor Henton Davies, that "it is no longer possible to state that worship in the days of the founding fathers of Israel can be described in terms of animism and the like".[2]

It is wiser to examine the religion of the patriarchs for what it is in itself than to identify it with something which it is not on the vain assumption that this can suffice to define it. To leap from the mention of a tree to the equation of the religion with something we find elsewhere, while completely ignoring the content of the narrative in which the tree is mentioned, does not seem the wisest use of evidence. In their wanderings the patriarchs would naturally come to places where there were springs, or would seek to find water in wells, and it is hard to see why this should make them animists. They would equally naturally come to places that were regarded as sacred, since these would be convenient stopping places. That they worshipped where they happened to be is not evidence that they participated in the established worship of these places, and nowhere do we read of the patriarchs participating in worship with others.[3] When Abraham returned from the rescue of Lot, he came to Salem[4] and presented a tenth of the spoil to

[1] Gen. 18. 23ff.   [2] In *I.D.B.* iv, 1962, p. 879b.
[3] Cf. below, p. 25 n. In *M.Q.*, 1963, p. 45 n, the present writer said that the patriarchs are represented as worshipping at the shrines of the local deities and thus recognizing the existence of more than one god. They may well have recognized the existence of more than one god, but it is doubtful if they worshipped more than one, though it is certain that members of their company did. The statement that the patriarchs are represented as worshipping at the shrines of the local deities goes beyond the evidence. There is no mention of these shrines in the records.
[4] Salem is commonly, and in my view rightly, identified with Jerusalem. Other identifications have been proposed; cf. H. W. Hertzberg, *J.P.O.S.* viii, 1928, pp. 169ff, where the Melchizedek incident is connected with Tabor. C. Mackay (*P.E.Q.* lxxx, 1948, pp. 121ff) identified it with Shechem, adducing Gen. 33.18 (where he renders "Jacob came to Shalem, a city of Shechem"; so also H. S. Nyberg, *A.R.W.* xxxv, 1938, pp. 357, 366f) and evidence from Eusebius that there was a Shalem near Shechem. S. Landersdorfer (*J.S.O.R.* ix, 1925, pp. 203ff) also locates Salem at Shechem, but this is rejected by E. Nielsen (*Shechem*, 1955, p. 343). A. P. Stanley (*Sinai and Palestine*, new edn, 1883, pp. 249f) argues that

Melchizedek, who blessed him.[1] Melchizedek was the priest of
El 'Elyon,[2] and it is probable that this deity is to be equated with
the god Zedek[3] or Shalem.[4] It is possible that Abraham went to

Melchizedek's sanctuary was on Mount Gerizim. But J. Simons (*O.T.S.*
ii, 1943, pp. 44ff; cf. *The Geographical and Topographical Texts of the
Old Testament*, 1959, pp. 215ff) has shown that there is no substantial
ancient evidence for a Shalem in the neighbourhood of Shechem. R. H.
Smith (*Z.A.W.* lxxvii, 1965, pp. 146ff) leaves open the question whether
Melchizedek's city was Shechem, Hebron, or Jerusalem. He rejects the
view that the Salem (Heb. *shālēm*) is the name of a place, but renders it
"subservient", holding that the incident records Melchizedek's surrender
to Abraham and the covenant meal which followed. Albright (*B.A.S.O.R.*,
No. 163, Oct. 1961, p. 52) holds the meaning to be "Melchizedek, a king
allied to him". The earliest identification of Salem with Jerusalem is in
the Genesis Apocryphon from Qumran, col. XXII, line 13.

[1] Gen. 14.18ff.   [2] Gen. 14.18.
[3] On Zedek as a divine name cf. H. Winckler, *K.A.T.*, 3rd edn. 1903,
p. 224; W. W. von Baudissin, *Adonis und Esmun*, 1911, pp. 247f, and
Kyrios als Gottesname, iii, 1929, pp. 398ff; A. Bertholet, *A History of
Hebrew Civilization*, E. Tr. by A. K. Dallas, 1926, p. 108; A. Lods,
Israel, E. Tr. by S. H. Hooke, 1932, p. 131; G. Widengren, *Accadian and
Hebrew Psalms of Lamentation*, 1937, pp. 71, 322; H. S. Nyberg, *A.R.W.*
xxxv, 1938, pp. 355ff; N. W. Porteous, *T.G.U.O.S.* x, 1943, pp. 1ff;
H. Ringgren, *Word and Wisdom*, 1947, pp. 83ff; R. A. Rosenberg, *H.U.C.A.*
xxxvi, 1965, pp. 161ff. This view is contested by C. F. Burney, *Judges*, 2nd
edn, 1920, pp. 41ff, and A. R. Johnson (*Sacral Kingship in Ancient Israel*,
1955, pp. 32f, 46) thinks it is uncertain. Cf. *Festschrift Alfred Bertholet*,
1950, p. 465, where the present writer thinks it probable. Cf. also the long
and valuable note of S. A. Cook, in W. R. Smith, *The Religion of the
Semites*, 3rd edn, 1927, pp. 655ff.
[4] On Shalem as a divine name, cf. H. Winckler, *K.A.T.*, 3rd edn, 1903,
p. 224; H. Zimmern, ibid., pp. 474f; J. Lewy, *R.H.R.* cx, 1934, pp. 60ff;
A. Jirku, *Z.D.M.G.* lxxxix, 1935, p. 380; G. Widengren, op. cit., p. 323;
H. S. Nyberg, *A.R.W.* xxxv, 1938, pp. 352ff; J. Gray, *J.N.E.S.* viii,
1949, pp. 72ff; A. R. Johnson, *Sacral Kingship*, p. 46; cf. also N. W.
Porteous, "Shalem-Shalom", *T.G.U.O.S.* x, 1943, pp. 1ff. C. F. Jean
(*Le Milieu biblique*, iii, 1936, p. 289) identifies Shalem with Shulman; so
also H. Winckler (*K.A.T.*, loc. cit.), Lewy (loc. cit. pp. 62f; cf. *J.B.L.* lix,
1940, pp. 519ff), Nyberg (loc. cit.), and A. Vincent (*La Religion des
Judéo-Araméens d'Éléphantine*, 1937, pp. 571 n, 657ff). Winckler (loc. cit.)
connects the name Solomon with this god (cf. T. J. Meek, *The Song of
Songs: a Symposium*, ed. by W. H. Schoff, 1924, pp. 53f). R. Dussaud
(*Les Découvertes de Ras Shamra et l'Ancien Testament*, 2nd edn, 1941,
p. 141) holds Shalem to have been the god of the evening peace (cf.
Porteous, loc. cit., p. 1, where this is thought to be unlikely), while
C. H. Gordon (*The Loves and Wars of Baal and Anat*, 1943, p. 3) equates

the shrine of Melchizedek, though there is no reference to this or even to the shrine itself in the story, but only the statement that Melchizedek went out to Abraham.[1] In any case there is no reason to suppose that Abraham shared in any ritual ceremony at Melchizedek's shrine or offered any worship to El 'Elyon.[2] For the study of Abraham's worship it is safer to rely on the recorded evidence rather than on what we reconstruct out of silence.

It is further remarkable that we nowhere find the patriarchs possessing or worshipping idols. It is, of course, true that we have the incident of Laban's teraphim being stolen by Rachel when Jacob departed from his father-in-law.[3] That the teraphim were idols of some sort is certain,[4] since Laban asks "Wherefore hast

Shalem with the Dusk, or Evening Star, and W. F. Albright (*A.f.O.* vii, 1931–2, p. 168) connects Shulman with the Underworld. Winckler (loc. cit.) equated Shalem-Shulman with Zedek, and so Nyberg (op. cit., p. 356), who equated both with El 'Elyon (so also I. Engnell, *Studies in Divine Kingship in the Ancient Near East*, 1943, p. 177) and all with 'Al (on whom cf. Nyberg, op. cit., pp. 329ff, and *Studien zum Hoseabuche*, 1935, pp. 58ff; G. R. Driver, *E.T.* l, 1938–9, pp. 92f; Johnson, *Sacral Kingship*, pp. 44f n; P. Ruben, *J.Q.R.* xi, 1898–9, p. 446, thought '*al* in some texts was a popular abbreviation of *Ba'al*). On the equation of Zedek or Shalem with El 'Elyon, cf. further H. Schmid, *Z.A.W.* lxvii, 1955, p. 177; E. Voegelin, *Israel and Revelation*, 1956, p. 277; Mowinckel, *The Psalms in Israel's Worship*, i, pp. 132f. G. Widengren (loc. cit.) regarded Zedek and Shalem as two different gods. A. R. Johnson (in *The Labyrinth*, ed. by S. H. Hooke, 1935, p. 84) suggests that El 'Elyon was thought of as the embodiment of *ṣedhek* = righteousness, rather than identified with a god of that name.

[1] Gen. 14.18.

[2] L. H. Vincent (*R.B.* lviii, 1951, p. 364) sees no reason why Abraham should not have offered worship to El 'Elyon by assimilation to El Shaddai. For my view of the origin and purpose of Gen. 14, which stands outside the main documents of the Pentateuch, cf. *Festschrift Alfred Bertholet*, 1950, pp. 461ff.

[3] Gen. 31.34.

[4] On the meaning of teraphim, see the richly documented note of A. R. Johnson, *The Cultic Prophet in Ancient Israel*, 2nd edn, 1962, pp. 32f; cf. also *M.G.*, 1963, pp. 22f. The nature of the teraphim of 1 Sam. 19.13ff is disputed (cf. ibid., pp. 22f n). Cf. further H. G. May, *J.B.L.* lx, 1941, pp. 127f. A. Lods (in *E.R.E.* vii, 1914, p. 141) doubts whether the word *terāphîm* means the same in all contexts. He connects it with *tōreph*, which in post-Biblical Hebrew means "foulness", and so finds it to be an opprobrious term which could be variously applied. On the Rachel incident cf. A. Vincent, *O.T.S.* viii, 1950, pp. 284ff and P. R. Ackroyd, *E.T.* lxii, 1950–1, pp. 378ff. In the David incident Ackroyd thinks

thou stolen my gods?"[1] It is now well known that evidence from Nuzu sheds light on Rachel's reasons for carrying them off. In Nuzu the possession of the teraphim by a woman's husband entitled him to the chief inheritance of his father-in-law's property,[2] and it may well be that Rachel's act was related in some way to this legal right, though we nowhere read of Jacob's claiming any inheritance in virtue of having them.[3] In any case Rachel's act can prove nothing for Jacob's religion. Similarly, when we read that Jacob buried all the foreign gods that were found in his household beneath the oak that was near Shechem,[4] this provides unexceptionable evidence that there was idolatry within the company of Jacob's family and servants, but it provides none that he worshipped idols. H. P. Smith supposes that when Jacob buried the idols, the divinities who inhabited the idols took up their abode

images designed to aid healing are intended, while in the Rachel incident he suggests that we have the introduction of the cult of the Mother goddess into Canaan from Mesopotamia. C. J. Labuschagne (*V.T.* xvi, 1966, pp. 115ff) connects the word *tᵉrāphîm* with the root *ptr* = "interpret".

[1] Gen. 31.30.

[2] Cf. S. Smith, *apud* C. J. Gadd, *R. Ass.* xxiii, 1926, p. 127, and *J.T.S.* xxxiii, 1932, pp. 33ff; C. H. Gordon, *R.B.* xliv, 1935, pp. 35f, *B.A.S.O.R.* No. 66, April 1937, pp. 27ff, *B.A.* iii, 1940, pp. 5f (in *Introduction to Old Testament Times*, 1953, pp. 116f, Gordon more recently says that since Jacob was bound for Canaan and was leaving Mesopotamia for good, it is not likely that the gods conveyed valuable property rights, and that their possession may rather have betokened clan leadership; repeated in *The World of the Old Testament*, 1960, p. 129); T. J. Meek, *Hebrew Origins*, revised edn, 1950, pp. 15f, and in *A.N.E.T.*, p. 219 n; H. M. Orlinsky, *Ancient Israel*, 1954, p. 19; E. A. Speiser, *I.E.J.* vii, 1957, p. 213, and *Genesis*, 1964, p. 250; A. E. Draffkorn, *J.B.L.* lxxvi, 1957, pp. 219ff. Sir James Frazer (*Folk-lore in the Old Testament*, ii, 1919, p. 399) conjectured that the purpose of Rachel's theft was to prevent the household gods from resenting and punishing any injury done to Laban.

[3] M. Greenberg (*J.B.L.* lxxxi, 1962, pp. 239ff) holds that Rachel's act was unrelated to Nuzu law, but was simply due to her desire to continue to worship her ancestral gods in a foreign country. In support of this he cites Josephus, *Ant.* XVIII. ix. 5 (340ff), where an account is given of a similar theft of household gods by the widow of a Parthian early in the Christian era, which W. Whiston (in a footnote to his translation of the passage) connected with Rachel's act. This is a far cry from the time of Rachel, and Greenberg admits that "it is not easy to forego a theory based (as is the Nuzi theory) on material coming almost from the same time and place as the patriarchs themselves" (p. 248).

[4] Gen. 35.2ff.

in the tree.[1] Clearly Jacob disapproved of the idols, and if the mention of sacred trees is held to imply the worship by the patriarchs of the spirits inhabiting them, it would be a strange mark of disapproval for Jacob to worship them. Moreover, the spirit supposedly believed to be already inhabiting the tree might be expected to object to being compelled to share his quarters with others. Oesterley suggests that Jacob's idea was to put the idols under the control of the spirit which dwelt in the tree.[2]

We may now turn from a consideration of what the religion of the patriarchs was not to see what, on the basis of the book of Genesis, it was. We may preface this by observing that a religion is not to be judged by the name of the god worshipped, but by the character of the religion itself and the quality of the life which it produces. In China Christian Bibles use the name Shang Ti for God, and Christian worship is offered to Shang Ti, the ancient God of China whose name appears in her oldest classics. That worship is filled to-day with a Christian content. It matters little whether God is called Shang Ti or Jehovah or Yahweh; what matters is how he is conceived and how he is worshipped. What names the patriarchs used for God are of less importance than the way they thought of him and what their worship meant for them. I have said that I hesitate to go so far as de Vaux and call the faith of the patriarchs monotheism.[3] Yet I now say that I think it was a practical monotheism.[4] The variety of divine names used does not seem to indicate a variety of divine beings who are set over against one another. By whatever name he was worshipped,

[1] *The Religion of Israel*, 1914, p. 17. E. Nielsen (*St. Th.* viii, 1955, pp. 103ff) argues from Gen. 35.5 that the burial of the gods had a magical purpose and is to be seen in connection with the Egyptian execration texts.

[2] In Oesterley and Robinson, *Hebrew Religion*, 2nd edn, p. 27.

[3] Above, p. 15.

[4] In *M.Q.*, 1963, pp. 35ff, the present writer has argued that the religion of Moses was not monotheism, but that it contained the seeds of monotheism. This is not to say that from the time of Moses all polytheism was eliminated from Israel. 1 Sam. 26.19 shows that long after the time of Moses Yahweh was thought of as one God among many. In now arguing that there was incipient or practical monotheism in the religion of the patriarchs, the writer is similarly not suggesting that polytheism was unknown in the stream of Israel's heritage from the time of Abraham. No family or community lives on a uniform religious level, and the recognition of the spiritual quality of an Abraham or a Moses should not be supposed to imply this.

the God they worshipped was thought of as one. They cannot have supposed that different gods came to them with the same promises, even claiming that the former promises were their own. This does not mean that we can describe the religion of the patriarchs as henotheism.[1] Our modern scientific labels do not seem to fit the facts. For henotheism is the worship of one god by people who believe there are many gods, all real though not all for them. The patriarchs neither deny nor affirm the existence of gods whom they did not worship. They ignore them.

There are passages which represent the patriarchs as offering sacrifice[2] or building an altar[3] or erecting and anointing with oil a pillar of stone.[4] In some of these stories, and particularly in the story of Jacob at Bethel, it is common to find an aetiological element, and to see in the story a justification of worship by the Israelites at an ancient shrine which existed before they came into the land.[5] While it is possible that this was so in the case of Bethel, we should remember that the Priestly writer records a theophany at Bethel,[6] and we can hardly suppose that he intended to legitimate the Bethel shrine, since for him Jerusalem was the only legitimate centre of worship. It is sometimes said that the tradition was here too strong for him.[7] But surely there was no necessity for him to include this. He could have passed it over without mention, as he passed over other things which offended his sense of what was right.

Moreover, we cannot suppose that all these stories which bring the patriarchs into association with trees and springs and stones

[1] Cf. J. Bright, *History of Israel*, 1960, p. 139: "Certainly Israel's faith was no polytheism. Nor will henotheism or monolatry do, for though the existence of other gods was not expressly denied, neither was their status as gods tolerantly granted."

[2] Gen. 22.13; 31.54; 46.1.

[3] Gen. 12.7f; 13.4, 18; 22.9; 26.25; 33.20; 35.7.

[4] Gen. 28.18; 35.14.

[5] So, for example, J. Skinner, *Genesis*, 1910, pp. xiif. Whereas nothing is said about these shrines much is said about the promises to the patriarchs, and Noth's view that these promises were at the heart of the patriarchal narratives (cf. above, p. 4, n. 1) seems to me better based than the aetiological theory which connects them with the shrines. Cf. J. Hoftijzer, *Die Verheissungen an die drei Erzväter*, 1956.

[6] Gen. 35.9.

[7] So J. E. Carpenter and G. Harford, *The Composition of the Hexateuch*, 1902, p. 232.

were intended to legitimate shrines. The tamarisk which Abraham planted at Beersheba[1] and the well which he dug there[2] may have been associated with the altar on which Jacob sacrificed there on his journey into Egypt,[3] and so be thought to legitimate the Israelite worship there in the post-Settlement period until the Deuteronomic reform.[4] Similarly, the tree under which Jacob buried the idols,[5] and the altar which he erected at Shechem,[6] may be thought to be intended to legitimate the sanctuary of Shechem. In the New Testament we read of Jacob's well in this neighbourhood,[7] though there is no mention of it in the Old Testament. But there are curious features here. Jacob's tree may have been the same as the oak of Moreh mentioned in connection with Abraham.[8] But Abraham is said to have built an altar here.[9] The compiler of the J document recorded the construction of these two altars. Which did he regard as the altar of the Shechem shrine, to be legitimated by the story? Similarly, we read of two altars at Bethel, one built by Abraham[10] and the other by Jacob,[11] but these are attributed to different documents. Moreover, what of the sacred spring of Beer-lahai-roi?[12] So far as we know, no shrine ever stood on this spot, and the story cannot be supposed to be legitimating anything. Abraham built an altar at the oaks of Mamre,[13] and at this spot he received the three visitors who came to renew the promise of a son and to forewarn him of the coming destruction of Sodom.[14] Probably here too the Abrahamic covenant was made.[15] Later we find both Isaac and Jacob at Mamre.[16] But of any shrine legitimated by all these things we read nothing in the Old Testament. Josephus writes of Abraham's oak,[17] which he locates six stadia from the city of Hebron, while Sozomen locates it fifteen stadia from the city and says Constantine built a church to mark the spot.[18] It may well be that all the stories are just ancient traditions and not aetiological stories intended to legitimate shrines.

But whatever the purpose of the stories, it is significant to note

[1] Gen. 21.33.   [2] Gen. 21.30.
[3] Gen. 46.1.   [4] Cf. Amos 5.5; 8.14.   [5] Gen. 35.4.
[6] Gen. 33.20.   [7] John 4.6.   [8] Gen. 12.6.
[9] Gen. 12.7.   [10] Gen. 12.8.   [11] Gen. 35.7.
[12] Gen. 16.14; cf. 24.62; 25.11.   [13] Gen. 13.18; cf. 14.13; 18.1.
[14] Gen. 18.1ff.   [15] Gen. 15.   [16] Gen. 25.9; 35.27.
[17] *B.J.* IV.ix.7 (533).   [18] *H.E.* ii.4.

that the only acts of worship associated with the patriarchs were acts which they performed individually. Where there was a sacrifice it was almost invariably on an altar erected by the patriarch himself. We read of altars at Bethel,[1] Shechem,[2] Mamre,[3] Beersheba,[4] Moriah,[5] and in Mizpah, east of the Jordan.[6] Nowhere do we read of priests. The patriarchs always performed the sacrifices themselves. Here we note that the Priestly writer records no sacrifice by a patriarch. It is generally believed that the reason is that for him sacrifice could not rightly be offered until it had been ordained by God and a duly authorized priesthood established to perform the rite. If this is true, it would appear that the Priestly writer did not hesitate to omit what seemed to him unedifying.

Such sacrifices as the patriarchs offered were apparently quite simple. We do not meet a variety of technical terms for particular types of sacrifices. The patriarchal offerings were the expression of their individual veneration for the deity and the vehicle of their personal worship rather than their participation in an established cultus. Sacrifice was a widespread form of religious worship, and it is not to be wondered at that the patriarchs should express their veneration for God in ways similar to those of the people around them, by sacrifice. When they believed they had a personal visitation from God, whether in the form of a divine or angelic visitor or by dream, or when they wished to call on the name of God and present themselves in worship before him, their sense of awe was expressed in this way. The form of the sacrifice is passed over lightly, and attention is rather drawn to their spirit of response to the approach of God to them or to their desire to approach God in calling upon his name. Their sacrifice was not a mere form of worship, but a genuine expression of their spirit and sense of God's presence. Professor John Bright rightly says that the religion of the patriarchs "was of a distinctive sort quite different from the official paganisms of the surrounding lands",[7] though he also says, wrongly I believe, "As the patriarchs entered Palestine,

---

[1] Gen. 12.8; 35.7. A. Alt (*In piam memoriam A. von Bulmerincq*, 1938, pp. 218ff = *Kleine Schriften*, i, 1963, pp. 79ff) has argued that Gen. 35.1–7 is concerned with a pilgrimage from Shechem to Bethel (cf. R. de Vaux, *A.I.*, p. 291).

[2] Gen. 12.7; 33.20.   [3] Gen. 13.18.   [4] Gen. 26.25.   [5] Gen. 22.9.

[6] Gen. 31.54. The altar is not itself mentioned here, but the sacrifice presupposes an altar on which it was offered.

[7] In *I.D.B.* ii, 1962, p. 561a.

their cults were carried on at local shrines, and their gods no doubt identified with the gods worshipped there".[1]

In one story we read how Abraham nearly sacrificed his son Isaac.[2] It is sometimes thought that child sacrifice, and in particular the sacrifice of firstborn sons, was once common in Israel. De Vaux has recently argued against this view,[3] and it need not concern us here. For Abraham does not propose to offer Isaac as a sacrifice because that was customary, and if it had been, Isaac would presumably have been aware of what was happening earlier than he was. Abraham felt constrained to offer Isaac as a sacrifice, not because it was a common duty or because Isaac meant so little to him, but because Isaac meant so supremely much to him, and because he wished to show the completeness of his own devotion to God. Our modern view of the sacredness of personality is irrelevant to the story, and would not arise in the mind of Abraham or Isaac. In a later age we read of Mesha offering his son in a moment of supreme national crisis as an appeal to his god to supreme exertion on behalf of his people.[4] We also read of

---

[1] Ibid. After the Settlement in Canaan the Israelites worshipped at the local shrines and by syncretism identified Yahweh with the local gods, who are called Baalim. It is significant that Baal as a divine name nowhere occurs in the patriarchal narratives, and it does not seem likely that the patriarchs identified their God with local Baals. The God they worshipped was El, who is other than Baal in the Ras Shamra texts. H. Cazelles (*S.D.B.*, vii, 1966, col. 146) says: "Même si El a des attaches locales, il est important de noter que les noms donnés à El ne sont pas des noms de Baals locaux." Since neither the local name for the god is used, and nor is there mention of attendance at any local shrine, and since, moreover, the patriarchs offered sacrifice themselves and did not avail themselves of the services of any priests of the shrines, there does not seem to be any evidence that they worshipped at these shrines. And if it be thought that the accounts have been purged of any mention of these things, it may be asked when this could be supposed to have taken place? Scarcely in the period of the Judges, when syncretism was so prevalent; scarcely in the period of the early monarchy, when syncretism was continued (cf. below, pp. 72ff); and scarcely in the age when the J document was written, since there is no polemic against the shrines and their worship and in that age the shrines were commonly resorted to, and there would be no reason to remove any mention of them. Moreover, if these stories were, as is commonly thought, intended to legitimate the shrines for Israel, it would have been foolish to eliminate any mention of them.

[2] Gen. 22.

[3] *A.I.*, pp. 441ff; *Studies in Old Testament Sacrifice*, 1964, pp. 52ff.

[4] 2 Kings 3.27.

Jephthah vowing a human sacrifice to God if he should return in victory as a similar appeal for all-out aid,[1] little realizing that his vow would entail the sacrifice of his daughter.[2] In both of these cases the sacrifice was intended to express the urgency of an appeal for help. No such motive appears in the story of Abraham and Isaac. It was not to extract something from God that Abraham was willing to sacrifice his son, but solely as an expression of his devotion to God. Mesha's sacrifice was dictated by selfishness, or at best by his patriotic regard for his people. Abraham's readiness to sacrifice Isaac was dictated by a religiously far superior motive, though he learned that if there is no sacrifice a man should be unwilling to make for God, there are some sacrifices God does not ask. When we look beneath the act to the spirit from which it arose, we find here a very lofty spirit of worship, which is the more remarkable when we reflect on the antiquity of the times of Abraham.

This narrowly averted sacrifice took place on one of the mountains in the land of Moriah,[3] which is identified by later Jewish tradition with the Temple site.[4] The Chronicler is the oldest writer to make this identification, and his is very late authority for it.[5] If there had been any intention on the part of the narrator to authenticate the Temple site by the story, we should have expected much earlier evidence of this. The Chronicler identifies the site with the place where God appeared to David,[6] where the reference is to the threshing floor of Araunah.[7] Again, if there were traditions identifying these sites, we should have expected them to be brought together much earlier. It is further doubtful if the compilers of the E document, in which the story of Abraham and Isaac has been preserved, had any suspicion that the reference was to the Temple site, since that document was almost certainly compiled in northern Israel after the breach between Israel and Judah, when the

---

[1] Judges 11.30f.   [2] Judges 11.34, 39.   [3] Gen. 22.2.

[4] Cf. Josephus, *Ant.* I. xiii. 1f (224, 226); VII. xiii. 4 (333); Jub. 18.13.

[5] 2 Chron. 3.1.

[6] Ibid. It is curious that though the Chronicler uses the name Mount Moriah, he makes no direct reference to the Abraham story. Moreover in Gen. 22.2 *one* of the mountains of the *land* of Moriah is mentioned, not *the* mountain. H. Gunkel (*Genesis*, 5th edn, 1922, pp 240f) suggests that the name of the mountain was originally Jeruel (cf. W. H. Bennett, *Genesis*, p. 237).

[7] 2 Sam. 24.16. He is called Ornan in 1 Chron. 21.15; 2 Chron. 3.1.

northern tribes no longer came to Jerusalem. Some scholars accordingly think that Mount Moriah was originally intended, as Samaritan tradition affirms, to be thought of as Gerizim.[1] A different aetiological significance has been proposed for the story by those who think it was originally intended to explain why human sacrifice was superseded in Israel, or, in particular, why the sacrifice of firstborn had ceased to be practised.[2] Here I am in agreement with Professor Speiser, who says: "If the author had intended to expose a barbaric custom, he would surely have gone about it in a different way."[3] Professor Speiser himself finds the story to mean no more than it appears to mean: "The object of the ordeal was to discover how firm was the patriarch's faith in the ultimate divine purpose."[4] If this was the object from God's side, from Abraham's it could only have been to express his supreme devotion to God, with no thought of gain, either immediate or future, but with a readiness to abandon in this sacrifice the very possibility of the realization of his hopes or the fulfilment of the promises he believed God had made to him. If the story is dismissed as fiction, its spiritual perception demands recognition; if it rests on actual experience, it is evidence of something higher than animism.

We cannot regard this story as a mere idealization of the past. There are sordid stories in the book of Genesis, which show that the writers are more concerned with the faithful transmission of traditions than with idealization. We read little of the worship of some of Jacob's sons, but much which is to their discredit. The

---

[1] So F. Bleek, *T.S.K.* iv, 1831, pp. 520ff; G. Grove, in Smith's *D.B.* ii, 1863, p. 122; A. P. Stanley, *Sinai and Palestine*, new edn, 1883, pp. 251f; J. Wellhausen, *Die Composition des Hexateuchs*, 3rd edn, 1899, p. 19; O. Procksch, *Genesis*, 1924, pp. 315f. S. R. Driver (in Hastings' *D.B.* iii, 1900, p. 437b) observes that Gerizim suits the distances of Gen. 22.4 better than Jerusalem, and is more conspicuously seen from a distance (cf. verse 4) than the Temple mount. L. H. Vincent (*R.B.* lviii, 1958, pp. 366ff) holds that Jerusalem is intended.

[2] So A. Dillmann, *Genesis*, 5th edn, 1886, p. 285; W. H. Bennett, *Genesis*, p. 237; J. Skinner, *Genesis*, 1910, p. 332 (Skinner observes however, that "the story contains no word in repudiation of human sacrifice, nor anything to enforce what must be supposed to be the main lesson, viz. that such sacrifices were to find no place in the religion of Abraham's descendants"). Cf. also J. L. McKenzie, *Scripture*, ix, 1957, pp. 79ff.

[3] *Genesis*, 1964, p. 165. [4] *Ibid.*, p. 166.

stories of Simeon and Levi at Shechem[1] or of Judah and Tamar[2] do not suggest that we have to do with men of high religious spirit. And Jacob's rebuke for Simeon and Levi[3] shows that it is not merely our more refined standards that are offended. Joseph's brothers treat him in a shameful way,[4] and the writer of the story clearly regards it so. But Joseph responds in a magnanimous way which makes the story forever impressive.[5] Instead of revenging himself on his brothers when he had them in his power, he forgave them in one of the most moving scenes in literature. The author or compiler of the stories was not set on idealizing the ancestors of his people. Nor was he set merely on telling stories with a good moral. Where there is a moral it comes out in the story itself and does not need to be pointed.

Jacob's character is not very exalted, and he reaps the fruits in having to flee from his brother's wrath and in the successive deceits or breaches of agreement he suffers at the hand of Laban,[6] and finally in the long grief he suffers by the deceit practised on him by Joseph's brothers.[7] But not every sinner suffers, and suffering is not always the fruit of sin. Joseph's brothers do not suffer in any degree comparable with their heartlessness towards him or with their cynical deceit of their father. On the other hand, Joseph suffers more from their sin against him than they do, and again in Egypt he is cast into prison for his very righteousness.[8] It is true that he ultimately achieves honour and wealth and position, but this does not explain the suffering through which he rose.

More important than sacrifice in the worship of the patriarchs is the fact that their worship is represented as a personal encounter with God. Abraham went out from Haran in response to the call of God.[9] It is idle to speculate on the form in which that call came to him. But in some way he was aware of a constraint which he believed to be of God. It may well be that it was connected with dissatisfaction with the religion of Haran, as late Jewish speculation affirmed.[10] His father Terah had earlier migrated with his family from Ur to Haran.[11] Some scholars have doubted the con-

---

[1] Gen. 34.   [2] Gen. 38.   [3] Gen. 49.5ff.   [4] Gen. 37.18ff.
[5] Gen. 45.1ff.   [6] Gen. 27.43ff; 29.23; 31.7, 41.
[7] Gen. 37.31ff.   [8] Gen. 39.7ff.   [9] Gen. 12.1ff.
[10] Judith 5.6ff. Cf. the collection of legends about Abraham in L. Ginzberg, *Legends of the Jews*, E. Tr. by Henrietta Szold, 1913 edn, i, pp. 195ff.
[11] Gen. 11.31.

nection of Abraham with Ur at all,[1] while in recent years it has been argued that the city from which Terah migrated was not the Ur of the Chaldees, the ancient city of Babylonia excavated by Woolley, but another Ur in the north, much nearer to Haran.[2] In favour of the Biblical tradition it is pointed out that Ur was the great centre of the worship of the Moon god Sin, and that Haran was also a second great centre of the worship of the same god, so that the two cities probably had some ancient connection which would explain migration from one to the other.[3] But the migration of Abraham from Haran cannot be so simply explained, and the fact that he exhibits a faith which consists in a personal encounter with God and leads to a remarkable loftiness of character suggests that in its origin as well as in its effect some dissatisfaction with the current religion around him entered into his call.

In the stories of Abraham he has repeated encounters with God, encounters bringing him the promise of a son which is fulfilled after years of waiting, during which his attitude to God

[1] So O. Procksch, *Genesis*, p. 498; H. Gunkel, *Genesis*, p. 157; W. F. Albright, *F.S.A.C.*, 2nd edn, 1946, p. 179 (cf. *Archaeology of Palestine and the Bible*, 1932, p. 209; but cf. *The Biblical Period*, rev. edn, 1963, p. 2, where this view appears to be abandoned: "We may never be able to fix the date of Terah's migration from Ur to Harran", where the context makes it clear that the Babylonian Ur is meant); G. E. Wright, *Biblical Archaeology*, rev. edn, 1962, p. 41a; E. A. Speiser, *Genesis*, 1964, p. 80. Cf. also S. R. Driver, *Genesis*, p. 142; J. Skinner, *Genesis*, p. 239; J. Bright, *History of Israel*, pp. 80f. J. C. L. Gibson (*J.S.S.* vii, 1962, pp. 58f) thinks Abraham's home was in Haran, but that he went to the southern Ur for a temporary visit and returned before leaving Haran for Canaan.

[2] So A. Lods, *Israel*, E. Tr. by S. H. Hooke, 1932, pp. 162ff (on this cf. H. Cazelles, in *S.D.B.*, Fasc. 36, 1961, col. 99); and in a different form C. H. Gordon, *J.N.E.S.* xvii, 1958, pp. 28ff, *Before the Bible*, 1962, pp. 27, 34, 288f, and in *Hebrew and Semitic Studies presented to G. R. Driver*, 1962, pp. 77ff (against this cf. H. W. Saggs, *Iraq*, xxii, 1960, pp. 200ff; cf. also H. Cazelles, in *S.D.B.*, vii, 1966, cols. 99f; W. F. Albright, *B.A.S.O.R.*, No. 163, October 1961, p. 44 n; D. J. Wiseman, *N.D.B.*, 1962, p. 1305; A. Parrot, *Abraham et son temps*, 1962, pp. 15ff; and R. de Vaux, *R.B.* lxxii, 1965, pp. 17ff). O. Eissfeldt (*C.A.H.*, rev. edn, Fasc. 31, 1965, p. 9) favours a location near Haran. An older view identified Ur with Edessa (cf. George Rawlinson, in Smith's *D.B.* iii, 1863, p. 1596b).

[3] Cf. P. (E.) Dhorme, *R.B.* xxxvii, 1928, pp. 379ff (= *Recueil Édouard Dhorme*, 1951, pp. 205ff).

seems to be unwavering. I have already noted that his devotion
to God makes him ready even to sacrifice the son of promise. The
promise of the land to his descendants is one whose fulfilment he
was not destined to see. Nowhere is Abraham a man who worships
God for what he gets out of it, but always as one whose devotion
to God is for God himself alone. In one of his encounters with
God we read that he asked how he should know that in his
descendants he was destined to inherit the land of promise.[1] There
follows the story of Abraham's covenant with God.[2] He is bidden
to take a heifer, a she-goat, a ram, a turtledove, and a pigeon, and
to cut them in pieces, save that the birds were not divided. Then
at sundown he fell asleep and the divine message came to him in
his sleep. Then he awoke to see a flaming torch pass between the
divided pieces, indicating, by a piece of ritual which we find
referred to elsewhere, God's ratification of the message in a
covenant which was visibly confirmed. Here is a sacrifice unlike
any other referred to in the patriarchal stories, and unlike any of
those prescribed in the ritual legislation of the Old Testament.[3]

[1] Gen. 15.8.   [2] Gen. 15.9ff.

[3] This covenant-making ceremony continued at least until the time of
Jeremiah; cf. Jer. 34.18f. The ceremony is commonly thought to be
connected with the Hebrew expression "to cut a covenant" (cf. W. F.
Albright, *B.A.S.O.R.*, No. 121, Feb. 1951, pp. 21f, for the parallel term
from Qaṭna). S. R. Driver (*Genesis*, p. 176) explains the symbolism by
saying: "The contracting parties pass between the divided victims, each
thereby symbolizing that, in case he breaks the terms agreed to, he is
willing to be parted asunder in like manner." This does not seem probable, since here only Yahweh, represented by the flaming torch, passes
between the pieces, and the idea of God's willingness to be dismembered
seems highly improbable. E. A. Speiser (*Genesis*, p. 112) thinks that in an
agreement between unequals only the weaker of the two passed between
the pieces. But again it seems improbable that Yahweh was thought to be
weaker than Abraham. It is far more likely that Skinner (*Genesis*, p. 283) is
right when he says that Yahweh alone passes between the pieces because
he alone contracts obligation. This seems to rule out W. Robertson
Smith's suggestion that "the parties stood between the pieces, as a symbol
that they were taken within the mystical life of the victim" (*Religion of the
Semites*, 3rd edn, with additional notes by S. A. Cook, 1927, pp. 480f). For
other theories cf. S. A. Cook, ibid., pp. 691f. In a covenant between men
divine sanctions might be invoked for its breach (Jer. 34.20), but it is
hard to see how God could be exposed to sanctions. In a human oath,
penalties for breach are invoked, but when God swears an oath (Gen.
22.16), nothing more can be read into it than a solemn undertaking. So
here, it is hard to see more than a solemn undertaking by God, sealed by

Professor Speiser finds evidences of magic in this story.[1] But again, what is important is not the ritual but the significance of the story. Abraham has an encounter with God, whose content is not born of the ritual but only confirmed by it after it has been experienced. More significant is the fact that Abraham's relation with God is now based in a covenant.[2] The covenant with Israel at Sinai laid obligations on Israel besides specifying the obligations

the dismemberment of the victim. Abraham has dismembered the victim, and God's passing between the pieces in the symbol of the flaming torch is his acceptance of the undertaking. Such a visible ceremony would give the concreteness of a bond to the undertaking. On Gen. 15 cf. L. A. Snijders, *O.T.S.* xii, 1958, pp. 261ff (on p. 273 Snijders quotes W. B. Kristensen's view of the significance of the ritual: "The death of a sacrificial animal was at the same time the death of the covenant, its sanctification; by means of the oath and the sacrifice, the covenant was transported into the world of absolute life. Then no deceit could annul its validity. It had been released from all transient relations." This seems to me doubtful). On the symbolism of the torch cf. A. G. Barrois, *Mélanges Syriens* (Dussaud Festschrift), i, 1939, pp. 101ff. On covenant and contract cf. G. M. Tucker, *V.T.* xv, 1965, pp. 487ff.

[1] *Genesis*, pp. 112ff.

[2] On the concept of Covenant in the Old Testament, cf. R. Valeton, *Z.A.W.* xii, 1892, pp. 1ff, 224ff, xiii, 1893, pp. 245ff; R. Kraetzschmar, *Die Bundesvorstellung im Alten Testament*, i, 1894; P. Karge, *Geschichte des Bundesgedankens im Alten Testament*, 1910; E. Lohmeyer, *Diatheke*, 1913; J. Pedersen, *Der Eid bei den Semiten*, 1914, pp. 21ff, and *Israel I–II*, E. Tr., 1926, pp. 263ff; L. G. da Fonseca, *Biblica*, viii, 1928, pp. 31ff, 161ff, 290ff, 418ff, ix, 1929, pp. 26ff, 143ff; G. Quell, "Diathēkē" in *Th.W.B.* ii, 1935, pp. 106ff (E. Tr. by G. W. Bromiley, ii, 1964, pp. 106ff); J. Hempel, *Gott und Mensch*, 2nd edn, 1936, pp. 162ff, and *R.G.G.* i, 3rd edn, 1957, cols. 1513ff; J. Begrich, *Z.A.W.* lx, 1944, pp. 1ff (reprinted in *Gesammelte Studien*, 1964, pp. 55ff); P. van Imschoot, *N.R.Th.* lxxiv, 1952, pp. 785ff, and "Alliance", in *Dictionnaire encyclopédique de la Bible*, 1960, cols. 46ff; E. Vogt, *Biblica*, xxxvi, 1955, pp. 565f; M. Noth, in *Mélanges Isidore Lévy*, 1955, pp. 433ff (reprinted in *Gesammelte Studien zum Alten Testament*, 1957, pp. 142f); H. W. Wolff, *V.T.* vi, 1956, pp. 316ff; J. Cadier, *E.Th.R.* xxxi, 1956, No. 4, pp. 10ff; V. Hamp, in *L.Th.K.* ii, 1958, cols. 770ff; A. Jepsen, in *Verbannung und Heimkehr* (Rudolph Festschrift), 1961, pp. 161ff; G. E. Mendenhall, "Covenant", in *I.D.B.* i, 1962, pp. 714ff; A. González Núñez, *Est. Bib.* xxiv, 1965, pp. 217ff. Cf. also O. Procksch, *Theologie des Alten Testaments*, 1950, pp. 572ff; P. van Imschoot, *Théologie de l'Ancien Testament*, i, 1954, pp. 237ff; L. Koehler, *Old Testament Theology*, E. Tr. by A. S. Todd, 1957, pp. 60ff; T. C. Vriezen, *Outline of Old Testament Theology*, E. Tr., 1958, pp. 139ff; W. Eichrodt, *Theology of the Old Testament*, E. Tr. by J. A. Baker, i, 1961 (built wholly on the Covenant).

which God freely accepted for himself. It has become common to compare the terms of that covenant with Hittite suzerainty treaties of the second millennium B.C.[1] This covenant lays no obligations on Abraham. God is so sure of him that no specifications are necessary. He but binds himself to do for Abraham all that he had promised.

Of Isaac we are told much less. We read of encounters he had with God,[2] but we are told nothing of his response to them. Jacob had an encounter with God at Bethel when fleeing from his brother,[3] and his response was quite other than Abraham's. In his dream he saw the angels of God ascending and descending and saw Yahweh above the ladder and heard the renewal of the promises made to Abraham and Isaac. His response was a vow that if God would indeed bless him, then he would worship God.[4] He makes a bargain with God, and shows nothing of the unmeasured trust of Abraham. His attitude to God was not *do ut des*, but *da ut dem*. On his return from Laban Jacob has another encounter with God in which he wrestles with the divine visitor by the ford of the Jabbok and emerges with a new name.[5] But

---

[1] Cf. G. E. Mendenhall, *Law and Covenant in Israel and the Ancient Near East*, 1955 (reprinted from *B.A.* xvii, 1954, pp. 26ff, 50ff); K. Balzer, *Das Bundesformular*, 2nd edn, 1964; F. C. Fensham, *Z.A.W.* lxxiv, 1962, pp. 1ff; D. J. McCarthy, *Treaty and Covenant*, 1963 (more cautious), and *C.B.Q.* xxvii, 1965, pp. 217ff. Cf. also J. Muilenburg, *V.T.* ix, 1959, pp. 347ff; S. Gevirtz, *V.T.* xi, 1961, pp. 137ff; Mendenhall, "Covenant", in *I.D.B.* i, 1962, pp. 714ff; J. Gray, *E.T.* lxxiv, 1962–3, p. 348; D. N. Freedman, *Interpretation*, 1964, pp. 419ff; F. Nötscher, *B.Z.* N.F. ix, 1965, pp. 181ff; W. Eichrodt, in *Gottes Wort und Gottes Land* (Hertzberg Festschrift), 1965, pp. 30ff; G. Fohrer, *Kerygma und Dogma*, xi, 1965, pp. 49ff; E. Gerstenberger, *J.B.L.* lxxxiv, 1965, pp. 38ff. J. Barr (in Hastings' one volume *D.B.*, rev. edn, 1963, p. 184a) says: "A recent attempt to invoke the similarities of covenant presentations to the Hittite treaties of sovereignty seems to the writer only to pick out points which might belong to any treaty supported by sacral sanctions, and not to explain more for the covenant in Israel than at most the form of certain more developed statements of it." Cf. also D. R. Hillers, *Treaty Curses and the Old Testament Prophets*, 1964 (on which see the review of P. Wernberg–Møller, *J.S.S.* x, 1965, pp. 281ff); G. M. Tucker, *V.T.* xv, 1965, pp. 487ff.

[2] Gen. 26.2ff.   [3] Gen. 28.12ff.   [4] Gen. 28.20f.

[5] Gen. 32.22ff. This strange and difficult story is often resolved into various aetiological elements, for example the explanation of the name Israel, the explanation of the name Penuel, the explanation of the food

before this interview he had sought God in prayer. His prayer arose out of his fear for himself, but it expressed a new humility. Hitherto he had trusted in his own cunning, or his mother's scheming. But now he cries to God: "I am not worthy of the least of all the mercies, and of all the truth, which thou hast shewed unto thy servant."[1] A third encounter with God reassured him when he took his journey into Egypt.[2]

Of Joseph we read of no similar encounters with God, but we read that Yahweh was with him, giving him favour in the sight of Potiphar[3] and later in the sight of the keeper of the prison.[4] When Potiphar's wife cast her eyes on him, Joseph's first thought is of the sin against God to which she would lure him.[5] Though we are

taboo of verse 32; or it is supposed that it rests on some myth of an encounter with the local spirit of the Jabbok (cf. H. P. Smith, *The Religion of Israel*, 1914, p. 24: "It may have been an old myth representing the dangerous temper of the Jabbok"). It is to be noted that the encounter is said to be with El, and the name Penuel is connected with El, and not with any local spirit of the stream; cf. O. Eissfeldt, in *Mélanges Bibliques* (Robert Festschrift), 1957, p. 80: "Vollends macht es die Fortsetzung der Erzählung Gn. 32, 23–33 deutlich, dass sie es von Haus aus mit der Offenbarung eines grossen Gottes, des Gottes El, nicht etwa irgend eines Fluss-oder Nachtdämons an Jakob zu tun hat" (cf. G. von Rad, *The Problem of the Hexateuch and Other Essays*, E.Tr. by E. W. T. Dicken, 1966, p. 59: "The narrative of Gen. xxxii. 25ff leaves no doubt that under cover of the spectral figure it is Yahweh himself who comes to Jacob"). It is tacitly assumed by many writers that it does not rest on any actual experience of Jacob. What that experience may have been in physical terms can no more easily be defined in relation to a river spirit than in relation to El, and no more easily in relation to another legendary figure than in relation to Jacob. F. van Trigt (*O.T.S.* xii, 1958, p. 303) sums up the chief significance of the story as "le dernier et suprême effort de Jacob pour verifier son caractère: faire tout pour obtenir le droit d'ainesse et le garder"; while G. A. Danell (*Studies in the Name Israel in the Old Testament*, 1946, p. 19) says: "With the new name Israel, Jacob has at last achieved the object he has coveted all his life, the inheritance from Abraham and Isaac." Of the considerable literature on this pericope, in addition to the commentaries of Gunkel, Skinner, and Procksch, the following may be noted: P. A. H. de Boer, *Ned. T.T.* i, 1946–7, pp. 149ff; K. Elliger, *Z.Th.K.* xlviii, 1951, pp. 1ff; J. Schildenberger, in *Miscellanea Biblica B. Ubach*, 1953, pp. 69-96; A. Jepsen, *Wissenschaftliche Zeitschrift der Karl-Marx-Universität Leipzig*, iii, 1953–4, pp. 273f; O. Eissfeldt, in *Mélanges Bibliques* (Robert Festschrift), pp. 77ff, and *O.L.Z.* lviii, 1963, cols. 325ff; F. van Trigt, loc. cit., pp. 38off. This story of Jacob is referred to in Hos. 12.3f (M.T. 4f) (on which cf. T. C. Vriezen, *O.T.S.* i, 1941–2, pp. 64ff).

[1] Gen. 32.10.　[2] Gen. 46.2ff.　[3] Gen. 39.2.　[4] Gen. 39.21.　[5] Gen. 39.9.

told little of the form of his worship, Joseph's religion is presented as a personal fellowship leading to righteousness.[1] In all these patriarchal narratives worship is less a matter of forms and ceremonies than a relation between man and God, and this is far more essential to the stories than the places where men are or the divine name that may stand in the narrative. The relation is one of reverence on the part of man, but not of terror. In writing of the pre-Mosaic period Kautzsch says: "The principal constituent of the yet rudimentary religious sense was fear of the constantly threatening but always incalculable influence of demonic powers."[2] Nothing could be farther from the truth so far as the patriarchs are concerned. The God of the patriarchs comes to them in friendliness and promise, and the relationship between them and God is one of intimacy. This is especially clear in the story of Abraham's intercession for Sodom,[3] where prayer rises far above the heights of Jacob's. Here Abraham is not concerned for himself but for his nephew Lot, and he pleads with God with great freedom for a city that ill deserves his intercession. The story is sometimes read as a typical bit of oriental barter, with Abraham steadily beating down the price for the sparing of the city. It may more fittingly be read as the story of a man whose intimacy with God was as devoid of selfish purpose as it was of terror of the deity.

It is particularly in the cases of Abraham and Joseph that we see the quality of life that issued from the religion of fellowship. It is true that Abraham is reported to have passed his wife off as his sister to avoid danger for himself,[4] as Isaac also is said to have done.[5] We do not need to condone this exposure of the wife to dishonour, and it is hard to suppose that the narrators found virtue in this act, whose consequences were averted only by divine aid. Rather should we see here a further instance of the fidelity of the narrators to tradition.[6] It is improbable that this was an oft

---

[1] On Wisdom elements in the Joseph story cf. G. von Rad, *Copenhagen Congress Volume* (S.V.T. i), 1953, pp. 120ff.

[2] In Hastings' *D.B.*, Extra Vol., 1904, p. 623b.   [3] Gen. 18.23ff.

[4] Gen. 12.10ff; 20.1ff. On the wife-sister relationship cf. E. A. Speiser, *Biblical and other Studies*, ed. by A. Altmann, i, 1963, pp. 15ff, and *Genesis*, 1964, pp. 91ff; R. de Vaux, *Theology Digest*, xii, 1964, p. 237.

[5] Gen. 26.6ff.

[6] E. A. Speiser (*I.E.J.* vii, 1957, pp. 212f) says, in the light of Nuzu evidence, that the passing of a wife off as a sister reflects the customs of the

repeated piece of deception, though it has come down in tradition in variant forms and attached to various names. It confirms that there was no intention to idealize the patriarchs. But though this incident, if it is rightly attached to the name of Abraham, shows the patriarch in a poor light, in all else he shows a rare nobility of character. And Joseph similarly rises to remarkable heights of integrity and magnanimity, and is unruffled by swift changes of fortune. Before we write off the religion of the patriarchs as animism, we should ask whether this is the quality of life that is associated with animism.[1] Of Isaac we have less knowledge, and as I have said he is a more colourless person.[2] Like Abraham he is a peaceable man, who is prepared to yield rather than have conflict, as the incident of the wells shows.[3] And if Jacob is set against Abraham and Joseph by the meaner level of character he attained, he equally appears in the tradition as a less deeply religious man. When he is tempted to be unscrupulous, he is undeterred by the thought of God,[4] as Joseph was.[5] Hope of gain could drive him to make a bargain with God,[6] and fear of man could drive him to confession and plea for divine help.[7] But his worship did not express itself in any thought of great sacrifice for God or intercession for others. Abraham and Joseph stand out as the two peaks among the patriarchs. Of Abraham John Skinner well observes: "From the religious point of view, the life of Abraham has a surprising inner unity as a record of the progressive trial and strengthening of faith . . . He is the Father of the faithful

period and is "totally devoid of any ethical implication whatsoever". He says: "A wife who had at the same time the status, though not necessarily the blood ties, of a sister happened to command greater protection and prestige than an ordinary wife" (p. 213). He believes that the full meaning of this custom had already been lost to the narrator of the Genesis story himself.

[1] H. Ringgren (*Israelitische Religion*, 1963, p. 24) rejects any idea that the religion of the patriarchs was primitive.

[2] Cf. R. W. Moss, in Hastings' one volume *D.B.*, 1909, p. 386b: "Isaac is a less striking personality than his father. Deficient in the heroic qualities, he suffered in disposition from an excess of mildness and the love of quiet. He was . . . a gracious and kindly but not a strong man."

[3] Gen. 26.18ff.

[4] Gen. 25.29ff. On the sale of birthright and parallels from Nuzu, cf. E. A. Speiser, *A.A.S.O.R.* xii, 1933, p. 44; C. H. Gordon, *B.A.* iii, 1940, p. 4, and *The Living Past*, 1940, p. 177.

[5] Gen. 39.9.   [6] Gen. 28.20ff.   [7] Gen. 32.9ff.

and the Friend of God. And that inward attitude of spirit is
reflected in a character of singular loftiness and magnanimity,
which reveals no moral struggle, but is nevertheless the fruit of
habitual converse with God."[1]

Worship in the patriarchal age, then, was simple and individual, and its known forms were sacrifice and prayer. Yet it rose
to heights of fellowship with God seldom surpassed, and worship
and life were closely related. It lacked the corporate element
which we so often think of as the essential element of worship
because the conditions under which the patriarchs lived made
corporate worship of that kind impossible. I find it hard to think
they mingled in the social worship of the Canaanite shrines of
their day, just because the atmosphere of worship reflected in
the traditions preserved in Genesis is so completely alien to all we
know of the Canaanite shrines.

[1] In Hastings' one volume *D.B.*, 1909, p. 6a. Cf. E. A. Leslie, *Old
Testament Religion*, 1936, p. 76: "Abraham, Isaac and Jacob we rightly
view as towering figures among the ancient Hebrews. Although shrouded
with mystery they must have been personalities of great religious genius
to have so permanently influenced Israel." I should subscribe to this with
less enthusiasm in the case of Isaac and Jacob than in that of Abraham.

2

From the Exodus to the Founding
of the Temple

In the patriarchal period we read only of individual worship, but
from now on our records are predominantly of corporate acts of
worship. Nevertheless, there are stories of individual encounters
with God. Of these the most familiar is the story of the call of
Moses at the Burning Bush,[1] while another is of Joshua's encounter before the fall of Jericho.[2] Both mark critical points in the
careers of these men, and in both cases they remove their shoes
from their feet[3] as the mark of their awed recognition that they
are in the presence of God.

In the account of Moses' experience at the Burning Bush,
Yahweh reveals his name to Moses and claims the Israelites in
Egypt as his people.[4] This is commonly understood to mean that
here for the first time Yahweh appears as the God of Israel, and
in the Priestly document it is expressly stated that God had been
known to the patriarchs as El Shaddai, but had not made his
name Yahweh known to them.[5] He identifies himself with the
God of the patriarchs, just as in the Christian Church in China
he is identified with Shang Ti; but whereas from now on Yahweh
normally replaces El Shaddai, in China it is Shang Ti who
replaces Yahweh. In both cases a new content is given to the conception of God conveyed by the name. It is hard to suppose that
Yahweh is here being identified with the variety of local spirits
of trees and springs that many scholars have read into the book
of Genesis,[6] but not difficult to understand his being identified
with the High God reflected in the accounts we have.

Nevertheless, as I have said, a new understanding of the

[1] Ex. 3.1ff.   [2] Josh. 5.13ff.   [3] Ex. 3.5; Josh. 5.15.
[4] Ex. 3.15, 7.   [5] Ex. 6.2f.   [6] Cf. above, p. 16.

character of God is now given. It is given not so much in word as in event. The God of the patriarchs was gracious in promise, and his holiness was offended by such human wickedness as was found in Sodom.[1] His presence gave Joseph favour in the sight of men[2] and also lifted him to great heights of character. He had chosen Abraham for blessing, and in the nobility of the spirit he attained Abraham justified his choice. Now he chose Israel to be the heir of that blessing, yet not because of her greatness or worth.[3] "The Lord did not set his love upon you, nor choose you, because ye were more in number than any people; for ye were the fewest of all peoples: but because the Lord loveth you."[4] "Not for thy righteousness, or for the uprightness of thy heart, dost thou go in to possess their land; . . . for thou art a stiffnecked people."[5] Israel was weak, despised, and oppressed. In due course God forced Pharaoh to release her, and when Pharaoh pursued he delivered her without the raising of a human hand. In all this he revealed himself as a compassionate God, a God against whom human oppression is an offence, an electing God, a mighty God, and a saving God.[6] Israel's faith was based not on speculation, but on experience, and just as the blind man healed by Jesus could say: "One thing, I know, that whereas I was blind now I see",[7] so they could say: "One thing we know, that whereas we were slaves

---

[1] Gen. 18.20.   [2] Gen. 39.3, 21.

[3] The historicity of the election of Abraham is sometimes denied. Cf. E. Jacob, *La Tradition historique en Israël*, 1946, p. 152: "L'élection ne remonte pas à l'époque patriarcale, mais à la sortie d'Egypte." Cf. K. Galling, *Die Erwählungstraditionen Israels*, 1928, p. 63. In *B.D.E.*, 1950, pp. 19ff, I have argued for the reliability of both traditions. Cf. F. F. Bruce, in *N.B.D.*, 1962, pp. 265f. S. H. Hooke (*In the Beginning*, 1947, pp. 62f) thinks the purpose of the Yahwist was to unite the two traditions. Cf. also T. C. Vriezen, *Die Erwählung Israels nach dem Alten Testament*, 1953 (on which see my review in *J.B.L.* lxxiii, 1954, pp. 116f); F. M. Th. de Liagre Böhl, in *Festschrift für Alfred Bertholet*, 1950, pp. 77ff (reprinted in *Opera Minora*, 1953, pp. 81ff); K. Koch, *Z.A.W.* lxvii, 1955, pp. 205ff; H. Wildberger, *Jahwes Eigentumsvolk*, 1960; G. E. Mendenhall, in *I.D.B.* ii, 1962, pp. 76ff; P. Altmann, *Erwählungstheologie und Universalismus im Alten Testament*, 1964.

[4] Deut. 7.7f. Cf. Deut. 4.37; 10.15.   [5] Deut. 9.5f.

[6] Cf. *U.B.*, 1953, pp. 65ff (p. 65: "The most significant things that are taught about God's character are deeply stamped on the Bible as a whole, and they all spring from Israel's experience of God in the period of the Exodus").

[7] John 9.25.

now we are free." Their experience was real, and in the texture of that experience lay the revelation of the character of God.

When Moses led the people out to the sacred mount, they entered into covenant with him.[1] Because he had delivered them they pledged themselves in gratitude to serve him, while he laid his commands upon them. The Covenant was not their bargain with God, but their response to what he had done for them.[2] Much interest to-day gathers round the similarity of the form of the Covenant to the Hittite suzerainty treaties, where the suzerain imposes his conditions upon the vassals and they pledge their loyalty to him.[3] The form is not confined to Hittite treaties and is largely begotten of the very nature of such treaties.[4] But whereas the suzerainty treaties were imposed and were born of the fear of the suzerain on the part of the lesser powers, Israel's Covenant was born of gratitude and was freely entered into. God's claim upon Israel was established by his deliverance of her, not by his conquest of her. It was therefore a moral obligation, which it would have been dishonourable of her to resist. It required her to obey the will of God: "If ye will obey my voice indeed, and keep

---

[1] On the covenant of Sinai cf. D. J. McCarthy, *Treaty and Covenant*, 1963, pp. 152ff. Cf. also J. Begrich, *Z.A.W.* lx, 1944, pp. 1ff (reprinted in *Gesammelte Studien*, 1964, pp. 55ff); L. Rost, *Th.L.Z.* lxxii, 1947, cols. 129ff; O. Eissfeldt, *Z.A.W.* lxxiii, 1961, pp. 137ff. M. Noth is doubtful if Moses had anything to do with the Sinai Covenant. He says (*History of Israel*, E. Tr., 2nd edn, 1960, p. 136), "This suggests that Moses had no historical connection with the event which took place on Sinai." A different view is taken by G. Fohrer, *Überlieferung und Geschichte des Exodus*, 1964, and W. Beyerlin, *Origins and History of the Oldest Sinaitic Traditions*, E.Tr. by S. Rudman, 1965.

[2] Cf. F. F. Bruce, in *N.D.B.*, 1962, p. 266b: "The promise of obedience was the only proper response on the part of the people to the grace which the covenant disclosed." Cf. E. Lohmeyer, *Diatheke*, 1913, p. 54; R. B. Y. Scott, *The Relevance of the Prophets*, 1944, p. 121. G. E. Wright (*The Challenge of Israel's Faith*, 1946, p. 90) treats it in terms of contract. But its basis was what God had done, freely and unconditionally.

[3] Cf. above, p. 32. Cf. also E. von Waldow, *Der traditionsgeschichtliche Hintergrund der prophetischen Gerichtsreden*, 1963, pp. 21ff; M. Noth, in *Mélanges Isidore Lévy*, 1955, pp. 433ff (reprinted in *Gesammelte Studien zum Alten Testament*, 1960, pp. 142ff).

[4] Cf. D. J. McCarthy, *Treaty and Covenant*, 1963, pp. 8off. W. Beyerlin (op. cit., p. 51) thinks "we may be dealing with what was basically an international covenant-form in the Near East of the second millennium B.C."

my covenant, then ye shall be a peculiar treasure unto me from among all peoples."[1]

The will of God is not defined primarily in terms of ritual acts, but in terms of behaviour. At the head of the commands given through Moses we find the Ten Commandments.[2] These have been widely denied to Moses and assigned to a much later date.[3] There are not wanting scholars, however, who are persuaded that in their original brief form they go back to the time of Moses,[4]

[1] Ex. 19.5. There is disagreement between scholars as to the document from which this verse comes. It is assigned to J by S. R. Driver, *L.O.T.*, 9th edn, 1913, p. 31, Oesterley and Robinson, *Introduction to the Books of the Old Testament*, 1934, p. 37; to E₁ by G. Beer, *Exodus*, 1939, p. 97; to E by O. Eissfeldt, *Hexateuch-Synopse*, 1922, p. 146*; to J or E by A. Weiser, *Introduction to the Old Testament*, E. Tr. by D. M. Barton, 1961, p. 112; to the JE redactor by J. E. Carpenter, *The Composition of the Hexateuch*, 1902, p. 517; to the D redactor by B. Baentsch, *Exodus-Leviticus*, 1903, p. 172, C. Steuernagel, *Lehrbuch der Einleitung in das Alte Testament*, 1912, p. 150, A. H. McNeile, *Exodus*, 2nd edn, 1917, p. 110, H. Trabaud, in *La Bible du Centenaire*, i, 1941, p. 94, C. A. Simpson, *The Early Traditions of Israel*, 1948, p. 199. Whatever its date it well represents the character of the Covenant, as expressed in the Decalogue. J. Muilenburg (*V.T.* ix, 1959, p. 352) says Ex. 19.3–6 is *in nuce* the *fons et origo* of the many covenantal pericopes which appear throughout the Old Testament.

[2] Ex. 20.2ff. In a slightly different form the same Decalogue stands at the beginning of the Deuteronomic Code in Deut. 5.6ff.

[3] To the period of the prophets by A. Kuenen, *Historico-Critical Inquiry into the Origin and Composition of the Hexateuch*, E. Tr. by P. H. Wicksteed, 1886, pp. 244f, W. E. Addis, in *E.B.* i, 1889, col. 1050, A. H. McNeile, *Exodus*, 2nd edn, 1917, pp. lviff, H. P. Smith, *The Religion of Israel*, 1914, p. 187, A. Lods, *Israel*, E. Tr. by S. H. Hooke, 1932, pp. 315f, J. Morgenstern, in *U.J.E.* iii, 1941, p. 510, and many others; to the disciples of Isaiah by S. Mowinckel, *Le Décalogue*, 1927, pp. 156ff., and *Jesaja-disiplene*, 1926, pp. 77ff; to the exilic period by C. Steuernagel, *Lehrbuch der Einleitung in das Alte Testament*, 1912, pp. 259ff, G. Hölscher, *Geschichte der israelitischen und jüdischen Religion*, 1922, p. 129, and others. For an original view cf. E. Nielsen, *Die zehn Gebote*, 1965.

[4] Among scholars who affirm or allow that the Decalogue may be Mosaic are H. Ewald, *G.V.I.* ii, 2nd edn, 1853, pp. 22f; T. K. Cheyne, *Exp.*, 4th series, v, 1892, p. 109; W. P. Paterson, in Hastings's *D.B.* i, 1898, p. 581b; C. F. Burney, *J.T.S.* ix, 1908, pp. 323ff; E. Kautzsch, in Hastings' *D.B.*, Extra Vol., 1909, p. 634b; S. R. Driver, *Exodus*, 1911, p. 415; G. A. Smith, *Deuteronomy*, 1918, p. 85; H. Schmidt in *Eucharistērion* (Gunkel Festschrift), i, 1923, pp. 78ff (with the exception of the fourth and fifth commandments); P. Volz, *Mose und sein Werk*, 2nd edn,

and I have more than once argued for this view and do not need to do so again here.[1] It requires exclusive devotion to Yahweh and abstention from idolatry, the honouring of the name of Yahweh and the observance of the sabbath, but for the rest it demands the honouring of parents and abstention from murder, adultery, theft, false witness, and envy. In the last command it penetrates beneath conduct to the spring of conduct, and the whole is commonly referred to as the Ethical Decalogue. Its entire emphasis is on standards of conduct in ordinary human relations, and not on ceremonial acts.

This does not mean that the religion of Yahwism was ever a religion without forms of worship. Amos asks: "Did ye bring unto me sacrifices and offerings in the wilderness?",[2] and this is commonly understood to be a denial that sacrifices were offered in that age. If that were really what Amos meant, we should have to conclude that he was ill informed; for all our older evidence shows that sacrifice was offered in that age.[3] Jeremiah says: "I spake not

1932, pp. 20ff; J. M. Powis Smith, *Origin and History of Hebrew Law,* 1931, pp. 3ff (excluding the second commandment); A. Weiser, *Introduction to the Old Testament,* E. Tr. by D. M. Barton, 1961, pp. 120f; A. S. Kapelrud, *St. Th.* xviii, 1964, pp. 81ff; J. P. Hyatt, *Encounter,* xxvi, 1965, pp. 199ff; W. Beyerlin, op. cit., p. 149; and many others (for fuller references see *M.G.,* 1963, pp. 1f).

[1] Cf. *Rel.B.,* 1942, pp. 6of; *M.M.O.T.,* 1945, pp. 18f; *R.O.T.,* 1946, pp. 85ff; *B.D.E.,* 1950, pp. 55f; *J.J.,* 1950, pp. 157ff; *M.G.,* 1963, pp. 1ff.

[2] Amos 5.25. I have discussed this passage in *B.J.R.L.* xxix, 1945–6, pp. 340ff, and *M.Q.,* 1963, pp. 73ff. D. B. Macdonald (*J.B.L.* xviii, 1899, pp. 214f) noted the unusual order of the Hebrew words and rendered: "Was it only flesh-sacrifices and meal-offerings that ye brought me in the wilderness?" where the answer to the rhetorical question should have been "We brought more than this; we brought true worship of heart and righteousness". This seems to me substantially correct, though I should not accept his rendering of the sacrificial terms. Cf. R. J. Thompson, *Penitence and Sacrifice in Early Israel,* 1963, pp. 165f; S. Amsler, in *Osée, Joël, Amos, Abdias, Jonas,* 1965, p. 215.

[3] It has always seemed to me curious that the scholars who hold that the patriarchs worshipped at the local shrines also press this text in the service of the view that the prophets opposed the whole cultus and declared that it was a Canaanite corruption of Israelite religion. If in pre-Mosaic times the ancestors of Israel had worshipped at shrines where sacrifices were offered, but in the Mosaic period a non-sacrificial worship had been established, we should have expected an explicit repudiation of sacrifice by Moses; and if the prophets believed that Mosaic worship was

unto your fathers, nor commanded them in the day that I brought them out of the land of Egypt, concerning burnt offerings and sacrifices: but this thing I commanded them, saying, Hearken unto my voice, and I will be your God, and ye shall be my people."[1] This accords precisely with what I have just said, that God's call at Sinai was for obedience and obedience as defined in the Decalogue was in terms of conduct and not of ritual.[2]

A widely held view,[3] and again one for which I have argued non-sacrificial they should have appealed to such an explicit repudiation. Documents which are older than the time of Amos, resting on traditions which are older still, say that it was for the purpose of sacrifice that Moses demanded from Pharaoh the release of the Israelites (Ex. 5.3, J). Of any alternative tradition, to which Amos may be supposed to be referring, we have no trace, and it would be remarkable for Amos to refer to it as though everyone were aware of it.

[1] Jer. 7.22. I have discussed this passage in *B.J.R.L.* xxix, 1945–6, pp. 345ff (cf. *U.B.*, p. 41 and *M.Q.*, pp. 73f). We have here an example of the comparative negative, of which there are several examples in the Bible, where "not this but that" means "less this than that". Cf. John 6.27: "Work not for the meat which perisheth, but for the meat which abideth unto eternal life."

[2] P. Reymond (*Th.Z.* xxi, 1965, pp. 314ff) argues that Jeremiah is not contesting that there were sacrifices in the Mosaic period, but saying that they were not instituted by Moses and were of less importance than the Covenant, which was so little heeded by his contemporaries.

[3] Cf. B. Stade, *G.V.I.* i, 1887, pp. 130f, and *Biblische Theologie des Alten Testaments*, i, 1905, pp. 42f; K. Budde, *Religion of Israel to the Exile*, 1899, pp. 17ff; T. K. Cheyne, in *E.B.* iii, 1902, col. 3208; G. A. Barton, *A Sketch of Semitic Origins*, 1902, pp. 272f, 275ff, and *Semitic and Hamitic Origins*, 1934, pp. 332f; C. F. Burney, *J.T.S.* ix, 1908, pp. 337f; B. D. Eerdmans, *Alttestamentliche Studien*, ii, 1908, pp. 44ff; H. P. Smith, *Old Testament History*, 1911, p. 57; H. Gressmann, *Mose und seine Zeit*, 1913, pp. 434f, 447ff; R. Butin, in *Catholic Encyclopedia*, iii, 1913, p. 776b; J. Morgenstern, *H.U.C.A.* iv, 1927, pp. 44ff; W. Vischer, *Jahwe der Gott Kains*, 1929; A. Lods, *Israel*, E. Tr. by S. H. Hooke, 1932, pp. 317f, 320ff; H. Schmökel, *J.B.L.* lii, 1933, pp. 212ff; E. A. Leslie, *Old Testament Religion*, 1936, pp. 78ff; A. Vincent, *La Religion des Judéo-araméens d'Éléphantine*, 1937, pp. 30ff; Oesterley and Robinson, *Hebrew Religion*, 2nd edn, 1937, pp. 148ff, 156; G. Beer, *Exodus*, 1939, p. 30; A. J. Wensinck, *Semietische Studiën uit de Nalatenschap A.J.W.*, 1941, pp. 23ff; M. Noth, *Evangelische Theologie*, 1946, p. 309; I. G. Matthews, *The Religious Pilgrimage of Israel*, 1947, pp. 49f; J. Muilenburg, *I.B.* i, 1952, p. 301; L. Koehler, *Old Testament Theology*, E. Tr. by A. S. Todd, 1957, pp. 45f; H. Cazelles, in *Moïse, l'homme de l'Alliance*, 1955, p. 18; G. von Rad, *Old Testament Theology*, E. Tr. by D. M. G. Stalker, i, 1962, pp. 9f; J. Gray, in Peake's *Commentary on the Bible*,

more than once,[1] is that Yahweh was the God of the Kenites before the days of Moses,[2] and that he was the God whose priest 2nd edn, 1962, p. 113a; G. W. Anderson, ibid., p. 161b; D. M. G. Stalker, ibid., pp. 212a, 226a; M. L. Newman, *The People of the Covenant*, 1965, pp. 26, 83f; and H. Heyde, *Kain, der erste Jahwe-Verehrer*, 1965, pp. 32ff. M. Noth, who denies that Moses had any connection with Sinai (cf. above, p. 39, n. 1), holds that the name Yahweh derives from the pre-Israelite worship of Sinai; cf. *History of Israel*, E. Tr., 2nd edn, p. 134. Among scholars who have rejected the view are A. R. Gordon, *The Early Traditions of Genesis*, 1907, pp. 106ff; E. König, *Geschichte der alttestamentlichen Religion*, 1912, pp. 162ff; R. Kittel, *G.V.I.* i, 6th edn, 1923, p. 392n; C. Toussaint, *Les Origines de la religion d'Israël*, i, 1931, p. 225; P. Volz, *Mose und seine Werk*, 2nd edn, 1932, p. 59; W. J. Phythian-Adams, *The Call of Israel*, 1934, pp. 72ff; A. J. Baumgartner, in Westphal's *Dictionnaire encyclopédique de la Bible*, ii, 1935, pp. 181f; T. J. Meek, *Hebrew Origins*, 2nd edn, 1950, pp. 94ff; M. Buber, *Moses*, 1947, pp. 94ff; F. V. Winnett, *The Mosaic Tradition*, 1949, p. 69; O. Procksch, *Theologie des Alten Testaments*, pp. 76f; C. H. W. Brekelmans, *O.T.S.* x, 1954, pp. 215ff; J. A. Motyer, in *N.D.B.*, 1962, pp. 688f. U. E. Simon (*A Theology of Salvation*, 1953, p. 88) dismisses it as "the acme of liberal inventiveness". W. F. Albright leaves open the possibility of its being right, saying (*C.B.Q.* xxv, 1963, p. 10): "Starting probably as a liturgical expression among the Hebrews (or possibly the Midianites), Yahweh was adopted by Moses as the official name of the God of Israel."

[1] Cf. *B.J.R.L.* xxii, 1938, pp. 285ff; *M.M.O.T.*, 1945, pp. 12ff; *B.D.E.*, 1950, pp. 26ff; *J.J.*, 1950, pp. 149ff; *M.G.*, 1963, pp. 16ff; *M.Q.*, 1963, pp. 48ff. My view has been criticized by C. H. W. Brekelmans, *O.T.S.* x, 1954, pp. 215ff, to whom I reply in *M.Q.*, pp. 52ff. On my view, the worship of Yahweh came into Israel in two different ways. It came into Judah and the tribes associated with her by gradual penetration from Kenite elements also associated with Judah, and so it was not dated at a particular point of time, but was carried back to the beginnings of time. It came into the tribes that came out of Egypt through Moses, and so was historically dated. Both of the Pentateuchal traditions are therefore explained. Moreover, it is probable that Moses had some Kenite blood in him on his mother's side, and this would explain his flight to Jethro when he was forced to flee from Egypt, just as Jacob went to his mother's kindred when he fled from his brother. The mother of Moses was named Jochebed, which appears to contain the divine name Yahweh, and this name could well have been a family name in her family. The two diverse Biblical traditions have therefore a point of connection. Every other view is compelled to jettison one or other of the Biblical traditions and leave it without explanation.

[2] For the view that Yahweh was one of the gods of Ras Shamra, cf. above, p. 12, n. 2. Even if that view is correct Yahweh was so insignificant a deity at Ras Shamra that Ugarit is unlikely to have been the source of the Israelite worship of him, and Israelite contacts with Ugarit are

Jethro, the father-in-law of Moses, was.[1] This does not mean that Moses simply mediated the Kenite religion to the Israelites.[2] What ultimately matters in religion is not the name of the God invoked, but the conception of the deity and the nature of the worship and the level of life to which it leads. Yahweh became the God of Israel, not because Moses taught them his name, but because he had saved them from the power of Egypt. What he meant to Israel, therefore, was something quite different from what he had meant to the Kenites, and it is not surprising that Israelite Yahwism had a new quality and was lifted to a new level. The Covenant of Sinai was based on gratitude for what Yahweh had done, and was the response to a moral obligation. It is not surprising, then, that the new Decalogue was an Ethical Decalogue, and not one simply taken over from the Kenites.

There is another Decalogue, found in Exodus 34, though now its terms are increased to thirteen, commonly referred to as the Ritual Decalogue.[3] Some of its provisions are also found scattered

unrecorded and improbable, whereas contacts with the Kenites are freely recognized in the Old Testament. J. Barr (*T.G.U.O.S.* xvii, 1959, p. 61) suggests that the word *yahweh* was known in patriarchal times, but not as the name of God in the strict sense, but as a phrase expressing his presence and action. This would not seem to explain the double tradition in the Pentateuch.

[1] J. P. Hyatt (*V.T.* v, 1955, pp. 130ff) argues that Yahweh was the God of one of Moses' ancestors through his mother, Jochebed (cf. also in *The Teacher's Yoke* (Trentham Festschrift), 1964, pp. 85ff). With this cf. *J.J.*, 1950, p. 160.

[2] Cf. what I have written in *M.M.O.T.*, pp. 17ff; *B.D.E.*, pp. 36f; *M.G.*, pp. 18f; *M.Q.*, pp. 57f; *J.J.*, pp. 156f. Cf. also K. Marti, *The Religion of the Old Testament*, E. Tr. by G. A. Bienemann, 1914, p. 62: "Even though Jahwe was originally the name of the God of Sinai, it immediately received a higher significance under the Israelites than that which it had possessed as the God of the confederate tribes of Mount Sinai." R. Butin (loc. cit.) rejects the view that the Israelites received "a great portion of their monotheistic theology" from the Kenites.

[3] In *M.G.*, 1963, pp. 7ff I discuss this Decalogue and indicate some of the many ways of reducing the thirteen to ten commandments proposed by different authors. Discussions of this Decalogue may be found in W. E. Barnes, *J.T.S.* vi, 1905, pp. 557ff; A. C. Knudson, *J.B.L.* xxviii, 1909, pp. 82ff; R. H. Kennett, in *Cambridge Biblical Essays*, ed. by H. B. Swete, 1909, pp. 95ff; G. Beer, *Pesachim*, 1912, pp. 23ff; C. H. Cornill, *Studien zur semitischen Philologie* (Wellhausen Festschrift), 1914, pp. 109ff; R. H. Pfeiffer, *J.B.L.* xliii, 1924, pp. 294ff; J. Morgenstern, *H.U.C.A.* iv, 1927, pp. 54ff; S. Mowinckel, *Le Décalogue*, 1927, pp. 19ff;

in the Book of the Covenant.[1] Like the other Decalogue the Ritual Decalogue demands the exclusive worship of Yahweh and abstention from idolatry and the observance of the sabbath, but for the rest its emphasis is on the observance of sacred festivals, the offering of sacrifices and firstfruits, and other ritual requirements: "All that openeth the womb is mine. . . . Three times in the year shall all thy males appear before the Lord. . . . Thou shalt not offer the blood of my sacrifice with leavened bread. . . . Thou shalt not seethe a kid in its mother's milk."[2] I have argued— though I did not originate the view—that this was the pre-Mosaic Kenite Decalogue.[3] Its expansion to thirteen commandments probably reflects accommodation to agricultural conditions. If the view that this was originally a Kenite Decalogue is correct, then the measure of the new thing · which Moses brought into the religion of Israel is to be found in the difference of the level of this Decalogue and the Ethical Decalogue. Significant is the common ground between the two Decalogues. Both demand the exclusive worship of Yahweh, forbid images,[4] and enjoin the observance

G. B. Gray, *J.T.S.* xxxvii, 1936, pp. 245ff; F. V. Winnett, *The Mosaic Tradition*, 1949, pp. 50ff. Further references may be found in *M.G.*, loc. cit.

[1] Cf. Ex. 20.23; 22.29f; 23.12, 14f, 17–19.

[2] Ex. 34.19, 23, 25, 26.

[3] *M.G.*, p. 18. The view that this Decalogue was of Kenite origin was advanced by J. Morgenstern, *H.U.C.A.*, iv, 1927, pp. 54ff.

[4] Here the term used means a molten image, whereas in the Ethical Decalogue the term used means a graven image. E. Kautzsch (in Hastings' *D.B.*, Extra Vol., p. 641b) takes this to mean that the rejection of a molten image permitted a graven image, but curiously thinks the rejection of a graven image included the rejection of a molten image. Cf. E. Sellin, *Introduction to the Old Testament*, E. Tr. by W. Montgomery, 1923, p. 45: "Particularly naïve is the assertion that Ex. 20 must be later than Ex. 34, because in the latter passage only molten images, whereas in the other images of all kinds, are forbidden, for if molten images are an offence against the Deity, carved images or those in plastic material can certainly be no less so." The worship of Yahweh appears to have been imageless from the beginning (cf. *M.G.*, 1963, pp. 23ff; also K. H. Bernhardt, *Gott und Bild*, 1956, pp. 110ff, 154f; H. Haag, in *Moraltheologie und Bibel*, ed. by J. Stelzenberger, 1964, p. 27). J. Morgenstern (*Amos Studies*, i, 1941, pp. 229ff, and *The Ark, the Ephod and the "Tent of Meeting"*, 1945, pp. 4 n, 107) maintained that in the inner shrine of the Temple there stood a golden image of Yahweh in human form until the reformation of Asa. More recently, however (*V.T.* x, 1960, p. 185), he holds that there was no image, but an empty throne. It is often held that the bulls of

of the sabbath.[1] These appear to be ancient and basic features of Yahwism, specifically continued in the Mosaic Decalogue. The remaining provisions, which were ritual, were replaced by the ethical demands which show that Yahweh is more interested in character than in ritual.

The Ritual Decalogue was not rejected, however. It was preserved in Israel, and has come down to us in Israelite documents. It was apparently taken over, but relegated to a secondary position. Moses did not invent a new ritual, because he was concerned with something far more fundamental than this.[2] He was welding a company of slaves into a people, whose bond of unity was their devotion to Yahweh, and before whom high ideals of character were set. He was achieving something unique in the history of religion, a people's commitment of itself in a Covenant to the God who had first chosen and delivered it.[3] Moses could hardly have contemplated a religion which did not express itself in some form of worship. But that could be taken over from the Kenites, so long as it was infused with the new spirit. When Jethro came to meet the delivered Israelites, he offered the sacrifice of thanksgiving for their deliverance.[4] This is fully consonant with the view that he was already the priest of Yahweh, but if he was

Jeroboam were images of Yahweh in the form of a bull. Many authors have held that they were pedestals, like the Canaanite pedestals on which Hadad stood, but with no image of Yahweh standing on them; cf. below, p. 82.

[1] For literature on the question of the sabbath, cf. below, p. 92, nn. 2, 6.

[2] The historicity of Moses was denied by E. Meyer (*Die Israeliten und ihre Nachbarstämme*, 1906, p. 451 n) while H. P. Smith (*Old Testament History*, 1911, pp. 52ff) thinks we can have little knowledge of him. For a survey of modern views on Moses cf. R. Smend, *Das Mosebild von Heinrich Ewald bis Martin Noth*, 1959.

[3] T. J. Meek (*Hebrew Origins*, 2nd edn, 1950, p. 96) sees nothing unique in this, and says that many peoples have adopted another religion. This is both true and beside the point. Conquest, infiltration, intermarriage, and various other causes have led to such adoption. But no other case is recorded of a people believing that God had first adopted and delivered them, and then committing themselves in an act of gratitude to him. K. Budde (*Religion of Israel to the Exile*, 1899, p. 38) says: "Israel's religion became ethical because it was a religion of choice and not of nature, because it rested on a voluntary decision which established an ethical relation between the people and its God for all time." This is inadequate, since choice is not inherently ethical. But gratitude is an ethical emotion, and a religion founded on gratitude is ethically based.

[4] Ex. 18.12.

the priest of some other god it would be very surprising for him to offer this sacrifice.[1] If he was the priest of Yahweh, it would be natural for him to initiate the Israelites into the forms of Yahweh worship.

It is not surprising that Israel should offer sacrifices to Yahweh, for sacrifice was widespread, and in the narratives of the patriarchs sacrifice had already figured.[2] It was for the purpose of offering sacrifice to Yahweh that Moses was sent to bring the people out of Egypt.[3] It is to be observed that in the Ritual Decalogue there was no provision for the individual sacrifice from time to time, as occasion demanded, though it is antecedently likely that such sacrifices would continue to be offered. The interest here is in the national festivals when the people were required to present themselves before God. Three times each year they were so to present themselves,[4] and they were required to bring an offering with them.[5]

There is, in particular, mention of the Passover,[6] which would thus appear to have been an observance of the religion of Yahweh among the Kenites before the time of Moses. It was observed by the Israelites in Egypt on the instructions of Moses at the time of the Exodus.[7] That the Passover was of great antiquity,[8] and that it was originally a sacrifice of nomads or semi-nomads, is

[1] T. J. Meek (*Hebrew Origins*, 2nd edn, 1950, pp. 94f; cf. *A.J.S.L.* xxxvii, 1920–1, p. 104) thinks Jethro was converted from the worship of his own god to the worship of Yahweh by the demonstration of the power of Yahweh in the deliverance of Israel. But in that case it would be very surprising for him to preside at his own initiation into the new religion. C. H. W. Brekelmans (*O.T.S.* x, 1954, pp. 215ff) thinks Jethro came to supplicate for a treaty with Moses, and that the sacrifice was for the ratification of the treaty, but of this there is no hint, and it would be surprising for the suppliant to preside at the meal and to go on to give advice on the administration of justice.

[2] Cf. above, pp. 22ff.   [3] Ex. 5.3.   [4] Ex. 34.23.
[5] Ex. 34.20.   [6] Ex. 34.25.   [7] Ex. 12.21ff.
[8] R. Smend (*Lehrbuch der alttestamentlichen Religionsgeschichte*, 1893, p. 127 n) says the Passover was originally unconnected with Yahweh and was older than the God of Israel. That it was older than Israelite Yahwism I would agree, but I believe it was connected with pre-Mosaic Yahwism. R. H. Pfeiffer (*Religion in the Old Testament*, 1961, p. 41) says: "Everything indicates that the festival had been celebrated by shepherds from time immemorial." Cf. S. R. Driver, *Exodus*, 1911, p. 410: "The Passover, at least in its primitive form, is in all probability a pre-Mosaic institution."

widely agreed.[1] That it was once quite separate from the Feast of Unleavened Bread, with which it was later associated, is generally believed,[2] though this view has been challenged by J. B. Segal.[3] Each family or group of families killed a male sheep or goat of a prescribed age, roasted it whole, and ate it with girt loins, after sprinkling the blood on the door-posts and lintel, and whatever remained uneaten had to be burned by fire before the morning.[4] The mention of door-posts and lintel presupposes houses, rather than tents, but this does not disprove the antiquity of the rite. Dhorme observes that it is due to the fact that the ceremony was continued from age to age after habitation in tents

[1] Cf. S. R. Driver, loc. cit.: "It is not . . . based upon agriculture, but reaches back into the nomadic stage." Cf. also W. H. Bennett, *Exodus*, p. 283; W. O. E. Oesterley, *Sacrifices in Ancient Israel*, 1937, p. 99; G. Beer, *Pascha*, 1911, pp. 13ff. On the other hand I. Engnell (*Orientalia Suecana*, i, 1952, p. 47) says it "is not primarily to be judged of as an old 'nomadic' or 'desert' feast". F. V. Winnett (*The Mosaic Tradition*, 1949, p. 156) conjectures that it may have been a Canaanite rite which was gradually adopted and merged with the specifically Israelite festival of Unleavened Bread (this reverses the more general view).

[2] So, for example, among recent authors, H. G. May, *J.B.L.* lv, 1936, pp. 65ff; E. Dhorme, *La Religion des Hébreux nomades*, 1937, p. 210; J. Pedersen, *Israel III–IV*, 1940, pp. 400f; R. Dussaud, *Les Origines cananéennes du sacrifice israélite*, 2nd edn, 1941, p. 207; P. van Imschoot, in *Dictionnaire encyclopédique de la Bible*, 1960, col. 1327; R. de Vaux, *A.I.*, p. 488, and *Studies in Old Testament Sacrifice*, E. Tr., 1964, p. 3; J. C. Rylaarsdam, in *I.B.D.* iii, 1962, p. 664a.

[3] *The Hebrew Passover*, 1963, p. 92ff (on which cf. the long review by H. Kosmala, *V.T.* xiv, 1964, pp. 504ff). R. de Vaux (*Studies in Old Testament Sacrifice*, p. 26 n) rejects this view. I. Engnell (loc. cit., p. 48), while holding that Passover and Unleavened Bread were originally separate, maintains that they were fused from the time of the Settlement, because they were at bottom really identical. A. Vincent (*La Religion des Judéo-Araméens d'Éléphantine*, 1937, pp. 306 n.) places their combination at the time of the Exodus, while H. J. Kraus (*Evangelische Theologie*, xviii, 1958, pp. 47ff) holds that Passover was celebrated at an amphictyonic shrine in the period of the Judges, and that Passover and Unleavened Bread were combined even before that. On the other hand E. Kutsch (*Z.Th.K.* lv, 1958, pp. 20ff, 34) held that Passover and Unleavened Bread were not combined until the Exile, while E. Auerbach (*V.T.* viii, 1958, pp. 1ff) maintained that the two feasts were first combined in P, and there for the first time given an historical interpretation.

[4] On the provision that the bones of the victim were not to be broken (Ex. 12.46) cf. J. Henninger in *Studi Orientalistici* (Levi della Vida Festschrift), i, 1956, pp. 448ff.

was discontinued,[1] and he says he can find no example more typical of the sacrifices of nomads.[2] The provision that nothing of the Passover sacrifice must remain over until the morning is found in the Ritual Decalogue.[3] It lies beyond my purpose to enter into a discussion of the question whether the Passover was originally a New Year festival, on which contrary views have been maintained,[4] or to consider the original significance of the ritual. That significance can only be conjectured,[5] and it is immaterial to

[1] *La Religion des Hébreux nomades*, p. 211.
[2] Ibid.   [3] Ex. 34.25.
[4] So S. H. Hooke, *The Origins of Early Semitic Ritual*, 1938, pp. 48ff; I. Engnell, loc. cit., pp. 48ff; J. B. Segal, op. cit., 114ff. Against this cf. N. H. Snaith, *The Jewish New Year Festival*, 1947, pp. 18ff; S. Mowinckel, *The Psalms in Israel's Worship*, E. Tr. by D. R. Ap-Thomas, 1962, p. 233. E. Auerbach (*V.T.* viii, 1958, pp. 1f) maintains that the word *ḥōdhesh* meant "month" only in post-exilic times and that before that it meant "new moon", and hence it would follow that Deut. 16.1 sets the Passover at the new moon of Abib. Cf. below, p. 91, for Snaith's view.
[5] Innumerable conjectures have been made, for example, that it was an offering of firstlings (so J. Wellhausen, *Prolegomena to the History of Israel*, E. Tr., pp. 89ff; W. R. Smith, *Religion of the Semites*, 3rd edn, 1925, pp. 464f; A. Lods, *Israel*, E. Tr. by S. H. Hooke, 1932, p. 292; W. O. E. Oesterley, *Sacrifices in Ancient Israel*, 1931, p. 100); that it was a threshold rite to preserve the house from harm (so H. C. Trumbull, *The Threshold Covenant*, 1896, pp. 203ff; C. A. Simpson, *I.B.* i, 1952, pp. 919f; cf. M. Joseph, in *U.J.E.* viii, 1942, p. 409a); that it was to enhance the fertility of the flocks (so S. Mowinckel, *Religion och Kultus*, 1953, pp. 58, 103f); that it was associated with a cultic limping dance connected with the ancient Near Eastern nature festival (so I. Engnell, loc. cit., pp. 46ff; cf. C. H. Toy, *J.B.L.* xvi, 1897, pp. 178f); that it was a common meal, intended to re-cement ties of kinship, into which magical ideas had been introduced (so T. H. Gaster, *Passover*, 1949, pp. 16ff); that it was not originally a springtime festival, but a rite used in times of pestilence to secure protection against the Destroyer (so I. Benzinger, in *E.B.* iii, 1902, col. 3595); that it was not a sacrifice of firstlings, but a springtime rite to protect against misfortune in the ensuing year (N. M. Nicolsky, *Z.A.W.* xlv, 1927, pp. 171ff, 241ff); that it was a circumcision festival, when all who had attained the proper age during the year were circumcised on the same day (so E. G. Hirsch, in *J.E.* ix, 1907, p. 554b); that it marked the removal of nomads from winter pasturage to summer pasturage (so L. Rost, *Z.D.P.V.* lvi, 1943, pp. 205ff; cf. M. Noth, *Überlieferungsgeschichte des Pentateuch*, 1948, p. 72f); that the slaying of the firstborn in Egypt goes back to the ritual slaying of the king (so S. H. Hooke, *Myth and Ritual*, 1933, p. 12). H. J. Kraus maintains that it was celebrated at the amphictyonic sanctuary of Gilgal from the

our purpose. We are concerned only with the forms and meaning of worship in ancient Israel, and since the conjectured original meaning of this rite does not figure in the Old Testament, it is of no moment to us to-day. For if a Kenite rite was continued, it was invested with a new meaning. From the time of the Exodus it was forever linked with the memory of the deliverance from Egypt and was a perpetual reminder to Israel of what God had wrought for them.[1] Its observance was thus a summons to renewed gratitude to God and to the renewal of the loyalty that was born of the gratitude the deliverance first aroused.

The requirement that men should present themselves before God three times a year implies some shrine or shrines at which they were to appear, and the bringing of firstfruits implies some priesthood to receive them. Moreover, since Jethro was a priest,[2] if Yahweh worship was Kenite before it was Israelite we have definite testimony to some priesthood, and since he offered the already mentioned sacrifice, it would seem that sacrifice by a priest was preferred to the practice we found in the patriarchal narratives, where the patriarchs offered sacrifices themselves. This does not necessarily mean that the services of a special priest were required for sacrifice, though it is antecedently probable that at any shrine to which the community was called to repair at national festivals some priest would be in charge.

In the Pentateuch we read of the construction of the Tabernacle[3] and of the hereditary Aaronite priesthood which served there,[4] together with vast numbers of Levites,[5] and we are told much of the ritual which is said to have been observed there. All this is in the Priestly document, and while it is agreed that many things in

days of the Judges (*Worship in Israel*, E.Tr., 1966, pp. 161ff; on the amphictyony see below, p. 58 n.). To the various theories as to the significance of the name for the Passover, *pesaḥ*, B. Couroyer (*R.B.* lxii, 1955, pp. 481ff) has added the proposal to give it an Egyptian derivation. For other derivations cf. H. Haag, in *S.D.B.* vi, 1960, cols. 1121f.

[1] For the view of J. Pedersen that Ex. 1—15 constituted a liturgical text annually read at the spring festival, recording not history but salvation history, cf. *Z.A.W.* lii, 1934, pp. 161ff, and for a criticism of it cf. S. Mowinckel, *St.Th.* v, 1952, pp. 66ff.

[2] Ex. 3.1; 18.1.

[3] Ex. 35—40. On the relation of the LXX text to M.T. cf. D. W. Gooding, *The Account of the Tabernacle*, 1959; also A. H. Finn, *J.T.S.* xvi, 1914–15, pp. 449ff.

[4] Ex. 28f.   [5] Num. 3f.

the ritual were of great antiquity, it is not to be doubted that the whole conception of the Tabernacle and its ministry was a projection into the past of the Temple and its ministry.[1] Nevertheless, we cannot doubt that there was some shrine, even in the period of the Wandering, where men could come into the presence of God.

The Tabernacle is said to have been always in the centre of the camp, or in the centre of the column in moving,[2] and according to Ex. 25.22 it was the place where God would commune with Moses and communicate his will. In the earlier E document, however, we read of a much simpler Tent of Meeting, to which everyone who sought the Lord might go.[3] Unlike the Tabernacle, this stood outside the camp afar off,[4] and it was kept by the Ephraimite, Joshua.[5] That this was not a temporary shrine, to be used only until the Tabernacle was constructed, is clear from the fact that it figures later in the story after the Tabernacle is said to have been prepared,[6] and this simple Tent fulfilled the need in the period of the Wanderings for a place where men might come into the presence of God. Of any form of worship in connection with this Tent, however, we are left without information, and it is significant that we never read of any act of sacrifice associated with this Tent. It would seem that where sacrifice is offered, it is on an *ad hoc* altar built for the occasion, similar to those we read of in the patriarchal age. When Jethro offered sacrifice, the altar is not mentioned but only implied,[7] and it must have been erected for the purpose. For we are told that Jethro came to meet Moses and the Israelites where they were encamped and sacrificed there, and afterwards returned to his own land. This sacrifice was not offered, therefore, at any shrine which Jethro kept as priest. Again, when the covenant sacrifice was offered, we are told that Moses rose early in the morning and erected an altar.[8] Similarly, in the story of the Golden Calf, Aaron is said to have erected an

---

[1] M. Haran (*J.B.L.* lxxxi, 1962, pp. 14ff) agrees that the account of the Tabernacle is largely imaginary, and that it never existed in Israel. But he suggests that it was derived from the tradition of the Shiloh shrine, which was presented in a Jerusalemite dress.

[2] Num. 2.

[3] Ex. 33.7ff. On the Tent traditions, cf. S. Lehming, in *Gottes Wort und Gottes Land* (Hertzberg Festschrift), 1965, pp. 110ff.

[4] Ex. 33.7.   [5] Ex. 33.11.   [6] Num. 11.16ff; 12.4ff.
[7] Ex. 18.12.   [8] Ex. 24.4.

altar.[1] Here I am not concerned with the question whether this story is a projection into the past of the northern bull-images, as is commonly thought, but merely with its testimony to the tradition that in the Wilderness period *ad hoc* altars were constructed as needed. The early law of the altar, found in the Book of the Covenant, laid it down that the altar should be made of earth, or else of unhewn stone, and that it should be erected in every place where God should record his name.[2] While, therefore, there was a portable shrine in the Wilderness period, there is no reason to think a portable altar accompanied it.

As to varieties of sacrifice in this period, apart from the Passover, we find references to whole burnt offerings and sacrifices,[3] where the general term for sacrifice is used. Thus, Jethro is said to have offered a whole burnt offering and sacrifices,[4] and Moses is said to have demanded from Pharaoh animals to offer as whole burnt offerings and sacrifices.[5] In the account of the covenant sacrifice we are told that whole burnt offerings and peace offerings were offered,[6] and in the law of the altar found in the Book of the Covenant the same terms are used.[7] The peace offering is better described as a communion offering[8] or shared offering, since it was shared between God, the priest, and the worshipper, and it is probable that in the passages referred to the general term is used for this variety of sacrifice.

There is little mention of any priesthood in the early records of this period. Jethro is described as a priest,[9] and, as has been said, he offered sacrifice when he was present. At the covenant sacrifice it was Moses who acted as the priest.[10] We are told that young men of the children of Israel offered whole burnt offerings and peace offerings, but since Moses disposed of the blood, it is apparent that he acted as the priest. The disposal of the blood is of particular importance in sacrifice, and always falls to the priest, where a professional priest is present. We are told that Moses cast half of it against the altar and sprinkled the rest upon the people.[11] On both of these occasions there was a sacred meal,[12] so that both were

---

[1] Ex. 32.5. [2] Ex. 20.24f. [3] '*Ōlôth* and *zᵉbhāḥîm*.

[4] Ex. 18.12. [5] Ex. 10.25. [6] Ex. 24.5. [7] Ex. 20.24.

[8] So R. de Vaux, *Studies in Old Testament Sacrifice*, 1964, p. 31. Cf. M. Noth's *Gemeinschafts-Schlachtopfer* in his translation in *Leviticus* in A.T.D., 1962. K. Elliger (*Leviticus*, 1966) has *Heilsmahlopfer*.

[9] Ex. 3.1; 18.1. [10] Ex. 24.4ff. [11] Ex. 24.6, 8. [12] Ex. 18.12; 24.11.

shared offerings. Similarly, in the story of the making of the Golden Calf, Aaron is said to have offered whole burnt offerings and peace offerings, after which there was a sacred meal.[1] It would therefore seem to have been the normal pattern of sacrifices, other than the whole burnt offering, to include a sacred meal in which the worshippers shared.

Of personal piety in this age we learn little. We should not omit to note, however, that prayer, which might be offered apart from any sanctuary or altar, figures in the story,[2] and in the account of Moses' intercession after the making of the Golden Calf,[3] atoning value is attributed to the prayer.[4] It is a noble prayer, far removed from the self-seeking prayer of Jacob at Bethel,[5] and more akin to Abraham's intercession for Sodom.[6] Moses seeks nothing for himself, but cries to God to forgive the people or to blot his name out of the book which he (God) had written. Here we are reminded of Paul's yearning over his fellow-Jews: "I could wish that I myself were anathema from Christ for my brethren's sake, my kinsmen according to the flesh."[7] Again, when the people rejected the minority report of the spies sent into the land of Canaan, Moses once more interceded for them and pleaded that they should be forgiven.[8] Worship is thus conceived as communion, not simply symbolized in the eating of a meal after part of the animal eaten had been offered on the altar, but expressing itself also in prayer. It should, moreover, be realized that obedience in the fulfilment of the Ten Commandments is also the service of God and therefore worship, for in Hebrew serve and worship are expressed by a common word.[9]

It is probable that the Ark of Yahweh comes from the Mosaic age. The elaborate description of the making of the Ark in the book of Exodus[10] belongs to the Priestly document and is part of its projection into the past of the later Temple. Apart from this we have no account of the making of the Ark in the book of

---

[1] Ex. 32.6.   [2] For example, Ex. 17.4; 33.12ff; Num. 11.2, 11ff; 12.13.
[3] Ex. 32.31f.   [4] Ex. 32.30.   [5] Gen. 28.20ff.
[6] Gen. 18.23ff.   [7] Rom. 9.3.   [8] Num. 14.13ff.
[9] It may be added that the same word denotes "work". It is doubtful if R. Martin-Achard (in *Vocabulary of the Bible*, ed. by J. J. von Allmen, E. Tr., 1958, p. 472a) is justified in deducing from this that "in Biblical thought there is no watertight division between daily work and the adoration of God".
[10] Ex. 37.1ff.

Exodus. Nevertheless, there are references to it which make it almost certain that it was as ancient as the time of Moses.[1] The book of Deuteronomy knows a tradition that Moses made the Ark,[2] and this is earlier testimony than the Priestly document and is in disagreement with it, since the latter attributes its construction to Bezalel, who is unmentioned in Deuteronomy. For its historical reminiscences Deuteronomy is largely dependent on the earlier JE, and it may well be that JE once contained an account of the making of the Ark,[3] which was ultimately discarded in favour of that of P. For there are references to the Ark in the older documents. A fragment of an ancient poem preserved in the book of Numbers indicates that when the Ark was taken up for journeying and when it came to rest Moses uttered a ritual cry, and that cry associates the Ark with the scattering of Israel's foes.[4]

In the Priestly account the Ark is housed in the Tabernacle and it is said to have contained the two tables of the Law on which the Ten Commandnments were inscribed.[5] The earlier accounts do not tell us where the Ark was kept. It is unmentioned in connection with the Tent of Meeting, though it is possible that it was kept there by the Ephraimite Joshua.[6] In a later age we find it in an

[1] Num. 10.33, 35f. E. Nielsen (*Oxford Congress Volume* (S.V.T. vii), 1960, pp. 61f) thinks it is impossible to conclude that the Ark had its origin in the Wilderness period, and proposes the view (pp. 63ff) that the Ark was particularly associated with the Benjamites and that it stood in the shrine of El-'Elyon at Shiloh. This view seems very improbable (cf. R. E. Clements, *God and Temple*, 1965, p. 34 n).

[2] Deut. 10.1, 3.

[3] Cf. S. R. Driver, *Deuteronomy*, 2nd edn, 1896, p. 118: "The consistency with which the retrospects of Deuteronomy are based upon JE's narrative in Exodus and Numbers renders it highly probable that the text of Exod. xxxiv.1–5 once told how Moses made the ark of acacia-wood, and deposited the tables in it . . .; but that when JE was combined . . . . with P, the passages containing those statements were omitted by the compiler." Cf. W. Beyerlin, op. cit., pp. 147f.

[4] Num. 10.35f.   [5] Ex. 40.20; cf. 31.18; 32.15; 34.29.

[6] Cf. R. de Vaux, *À la Rencontre de Dieu* (Mémorial Gelin), 1961, pp. 55ff. G. von Rad (*Old Testament Theology*, E. Tr. by D. M. G. Stalker, i, 1962, p.235; cf. also *The Problem of the Hexateuch and Other Essays*, E.Tr., 1966, pp. 103ff) holds that Ark and Tent were two cult objects existing independently of each other. M. Noth (*Exodus*, E. Tr. by J. S. Bowden, 1962, pp. 254ff) observes that the concept of the tent is quite substantially different from the concepts associated with the Ark. Cf. also M. Haran, *J.S.S.* v, 1960, pp. 50ff; M. L. Newman, *The People of the Covenant*, 1965, p. 65.

Ephraimite shrine,[1] and the young Ephraimite Samuel slept beside it.[2] Deuteronomy, which is older than the Priestly document and which may here again be dependent on lost older sources, preserves the tradition that it contained the tables of the Law.[3]

The fragment of poetry just referred to is our most ancient reference to the Ark, and its testimony to the association of the Ark with war is supported by other passages. It was regarded as the symbol of the presence of God himself with his people.[4] In the battle against the Amalekites and Canaanites, in which the Israelites fought contrary to the orders of Moses and in which they were defeated, we are told that the Ark did not leave the camp for the battlefield.[5] In the attack on Jericho the ritual procession of the Ark played an important part.[6] Later, in the days of Eli the Ark was taken from the Shiloh shrine to the battlefield of Aphek and there captured by the Philistines.[7] When the Ark was brought on to the battlefield it was greeted with a great shout by the Israelites,[8] and when the Philistines learned the reason they said: "God is come into the camp", doubtless reflecting the Israelite belief that the Ark was the symbol of God's presence.[9] All of this points to the antiquity of the Ark, and to its associations with war. For war was a sacred undertaking in the eyes of Israel, and ritual commands were laid upon the warriors.[10]

[1] 1 Sam. 3.3.

[2] Ibid. J. Maier (*Das israelitische Ladeheiligtum* (B.Z.A.W. 93), 1965) holds that all references to the Ark prior to its appearance at Shiloh are unhistorical. He surmises that it may have been associated with anti-Philistine propaganda, and may have been a treasure chest for offerings for the rising against the Philistines.

[3] Deut. 10.2, 5.

[4] A. R. Johnson (*The One and the Many in the Israelite Conception of God*, 2nd edn, 1961, pp. 19ff) prefers to speak of it as an "extension" of the personality of God.

[5] Num. 14.44.   [6] Josh. 3ff.   [7] 1 Sam. 4.

[8] 1 Sam. 4.5.   [9] 1 Sam. 4.7.

[10] Cf. J. Pedersen, *Israel III–IV*, 1940, pp. 1ff; R. de Vaux, *A.I.*, pp. 213ff; G. von Rad, *Der heilige Krieg im alten Israel*, 1951, and *Studies in Deuteronomy*, E. Tr. by D. M. G. Stalker, 1953, pp. 45ff; O. Bauernfeind, *Th.W.B.* vi, 1960, pp. 507ff; also H. Frederiksson, *Jahwe als Krieger*, 1945; O. Eissfeldt, "Jahwe Zebaoth", in *Miscellanea Academica Berolinensia*, iii, 1950, pp. 128ff; B. N. Wambacq, *L'Épithète divine Jahvé S^eba'ôt*, 1947; and P. D. Miller, *Interpretation*, xix, 1965, pp. 39ff.

In this connection we recall the custom of the ban,[1] by which all enemy persons and property were destroyed as a religious act. This probably concerned only the first battle of a campaign or some critical encounter, when everything was vowed to destruction as an act of worship and appeal to God. There can be no reason to doubt that this custom was observed at Hormah,[2] since the very name reflects the word ḥērem, or ban, and at Jericho. When Achan was found to have violated the vow and to have retained some of the spoil, he himself and all his family and possessions were themselves destroyed so as to eliminate from Israel the iniquity that had been wrought.[3] In a later age we find the same ban put into operation against the Amalekites at the instigation of Samuel, though only partially applied by Saul.[4] A somewhat milder form of ban is referred to in some passages, where we read of the massacre of all men, women, and children, but the retention of animal and material spoil by the victors.[5] Here there is nothing peculiar to Yahwism, and this savage custom is not part of the new thing mediated to Israel by Moses. As the inscription of Mesha tells us,[6] the Moabites no less than the Israelites had this custom, and it is probable that we have here something that Israel took over from the world in which she was set.[7] She looked to God for victory when she was the aggressor and for deliverance when she was attacked, and in a crisis she could show the same willingness to express her plea for help in the terms used by her neighbours. But we need not regard this as a form of worship which belonged in its origin to Yahwism. Like the institution of sacrifice, it was shared with the peoples around

---

[1] On the ban cf. A. Fernández, *Biblica*, v, 1924, pp. 1ff; C. H. W. Brekelmans, *De Ḥerem in het Oude Testament*, 1959.

[2] Num. 21.1ff.   [3] Josh. 7.   [4] 1 Sam. 15.

[5] Cf. Deut. 2.34f; 3.6f; 7.2; Josh. 11.14. In Deut. 20.10ff there is a further relaxation of the severity of the ban, since here only the males were put to death.

[6] Line 17 (cf. *N.S.I.*, 1903, pp. 1, 3, or *D.O.T.T.*, 1958, p. 197).

[7] Cf. W. F. Albright, *F.S.A.C.*, 2nd edn, 1946, p. 213: "The practice of devoting a recalcitrant foe to destruction as a kind of gigantic holocaust to the national deity was apparently universal among the early Semites." Cf. A. Lods, *Israel*, E. Tr. by S. H. Hooke, 1932, p. 288, where it is shown that the custom was wider than a Semitic one. Lods says, "The effect of the ḥerem is to release fatal power. But the blind working of this force, which may destroy friends as well as foes, suggests that originally it was not conceived of as personal."

Israel. But unlike the institution of sacrifice, which could become the vehicle of religious experience and which persisted throughout the Old Testament period until the final destruction of the Temple, the ban fell into desuetude within the period of the Old Testament, and it figures as an historical act only in the early records.[1]

We must now turn to the age of Joshua and the Judges. The age of Joshua was the age of entry into the land west of the Jordan and consequently the age of struggle to secure a foothold in the land. We therefore learn of much fighting, but little worship. We are told of an altar that Joshua built on Mount Ebal in fulfilment of the command of Moses,[2] and while this is commonly assigned to the Deuteronomic redactor, the passage in Deuteronomy containing the instruction is commonly assigned to JE.[3] The story of the erection of an altar on the east of Jordan by the eastern tribes and of the threat of war against them by the other tribes because they were turning from the Tabernacle and its altar[4] belongs to the Priestly writer's projection into the past of the law of the single sanctuary and its ritual.[5] The JE tradition tells of the carrying of stones from the Jordan to Gilgal, where they were set up as memorial stones,[6] and since an important shrine is known to have stood at Gilgal, where the tribes from time to time rallied on great occasions, when sacrifice is known to have been offered,[7] it is probable that a Yahweh shrine was established there at this time.

[1] In none of the later occurrences of the word in the Old Testament does it refer to Israel's practice of this custom. In Jer. 50.26 and 51.3 it refers in prophecy to the coming treatment of Jerusalem by the Chaldaeans; in Isa. 34.5 it refers to the coming divine judgement on Edom. In Isa. 43.28 it refers to the coming divine judgement on Israel; in Mal. 4.6 (M.T. 3.24) it refers to the judgement on the earth that shall be averted; and in Zech. 14.11 Jerusalem is promised protection against such treatment.

[2] Josh. 8.30f.   [3] Deut. 27.4ff.   [4] Josh. 22.10ff.

[5] K. Möhlenbrink (Z.A.W. lvi, 1938, pp. 246ff) thinks it was a polemic of Shiloh against Gilgal. C. A. Simpson (The Early Traditions of Israel, 1948, p. 399) thinks that while verse 11 implies that the altar was east of Jordan, verse 10 shifts it to the west, and this necessitated the dropping of the name of the originally East Jordan altar in verse 34.

[6] Josh. 4.2ff.

[7] Josh. 14.6; 1 Sam. 7.16; 11.14f; 13.4; 15.12; Hos. 12.11 (M.T. 12); Amos 4.4; 5.5.

In the post-Settlement period, as reflected in the book of Judges, we find abundant signs of a new syncretism, which fused Yahwism with the religion of Canaan and brought it down to the level of Canaanite religion. This was fertility religion, marked by practices quite alien to the religion of the Decalogue. The Israelites were surrounded by Canaanites and offered worship at existing local shrines according to Canaanite customs, learning the arts of agriculture and viticulture and taking over with them the local rites associated with them. It is not surprising, therefore, that we find the deterioration of moral standards, such as appears especially in the stories in the appendix to the book of Judges. The theft of the property and priest, even of a fellow-Israelite,[1] was not condemned by men's consciences, and the Benjamites rallied round the men of Gibeah, whose conduct shocked the rest of the Israelites.[2]

While the tribes sometimes act together in the face of common dangers, often they are in conflict with one another,[3] and rarely do we find all the tribes acting together. It is common to-day to speak of the amphictyony of the twelve tribes of Israel and to suggest that they formed a military confederation on a religious basis with a single amphictyonic sanctuary.[4] I am not persuaded of

[1] Judges 18.14ff.   [2] Judges 19ff.   [3] Judges 8; 12; 20.
[4] The idea of an Israelite amphictyony was advanced by A. H. Sayce, *P.S.B.A.* xi, 1888–9, p. 347. It was presented by M. Noth (*Das System der zwölf Stämme Israels*, 1930, pp. 39ff) so persuasively that it has become widely accepted (cf. also J. Pedersen, *Israel III–IV*, 1940, pp. 677f, and the references given there). Noth maintained (pp. 107f) that there was a twelve-tribe amphictyony based on Shechem, and that Judah belonged to this and also to another amphictyony based on Hebron, which was partly non-Israelite and partly Israelite. T. J. Meek (*Hebrew Origins*, 2nd edn, 1950, p. 26) believed the amphictyony organized by Joshua at Shechem was only for the Joseph tribes (cf. G. A. Danell, *Studies in the name Israel in the Old Testament*, 1946, p. 46; H. S. Nyberg, *A.R.W.* xxxv, 1938, p. 367). In my view the Shechem covenant of Josh. 24 really concerns what happened in the time of Jacob and had nothing to do with Joshua originally (cf. *J.J.*, 1950, pp. 43f, 126ff). It is to be noted that the building of an altar at Shechem is attributed to Jacob (Gen. 33.20) and to Joshua (Josh. 8.30), strange gods are said to have been put away by Jacob (Gen. 35.2ff) and by Joshua (Josh. 24.20ff), and Jacob (Gen. 34) and Joshua (Josh. 24.25) are both said to have established covenants at Shechem (LXX reads Shiloh for Shechem, and this is followed by H. A. Poels (*Examen critique de l'histoire du Sanctuaire de l'Arche*, i, 1897, pp. 69f), but the reading of M.T. is to be preferred). K. Möhlenbrink

this.[1] If at the time of the battle of Taanach Reuben and Dan and Asher had been pledged by solemn oath to join the tribes that resisted Sisera, there would have been curses pronounced on them in the Song of Deborah instead of the mild reproaches that we find.[2] The Song implies that there was some reason to expect help, some moral obligation on them to share in the battle, but it scarcely implies a binding oath. When the Ammonites attacked the Gileadites, no appeal was made to an amphictyony for help, or recourse had to an amphictyonic sanctuary, but Jephthah was appealed to for help and recourse had to the shrine of Mizpah, east of the Jordan, where a solemn compact with Jephthah was made.[3] When the other tribes gathered to attack Benjamin, it was to the shrine of Mizpah, west of the Jordan, that they repaired,[4] while later we read that they went to Bethel to consult Yahweh.[5] We are told that the Ark of God was there,[6] though later we find it at Shiloh.[7] If it was at Bethel, we should expect that to be the centre of any amphictyony, and the sacred oath that preceded the battle with Benjamin might have been expected to be sworn there. I find no evidence, then, of a single sanctuary for the whole confederation of the Israelite tribes, and it seems to me more consonant with the evidence to find that there was no central authority, religious or political, but that groups of tribes entered into alliance for particular purposes from time to time. The bond between them was the recognition of some kinship and the common acceptance of Yahweh as their national God.

At the end of the period of the Judges the Ark was certainly at

(*Z.A.W.* lvi, 1938, pp. 250ff) says the Shechem covenant cannot have antedated the time of Abimelech, and postulates a Gilgal amphictyony, which was later replaced by a Shiloh amphictyony, while Mowinckel argues for a Kadesh amphictyony (*Norsk Geografisk Tidsskrift*, ix, 1942, pp. 13f). This proliferation of amphictyonies is not reassuring. On the history and archaeology of Shechem, cf. E. Nielsen, *Shechem*, 1955; G. E. Wright, *Shechem*, 1965; S. H. Horn, *J.E.O.L.*, No. 18, 1965, pp. 284ff.

[1] Cf. *I.D.B.* ii, 1962, p. 754a; *J.S.S.* x, 1965, p. 99. Cf. also R. Smend, *Jahwekrieg und Stämmebund*, 1963, where the analogy of the Israelite tribal organization with the Greek amphictyony is rejected. Cf. also O. Eissfeldt, *C.A.H.*, rev. edn, Fasc. 32, 1965, pp. 16f. R. de Vaux (*A.I.*, 1961, p. 93) thinks the comparison is helpful, provided we do not press it too far. Cf. also S. Herrmann, *Th.L.Z.* lxxxvii, 1962, cols. 561ff.

[2] Judges 5.17.   [3] Judges 11.4ff.   [4] Judges 20.1.
[5] Judges 20.26.   [6] Judges 20.27.   [7] 1 Sam 3.3; 4.3.

Shiloh in the custody of Eli,[1] and this would imply that the Shiloh shrine was a specifically Yahweh shrine. There may have been others, but certainly all shrines were not. At Ophrah there was a shrine at which the Israelites were worshipping, yet quite certainly not a specifically Yahweh shrine, but a pre-Israelite Canaanite shrine.[2] When Gideon experienced a theophany he immediately built a Yahweh altar,[3] just as the patriarchs had done. Later, he broke down the other altar,[4] which he called a Baal altar. It will be observed that Gideon found no difficulty in building an altar to Yahweh in the neighbourhood of an existing altar of Baal in a shrine to which his fellow-Israelites were accustomed to go. This would suggest that in the stories of the patriarchs there is no necessity to assume that they went to pre-existing shrines when we read that they built an altar. They could as easily mark the scene of a theophany by an altar as Gideon could. Later we read that Manoah used a rock in the field as an altar and offered sacrifice,[5] where we are not told the location and have no reason to suppose that a shrine marked the spot, either previously or subsequently. From the story of Gideon it would seem that in the post-Settlement period the Israelites often worshipped at local shrines according to Canaanite rites, yet were conscious that Yahweh was their national God, and in times of crisis they could set Yahweh worship over against Baal worship.

That there was declension from the standards of Mosaic Yahwism is in no way surprising. Under the powerful influence of Moses and following the deliverance from Egypt a new impulse is understandable. But the story of the Wilderness period shows that Moses was often faced by people who did not share his moral and religious strength. In the period following the Settlement, when there was no figure comparable with Moses and when all around the Israelites were people more advanced in the arts of settled life but on an inferior religious level, it is not surprising that the heights of Mosaic Yahwism were often forgotten. Yahweh's abode was still thought to be at the sacred mount in the wilderness, and Deborah sang of his setting forth from Seir to give victory to his people.[6] But the mount was far away. Yahweh altars might mark spots where he had revealed himself in theophanies to his people. But these were few. It is not surprising

[1] 1 Sam. 4.4ff.   [2] Judges 6.28ff.   [3] Judges 6.24.

[4] Judges 6.25ff.   [5] Judges 13.19.   [6] Judges 5.4.

that men repaired to the local sanctuaries for agricultural festivals or for ordinary occasions of sacrifice, and that their standards were accommodated to those of the people around them. Of the extent of that accommodation the book of Judges gives clear indication. I have said that Yahwism seems to have been an imageless cult even before the time of Moses.[1] Yet now, in the period of the Judges, we read that Gideon made an ephod of the gold and other offerings of the people,[2] and it is clear that this was some sort of idol.[3] Again, we read that Micah's mother used the silver which he stole from her and later restored to make an image,[4] and this was placed in a shrine along with an ephod and teraphim.[5] The contents of this shrine were later seized by the migrating Danites and carried to the city of Dan to be installed in its shrine.[6] Gideon's ephod and Micah's image may have been images of Yahweh, though we are not expressly told this.[7] The teraphim are unlikely to have been images of Yahweh, but may have been household images, such as those stolen from Laban by Rachel,[8] or figures used for divination. But even if Gideon and Micah made images of Yahweh, this would not prove that during this period no law against images in the religion of Yahweh had been made. When the prophets condemn the adultery that took place around them, this does not prove that no law against adultery was known. The breach of law cannot prove the absence of law. Moreover, laws can fall into desuetude and be ignored so that those who break them are not conscious of guilt.

During this period we find some development of the priesthood. No special law of the priesthood is found in JE, though it would appear that Moses acted as a priest.[9] Micah established one of his sons as priest in his private shrine,[10] but later engaged a wandering Levite to serve as his priest.[11] This Levite proved to be the

---

[1] Cf. above, pp. 41, 45.   [2] Judges 8.26f.

[3] This is not agreed by all scholars, but is the most natural understanding of the passage. Cf. C. F. Burney, *The Book of Judges*, 1920, pp. 236ff, where much special pleading is resorted to to avoid this conclusion.

[4] Judges 17.4.   [5] Judges 17.5.   [6] Judges 18.17ff.

[7] Cf. *M.G.*, 1963, pp. 21f n.

[8] Gen. 31.19. On teraphim see above, p. 19, n. 4.   [9] Ex. 24.4ff.

[10] Judges 17.5. J. Hoschander (*The Priests and Prophets*, 1938, p. 235) says: "We may rest assured that . . . such a custom was general and old."

[11] Judges 17.12.

grandson of Moses.[1] In Genesis the Levites are a secular clan, who joined with Simeon in a treacherous attack on Shechem[2] and incurred their father's severe rebuke,[3] and in the Blessing of Jacob the two tribes come under their father's common curse,[4] and it is predicted that they will be scattered in Israel.[5] Simeon for a time found a home in the south of Judah, but gradually disappeared or was incorporated in Judah.[6] The Levites seem to have achieved no territorial integrity, but we have various references to Levites who were connected with Judah.[7] From the

---

[1] Judges 18.30. The M.T. reads Manasseh, but with the *n* suspended. It is not to be doubted that the original reading was Moses (so Vulg. and Talmudic tradition; cf. T. B. *Baba bathra*, 109b). M. J. Lagrange (*Le Livre des Juges*, 1903, pp. 288ff) vigorously emends the text and distinguishes between Micah's priest and the grandson of Moses, making the latter the Danite tribal priest before the migration of Dan. On this cf. C. Hauret, in *Mélanges Bibliques* (Robert Festschrift), 1957, pp. 105ff.

[2] Gen. 34.25ff.   [3] Gen. 34.30.

[4] Gen. 49.5ff. With this contrast the blessing on Levi in Deut. 33.8ff.

[5] Gen. 49.7.

[6] It is significant that Simeon does not figure in the Blessing of Moses (Deut. 33). Moreover, as C. A. Simpson says (in Hastings' one volume *D.B.*, rev. edn, ed. by F. C. Grant and H. H. Rowley, 1963, p. 915b): "Most of the cities assigned to Simeon in Jos19[1-9] reappear elsewhere as cities of Judah (cf Jos 15[26-32, 42], 1 K 19[3], Neh 11[26-29], 1 S 27[6], 30[30]. The inference to be drawn is that following the disaster alluded to in Gen. 49[5-7] the survivors of Simeon were absorbed into Judah." E. Nielsen (*Shechem*, 1955, p. 261 n) observes that Simeon nowhere appears in the historical traditions of Samuel–Saul–David, although "Simeonite" cities such as Beersheba, Ziklag, and Hormah are mentioned. J. Hoschander (*The Priests and Prophets*, 1938, p. 237) thinks there is scarcely any room to doubt that Simeon was almost annihilated shortly after the conquest of Canaan. Cf. S. A. Cook, "Simeon and Levi", *A.J.Th.* xiii, 1909, pp. 370ff.

[7] Cf. Judges 17.7; 19.1. On the Levites cf. S. A. Cook, loc. cit., and *E.Brit.*, 11th edn, xvi, 1911, pp. 512ff; K. Möhlenbrink, *Z.A.W.* lii, 1934, pp. 184ff. In Minaean inscriptions *lw'* and *lw't* are held to mean "priest" and "priestess" (cf. G. Hölscher in Pauly-Wissowa, *R.E.* xii, 1925, col. 2161), but these inscriptions are of uncertain date (cf. G. B. Gray, *Sacrifice in the Old Testament*, 1925, pp. 242ff). Hölscher (loc. cit.) concludes that the Levites never were a secular tribe (so also E. Nielsen, *A.S.T.I*, iii, 1964, pp. 16ff), but that the term was always functional in Israel. But it is hard to see how Simeon and Levi could ever have been joined in a common curse if this were so. Though they did not share a common fate, since Simeon was absorbed in Judah whereas Levi survived in a functional rôle, it is clear that when Gen. 49.7 was written it was

story of Moses' grandson it would seem that there was a tendency for them to become priests as opportunity offered, for Micah seems to have found great satisfaction when he obtained a Levite to serve in his shrine.[1]

Of the kind of worship that went on in the shrines during this period we have little knowledge. Sacrifice was offered there, though the act of sacrifice does not appear to have been restricted to a resident priesthood. For Samuel is said to have offered sacrifice at more than one shrine. He sacrificed at Mizpah,[2] west of the Jordan, and built an altar at Ramah,[3] and planned to offer sacrifice at Gilgal,[4] though in this Saul forestalled him.[5] When we are told that he judged Israel in Bethel,[6] in addition to these places, we are probably justified in assuming that he also offered sacrifice there.

Here it is legitimate to conclude that no law of a single sanctuary was known at this time. For Samuel was a devotee of Yahweh, who recalled the people to loyalty to him and rekindled their patriotic and religious ardour, who might therefore have been expected to observe the law, if he had known of it. Moreover, as has been said, the Book of the Covenant knows no law of a single sanctuary, but freely presupposes a multiplicity,[7] and this is the oldest law-book of the Pentateuch.

The shrine of Shiloh was a centre of festival worship as we learn from the final story of the book of Judges, where the maidens were gathered for a festal dance when the Benjamites seized them and carried them off as brides.[8] In the time of Eli Shiloh was still a centre of festival worship, to which we read that Elkanah went

expected that they would. R. de Vaux (*A.I.*, 1961, pp. 369f) denies that *lw'* and *lw't* mean "priest" and "priestess", and says that if anyone borrowed the word it was the Minaeans. T. J. Meek (*Hebrew Origins*, 2nd edn, 1950, p. 130) thinks that some of the Levites migrated southwards into Arabia and there became priests, and by this means he explains the Minaean references. S. Mowinckel (*Norsk Geografisk Tidsskrift*, ix, 1942, pp. 22f) connects the name Levi with the ecstatic dance, and thinks the Levites were originally cultic officials of Kadesh. Cf. also J. Pedersen, *Israel III–IV*, 1940, pp. 170ff; A. Haldar, *Associations of Cult Prophets among the Ancient Semites*, 1945, pp. 91ff; E. Nielsen, *Shechem*, 1955, pp. 264ff; R. de Vaux, *A.I.*, pp. 369ff.

[1] Judges 17.13. [2] 1 Sam. 7.9. [3] 1 Sam. 7.17.
[4] 1 Sam. 10.8. [5] 1 Sam. 13.9; cf. also 11.15; 15.21.
[6] 1 Sam. 7.16. [7] Ex. 20.24. [8] Judges 21.19ff.

yearly to offer sacrifice.[1] Doubtless the other shrines were similarly resorted to at festivals, though we are not given accounts of them. After the capture of the Ark by the Philistines,[2] Shiloh appears to have been destroyed,[3] and festivals could no longer take place there. This would doubtless increase the desire to go to other shrines to celebrate the festivals.

The shrine of Ramah was the scene of a sacrificial meal on the day when Saul went there to consult Samuel about his father's lost asses, and we are told that Samuel presided at the meal.[4] This would not appear to be one of the great festivals, or Saul would presumably have known of it. It was therefore probably the private offering of some man and his guests to mark something in his own experience. We may therefore reasonably conclude that the shrines were resorted to for private acts of worship, as well as on the annual festivals.

They were also resorted to in times of national crisis on public occasions. As has been already said, tribes or groups of tribes used the shrines for the making of solemn oaths before God, such as that which the Gileadites swore to Jephthah.[5] Similarly, the other tribes swore an oath at the Mizpah west of the Jordan to take vengeance on Benjamin and not to give their daughters in marriage to members of that tribe.[6] Vows could be made elsewhere than at a sanctuary, and there is no reason to suppose that Jephthah's vow which resulted in the sacrifice of his daughter was made at a sanctuary.[7] A vow wherever made was a religious act, and Jephthah felt under obligation to fulfil his vow. It is clear that he did not expect it to involve his daughter, but he did contemplate a human sacrifice.[8] This does not prove that human sacrifice was common in Israel at this time or that human sacrifice

---

[1] 1 Sam. 1.3ff.   [2] 1 Sam. 4.

[3] This was long surmised (cf. H. Ewald, *G.V.I.* ii, 2nd edn, 1853, p. 540), but has been made almost certain by the Danish excavations (cf. H. Kjaer, *P.E.F.Q.S.*, lix, 1927, pp. 202ff, lxiii, 1931, pp. 71ff). For the date of this destruction cf. W. F. Albright, *B.A.S.O.R.*, No. 35, Oct. 1929, p. 4; H. Kjaer, *J.P.O.S.* x, 1930, pp. 37ff; A. Mallon, *Biblica*, x, 1929, pp. 369ff; L. Hennequin, in *S.D.B.* iii, 1936, col. 378.

[4] 1 Sam. 9.13, 34.   [5] Judges 11.11.

[6] Judges 21.1.   [7] Judges 11.30f.

[8] A.V. and R.V. have "whatsoever cometh forth", but R.S.V. rightly has "whoever comes forth". Cf. C. F. Burney, *Judges*, 2nd edn, 1920, p. 319: "From the first a *human* sacrifice is contemplated."

had hitherto been regarded as normal in Yahwism.[1] In a later age the king of Moab offered his son in sacrifice to his god in a national crisis,[2] and Jephthah's vow is to be seen in relation to this. As he led his troops into battle there was no opportunity to offer such a sacrifice, and as Jephthah had no son he could not offer a son. So he vowed to sacrifice the first person who should issue from his house on his victorious return. His purpose, like Mesha's, was to stimulate his God to the utmost effort to help him,[3] and in his vow and the subsequent sacrifice of his only child Jephthah was reflecting the standards of the peoples around him, and not

[1] L. Rost (in *Von Ugarit nach Qumran* (Eissfeldt Festschrift), 1958, pp. 181f) has suggested the possibility that the burnt offering may have been originally a human sacrifice. But there is no evidence that it was such in Israel in historical times. De Vaux (*Studies in Old Testament Sacrifice*, 1964, pp. 63ff) has carefully examined the evidence and shown that it cannot establish that human sacrifices were ever lawful in Israel. That children were offered in sacrifice in the seventh century cannot prove the contrary. These, as de Vaux insists, were limited to a particular age and were condemned by all who stood for Yahwism. They represented a foreign custom which was brought into Israel from outside (cf. L. Moraldi, *Espiazione sacrificale e riti espiatori*, 1956, pp. 99ff). On the question whether these were offered to the god Moloch, de Vaux follows the view of O. Eissfeldt (*Molk als Opferbegriff im Punischen und Hebräischen und das Ende des Gottes Moloch*, 1935; cf. also *P.E.Q.* lxxix, 1947, pp. 85f) that Molk was the name of a type of sacrifice and not of the god to whom it was offered (cf. de Vaux's earlier review, *R.B.* xlv, 1936, pp. 278ff), but believes that the Israelites misunderstood the word when they borrowed it, and thought these sacrifices were destined for a king-god (pp. 87ff). Cf. also R. Dussaud, *Les Origines cananéennes du sacrifice israélite*, 2nd edn, 1941, pp. 352f; J. Friedrich, *Phönizisch-Punische Grammatik*, 1951, p. 86; H. Cazelles, in *S.D.B.* v, 1957, cols. 1337ff; W. J. Harrelson, in Hastings' one volume *D.B.*, rev. edn, 1963, p. 669. In *Ras Schamra und Sanchunjaton*, 1939, pp. 69f, Eissfeldt holds that these sacrifices ceased to be offered in Phoenicia in the seventh century B.C. Eissfeldt's view has been rejected by E. Dhorme, *La religion des Hébreux nomades*, 1937, pp. 213f; A. Bea, *Biblica*, xviii, 1937, pp. 95f; A. Jirku, *A.R.W.* xxxv, 1938, pp. 178f; K. Dronkert, *De Molochdienst in het Oude Testament*, 1953 (cf. my review, *Bi.Or.* x, 1953, pp. 196f); A. van den Born, in *Dictionnaire encyclopédique de la Bible*, 1960, col. 1213. J. Gray (*The Legacy of Canaan* (S.V.T. v), 1957, p. 126 n, and in *I.D.B.* iii, 1962, pp. 422f) leaves it an open question.

[2] 2 Kings 3.27.

[3] Cf. C. F. Burney, *Judges*, p. 320: "It is an extraordinary sacrifice, offered in a great emergency as a supreme bid for the active co-operation of the deity."

testifying to the demands of the Yahwism that had been mediated by Moses.

A further purpose for which shrines were resorted to was the consultation of the oracle. When the Danite representatives were scouting for fresh territory to occupy, they came to Micah's shrine and asked his priest to inquire of the sacred oracle to see if their mission should be successful.[1] The consultation of the oracle was an ancient priestly function. When Jethro came to meet the Israelites, he found that Moses was already acting as judge and as the consultant of the oracle,[2] and this continued to be a priestly function. At the battle of Michmash Saul consulted the oracle through Ahijah the priest,[3] whose function could therefore be exercised other than in a shrine, though it would doubtless be normally exercised in a shrine. We are not told the method whereby Micah's priest consulted the oracle, but since there was an ephod in his shrine and elsewhere the ephod is mentioned in this connection,[4] it is probable that this was used by Micah. In the case of Ahijah we find that at first the ephod is mentioned— though the Hebrew text here has "the Ark" instead of "the ephod"[5]—but later we find the Urim and Thummim if we follow the superior Greek text.[6] Into the variety of theories on the ephod[7] and the Urim and Thummim[8] we cannot go here. The ephod is sometimes quite certainly a garment,[9] while Gideon's

[1] Judges 18.5f.   [2] Ex. 18.13ff.   [3] 1 Sam. 14.18.
[4] Cf. 1 Sam. 23.9ff; 30.7f.
[5] 1 Sam. 14.18; cf. S. R. Driver, *Notes on the Hebrew Text of the Books of Samuel*, 2nd edn, 1913, p. 110.
[6] 1 Sam. 14.41f (R.S.V.); cf. S. R. Driver, op. cit., pp. 117f.
[7] Cf. T. C. Foote, *J.B.L.* xxi, 1902, pp. 1ff; E. Sellin, in *Orientalische Studien* (Nöldeke Festschrift), ii, 1906, pp. 699ff, *J.P.O.S.* xiv, 1934, pp. 1ff, xvii, 1937, pp. 236ff; H. J. Elhorst, *Z.A.W.* xxx, 1910, pp. 259ff; W. R. Arnold, *Ephod and Ark*, 1917; C. F. Burney, *The Book of Judges*, 2nd edn, 1920, pp. 236ff; K. Budde, *Z.A.W.* xxxix, 1921, pp. 1ff; H. Thiersch, *Z.A.W.* liii, 1935, pp. 180ff; J. Morgenstern, *The Ark, the Ephod, and the "Tent of Meeting"*, 1945, pp. 114ff; K. Elliger, *V.T.* viii, 1958, pp. 19ff.
[8] Cf. A. R. S. Kennedy, in Hastings' *D.B.* iv, 1902, pp. 838ff; G. F. Moore, in *E.B.* iv, 1903, cols. 5235ff; W. Muss–Arnolt, in *J.E.* xii, 1907, pp. 384f; A. Jeremias, in *Assyriologische und archäologische Studien* (H. V. Hilprecht Festschrift), 1909, pp. 223ff; E. Kautzsch, in *The New Schaff-Herzog Encyclopedia*, xii, 1912, pp. 107ff; J. Paterson, in Hastings' one volume *D.B.*, rev. edn, 1963, pp. 1019f.
[9] Cf. 1 Sam. 2.18, 28; 2 Sam. 6.14; Ex. 28.6ff.

ephod seems equally certainly to be some sort of idol.[1] One view is that the oracular stones were carried in a pocket on the idol,[2] as the Urim and Thummim are said later to have been carried on the person of the High Priest,[3] and that they were consulted by shaking the idol or by the priest bringing them out of the pocket of the worn ephod with his hand.[4] In either case it is probable that the Urim and Thummim were the actual means of consultation. Here again one of several views is that they were flat stones, one side of which was the auspicious side and the other the inauspicious.[5] If they fell or were drawn out showing different sides there was no answer, but if they showed the same side the answer was auspicious or inauspicious according to which side it was.[6] All of this conjecture, however, is immaterial to our present

[1] Judges 8.26f; so K. Budde, *Richter*, 1897, pp. 67f; G. F. Moore, *Judges*, 2nd edn, 1898, pp. 232f. B. Stade (*Biblische Theologie des Alten Testaments*, i, 1905, p. 120) thought it was made of wood with gold covering. Cf., however, C. F. Burney, *The Book of Judges*, 2nd edn, 1920, pp. 240ff, where it is argued that there is nothing to compel us to believe that Gideon's ephod was an idol. It is to be noted that in 1 Sam 23.6 Abiathar fled to David with an ephod "in his hand". The view of W. R. Arnold (op. cit.), that wherever a solid article appears to be referred to we should read "Ark" for "ephod", is rejected by J. Morgenstern (op. cit., p. 115), and seems arbitrary.

[2] Cf. J. Pedersen, *Israel III–IV*, 1940, p. 224.   [3] Lev. 8.8.

[4] Cf. I. Mendelsohn, in *I.D.B.* iv, 1962, p. 740b.

[5] This derives the two words from geminate verbs (*'ārar* and *tāmam*) and both are then of the same form (cf. J. Wellhausen, *Prolegomena to the History of Israel*, E. Tr., 1885, p. 394 n). On this and other proposed derivations cf. A. R. Johnson, *The Cultic Prophet in Ancient Israel*, 2nd edn, 1962, p. 6 n. R. Press (*Z.A.W.* li, 1933, p. 229) also sees in Urim the inauspicious answer, but does not favour the attempt to determine the etymology by the use of the Urim and Thummim (cf. R. de Vaux, *A.I.*, p. 352). I. Engnell (*Gamla Testamentet*, 1945, p. 70 n; cf. *S.B.U.* ii, 1952, col. 1517) takes Urim and Thummim to be a hendiadys, meaning "the true lights".

[6] So H. P. Smith, *The Religion of Israel*, 1914, p. 122; Oesterley and Robinson, *Hebrew Religion*, 2nd edn, 1937, p. 166. This is the view that seems to me most probable (cf. *Prophecy and Religion in Ancient China and Israel*, 1956, p. 7 n). A similar device was used in Chinese divination (cf. H. Doré, *Recherches sur les superstitions en Chine*, I ii, 1912, p. 243). A. R. S. Kennedy (in Hastings' *D.B.* iv, 1902, p. 840a; cf. I. Mendelsohn, in *I.D.B.* iv, 1963, p. 740b) thinks that they were in the form of dice, and G. F. Moore (in *E.B.* iv, 1907, col. 5236) that one stone was called Urim and the other Thummim. J. Lindblom (*Israels Religion*, 2nd edn, 1953,

purpose, which is but to note that resort to the oracle was a priestly function, and that one of the purposes for which men visited the shrines was to consult the oracle. In this there was nothing peculiar to Yahwism, and indeed there is little reference to the consultation of the oracle in the later period of Old Testament history.[1] It is, indeed, of interest to note that when Moses consulted God he is not said to have used mechanical means, but to have gone into the Tent of Meeting to consult God in a personal encounter.[2]

Amid so much that fell so far below Mosaic Yahwism, it is pleasant to note that in all the throng of a festival at Shiloh Hannah could bring her private petition to God and pour out her misery before him.[3] Of the ritual of the worship on the occasion we have no knowledge; but it was the occasion of the individual encounter with God of an unhappy woman, and her prayer was answered. The simple plea of Hannah and the kindly response of Eli when he perceived that she was a troubled soul[4] show that not all the religion of that age was ignoble, though as a whole it was no exalted period, but a rough age in which every man did that which was right in his own eyes.[5] Prayer figures, of course, in other stories, both in the shrine and elsewhere. Joshua could pray for the help of the elements when he went to the relief of Gibeon,[6] and Samson could pray when he was being tormented for the sport of the Philistines.[7] Worship is always encounter, whether accompanied by a ritual act or not, and is never to be estimated merely in terms of ritual.

Something should be said here about the prophets, who come prominently before us in this period. They appear as devotees of

pp. 60f) suggests that the Urim and Thummim were adopted from the Kenite cult at Kadesh (cf. W. Eichrodt, *Theology of the Old Testament*, E. Tr. by J. A. Baker, i, 1959, p. 113, where they are said to be taken over from the priests of Kadesh). J. Schoneveld (*Orientalia Neerlandica*, 1948, pp. 216ff) maintains that the Urim and Thummim were not used together but separately, the Urim when information about the future was wanted, and the Thummim in judicial cases.

[1] Cf. A. R. S. Kennedy, in Hastings' *D.B.* iv, p. 840b: "It cannot be a mere coincidence that the use of Urim and Thummim is never mentioned in the historical narratives after the time of David."

[2] Ex. 33.9. Cf. also Num. 12.7f (on this passage cf. A. R. Johnson, *The Cultic Prophet in Ancient Israel*, 2nd edn, pp. 46ff).

[3] 1 Sam. 1.10f.   [4] 1 Sam. 1.17.   [5] Judges 17.6; 21.25.
[6] Josh. 10.12f.   [7] Judges 16.28.

Yahweh, who stirred men to patriotic fervour against the Philistine foe by reviving their confidence in Yahweh, the national God.[1] They were certainly religious figures, though they do not seem to have been functionaries of the shrines comparable with the priests —at least in this period. How far it is legitimate to think of them as Temple personnel in a later age we must consider in a subsequent chapter, and it will be best to reserve until then the consideration of the prophetic office. Here it must suffice to say that the prophets we read of in the period before the founding of the monarchy were not, in general, figures of the stature of the eighth- and seventh-century prophets, calling men to a deeper understanding of the will of God. In fairness to them it should be said, however, that without their revival of the national spirit and the stemming of the Philistine tide, Israel might well have ceased to be distinguishable from her neighbours and the religion of Yahwism might have been submerged in the corrupting influences of that age. Outstanding among the prophets of that age was Samuel, who, even when we have stripped away all the idealization of a later age, stands out as a dominant figure, calling the people to a new confidence in God and a new loyalty to him, and awakening them to new efforts to preserve their identity and their faith.

There are passages in which Moses is called a prophet, though this function is commonly denied him.[2] Hosea says "By a prophet the Lord brought Israel up out of Egypt",[3] where Moses is clearly referred to, while Deuteronomy 33 is said to be the Blessing of Moses, the "man of God",[4] and the same title is given to him in Josh. 14.6. In Num. 12.6ff we read: "If there be a prophet among you, I the Lord will make myself known unto him in a vision, I

---

[1] 1 Sam. 10.5, 10.

[2] Cf. K. Marti, *The Religion of the Old Testament*, E. Tr. by G. A. Bienemann, 1914, pp. 63f: "He is only rightly understood when he is conceived as a prophet"; C. R. North, *The Old Testament Interpretation of History*, 1946, pp. 170f: "The Hebrew estimate of him was that he was a prophet, indeed the greatest of the prophets. If the function of the prophet was to act as interpreter between Yahweh and his people, that estimate does not seem exaggerated." Abraham is also called a prophet in Gen. 20.7, 17, but he is nowhere represented as mediating the word of God to men. The only prophetic function which he exercises (cf. below, p. 163) is intercession.

[3] Hos. 12.13.   [4] Deut. 33.1.

will speak unto him in a dream. My servant Moses is not so; he is faithful in all mine house: with him will I speak mouth to mouth, even manifestly, and not in dark speeches; and the form of the Lord shall be behold." That this is not intended to dissociate Moses from the prophets, but rather to exalt him as the supreme prophet, is suggested by Deut. 34.10: "And there hath not arisen a prophet since in Israel like unto Moses, whom the Lord knew face to face." Moreover, we read in Deut. 18.18: "I will raise them up a prophet from among their brethren, like unto thee (i.e. Moses); and I will put my words in his mouth, and he shall speak unto them all that I shall command him." We make our own definitions of a prophet and try to force them on the Old Testament instead of asking how the prophet was conceived in Israel. The passage I have last quoted makes it clear that the prophet was conceived of as the mouthpiece of God,[1] and when Jeremiah denounces the false prophets it is for uttering a word which has no deeper source than their own hearts.[2] If the function of the prophet is indeed to be the mouthpiece of God, no Old Testament figure more deserves this title than Moses. The glory of the eighth- and seventh-century prophets is commonly held to be their insistence on the ethical quality of true religion. They were building on the work of Moses, who established Israelite Yahwism on an ethical basis and gave it an ethical character in the Ten Commandments from the start. If, as some define him, the prophet was the man who was called of God to his office, then again Moses deserves this title as much as any. If Abraham was the supreme figure of the period dealt with in the previous chapter, Moses was the supreme figure of the period under survey in this.

[1] Cf. J. Muilenburg, in *The Bible in Modern Scholarship*, ed. by J. P. Hyatt, 1965, p. 97: "They [the prophets] are speakers for Yahweh, proclaimers of the law, apostles sent to particular times to speak particular words."

[2] Jer. 23.16, 26.

3

The Temple and its Place in Worship

The founding of the monarchy in Israel brought little immediate change in the forms of worship. There was a renewed sense that Yahweh was the God of Israel and that he had delivered them from the Philistine menace, though that menace was not wholly removed. At the beginning of the reign of Saul the Philistines were established in the heart of the country at Gibeah,[1] but after the victory of Michmash[2] the central highlands were freed of their domination. They were still trying to re-enter, however, and at the battle of Ephes-dammim,[3] with which David's encounter with Goliath is associated, they were trying to force their way from the lowlands into Judah. Though they were halted there, they extended their influence up the coast and into the Vale of Esdraelon, and at the battle of Gilboa were attacking the central highlands from the north,[4] and for a time regained their influence.[5]

[1] I Sam. 13.3, where we should read Gibeah, with LXX and Targ., instead of M.T. Geba; cf. I Sam. 10.5, 10, where we see that the Philistine garrison was at Gibeah (a name which means "hill"). The word rendered "garrison" may mean "pillar" (Gen. 19.26), "prefect" or "deputy" (I Kings 4.19), but here probably means "garrison" (cf. Vulg.; Targ. has "soldiers"); cf. S. R. Driver, *Notes on the Hebrew Text of the Books of Samuel*, 2nd edn, 1913, p. 80. "It appears from this verse (I Sam. 10.5) that a large area of Central Palestine was now in the hands of the Philistines" (so Driver, ibid.).

[2] Cf. I Sam. 14.46.

[3] I Sam. 17. Ephes-dammim is called Pas-dammim in I Chron. 11.13.

[4] I Sam. 31.

[5] J. Bright (*History of Israel*, 1960, p. 174) says: "The debacle at Gilboa left Israel at the mercy of the Philistines, who apparently followed up their advantage and occupied at least as much of the land as they had held before Saul came upon the scene. While they did not venture into Transjordan, ... their garrisons were once more established in the central

Throughout this period worship continued to be offered at various shrines, though the shrine of Shiloh had been destroyed,[1] and when we next hear of the family of Eli it is found at a shrine at Nob,[2] a place which is scarcely mentioned elsewhere in the Bible[3] and whose shrine is of so little importance that it is nowhere mentioned again. The family of Eli is wiped out by Saul[4] because of its friendly reception of David,[5] save that a single member, Abiathar, escaped to join David.[6] It was not until David had come to the throne and had united Israel under his rule, and had conquered Jerusalem and broken the power of the Philistines, that any notable step was taken. For David established his capital in Jerusalem[7] and made it the location of a royal shrine. Political and military considerations may have led to the choice of Jerusalem as the capital, but the royal shrine was more than the shrine that happened to be established in that city. The Temple was not built until the reign of Solomon, but significant steps had already been taken. For David had brought the Ark from the obscurity of Kiriath-jearim, where it had lain since it was returned by the Philistines,[8] into Jerusalem.[9] By bringing this ancient symbol of Yahwism which had come down from the time of Moses into the city, he gave religious prestige to his new capital, and manifested to all his people his exaltation of the national God. He also, as we shall see, attached national and religious sentiment to Jerusalem in a way that survived the disruption of the kingdom.

It is improbable that David did anything to check the syncretism

mountain range." M. Noth (*History of Israel*, E. Tr., 2nd edn, 1960, p. 178) thinks they occupied Transjordan also, but the fact that Saul's son established his capital in Transjordan (2 Sam. 2.8) suggests that Philistine influence did not extend there.

[1] Cf. above, p. 64, n. 3.

[2] 1 Sam. 21.1 (M.T. 2). H. A. Poels (*Histoire du sanctuaire de l'Arche*, 1897, pp. 282ff) maintained that Nob is to be located at Gibeon, and that Gibeonites were massacred by Saul with priests, giving rise to the blood feud which was ended in the reign of David (2 Sam. 21.1ff) by the hanging of seven of Saul's descendants. Cf. also T. K. Cheyne (in *E.B.* iii, 1902, col. 3430), A. Bruno (*Gibeon*, 1923, pp. 69ff), and I. Hylander (*Der literarische Samuel-Saul-Komplex*, 1932, pp. 291f), who identify Nob with Gibeon.

[3] Cf. Isa. 10.32; Neh. 11.32. T. K. Cheyne (in *E.B.* iii, 1902, col. 3430) rejects the reading in the former of these passages.

[4] 1 Sam. 22.18.   [5] 1 Sam. 21.1ff (M.T. 2ff).   [6] 1 Sam. 22.20.
[7] 2 Sam. 5.9.   [8] 1 Sam. 7.1f.   [9] 2 Sam. 6.

with Canaanite religion that had been going on since the Settlement. We soon find the Ark in the care of two priests, Abiathar, the descendant of Eli, and Zadok,[1] whose genealogy is unknown,[2] though he was subsequently supplied with one going back to Aaron.[3] It is probable that Zadok was the Jebusite priest of Jerusalem before the capture of the city,[4] and that while the Ark

[1] 2 Sam. 15.24ff; 20.25.

[2] In 2 Sam. 8.17 he is said to be the son of Ahitub, but the text of this verse is clearly corrupt. The priests here are said to be Zadok and Ahimelech, but the Abiathar who fled to David (1 Sam. 22.20) and who stood beside Zadok in David's reign (2 Sam. 20.25) was still priest at Solomon's accession (1 Kings 1.7), until he was dismissed by Solomon (1 Kings 2.26). Moreover, Ahimelech is said to be the son of Abiathar, whereas Abiathar was the son of Ahimelech (1 Sam. 22.20). Further, Zadok is said to be the son of Ahitub, who is apparently the same person as Abiathar's grandfather. K. H. Graf (De templo Silonensi commentatio, 1855, p. 13) accepted this, and so made Zadok the uncle of Abiathar, and both the descendants of Eli. But 1 Sam. 2.27ff is usually held to refer to the supersession of the house of Eli by the house of Zadok, and so to distinguish them, and when the Chronicler provided Zadok with a genealogy (see next note) he traced him back to the house of Eleazar and not to the house of Ithamar, to which Eli belonged. We should therefore probably read in 2 Sam. 8.17 "Zadok, and Abiathar the son of Ahimelech the son of Ahitub" (so F. J. V. D. Maurer, Commentarius grammaticus criticus in Vetus Testamentum, i, 1835, p. 184; F. Hitzig, in O. Thenius, Die Bücher Samuels, 1842, p. 166; so also W. Nowack, Samuel, 1902, p. 184; K. Budde, Samuel, 1902, p. 243; P. Dhorme, Samuel, 1910, p. 341; H. W. Hertzberg, Samuel, E. Tr. by J. S. Bowden, 1964, pp. 292ff) J. Wellhausen proposed the order "Abiathar the son of Ahimelech the son of Ahitub, and Zadok" (Der Text der Bücher Samuelis, 1871, p. 177; so also A. R. S. Kennedy, Samuel, p. 233). Syr. has "Abiathar the son of Ahimelech" but retains "Zadok the son of Ahitub", and so H. P. Smith (Samuel, 1899, p. 309), S. R. Driver (op. cit., p. 283), and M. Rehm (Textkritische Untersuchungen zu den Parallelstellen der Samuel-Königsbücher und der Chronik, 1937, p. 126, and Echt.B., Altes Testament, ii, 1956, p. 95).

[3] 1 Chron. 6.4ff, 50ff (M.T. 5.30ff; 6.35ff).

[4] Cf. H. H. Rowley, "Zadok and Nehushtan", J.B.L. lviii, 1939, pp. 113ff. This view was proposed by S. Mowinckel, Ezra den Skriftlærde, 1916, p. 109 n; H. R. Hall, in The People and the Book, ed. by A. S. Peake, 1925, p. 11; A. Bentzen, Studier over det Zadokidiske Præsterkabs historie, 1931, pp. 10f (cf. Z.A.W. li, 1933, p. 174). It is followed by K. Möhlenbrink, Z.A.W. lii, 1934, p. 204; H. S. Nyberg, A.R.W. xxxv, 1938, p. 375; G. Widengren, Psalm 110 och det sakrale kungadömet i Israel, 1941, p. 21; H. Ringgren, in S.B.U. ii, 1952, col. 1004; G. B. Caird, I.B. ii, 1953, p. 1091; H. G. Judge, J.T.S., N.S. vii,

was temporarily housed in a tent when it was first brought into Jerusalem,[1] it was later brought into the shrine where Zadok officiated,[2] and remained there until the Temple was built by Solomon. If this view is right, it would seem that David identified the ancient God of Jerusalem, called El 'Elyon in the story of

1956, p. 71; N. H. Snaith, in Peake's *Commentary on the Bible*, 2nd edn, ed. by M. Black and H. H. Rowley, 1962, p. 246a; R. W. Corney, in *I.D.B.* iv, 1962, p. 928b; C. E. Hauer, *J.B.L.* lxxxii, 1963, p. 90; D. R. Jones, in Hastings' one volume *D.B.*, rev. edn, 1963, pp. 794a; W. Harrelson, *Interpreting the Old Testament*, 1964, p. 421; M. L. Newman, *The People of the Covenant*, 1965, p. 161. Cf. also A. R. Johnson, *Sacral Kingship in Ancient Israel*, 1955, p. 46 n. Hauer (loc. cit., pp. 91ff) suggests, on the basis of 1 Chron. 12.28, that Zadok had deserted to David with a company of priests prior to the capture of Jerusalem. E. Auerbach (*Z.A.W.* xlix, 1931, pp. 327f) argues, on the basis of 1 Chron. 16.39, that Zadok was priest at the Wilderness shrine at Gibeon. This view was earlier presented by Keil and Delitzsch (*The Books of Samuel*, E. Tr. by J. Martin, 1866, p. 365) and C. F. D. Erdmann (*The Books of Samuel*, E. Tr. by C. H. Toy and J. A. Broadus, 1877, p. 453), and criticized by W. W. von Baudissin (*Geschichte des alttestamentlichen Priesterthums*, 1889, p. 204; cf. also *J.B.L.* lviii, 1939, p. 119). J. Hoschander (*The Priests and Prophets*, 1938, p. 143) suggests that Zadok was priest at Hebron, and that he was transferred to Gibeon when the capital was transferred to Jerusalem, to the disgust of Abiathar. This is wholly without evidence. E. Sellin (*Geschichte der israelitisch-jüdischen Volkes*, i, 2nd edn, 1935, pp. 167, 169f) thought Zadok was priest at Gibeon, but migrated from there to Kiriath-jearim, and that he was the brother of Uzzah (on this cf. *J.B.L.*, loc. cit., pp. 120f). J. A. Poels (*Examen critique de l'histoire du sanctuaire de l'Arche*, 1897, pp. 163ff) equates Kiriath-jearim with Gibeon. J. Dus (*V.T.* x, 1960, pp. 353ff) maintains that the Gibeon sanctuary was a shrine of Shamash the Sun god.

[1] 2 Sam. 6.17.

[2] 2 Sam. 7.2 says that the Ark was housed in a tent at the time of Nathan's oracle, and 1 Kings 8.4 say it was taken from a tent to Solomon's Temple. But 2 Sam. 7.6 states unhistorically that until the time of David the Ark had never been housed in anything but a tent (for the abundant evidence that the Shiloh sanctuary was not a tent cf. K. H. Graf, *De templo Silonensi commentatio*, 1855, pp. 6f; moreover there is no reason to suppose that it was in a tent in the house of Abinadab (1 Sam. 7.1) or in the house of Obed-edom (2 Sam. 6.10f); for an attempt to prove the contrary cf. H. A. Poels, op. cit., pp. 117ff), and 1 Kings 8.4 was dictated by later orthodoxy, as is shown by its post-exilic distinction between priests and Levites. 2 Sam. 7.2 does not involve the conclusion that the Ark remained in a tent throughout the reign of David. The king purposed to build a Temple, and when he was dissuaded from doing so may have transferred it to a more permanent home.

Abraham and Melchizedek,[1] but also called Zedek and Shalem,[2] with Yahweh. In this there is nothing more surprising than in the identification of Yahweh with El Shaddai, which we have already noted. And that Yahweh was in fact identified with El 'Elyon in later Israelite thought is beyond doubt.[3] No more suitable occasion for the identification could be found than this, and it would serve to weld together the Jebusite population of Jerusalem and the Israelite people of the conquering king, especially if it were associated with the recognition of the Jebusite priest alongside the Israelite priest.[4]

We are told that David contemplated the erection of a shrine for the Ark, but was dissuaded by Nathan the prophet, acting as God's messenger,[5] and the Chronicler says that though he did not

[1] Gen. 14.18. R. H. Smith (*Z.A.W.* lxxvii, 1965, p. 148) is not persuaded that there was any connection between El 'Elyon and Jerusalem. On the other hand, O. Eissfeldt (*Forschungen und Fortschritte*, xxxix, 1965, p. 300) thinks the equation of Yahweh with El 'Elyon points to the time of David's reign in Jerusalem.

[2] See above, p. 18. G. Widengren (op. cit., p. 71) finds some references to Zedek as a divine name in Ps. 85.10, 11, 13 (M.T. 11, 12, 14) and 89.14 (M.T. 15), where most translate the word as "righteousness". Cf. G. W. Ahlström, *Psalm 89*, 1959, pp. 79f.

[3] Cf. Ps. 7.17 (M.T. 18); 47.2 (M.T. 3); also 9.2 (M.T. 3); 18.13 (M.T. 14); 21.7 (M.T. 8); 83.18 (M.T. 19); 91.9; 92.1 (M.T. 2).

[4] O. Eissfeldt (*C.A.H.*, rev. edn, Fasc. 32, 1965, p. 68) conjectures that the Disruption may have been partly due to Zadok's promotion of Canaanite usage.

[5] 2 Sam. 7.1ff; 1 Chron. 17.1ff. G. W. Ahlström (*S.E.Å.* xxv, 1960, pp. 5ff; *V.T.* xi, 1961, pp. 113ff) maintains that Nathan was the spokesman of the Jebusite party, whose objection to the building of the Temple was that it would rival the ancient Jebusite shrine. He locates that shrine on the threshing-floor of Araunah, in whom he sees the Jebusite king. A. Weiser, on the contrary, thinks Nathan's word was not directed against a Temple building as such, but against the danger of linking Yahweh with a sacred dwelling place of a Canaanite type (*Z.A.W.* lxxvii, 1965, pp. 153ff). Of the considerable literature on Nathan's oracle the following may be noted: L. Rost, *Die Überlieferung von der Thronnachfolge Davids*, 1926, pp. 47ff; S. Mowinckel, *S.E.Å.* xii, 1947, pp. 220ff; H. van den Bussche, *Le Texte de la prophétie de Nathan sur la dynastie Davidique* (reprinted from *E.Th.L.* xxiv, 1948, pp. 354ff), 1948; H. J. Kraus, *Die Königsherrschaft Gottes im Alten Testament*, 1951, pp. 35ff; Marcel Simon, *R.H.P.R.* xxxii, 1952, pp. 41ff; G. Widengren, *Sakrales Königtum im Alten Testament und im Judentum*, 1955, pp. 59ff; M. Noth, in *Mélanges Bibliques* (Robert Festschrift), 1957, pp. 122ff (reprinted in *Gesammelte Studien zum Alten Testament*, 1960, pp. 309ff); G. W. Ahlström, *V.T.* xi,

build the Temple, he amassed the means for it to be built.[1] It is probable that the site of the future Temple was chosen in the time of David. In the closing story of the appendix to the books of Samuel, which tells of David's numbering of the people and the subsequent plague,[2] we are told that the angel of the Lord stayed at the threshing-floor of Araunah[3] and that David acquired the site and erected an altar there.[4] The site of this altar may have been the site of the altar in Solomon's Temple, though this is not specifically stated. The site of the Temple is to-day marked by the mosque known as the Dome of the Rock, and scholars discuss whether the Rock was once under the Holy of Holies or the great altar of the Temple.[5] In the story of the threshing-floor of Araunah no rock is mentioned, and it is both unnecessary and impossible for us to determine exactly what its relation was to the structure of the Temple. If, as is probable, and as the Chronicler specifically states,[6] the threshing-floor of Araunah was incorporated in the site of the Temple, this would mean that the site of the Temple was chosen by Yahweh. For the staying of the plague at this point is equivalent to a theophany, and the erection of an altar here would be in accordance with the practice of the patriarchs[7] and also in accordance with the law of the altar found in the Book of the Covenant.[8] The Chronicler states that Yahweh appeared unto David at this spot,[9] and also identifies the site with Mount

1961, pp. 113ff; E. Kutsch, *Z.Th.K.* lviii, 1961, pp. 137ff; A. Caquot, in *Bonn Congress Volume* (S.V.T. ix), 1963, pp. 213ff; M. Tsevat, *H.U.C.A.* xxxiv, 1963, pp. 71ff, and *Biblica*, xlvi, 1965, pp. 353ff; H. Gese, *Z.Th.K.* lxi, 1964, pp. 10ff; R. A. Carlson, *David the Chosen King*, 1964, pp. 97ff. On the election of David and his dynasty cf. S. Amsler, *David, Roi et Messie*, 1963, pp. 37ff; R. A. Carlson, op. cit.

[1] 1 Chron. 22.2ff.   [2] 2 Sam. 24.1ff.
[3] 2 Sam. 24.16.   [4] 2 Sam. 24.25.
[5] Cf. H. Schmidt, *Der Heilige Fels in Jerusalem*, 1933; K. Galling, *B.R.L.*, 1937, col. 519 (cf. M. Noth, *History of Israel*, E. Tr., 2nd edn, 1960, p. 208); R. de Vaux, *A.I.*, 1961, pp. 318f; K. Möhlenbrink, *Der Tempel Salomos*, 1932, p. 36; J. de Groot, *Die Altäre des Salomonischen Tempelhofes*, 1924, p. 31; H. W. Hertzberg, *J.P.O.S.* xii, 1932, pp. 32ff; F. V. Filson, *B.A.* vii, 1944, p. 81. Cf. also G. B. Gray, *Sacrifice in the Old Testament*, 1925, pp. 132ff; A. Lods, *Israel*, E. Tr. by S. H. Hooke, 1932, p. 362; J. Simons, *Jerusalem in the Old Testament*, 1952, pp. 381ff; L. H. Vincent and A. M. Steve, *Jérusalem de l'Ancien Testament*, 1956, pp. 526ff.

[6] 2 Chron. 3.1; Araunah is here called Ornan, as in 1 Chron. 21.15.
[7] See above, pp. 23f.   [8] Ex. 20.24.   [9] 2 Chron. 3.1.

Moriah,[1] but this is at best evidence that by his time Jewish tradition had accepted this identification, and at worst simply the expression of his own desire to magnify the sacredness of this spot, just as he magnified its importance by turning the fifty shekels of silver which we are told in 2 Samuel David gave for it[2] into 600 shekels of gold.[3] It is improbable that Araunah's threshing-floor is to be identified with the site of Abraham's sacrifice, since if it were true, we should have expected it to be a sacred site before David purchased it from Araunah, and not to be a threshing-floor.[4] Pre-exilic tradition knows nothing of this identification.

This does not affect the question of the belief that the site was divinely chosen, a belief resting on the staying of the plague and on the presence of the Ark in Jerusalem. When David first sought to bring the Ark into the city on a cart, there was a mishap, resulting in the death of Uzzah.[5] David was immediately nervous lest this meant that Yahweh disapproved of the bringing of the Ark here, and put the Ark in the house of Obed-edom.[6] When he found that no misfortune befell Obed-edom he tried again to bring the Ark into the city,[7] this time with great caution. In the Ark Jerusalem had the token and pledge of the presence of Yahweh himself. And if he had come to dwell in Jerusalem, it was because he had chosen it for his residence. In some of the Psalms it is declared that Yahweh had chosen Zion,[8] and when Jerusalem was identified with the unnamed central sanctuary of the book of Deuteronomy, it would inevitably be thought of as the place which Yahweh had chosen to cause his name to dwell there.[9]

In accordance with the older law of JE, David does not seem to have observed any special sacred ordinance regulating the personnel of the shrine. He himself is said to have offered sacrifice

---

[1] 2 Chron 3.1.   [2] 2 Sam. 24.24.   [3] 1 Chron. 21.25.
[4] G. W. Ahlström (*S.E.Å.* xxv, 1960, pp. 7ff; *V.T.* xi, 1961, pp. 115ff) deduces from the word *gōren*, or threshing-floor, that the site was already a sacred one, and adduces evidence for the practice of fertility rites on the threshing-floor. But there is no evidence that the threshing-floor was necessarily the location of a shrine, and the fact that David built an altar on the threshing-floor of Araunah (2 Sam. 24.25) would seem to be evidence that it was not already the site of a shrine. W. Fuss (*Z.A.W.* lxxiv, 1962, pp. 145ff) offers a literary analysis of the chapter, and argues that it rests on an originally Jebusite aetiological source.
[5] 2 Sam. 6.6f.   [6] 2 Sam. 6.10.   [7] 2 Sam. 6.12ff.
[8] Ps. 132.13.   [9] Deut. 12.5, 11; 14.23; 16.2, 11; 26.2.

before the Ark when it was brought into Jerusalem,[1] and to have worn an ephod,[2] which we have seen to be a priestly garment. That Abiathar, who had been with David in his outlaw days and who was descended from the priesthood of Shiloh,[3] should be continued as priest is not surprising, but if Zadok was a Jebusite priest his being put in joint charge of the Ark is evidence that neither Aaronic nor Levite nor even Israelite descent was regarded by David as essential to the priesthood. We are also told that David consecrated his own sons as priests.[4]

When Solomon built the Temple, it stood beside his royal palace,[5] and it was not built to be the sole shrine of the land. It was a royal shrine, not in the sense of being a private chapel,[6] but in being the official shrine for the royal rites of the kingdom. Its importance lay rather in what it became than in what it was at the start, though when we come to consider the royal rites we shall see that it must at once have had a special position. At the Disruption, Jeroboam I constituted Bethel and Dan as royal shrines for the north.[7] This was due not only to jealousy of the prestige of Jerusalem, but to the fact that here the royal rites of the kings of Judah were observed. He required a shrine or shrines which marked the scene of a theophany or had some special association with the great events of Israel's religious history, and so he chose Bethel which was associated in tradition with a theophany to Jacob,[8] the father of all the tribes, and Dan in the far north, which had a priesthood tracing its descent from Moses,[9] the great charismatic leader who had mediated Yahwism to Israel. Here the royal rites of the northern kingdom, of which we have scant knowledge,

---

[1] 2 Sam. 6.13.   [2] 2 Sam. 6.14.
[3] 1 Sam. 14.3; 22.20.   [4] 2 Sam. 8.18.

[5] 1 Kings 7.1ff. The great court (1 Kings 7.12) appears to have included both the royal palace and the Temple. On the relation of palace to Temple cf. K. Möhlenbrink, *Der Tempel Salomos*, 1932, pp. 48ff.

[6] Cf. R. E. Clements, *Prophecy and Covenant*, 1965, p. 58: "It was no more private than the King himself could have been called a private person" (cf. also *God and Temple*, 1965, p. 68). Cf. also H. Vincent, in *Mélanges Bibliques* (Robert Festschrift), 1957, pp. 137ff; R. de Vaux, *A.I.*, p. 320.

[7] 1 Kings 12.28f. On Jeroboam's festival of dedication and its relevance to calendar changes cf. J. Morgenstern, *Amos Studies*, i, 1941, pp. 146ff; and, for a modification of his view, *J.B.L.* lxxxiii, 1964, pp. 109ff.

[8] Gen. 28.11ff.   [9] Judges 18.30; see above, p. 62, n. 1.

were observed. But though his shrines had older traditions and associations than the shrine of Jerusalem, they had not the splendour of the Temple and they lacked the Ark, which was an unrivalled symbol of Yahwism, and which was associated with Moses and the wilderness period, when Yahwism was established in Israel.

In its structure there was nothing peculiarly Yahwistic about the Temple. I have already said that the account of the Tabernacle in the Wilderness is but a projection of the Temple into the past. Hence the Temple was not conformed to a pre-existing plan of what a Yahweh shrine should be. Tyrian workmen were engaged for its erection,[1] and it was designed to be a more magnificent shrine than any other in the land, one befitting the wealth and splendour of the king himself. With equal readiness Solomon built shrines to other gods than Yahweh for the use of his foreign wives,[2] and there is no evidence that the forms of the ritual of the Temple, other than the royal rites, were peculiar to Yahwism, or that the ornamentation of the Temple was so peculiar.[3]

The Temple proper consisted of a porch,[4] beyond which was a large chamber, later called the Holy Place, and beyond this a smaller inner shrine, or Holy of Holies, into which the Ark[5] was brought.[6] This was called the *deḇhîr*, which is rendered "oracle"

---

[1] 1 Kings 5.2ff. On possible variations in the orientation of the Temple in the course of its history cf. L. A. Snijders, *O.T.S.* xiv, 1965, pp. 214ff.

[2] 1 Kings 11.8.

[3] On the Temple cf. A. Parrot, *The Temple of Jerusalem*, E. Tr. by B. E. Hooke, 1957; K. Möhlenbrink, *Der Tempel Salomos*, 1932; K. Galling, *Z.D.P.V.* lv, 1932, pp. 245ff, and in *R.G.G.* 3rd edn, vi, 1962, cols. 684ff; R. de Vaux, *A.I.*, pp. 312ff; W. F. Stinespring, in *I.D.B.* iv, 1962, pp. 534ff. Cf. also G. E. Wright, *B.A.* vii, 1944, pp. 73ff, and *Biblical Archaeology*, 2nd edn, 1962, pp. 137ff.

[4] 1 Kings 6.3.

[5] On the question whether the Ark was conceived of as the throne of Yahweh cf. R. E. Clements, *God and Temple*, 1965, pp. 28ff, and the literature there cited.

[6] 1 Kings 8.6. That the Ark was brought into the Temple is not to be doubted, but the account given in 1 Kings 8.1ff cannot be accepted in its details. It states that the Ark was brought up together with the Tent of Meeting from the city of David. The implication that this was the tent prepared in the time of Moses will not bear examination. For the tent in which David placed the Ark when he first brought it to Jerusalem was one which he pitched for it (2 Sam. 6.17), and there is no suggestion that it

in R.V.,[1] and "inner sanctuary" in R.S.V. It was a perfect cube in shape, twenty cubits each way,[2] and without light. "The Lord hath said that he would dwell in the thick darkness" we read in I Kings 8.12, in a passage which the LXX says stood in "The Book of Songs" (which is perhaps the same as the Book of Jashar, which is cited in the book of Joshua,[3] and which contained David's Lament over Saul and Jonathan[4]). This is probably a reference to the *debhîr*. It seems likely that this inner shrine was on a higher level than the outer,[5] and was separated from the latter by a thin partition.[6] In the description of the Tabernacle, which we have said was a projection of the Temple into the past, the division consisted of a veil,[7] as in the Temple of Herod.[8] The whole of the Temple proper was surrounded by a courtyard.[9]

We need not linger over the details of the building, since many of them are not certainly recoverable from the description given in the account of the construction of Solomon's Temple. We

was of higher antiquity. The Ark was not housed in a tent, but in a temple (1 Sam. 1.9), at Shiloh (in Josh. 18.1 and 19.51 the Tent is said to have been at Shiloh, but there is no mention of the Ark; these passages are late and of doubtful historicity; cf. de Vaux, *A.I.*, pp. 297, 304), and later it was in the house of Abinadab in Kiriath-jearim (1 Sam. 7.1). According to Judges 20.27, there had been a time when the Ark was in Bethel, but nowhere is there any suggestion that the Tent was ever there. The Chronicler states in 2 Chron. 1.3 that at the beginning of the reign of Solomon the Tent of Meeting was in Gibeon, and clearly differentiates it from the tent which David had pitched in Jerusalem. As there is nowhere any suggestion that the Ark was ever in Gibeon, it is impossible to suppose that there had been any continuous association of the Tent and the Ark from the days of the Settlement, or that Solomon brought the Mosaic tent from Zion into the Temple. Cf. G. von Rad (*Old Testament Theology*, E. Tr. by D. M. G. Stalker, i, 1962, p. 236): "After the Settlement of Israel in Canaan the Tent disappears from the history." M. L. Newman (The *People of the Covenant*, 1965, pp. 67f, 161f) suggests that the Tent, which was unassociated with the Ark before the time of David, had been at Hebron and was brought from there to Jerusalem.

[1] 1 Kings 6.5, 16, etc.; 7.49; 8.6, 8; Ps. 28.2.
[2] 1 Kings 6.20. On the description of the *debhîr* in the M.T. and LXX cf. D. W. Gooding *V.T.* xv, 1965, pp. 405ff.
[3] Josh. 10.13.   [4] 2 Sam. 1.18.   [5] Cf. R. de Vaux, *A.I.*, p. 314.
[6] Cf. de Vaux, ibid. pp. 313f.   [7] Ex. 26.33.
[8] Cf. Matt. 27.51; Mark 15.38; Luke 23.45; also Josephus, *B.J.* V.v.5 (219).
[9] 1 Kings 6.36.

may, however, note that the general lay-out of the Temple can be paralleled from non-Israelite shrines uncovered by the spade of the archaeologist, and de Vaux points out that the parallels are particularly close in the case of Syrian and Palestinian shrines.[1] This confirms that there is nothing particularly Yahwistic in the general plan of the Temple.

In front of the porch stood two pillars, called Jachin and Boaz.[2] It is uncertain whether they were free-standing pillars or not, but in either case they can be paralleled from other ancient sites.[3] There has been much speculation as to the meaning of the names and many theories have been advanced, but no certainty is attainable, and since these names can contribute little to our understanding of the forms or meaning of Israelite worship they need not detain us.[4] As to the pillars themselves, de Vaux is of the

[1] *A.I.*, pp. 317f. Cf. also O. Eissfeldt, *C.A.H.*, rev. edn, Fasc. 32, 1965, p. 63.

[2] 1 Kings 7.15ff.

[3] Cf. S. A. Cook, *The Religion of Ancient Palestine in the Light of Archaeology*, 1930, pp. 166f; H. G. May, *B.A.S.O.R.*, No. 88, Dec. 1942, p. 20; A. Parrot, *The Temple of Jerusalem*, E. Tr. by B. E. Hooke, 1957, p. 27; R. de Vaux, *A.I.*, p. 314. Albright (*B.A.S.O.R.*, No. 85, Feb. 1942, pp. 18ff, and *A.R.I.*, 3rd edn, 1953, pp. 144ff; cf. W. Robertson Smith, *Religion of the Semites*, 3rd edn, 1927, pp. 487ff) suggested that they were cressets. N. H. Snaith (*I.B.* iii, 1954, p. 62) thinks the most probable explanation is that they represented the two mountains which flanked the path to the mountain of the gods away to the north. On these pillars cf. also S. Yeivin, *P.E.Q.* xci, 1959, pp. 6ff; W. Kornfeld, *Z.A.W.* lxxiv, 1962, pp. 50ff.

[4] R. B. Y. Scott (*J.B.L.* lviii, 1939, pp. 143ff; cf. *I.D.B.* ii, 1962, pp. 780f) suggested that they were the first words of two inscriptions, perhaps "He [Yahweh] will establish the throne of David, and his Kingdom to his seed forever" and "in the strength of Yahweh shall the King rejoice". For the former Albright (*A.R.I.*, p. 139) suggests "Yahweh will establish thy throne for ever". J. Gray (*Kings*, 1964, p. 175) thinks the names reflect the relationship of God and the King: "He (God) establishes", and "By Him (i.e. God) he (the King) is mighty". J. Obermann (*J.B.L.* lxviii, 1949, pp. 317f) thinks the two words are epithets of God, "Sustainer, Maintainer, Establisher" (cf. Albright, *J.B.L.* xliii, 1924, p. 375 "Creator") and "Smiter, Undoer". For other suggestions cf. T. Witton Davies, in Hastings' *D.B.* i, 1898, pp. 308f; H. G. May, *B.A.S.O.R.*, No. 88, Dec. 1942, pp. 19ff; P. L. Garber, *B.A.* xiv, 1951, pp. 8ff; A. Parrot, *The Temple of Jerusalem*, pp. 26ff; W. Kornfeld, *Z.A.W.* lxxiv, 1962, pp. 50ff. For Boaz LXX^B has *Balaz* and there is another MS. reading *Boolaz*, whence J. A. Montgomery (*J.Q.R.* xxv, 1934–5, p. 265) suggests the meaning "master of strength".

opinion that they were *maṣṣēbhôth*,[1] comparable with those of the old Canaanite shrines. Jacob's pillar at Bethel was a *maṣṣēbhāh*,[2] and there are frequent references in the Old Testament to pillars of this kind at the high places.[3] In Deuteronomy they are condemned,[4] but there is no evidence that the earlier conscience of Israel condemned them.[5]

In the court surrounding the Temple proper was the Sea of Bronze, which stood on twelve bulls of bronze.[6] Here, once more, there is nothing particularly Yahwistic, and de Vaux cites the parallel of a stone basin from Cyprus and the *apsû* of some Mesopotamian temples.[7] The bull was a common Canaanite symbol of fertility,[8] and it is probably borrowed here in the ornamentation of the Temple from Canaanite sources. It will be remembered that Jeroboam I set up bull figures in his temples at Bethel and Dan.[9] Archaeology has brought to light bull figures with the images of a god standing on them,[10] and H. T. Obbink has argued that the bulls of Jeroboam were not intended to be images of Yahweh, but pedestals with no figure standing on them,[11] since Yahwism was a religion without idols, prohibiting figures of Yahweh. While this is probably true,[12] the bull images

---

[1] *A.I.*, p. 314. This view was found in older writers, for example R. Kittel, *Könige*, 1900, p. 63; J. Skinner, *Kings*, p. 125; J. de Groot, *Die Altäre des Salomonischen Tempelhofes*, 1924, p. 17. The term used here, however, is a different one.

[2] Gen. 28.18.

[3] Cf. J. W. Wevers, in Hastings' one volume *D.B.*, rev. edn, 1963, pp. 772f.

[4] Deut. 16.22.   [5] Cf. Hos. 3.4.

[6] 1 Kings 7.23ff. On this cf. C. Bagnani, in *The Seed of Wisdom* (Meek Festschrift), 1964, pp. 114ff.

[7] *A.I.*, p. 319.

[8] Cf. Albright, *F.S.A.C.*, 2nd edn, 1946, p. 230; W. J. Harrelson, in *I.B.D.* i, 1962, p. 489a.

[9] 1 Kings 12.28ff.

[10] Harrelson gives an illustration of one, loc. cit., p. 488b, and D. J. Wiseman another in *N.B.D.*, 1962, p. 497a.

[11] *Z.A.W.* xlvii, 1929, pp. 267f. Cf. also W. Eichrodt, *Theology of the Old Testament*, E. Tr., i, 1961, p. 117; J. Hempel, *Gott und Mensch*, 2nd edn, 1936, pp. 265ff, and *Z.A.W.* lvii, 1939, pp. 72f; W. F. Albright, *J.B.L.* lvii, 1938, p. xviii, and *F.S.A.C.*, 2nd edn, 1946, pp. 228ff; N. H. Snaith in Hastings' one volume *D.B.*, rev. edn, 1963, p. 119b. H. J. Kraus (*Worship in Israel*, E.Tr., 1966, pp. 149f) is doubtful of this view.

[12] O. Eissfeldt (*Z.A.W.* lviii, 1940–1, pp. 190ff) regards the bulls as small transportable objects similar to one exemplified at Mari, while L. Waterman (*A.J.S.L.* xxxi, 1914–15, pp. 229ff) argued that they were "bull colossi".

were condemned by the later conscience,[1] probably because, though they may not have been created to be regarded as images of Yahweh, they had become so regarded by the people. It should be added that there were in the court of the Temple ten smaller lavers of bronze,[2] and that these again can be paralleled elsewhere.[3] In the outer shrine there was the table of shewbread and ten candlesticks.[4] It will be recalled that there was shewbread at the shrine of Nob when David visited it,[5] so that this figured in the shrine there before the building of the Temple. Parallels can be found outside Israel,[6] and in the Apocrypha in the story of Bel and the Dragon the pretence that the god ate this bread is ridiculed. There is no likelihood that such a pretence was made in Israel, since in the story of David we are told that hot bread was put in its place on the day when it was taken away,[7] and in the Law of Holiness, where we are told about the making of the shewbread,[8] we are told that it was placed in the sanctuary on the sabbath day and eaten by the priests when it was removed.[9] There were twelve loaves, and the number perhaps represents the twelve tribes.[10] The bread was perhaps placed on a cedar table.[11] In the

[1] Cf. 1 Kings 14.9, where Jeroboam is said to have made "other gods and molten images", apparently with reference to the bull images. Cf. also Hos. 8.5f; 13.2; 2 Kings 17.16; 2 Chron. 13.8.

[2] 1 Kings 7.38.

[3] Cf. de Vaux, A.I., p. 319. 2 Chron. 4.6 says that the lavers were to wash the sacrificial gifts and the sea for the priests to wash in. It is generally thought that both the sea and the lavers originally had a symbolic meaning, the sea representing the primeval waters and the lavers the clouds (cf., for example, W. R. Harvey-Jellie, *Chronicles*, p. 194; E. L. Curtis and A. A. Madsen, *Chronicles*, 1910, p. 332). But de Vaux (*A.I.*, pp. 328f) holds that it is improbable that the lavers represented the clouds, though he allows the possibility that the sea represented the primeval waters.

[4] 1 Kings 7.48f.   [5] 1 Sam. 21.6. (M.T. 7).

[6] Cf. P. R. Ackroyd, in Hastings' one volume *D.B.*, rev. edn, 1963, p. 912a; H. F. Beck, in *I.D.B.* i, 1962, p. 464.

[7] 1 Sam. 21.6.   [8] Lev. 24.5ff.   [9] Lev. 24.8f.

[10] So de Vaux, *A.I.*, p. 422. It is possible, however, that the number twelve originally had a different significance, perhaps connected with the signs of the Zodiac or the calendar. For the Babylonians placed loaves in twelves or multiples of twelve before their gods (cf. *K.A.T.*, 3rd edn, 1903, p. 600).

[11] 1 Kings 6.20. The Hebrew says "he covered the altar with cedar" (so A.V., R.V.); but LXX reads "he made the altar" ("of cedar" having

description of the Tabernacle the table is said to have been made
of shittim wood and to have been overlaid with gold.[1]

In the description of the Temple in the book of Kings, we are
told that there was a golden table[2] beside the table of shewbread,
and this is held to be the altar of incense,[3] but by many scholars
rejected as an anachronism[4] on the ground that incense was not
used in the worship until post-exilic days.[5] There are two words
which are rendered "incense", but R.S.V. usually distinguishes
between them and renders one "incense" and the other "frankincense". There is no reason to doubt that frankincense was used in

perhaps fallen out), and R.S.V. follows this reading. In 1 Kings 7.48 the
table of shewbread is said to have been made of gold, but that passage is
generally held to have been a late interpolation. 2 Chron. 4.19 speaks of
the tables of shewbread, but says nothing of the material. The altar of
1 Kings 6.20 is generally understood to refer to the table of shewbread
(cf. A. R. S. Kennedy, in *D.B.* iv, 1902, p. 495b), but this is not clear.
De Vaux (*A.I.*, p. 319) understands it to refer to the altar of incense,
which is held by many scholars to be excluded on the ground that incense
was not used in the pre-exilic Temple. This argument is not conclusive,
however, and it is probable that incense was used in pre-exilic times (see
below). This does not necessarily imply that there was an altar of incense
in pre-exilic times, since incense could have been burned in censers, as in
the ritual of the Day of Atonement (Lev. 16.12f.). B. D. Eerdmans
(*Alttestamentliche Studien*, iv, 1912, pp. 28ff) maintains that there was an
incense altar in the pre-exilic Temple, but none in the post-exilic.

[1] Ex. 25.23ff.   [2] 1 Kings 7.48.

[3] So de Vaux, *A.I.*, p. 319. As noted above (p. 83, n. 11) this verse
is held by many to be a late addition to the text. R. de Langhe (*Biblica*,
xl, 1959, pp. 476ff) has argued that the words "altar of gold" should be
rendered "altar of incense", and offers evidence that *zāhābh* carried the
meaning of "incense" as well as of "gold". On this de Vaux comments
(*A.I.*, p. 411) that while this rendering is possible, the meaning must have
been very soon lost. That no altar of gold stood in the pre-exilic Temple is
rendered probable by the fact that none is mentioned among the treasures
carried away by the Babylonians at the destruction of the Temple (2 Kings
25.13ff). Cf. R. de Langhe, *Het Gouden Altaar in de israëlietische eredienst*,
1952, and in *Studia Biblica et Orientalia*, i, 1959, pp. 342ff. A. van Hoonacker (*R.B.*, N.S. xi, 1914, pp. 177f) thought that Judas Maccabaeus may
not have replaced the altar by a golden one when he restored the Temple.

[4] But cf. J. de Groot, *Die Altäre des Salomonischen Tempelhofes*, 1924,
p. 11.

[5] So J. Wellhausen, *Prolegomena to the History of Israel*, E. Tr., 1885,
pp. 64f. Cf. J. A. Selbie, in Hastings' *D.B.* ii, 1899, pp. 467f; G. F. Moore,
in *E.B.* ii, 1901, col. 2166; J. D. Eisenstein, in *J.E.* vi, 1907, p. 569;
Oesterley and Robinson, *Hebrew Religion*, 2nd edn, 1937, p. 334.

pre-exilic times. It is referred to by Jeremiah as imported from
Sheba,[1] and mentioned in connection with sacrifice.[2] In the
passage from the Law of Holiness about the shewbread, it is said
that frankincense is to be placed alongside the shewbread on the
table of shewbread.[3] The use of incense is not peculiar to Israel,
and there is no reason to doubt that it was used in Israel. There
is, however, some reason to doubt that there was a separate table
of incense in Solomon's Temple in view of the passage from the
Law of Holiness already mentioned.[4] So far as the other term for
incense is concerned, it is improbable that it was used with this

[1] Jer. 6.20. Cf. G. van Beek, B.A. xxiii, 1960, pp. 70ff.
[2] Jer. 17.26; 41.5; Isa. 43.23.   [3] Lev. 24.7.
[4] W. Corswant (A Dictionary of Life in Bible Times, E. Tr. by A. W.
Heathcote, 1956, p. 273) says: "For a long time it was thought that there
was no altar of incense in this first Jerusalem Temple, but at the present
time, on the contrary, its presence beside the table for shewbread is
fairly generally admitted." This goes somewhat farther than the present
writer goes. More cautious is H. F. Beck, in I.D.B. ii, 1962, p. 698a, who
observes: "There is no conclusive proof that the offering of incense was
unknown in Israel before the seventh century." G. B. Gray (Sacrifice in
the Old Testament, 1925, pp. 142f) rightly notes that the incense altars
found in excavations are not evidence for a pre-exilic altar of incense in the
Temple (cf. M. Haran, V.T. x, 1960, p. 120). M. Löhr (Das Räucher-
opfer im Alten Testament (in Schriften der Königsberger Gelehrten
Gesellschaft, Geisteswiss. Klasse, iv, 1927), p. 179) thinks the probability
that there was an incense altar in the pre-exilic Temple greater than that
there was not, but finds certainty unattainable. Cf. also B. D. Eerdmans,
Alttestamentliche Studien, iv, 1912, pp. 28ff. H. Ingholt (in Mélanges
Syriens (Dussaud Festschrift), ii, 1939, pp. 795ff) argued that the word
ḥammān (Isa. 17.8; 27.9; Lev. 26.30; Ezek. 6.4, 6; 2 Chron. 14.5 (M.T.
4); 34.4, 7), which is rendered "sun image" in R.V., means a portable
incense stand, and this view has been accepted by K. Elliger (Z.A.W.
lvii, 1939, pp. 256ff—against the view of J. Lindblom (Die Jesaja-
Apokalypse, 1938, pp. 91ff) that it was a maṣṣebhāh), W. F. Albright
(A.R.I., pp. 215f), K.B. (p. 311b), R. de Langhe (Biblica, xl, 1959,
p. 486), S. H. Horn (Seventh Day Adventist Bible Dictionary, 1960,
p. 503a), R. de Vaux (A.I., pp. 286f), K. Galling (in I.D.B. ii, 1962,
p. 699), N. H. Snaith (in Peake's Commentary on the Bible, 2nd edn, 1962,
p. 253a), A. S. Herbert (ibid., p. 357b), J. Muilenburg (ibid., p. 573b),
F. F. Bruce (in Hastings' one volume D.B., rev. edn, 1963, p. 24b), and is
followed by R.S.V. M. Haran (V.T. x, 1960, p. 121) expresses doubt on
this question. But this is of little relevance for our purpose, in view of the
fact that these ḥammānîm are condemned as heathen cultic articles and in
view of the lateness of the references. As de Vaux says (loc. cit.), none is
pre-exilic, as Isa. 17.7f is commonly considered to be an addition.

meaning in pre-exilic times. It means "smoke", and the verb "to cause smoke to ascend" was used in pre-exilic times for the causing of the smoke of sacrifice to ascend, and the noun meant the smoke of sacrifice.[1] The fact that this word was used of the aromatic smoke of incense in post-exilic times does not mean that incense was first used after the exile. Montgomery says: "The earlier objection . . . , that incense did not reach Palestine until a much later age, is now fully disposed of by the discovery of numerous and highly elaborate censers, . . . while they appear to have been of common domestic use, going back well into the second millennium."[2] In the Priestly law we are given the directions for making incense, and are told that it was made of four ingredients, together with a seasoning of salt.[3] Josephus tells us that in his time thirteen ingredients went into incense.[4] It would therefore seem that in pre-exilic times the incense used in the Temple consisted only or mainly of frankincense, and that when in post-exilic times a more compound incense was used and a different term was needed for it, it was called "holy smoke".

It is curious that the altar of burnt offerings, which stood in the court outside the Temple proper, is unmentioned in the account of the construction of the Temple, though there are allusions to it elsewhere.[5] De Vaux thinks it may have been a movable bronze altar and that it was unmentioned in the account of the building of the Temple because it did not conform to Israelite custom as expressed in the Book of the Covenant,[6] where we are told that the altar should be of earth or else of unhewn stone.[7]

In none of these respects is there reason to suppose that the furnishing or ornamentation of the Temple differentiated it from

---

[1] 1 Sam. 2.15f (cf. Lev. 17.6 H; Num. 18.17 P); 2 Kings 16.13, 15; Amos 4.5. In a number of other pre-exilic passages the expression could refer to incense or sacrifice, but is more probably used of the latter. On the other hand the passages where the reference is certainly to incense are all later.

[2] *Kings*, 1951, p. 104. Cf. A. van Hoonacker, *R.B.* N.S. xi, 1914, pp. 161ff; A. Eberharter, *Z.K.Th.* l, 1926, pp. 89ff; K. Galling, *B.R.L.*, 1937, cols. 13ff; A. G. Barrois, *Manuel d'archéologie biblique*, ii, 1953, pp. 380ff; W. Corswant, op. cit., p. 27.

[3] Ex. 30.34ff. Cf. Jub. 16.24, where seven ingredients are named.

[4] *B.J.* V.v.5 (218).   [5] 1 Kings 8.22, 54, 64; 9.25.

[6] *A.I.*, p. 410. On the altar among Israel's neighbours cf. K. Galling, *Der Altar in den Kulturen des alten Orients*, 1925.

[7] Ex. 20.24ff.

other shrines of the period, and the workmen employed by Solomon seem to have created only a more splendid version of the shrines of Syria and Palestine of those times.

In a later age we read of a Brazen Serpent which stood in the Temple, and which Hezekiah destroyed because it was associated with idolatry.[1] We are not told when it was brought into the Temple, though we are given an account of its making in the Wilderness period, when Moses is said to have been responsible for its creation.[2] It is curious that we hear nothing of its history from the time of Moses to the time of its destruction, and we are not told where it was in the age of the Judges or whence it was conveyed to the Temple. There is no reason to suppose that it was with the Ark at Shiloh, or that it accompanied the Ark into the land of the Philistines or was at Kiriath-jearim or was brought to Jerusalem by David, and if Solomon had brought this symbol with associations with Moses into the Temple at the time of the construction of the Temple we should expect some account of it comparable with the account of the bringing of that other symbol which came from Mosaic times, the Ark, into Jerusalem. It is, indeed, very probable that it was a Jebusite sacred symbol in Jerusalem before David captured the city, and that it was transferred from the Jebusite shrine to the Temple when it was built and when Zadok removed from the older shrine to the new.[3] Once more, therefore, there is no reason to find in the new building or its contents anything which of itself shows anything to differentiate the worship of Israel from that of her neighbours, with the exception of the sacred symbol of the Ark.

The Temple was resorted to on the three great festivals of the year. These were the agricultural festivals of Unleavened Bread,

[1] 2 Kings 18.4.   [2] Num. 21.8f.

[3] Cf. what I have written in *J.B.L.* lviii, 1939, pp. 113ff and in *Festschrift für Alfred Bertholet*, 1950, pp. 461ff. Cf. also R. Kittel, *Könige*, 1900, pp. 278f; A. Lods, *Israel*, E. Tr., 1932, pp. 361f, 404, and *The Prophets and the Rise of Judaism*, E. Tr. 1937, p. 114; J. A. Montgomery, *Kings*, p. 481; N. H. Snaith, *I.B.* iii, 1954, p. 290; H. J. Boecker, in Reicke and Rost, *Biblisch-historisches Handwörterbuch*, i, 1962, col. 371; J. Mauchline, in Hastings' one volume *D.B.*, rev. edn, 1963, p. 898a; J. Gray, *Kings*, 1964, p. 608. On serpent worship in Jerusalem cf. I. Benzinger, *Hebräische Archäologie*, 3rd edn, 1927, p. 327; S. A. Cook, *Religion of Ancient Palestine*, 1930, pp. 82, 99 n; K. Galling, *B.R.L.*, 1937, col. 459.

the Harvest Festival (also called the Feast of Weeks[1] and, in the the New Testament, Pentecost), and the Feast of Ingathering[2] (also called the Feast of Tabernacles).[3] These feasts were in all probability taken over from the Canaanites after the Settlement of the Israelites,[4] though they were given Israelite features. Thus, de Vaux is of the opinion that the Feast of Unleavened Bread at first always extended from sabbath to sabbath,[5] and as the sabbath does not seem to have been a Canaanite observance[6] this may have been a peculiarly Israelite feature.[7] If so, it lost this character when it became attached to the Passover, which did not always fall on the sabbath. That Passover and Unleavened Bread were originally two distinct and unconnected festivals is not to be doubted, though J. B. Segal has recently challenged it.[8] But there is no reason to think that Passover was a Canaanite festival. Unlike the agricultural feast of Unleavened Bread, it was of pastoral origin, and there is no reason to doubt that the Israelites brought it with them into Canaan, and that it was the festival which most clearly distinguished Israelite religion from Canaanite. Through the Exodus it was given an historical association and it was celebrated to proclaim the mighty acts of God for his people Israel.[9] Through the linking together of Passover and Unleavened Bread the association with Israel's history and the memory of her deliverance was extended to the Feast of Unleavened Bread.

The Harvest Festival is mentioned in the old Gezer Calendar,[10]

[1] Ex. 34.22; Deut. 16.16.   [2] Ex. 23.16; 34.22.   [3] Deut. 16.16.
[4] Cf. de Vaux, *A.I.*, p. 491: "The feast of Unleavened Bread was, therefore, an agricultural feast, and was not observed until the Israelites had settled in Canaan. It is quite possible, then, that the Israelites adopted this feast from the Canaanites"; p. 494: "The feast of Weeks was a feast for farmers living a settled life; Israel adopted it only after its entry into Palestine, and must have taken it from the Canaanites"; p. 501: "The feast [of Tabernacles] could not have been instituted until after the settlement in Canaan, and the presumption is that it was adopted from the Canaanites."
[5] *A.I.*, p. 491.
[6] Cf. de Vaux, ibid. On the sabbath cf. *M.G.*, pp. 25ff; de Vaux, *A.I.*, pp. 475ff.
[7] So de Vaux, *A.I.*, p. 491.   [8] Cf. above, p. 48.
[9] G. Fohrer (*Überlieferung und Geschichte des Exodus*, 1964, pp. 92ff) thinks Passover was first associated with the memory of the Exodus in Deuteronomy.
[10] Line 5. Cf. M. Lidzbarski, *Ephemeris für semitische Epigraphie*, iii, 1915, pp. 36ff; D. Diringer, *Le iscrizioni antico-ebraiche palestinesi*, 1934, pp. 1ff; J. Mauchline, in *D.O.T.T.*, pp. 201ff.

and it too was probably of pre-Israelite origin and was taken over from the Canaanites. Both this and the Feast of Ingathering were at a later date associated with Israel's history. A passage in Deuteronomy presents a liturgy for use at the Harvest Festival,[1] recalling the Descent into Egypt as the result of famine, the oppression in Egypt, the deliverance from task-work, and the gift of the land. The Feast of Ingathering was associated through the booths in which it was celebrated with the wanderings in the Wilderness, when the people had no settled homes. In neither of these cases did the historical association displace the agricultural character of the feasts, as the historical association of Passover displaced the original significance of that feast, so that we are left with no more than conjecture as to what the original significance of Passover was.

Once more, there is nothing peculiar to the Temple in the fact of the observance of these feasts. Before the Temple was built we read of the execution of seven of Saul's descendants at Gibeon at the beginning of the barley harvest,[2] which was the time of the Feast of Unleavened Bread,[3] and there is no reason to doubt that it continued to be celebrated at the local shrines through most of the pre-exilic period. Similarly, Passover was celebrated at local shrines until the Deuteronomic reform in the time of Josiah centralized the celebration in Jerusalem.[4] The Feast of Ingathering,

[1] Deut. 26.1ff.

[2] 2 Sam. 21.1ff. On this incident and its connections with the fertility cult, cf. A. S. Kapelrud, in *Interpretationes ad Vetus Testamentum pertinentes* (Mowinckel Festschrift), 1955, pp. 113ff, *Z.A.W.* lxvii, 1955, pp. 198ff, and in *The Sacral Kingship* (Supplements to *Numen*, iv), 1959, pp. 294ff; H. Cazelles, *P.E.Q.* lxxxvii, 1955, pp. 165ff. A. Malamat (*V.T.* v, 1955, pp. 1ff) examines this incident in the light of a Hittite parallel. Cf. also J. Prado, *Sefarad*, xiv, 1954, pp. 43ff.

[3] The barley harvest was the first to be reaped (cf. Gezer Calendar, line 4), and Lev. 23.9ff places the presentation of the first sheaf fifty days before the feast of Pentecost (verses 15ff), and therefore at the beginning of the feast of Unleavened Bread. Cf. M. Noth, *Leviticus*, E. Tr. by J. E. Anderson, 1965, pp. 170ff.

[4] Cf. 2 Kings 23.22f, where it is stated that no Passover like Josiah's, which was kept in Jerusalem, had been previously kept. 2 Chron. 30.1ff. attributes to Hezekiah the holding of a similar Passover in Jerusalem. That Hezekiah carried through a reform is to be accepted (cf. *M.G.*, pp. 126ff) despite denials by J. Wellhausen (*Prolegomena to the History of Israel*, E. Tr., p. 25), B. Stade (*G.V.I.* i, 1889, p. 607), T. K. Cheyne (in *E.B.* ii, 1901, cols. 2058f), G. Hölscher (*Geschichte der israelitischen und*

which was the time of the vintage harvest,[1] was celebrated at Shiloh during the period of the Judges,[2] and it was probably the feast for which Elkanah came with his wives to Shiloh.[3] For at this feast there seems to have been much drinking of wine and this would account for Eli's thought that Hannah might be drunk.[4] Isaiah's Song of the Vineyard[5] may have been modelled on a vintage song which was sung at this festival.

There are references to sabbath and new moon as special religious days,[6] and it is probable that numbers resorted to the Temple on these days. Isaiah probably has the Jerusalem Temple in mind in his denunciation of the religious observances of his day,[7] and here he mentions new moon and sabbath.[8] So far as the sabbath is concerned we have a clear indication in the account of the coronation of Joash that large numbers went to the Temple on the sabbath day.[9] The coronation of the young prince was timed to take place on the sabbath day, when we are told that the two companies of guards normally on duty at the royal palace exchanged duties with the single company normally on duty in the Temple,[10] and this would imply that larger numbers of people were to be found in the Temple on the sabbath than on other days. But again, we find references to new moon and sabbath where there is no reference to the Jerusalem Temple,[11] and other shrines must have been similarly attended on these days. Both Amos and Hosea speak of new moon and sabbath,[12] and as they were both prophesying in the northern kingdom, they presumably were thinking of religious observances in the shrines there. From

jüdischen Religion, 1922, p. 99), and A. Lods (*The Prophets and the Rise of Judaism*, E. Tr., 1937, p. 115). But the account of his Passover given by the Chronicler is less trustworthy, though it has been defended by S. Talmon (*V.T.* viii, 1948, pp. 58ff), H. J. Kraus (*Evangelische Theologie*, xviii, 1958, pp. 63ff), and H. Haag (in *S.D.B.* vi, 1960, col. 1133). For the Chronicler himself denies it in 2 Chron. 35.18. Cf. Curtis and Madsen, *Chronicles*, 1910, pp. 470f; W. A. L. Elmslie, *Chronicles*, 1916, p. 310; W. Rudolph, *Chronikbücher*, 1955, p. 299; H. Cazelles, *Chroniques*, 2nd edn, 1961, pp. 214, 218; R. de Vaux, *Studies in Old Testament Sacrifice*, 1964, p. 2 n. K. Galling (*Chronik, Esra, Nehemia*, 1954, pp. 159f) assigns 2 Chron. 30.1ff. to a secondary hand.

[1] Deut. 16.13.   [2] Judges 21.19ff.   [3] 1 Sam. 1.3ff.
[4] 1 Sam. 1.13.   [5] Isa. 5.1ff.
[6] Cf. 2 Kings 4.23; Ezek. 45.17; 46.3; Hos. 2.11 (M.T. 13); 2 Chron. 2.4.
[7] Isa. 1.10ff.   [8] Isa. 1.13.   [9] 2 Kings 11.4ff.   [10] 2 Kings 11.5ff.
[11] 2 Kings 4.23; Hos. 2.11 (M.T. 13).   [12] Amos 8.5; Hos. 2.11 (M.T. 13).

the story of Elisha's raising of the Shunammite's son we gather
that these days were normal days for the consultation of prophets.[1]
Some scholars have thought that the linking together of sabbath
and new moon means that the sabbath was at one time a monthly
observance,[2] and Professor Snaith has argued that the month
formerly began at the full moon, so that what is normally called
the new moon should really be translated "new moon day", i.e.
full moon, and that the sabbath was the day of the new moon.[3]
Against this is to be set the fact that in the oldest Decalogue,
which is probably of pre-Israelite, Kenite, origin,[4] as well as in
the familiar Decalogue of Exodus 20 and Deuteronomy 5, the
sabbath is clearly a weekly celebration.[5] The sabbath appears to
have been a distinctively Israelite observance, not shared with the
Canaanite neighbours.[6]

[1] 2 Kings 4.23.
[2] Cf. J. Meinhold, Sabbat und Woche im Alten Testament, 1905,
pp. 3ff; T. J. Meek, J.B.L. xxxiii, 1914, pp. 201ff; G. Hölscher, Geschichte
der israelitischen und jüdischen Religion, 1922, p. 80; S. Mowinckel, Le
Décalogue, 1927, pp. 75ff; A. Lods, Israel, E. Tr., pp. 438ff; O. Procksch,
Theologie des Alten Testaments, 1950, p. 544. R. de Vaux (A.I., p. 480)
observes: "One thing is certain: it is useless to try to find the origin of the
Sabbath by connecting it in some way with the phases of the moon."
Other scholars who reject this view include B. D. Eerdmans, Alttestamentliche Studien, ii, 1910, pp. 138ff; E. König, Geschichte der alttestamentliche Religion, 1912, pp. 238f; R. Kittel, G.V.I. i, 6th edn, 1923,
p. 447; B. Jacob, J.Q.R., N.S. xiv, 1923-4, pp. 157f; K. Budde, J.T.S.
xxx, 1929, pp. 7ff, and Z.A.W. xlviii, 1930, pp. 144f.
[3] Cf. The Jewish New Year Festival, 1947, pp. 103ff.
[4] Cf. M.G., pp. 18ff.
[5] Ex. 34.21. J. and H. Lewy (H.U.C.A., xvii, 1942-3, pp. 1ff) hold that
the seven-day week was a development from a fifty-day period in the time
of Ezra. The Ritual Decalogue and the Ethical Decalogue are both
certainly older than this and both present it as a seven-day period.
[6] Of the enormous literature on the Sabbath the following may be
noted: H. Zimmern, Z.D.M.G. lviii, 1904, pp. 199ff; J. Meinhold, op. cit.,
1905, Z.A.W. xxix, 1919, pp. 81ff, and Z.A.W. xlviii, 1930, pp. 121ff;
E. König, op. cit., pp. 235ff; T. J. Meek, J.B.L. xxxiii, 1914, pp. 201ff;
J. E. McFadyen, Exp., 8th series, xi, 1916, pp. 311ff; A. H. McNeile,
Exodus, 2nd edn, 1917, pp. 121ff; W. Nowack, in Abhandlungen zur
semitischen Religionskunde (Baudissin Festschrift), 1918, pp. 390ff; R.
Kittel, G.V.I. i, 6th edn, 1923, pp. 446ff; B. Jacob, J.Q.R., N.S. xiv,
1923-4, pp. 153ff; B. D. Eerdmans, in Vom Alten Testament (Marti
Festschrift), 1925, pp. 79ff; S. Mowinckel, Le Décalogue, 1927, pp. 75ff;
K. Budde, J.T.S. xxx, 1929, pp. 1ff, and Z.A.W. xlviii, 1930, pp. 138ff;
A. Lods, Israel, E. Tr., pp. 437ff; P. Volz, Mose und sein Werk, 2nd edn,

Most of our information about the observance of these sacred festivals and days comes from the Priestly law, and it tells us how they were observed in post-exilic times in the Second Temple. There is no reason to doubt that much of the ritual went back to pre-exilic days, though we have little means of knowing exactly how much. The ritual of the day of Atonement[1] is particularly a case in point. We have no information from the pre-exilic age of this solemn occasion, but it is generally agreed that the ritual of the Scapegoat is very ancient and must go back far into the past.[2] Two goats were chosen and of these one was driven out into the wilderness, while the other was sacrificed. It is sometimes suggested that in sacrifice the sacrificer laid his hand on the head of the victim[3] to transfer his sin to it;[4] but the ritual of the Scapegoat

---

1932, pp. 46ff; W. W. Cannon, *Z.A.W.* li, 1931, pp. 325ff; E. G. Kraeling, *A.J.S.L.* xlix, 1932–3, pp. 218ff; S. Langdon, *Babylonian Menologies and the Semitic Calendars*, 1935, pp. 89ff; J. and H. Lewy, *H.U.C.A.* xvii, 1942–3, pp. 1ff; H. Cazelles, *Études sur le Code de l'Alliance*, 1946, pp. 92ff; M. Buber, *Moses*, 1946, pp. 80ff; N. H. Snaith, loc. cit.; N. H. Tur-Sinai, *Bi.Or.* viii, 1951, pp. 14ff; R. North, *Biblica*, xxxvi, 1955, pp. 182ff; E. Vogt, *Biblica*, xl, 1959, pp. 1008ff; E. Lohse, in *Th.W.B.* vii, 1964, pp. 1ff; R. de Vaux, *A.I.* pp. 475ff; J. Morgenstern, in *I.D.B.* iv, 1962, pp. 135ff; H. J. Kraus, *Worship in Israel*, E.Tr., 1966, pp. 78ff; W. Rordorf, *Der Sonntag*, 1962, pp. 11ff. R. H. Pfeiffer (*Religion in the Old Testament*, 1961, p. 92) says the Sabbath was taken over from the Canaanites, but of this there is no evidence. Other authors who think a weekly Sabbath cannot have been observed prior to the Settlement are R. Smend, *Lehrbuch der alttestamentlichen Religionsgeschichte*, 2nd edn, 1899, p. 160; B. Stade, *Biblische Theologie des Alten Testaments*, i, 1905, p. 177; W. E. Addis, *The Documents of the Hexateuch*, i, 1892, pp. 139f n; T. J. Meek, *J.B.L.* xxxiii, 1914, p. 204. J. N. Schofield (*The Religious Background of the Bible*, 1944, p. 144) thinks the prophets would not have recognized the Sabbath as divinely ordained even as late as the time of Jeremiah. R. de Vaux (*A.I.*, p. 480) holds that the weekly Sabbath goes back to the first origins of Yahwism, and A. Weiser (*Introduction to the Old Testament*, E. Tr. by D. M. Barton, 1961, pp. 120f) says it cannot be proved that it was not observed in the wilderness (cf. E. Sellin, *Introduction to the Old Testament*, E. Tr. by W. Montgomery, 1923, p. 41).

[1] Lev. 16.1ff; also 23.26ff; Ex. 30.10; Num. 29.7ff.

[2] Cf. G. B. Gray, *Sacrifice in the Old Testament*, 1925, p. 315; R. de Vaux, *A.I.*, p. 509; J. Barr, in Hastings' one volume *D.B.*, rev. edn, 1963, pp. 79f.

[3] Lev. 1.4; 3.2, 8, 13, etc.

[4] Cf. M. Noth, *Leviticus*, E. Tr., 1965, pp. 38f: "the transference to the animal of the guilt, conceived in some quite solid sense". W. Eichrodt, on

does not favour this view. For here the sin is transferred to the Scapegoat, which is not sacrificed, whereas the goat that is sacrificed does not similarly have the sin transferred to it.[1] That the rite is very ancient is indicated by the fact that we do not know the meaning of Azazel,[2] to whom, or to which, the Scapegoat is sent. One goat is designated as for Yahweh, and the other as for Azazel. Professor Driver thinks "for Azazel" means "for the precipice",[3] but de Vaux thinks this would be a poor parallel to "for Yahweh", and thinks Azazel must be some demonic spirit.[4] There are parallels to this ceremony outside Israel,[5] though none that sheds light on the meaning of Azazel. It is to be noted, however, that though this rite is ancient and almost certainly goes back to pre-exilic days, this does not mean that the observance of the

the other hand, says (*Theology of the Old Testament*, E. Tr. by J. A. Baker, i, 1961, p. 165): "The substitutionary value of the victim is restricted to the quite general principle that, if man were to omit the prescribed form of expiation, he would *irrevocably* fall under the just and annihilating wrath of God. . . . Similarly the resting or placing of the hands of the offerer upon the victim . . . means no more than that the close relation between the offerer and the victim ought to take the form of a readiness on the part of the offerer to surrender that which belongs to him" (cf. p. 165 n for the principal objections to a substitutionary view). Cf. also H. W. Robinson, *J.T.S.* xliii, 1942, p. 130: "The natural meaning of the laying of hands on the sacrifice is the closer identification of the offerer with his offering. . . . By placing them on the animal the offerer says intensively, 'This is mine, and it is I who offer it.' He does not say, 'This is I; let it suffer in my place', for there is nowhere in the Old Testament the suggestion of penalty suffered by the sacrificial victim." Cf. also R. de Vaux, *Studies in Old Testament Sacrifice*, 1964, p. 63: "The offerer thus shows that *this* victim is *his* victim, and that it is about to be sacrificed for his benefit and not in his place." L. Moraldi (*Espiazione sacrificale e riti espiatori*, 1956) opposes the substitutionary view of Old Testament sacrifice (so also A. Metzinger, *Biblica*, xxi, 1940, pp. 159ff, 247ff, 353ff), while A. Médebielle (in *S.D.B.* iii, 1938, cols. 48ff) maintains it.

[1] Cf. H. W. Robinson, *J.T.S.* xliii, 1942, p. 131.
[2] M. Noth (*Leviticus*, E. Tr. by J. E. Anderson, 1965, p. 125) thinks the whole rite had a history before it came into the cleansing ritual of Lev. 16.
[3] Cf. *J.S.S.* i, 1956, pp. 97ff.
[4] Cf. *A.I.*, p. 509. On Azazel cf. S.R. Driver, in Hastings' *D.B.* i, 1898, pp. 207f; I. Benzinger, in *E.B.* i, 1899, cols. 394f; S. Landersdorfer, *Studien zum Biblischen Versöhnungstag*, 1924, pp. 13ff; W. H. Gispen, in *Orientalia Neerlandica*, 1948, pp. 156ff.
[5] Cf. *A.I.*, p. 508. Cf. also James Frazer, *The Scapegoat*, 3rd edn, 1936.

Day of Atonement goes back to pre-exilic days.[1] The rite has been combined with the ritual of the day of Atonement,[2] but we have no means of knowing what place it may have had in the pre-exilic ritual, either in the Temple or elsewhere in Israelite shrines. In the Priestly law we read of daily sacrifices in the Temple.[3] There are few references to these in pre-exilic sources, but there seems no reason to doubt that they were offered.[4] We read that in the time of Ahaz these sacrifices were offered in the Temple,[5] and in the account of Elijah's sacrifice on Mount Carmel we are told that this was offered at the time of the evening sacrifice.[6] As Elijah was a northern prophet, there is no reason to suppose that the reference here was to the Jerusalem Temple, and we are once more justified in concluding that such sacrifices were offered elsewhere than in the Temple.

[1] Cf. *A.I.* p. 509: "The Levitical ritual has therefore incorporated an old custom of unknown origin into its liturgy. . . . This does not mean, however, that the Day of Atonement and its ritual are of very ancient origin." De Vaux himself thinks it had not been instituted in the time of Ezra and Nehemiah (p. 510), but A. Médebielle (in *S.D.B.* iii, 1938, col. 63) thinks this very improbable. W. O. E. Oesterley (*Sacrifices in Ancient Israel*, 1937, pp. 226ff) holds that the Day of Atonement was a post-exilic institution (p. 226), but says: "Most of the ideas, as well as the rites, in connexion with the Day of Atonement go back to pre-exilic times" (p. 229). C. von Orelli (in *New Schaff-Herzog Encyclopedia of Religious Knowledge*, i, 1908, pp. 356f) and B. D. Eerdmans (*Alttestamentliche Studien*, iv, 1912, pp. 73ff) maintain a pre-exilic date for the observance.

[2] On the Day of Atonement cf. J. Wellhausen, *Prolegomena to the History of Israel*, E. Tr., 1885, pp. 110ff; B. Stade, *G.V.I.* ii, 1888, pp. 257ff; A. Dillmann, *Exodus and Leviticus*, 3rd edn, ed. by V. Ryssel, 1897, pp. 571ff; S. R. Driver and H. A. White, in Hastings' *D.B.* i, 1898, pp. 199ff; I. Benzinger and T. K. Cheyne, in *E.B.* i, 1899, cols. 383ff; C. von Orelli and J. F. McCurdy, in *New Schaff-Herzog Encyclopedia of Religious Knowledge*, i, 1908, pp. 356f; B. D. Eerdmans, *Alttestamentliche Studien*, iv, 1912, pp. 73ff; S. Landersdorfer, op. cit.; G. B. Gray, *Sacrifice in the Old Testament*, 1925, pp. 306ff; W. O. E. Oesterley, *Sacrifices in Ancient Israel*, 1937, pp. 226ff; A. Médebielle, in *S.D.B.* iii, 1938, cols. 61ff; R. Rendtorff, *Die Gesetze in der Priesterschrift*, 1954, pp. 59ff; R. de Vaux, *A.I.*, pp. 507ff; J. C. Rylaarsdam, in *I.D.B.* i, 1962, pp. 313ff.

[3] Ex. 29.38ff; Num. 28.2ff.

[4] W. O. E. Oesterley (*Sacrifices in Ancient Israel*, p. 221) thinks that in pre-exilic days only the morning sacrifice was offered, and so de Vaux (*A.I.*, p. 469). On this see below, p. 122.

[5] 2 Kings 16.15.   [6] 1 Kings 18.29.

For all of these occasions of communal resort to the Temple or of public rites there does not seem, therefore, to be any limitation to the Temple, prior to the reform of Josiah. Both the Temple and the local shrines were resorted to by individuals for the offering of their personal or family offerings on particular occasions. But to the question of sacrifices we shall return.

Of the priesthood of the Temple we are less informed than we could wish.[1] Abiathar, who was descended from Eli,[2] the priest of Shiloh, was cashiered before the Temple was built,[3] and retired to Anathoth, leaving Zadok in charge of the Ark, and later of the Temple. The Temple must have required the care of more than one priest, however, and who the others were, or where they came from, we do not know. David himself offered sacrifice when the Ark was brought into Jerusalem,[4] but this does not mean that he served as a priest on ordinary occasions, or should be described as a priest-king. In a later age Uzziah is said to have performed a priestly act and for this he is condemned by the Chronicler,[5] who attributes his leprosy to this act. Clearly it was regarded as improper by the time of the Chronicler for anyone but a professional priest to perform priestly duties, but equally clearly we cannot carry this back to the time of the early monarchy. There is nothing improbable in the king being regarded as competent to sacrifice on occasion without turning him into a regular priest. But when we are told that David made his sons priests,[6] this would

[1] The literature on the priesthood is considerable. Here it must suffice to note the following: W. W. von Baudissin, *Geschichte des alttestamentlichen Priesterthums*, 1889, and in Hastings' *D.B.* iv, 1902, pp. 67ff; A. van Hoonacker, *Le sacerdoce lévitique*, 1899; W. R. Smith and A. Bertholet, in *E.B.* iii, 1902, cols. 3837ff; J. Köberle, in *P.R.E.* 3rd edn, xvi, 1905, pp. 32ff; A. C. A. Hall, in *The New Schaff-Herzog Encyclopedia of Religious Knowledge*, ix, 1911, pp. 248ff; H. Lesêtre, in Vigouroux's *D.B.* v, 1912, cols. 640ff; H. P. Smith, in Hastings' *E.R.E.* x, 1918, pp. 307ff; G. Hölscher, in Pauly-Wissowa, *R.E.* xii, 1925, cols. 2155ff; G. B. Gray, *Sacrifice in the Old Testament*, 1925, pp. 179ff; R. H. Kennett, *Old Testament Essays*, 1928, pp. 59ff; G. Schrenk, in *Th.W.B.* iii, 1950, pp. 257ff; R. de Vaux, *A.I.*, 1961, pp. 345ff; R. Abba, in *I.B.D.* iii, 1962, pp. 876ff; D. A. Hubbard, in *N.B.D.*, 1962, pp. 1028ff; D. R. Jones, in Hastings' one volume *D.B.*, rev. edn, 1963, pp. 793ff; A. H. J. Gunneweg, *Leviten und Priester*, 1965.
[2] Cf. 1 Sam. 14.3; 22.20.   [3] 1 Kings 2.26.   [4] 2 Sam. 6.13.
[5] 2 Chron. 26.16ff. On Uzziah's sin cf. J. Morgenstern, *Amos Studies*, i, 1941, pp. 127ff.
[6] 2 Sam. 8.18.

seem to mean that they were made regular priests, and this would imply that the priesthood was not yet regarded as hereditary or as limited to the tribe of Levi. We have seen that during the period of the Judges there developed a preference for a Levite as priest,[1] and the priesthood of Dan, though Levite, was not Aaronic, since it claimed descent from Moses.[2] While all of this concerned the period before the construction of the Temple, there is no reason to suppose that the building of the Temple immediately made any difference.

In the book of Deuteronomy the priests are equated with the Levites.[3] This book was probably written early in the reign of Manasseh as a programme for reform when occasion should offer,[4]

---

[1] Cf. above, p. 63.   [2] Judges 18.30.

[3] Deut. 18.1ff. Cf. J. E. Carpenter, *The Composition of the Hexateuch*, 1902, p. 127: "The Levitical priests are expressly equated with 'the whole tribe of Levi'"; G. B. Gray, *Critical Introduction to the Old Testament*, 1913, p. 35: "Priests and Levites are co-extensive terms"; S. R. Driver, *Introduction to the Literature of the Old Testament*, 9th edn, 1913, p. 82: "In Dt. it is implied that *all* members of the tribe of Levi are qualified to exercise priestly functions"; R. H. Pfeiffer, *Introduction to the Old Testament*, 1941, p. 263: "In D the terms 'Levites' and 'priests' were synonymous." This view has been challenged by G. E. Wright (*V.T.* iv, 1954, pp. 325ff), to whom J. A. Emerton has replied (*V.T.* xii, 1962, pp. 129ff). Deuteronomy distinguishes between the Levites at the central sanctuary and the country Levites, but the distinction is one of opportunity and not of status. It recognizes the right of any Levite to come to the central sanctuary to exercise the priestly office (cf. G. B. Gray, loc. cit.). As R. de Vaux observes (*A.I.*, p. 363): "Every Levite retained his priestly rights, and when he came to the central sanctuary, he not only officiated there but received a stipend equal to that of his brother Levites who were attached to the sanctuary."

[4] Cf. H. H. Rowley, *The Growth of the Old Testament*, 1950, pp. 29ff; also A. R. Siebens, *L'Origine du Code Deutéronomique*, 1929, p. 96. Other scholars who date Deuteronomy in the reign of Manasseh are: H. Ewald, *G.V.I.* i, 3rd edn, 1864, pp. 186f, iii, 2nd edn, 1853, pp. 682ff; S. Davidson, *Introduction to the Old Testament*, i, 1863, p. 383; H. E. Ryle, in Hastings' *D.B.* i, 1898, p. 603a; S. R. Driver, *Introduction to the Literature of the Old Testament*, 9th edn, 1913, p. 87; J. Meinhold, *Einführung in das Alte Testament*, 3rd edn, 1932, p. 211; Oesterley and Robinson, *Introduction to the Books of the Old Testament*, 1934; A. Lods, *Histoire de la littérature hébraïque et juive*, 1950, p. 371; C. Kuhl, *The Old Testament: its origins and composition*, E. Tr. by C. T. M. Herriott, 1961, p. 84; M. Noth, *History of Israel*, E. Tr., 2nd edn, 1960, p. 275. J. Hempel (*Die Schichten des Deuteronomiums*, 1914, p. 259) suggested that Deuteronomy was perhaps composed towards the end of Hezekiah's reign.

and when it was found in the Temple in the reign of Josiah, the reform was largely carried through. But not wholly. For while Deuteronomy distinguished between the country Levites and those of the central sanctuary,[1] it accorded all equal status and laid it down that the country Levites were entitled to come to the central sanctuary and offer sacrifices there. This provision could not be put into effect, however, and the account of the reform tells us that the priests of the high places did not come to the altar of the Lord in Jerusalem.[2] Presumably the Jerusalem priesthood

[1] Deut. 18.6ff.

[2] 2 Kings 23.9. This seems to render highly improbable the view that the Deuteronomic law was composed with the connivance of the Jerusalem priests just before Josiah's reform, with a view to that reform, since in that case a provision would not have been included in the law and immediately opposed when the reform was carried through. Many older writers dated Deuteronomy immediately before the reform, including W. W. von Baudissin, *Einleitung in die Bücher des Alten Testamentes*, 1901, p. 113; K. Budde, *Z.A.W.* xliv, 1926, p. 222; C. F. Kent, *Growth and Contents of the Old Testament*, 1926, p. 189; E. Sellin, *Einleitung in das Alte Testament*, 6th edn, 1933, pp. 47ff (cf. earlier view below). A number of scholars have held the view that Deuteronomy was the basis of Hezekiah's reform; so J. G. Vaihinger, in *P.R.E.*, 1st edn, xi, 1859, p. 328; A. Westphal, *The Law and the Prophets*, E. Tr. by C. du Pontet, 1910, p. 304; C. Steuernagel, *Lehrbuch der Einleitung in das Alte Testament*, 1912, pp. 191ff; E. König, *Deuteronomium*, 1917, pp. 48ff; G. A. Smith, *Deuteronomy*, 1918, p. cii; E. Sellin, *Introduction to the Old Testament*, E. Tr. by W. Montgomery (based on 3rd German edn), 1923, pp. 73ff; H. Junker, *Biblica*, xxxiv, 1953, pp. 493f. Some have argued for its composition in the early monarchical period (so T. Oestreicher, *Das deuteronomische Grundgesetz*, 1923, and *Z.A.W.* xliii, 1925, pp. 246ff; A. C. Welch, *The Code of Deuteronomy*, 1924; W. Staerk, *Das Problem des Deuteronomiums*, 1924, and in *Sellin Festschrift*, 1927, pp. 139ff), or to the time of Samuel (so E. Robertson, *B.J.R.L.* xxvi, 1941–2, pp. 183ff; cf. R. Brinker, *The Influence of Sanctuaries in Early Israel*, 1946, pp. 205ff). Yet others have maintained a date after the fall of Jerusalem to Nebuchadrezzar (so C. W. P. Gramberg, *Kritische Geschichte der Religionsideen des Alten Testaments*, i, 1829, pp. xxvi, 153ff, 308ff; W. Vatke, *Die Religion des Alten Testamentes*, 1835, pp. 504ff; G. d'Eichtal, *Mélanges de critique biblique*, 1886, pp. 81ff (cf. M. Vernes, *M. Gustave d'Eichtal et ses travaux sur l'Ancien Testament*, 1887, pp. 33ff); M. Vernes, *Précis d'histoire juive*, 1889, pp. 468ff, 795 n; L. Horst, *R.H.R.* xvi, 1887, pp. 28ff, xvii, 1888, pp. 1ff, xviii, 1888, pp. 320ff, xxiii, 1891, pp. 184ff, xxvii, 1893, pp. 119ff; R. H. Kennett, *Deuteronomy and the Decalogue*, 1920, pp. 1ff, and *J.T.S.* vi, 1905, pp. 161ff, vii, 1906, pp. 481ff; G. Hölscher, *Z.A.W.* xl, 1922, pp. 161ff; G. R. Berry, *J.B.L.* xxxix, 1920, pp. 44ff, lix, 1940, pp. 133ff;

was too strong to allow of this. The reformers realized that even if this had been put into effect, the country Levites would suffer great diminution of their livelihood, through the closing of the country shrines, and therefore Deuteronomy commended the Levites to the charity of the people along with the widows and orphans.[1]

In the Blessing of Moses, which probably dates from the period of the monarchy,[2] perhaps before the fall of the northern kingdom,

F. Horst, *Z.A.W.* xli, 1923, pp. 99ff, and *Z.D.M.G.* lxxvii, 1923, pp. 220ff; S. A. Cook, in *C.A.H.* iii, 1925, pp. 406f, 481ff; E. König, *Z.A.W.* xlviii, 1930, pp. 43ff; A. Loisy, *Religion d'Israël*, 3rd edn, 1933, pp. 200ff; J. Pedersen, *Israel III–IV*, 1940, pp. 569ff; J. N. Schofield, in *Studies in History and Religion* (Wheeler Robinson Festschrift), 1942, pp. 44ff). R. Frankena (*O.T.S.* xiv, 1965, pp. 122ff) based on the links with the vassal treaties of Esarhaddon the view that at least the kernel of Deuteronomy must have been written in the seventh century B.C. R. H. Pfeiffer (*Introduction to the Old Testament*, 1941, pp. 178ff) thinks the original work was composed in 621 B.C. and that it received a series of additions down to about 400 B.C. For critical examinations of these various views cf. H. Gressmann, *Z.A.W.* xlii, 1924, pp. 313ff; W. Nowack, in *Vom Alten Testament* (Marti Festschrift), 1925, pp. 221ff; S. A. Cook, *J.T.S.* xxvi, 1925, pp. 162ff; R. Kittel, *G.V.I.* ii, 7th edn, 1925, pp. 439ff; J. Battersby Harford, *Exp.*, 9th series, iv, 1925, pp. 323ff; K. Budde, *Z.A.W.* xliv, 1926, pp. 177ff; W. C. Graham, *J.R.* vii, 1927, pp. 396ff; J. A. Bewer, *J.B.L.* xlvii, 1928, pp. 305ff; L. B. Paton, *J.B.L.*, ibid., pp. 322ff; W. Baumgartner, *Th.R.*, N.F. i, 1929, pp. 7ff; O. Eissfeldt, *The Old Testament: an Introduction*, E. Tr. by P. R. Ackroyd, 1965, pp. 171ff; *M.Q.*, 1963, pp. 187ff. For a recent defence of the Mosaic origin of the book in its earliest form, cf. M. H. Segal, *J.Q.R.*, N.S. xlviii, 1957–8, pp. 315ff.

[1] Cf. A. Causse, *R.H.P.R.* xiii, 1933, pp. 289ff.

[2] O. Eissfeldt (op. cit., p. 228) says it is certainly pre-exilic, and also certainly older than the fall of the northern kingdom (cf. A. Weiser, *Introduction to the Old Testament*, E. Tr., 1961, p. 118). It is commonly ascribed to the period of Jeroboam II (so E. Reuss, *La Bible: Ancien Testament*, III ii, 1879, pp. 360f; A. Kuenen, *Origin and Composition of the Hexateuch*, E. Tr. by P. H. Wicksteed, 1886, p. 240; B. Stade, *G.V.I.*, 2nd edn, i, 1889, pp. 150, 152; C. Steuernagel, *Deuteronomium*, 1898, p. 122; G. F. Moore, in *E.B.* i, 1899, col. 1090; E. Kautzsch, in Hastings' *D.B.* v, 1904, p. 650a; C. Cornill, *Introduction to the Canonical Books of the Old Testament*, E. Tr. by G. H. Box, 1907, p. 125; H. Wheeler Robinson, *Deuteronomy and Joshua*, p. 234; T. André, in *La Bible du Centenaire*, i, 1941, p. 286; A. Lods, *Histoire de la littérature hébraïque et juive*, 1950, p. 56; A. Bentzen, *Introduction to the Old Testament*, 2nd edn, ii, 1952, pp. 58f; R. Tournay, *R.B.* lxv, 1958, pp. 181ff), but by some to the time of Jeroboam I (so A. Dillmann, *Numeri, Deuteronomium und Josua*, 1886, p. 415; S. R. Driver, *Deuteronomy*, 2nd edn, 1896, pp. 387f;

the priestly office is assigned to the tribe of Levi.[1] This is in agreement with Deuteronomy's equation of priests and Levites. It would therefore appear that gradually over the period of the monarchy Levites were regarded as not merely to be preferred for the office of priest, but to be essential. How far all the people who were now called Levites were actually of Levitical descent we have no means of knowing. Presumably the Zadokites were by now regarded as Levites, since we know that the Deuteronomic reform did not displace the Jerusalem priesthood, and we find Zadok later supplied with a genealogy tracing him back to Eleazar, the son of Aaron.[2] De Vaux is of the opinion that the Law of Holiness, found in Leviticus, was put forward by the Zadokites of Jerusalem as a rival code to the book of Deuteronomy.[3] This does not seem to me to be very probable, since Deuteronomy did so much to exalt the status of the Jerusalem priesthood. There is some reason to think that this was not the intention of the compilers of Deuteronomy, since they may have had a northern shrine in mind as the central sanctuary,[4] but in actual fact this is what the Deuteronomic reform achieved. For while Deuteronomy accorded nominal equality of status to the country priests, it clearly recognized that they could never have equality of opportunity, and since the Jerusalem priests successfully prevented any exercise of the priesthood in the Temple by the country Levites they could be well content with what the Deuteronomic reform had done for them.

It is certain, however, that some struggle for the priesthood went on. For Ezekiel, in his sketch of the future Temple and its ministry, proposed to rationalize the superior status of the Jerusalem priesthood by reserving the priesthood proper to them

J. A. Bewer, *The Literature of the Old Testament*, 1922, p. 19). Earlier origin, in the period of the Judges, has been maintained by E. König (*Deuteronomium*, 1917, pp. 236f) and E. Sellin (*Introduction to the Old Testament*, E. Tr. by W. Montgomery, 1923, p. 39), or in the eleventh century B.C. by F. M. Cross and D. N. Freedman (*J.B.L.* lxvii, 1948, p. 192), while H. Ewald (*G.V.I.* i, 3rd edn, 1864, pp. 187f) ascribed it to the period of Josiah. The oracle on Levi is held to be post-exilic by R. H. Pfeiffer (*Introduction to the Old Testament*, 1941, pp. 278f) and C. Kuhl (*The Old Testament: its Origins and Composition*, E. Tr. by C. T. M. Herriott, 1961, p. 87). On the Blessing of Moses cf. also H. J. Kittel, *Die Stammessprüche Israels*, 1959; H. J. Zobel, *Stammesspruch und Geschichte*, 1965.

[1] Deut. 33.8ff. With this contrast Gen. 49.5ff, where Levi is cursed instead of blessed, and where there is no reference to any priestly function.
[2] 1 Chron. 6.4ff (M.T. 5.30ff).   [3] Cf. *A.I.*, p. 376.   [4] Cf. p. 106.

and reducing the country Levites to the more menial tasks of the Temple, on the ground that the country Levites had not maintained a pure worship, but had worshipped idols.[1] Ezekiel's own description of what went on in the Temple prior to its destruction is an odd commentary on this piece of rationalization.[2] It is to be noted, however, that Ezekiel gives to the Zadokites the title Levites,[3] as he does to those to be given the menial tasks. Levite had become a professional title, though the fiction was preserved that it was also a tribal one. To make way for the country Levites, or priests of the high places, Ezekiel proposed that other Temple servants, whom he describes as aliens, should be dismissed.[4] At the time of the coronation of Joash, to which reference has been made, the Temple and palace guards are described as Carites.[5] These appear to have been foreign mercenaries,[6] and since it was contrary to the later law and certainly contrary to the practice in the days of the Chronicler to have any but Levites in the service of the Temple, the Chronicler turns them into Levites.[7] How far non-Israelites may have been engaged in other services in the Temple we do not know.

The solution of Ezekiel, that the Zadokites should have a higher status and the country Levites a lower, was not accepted. The non-Zadokite priests successfully secured a compromise, which is reflected in the Priestly Code, and which continued in force until New Testament times.[8] The priesthood was now reserved to those who were classed as Aaronites, while the others had the lower status of Levites,[9] and the Aaronites were divided into the

---

[1] Ezek. 44.10ff.   [2] Ezek. 8.6ff.

[3] Ezek. 44.15. On Ezekiel and the Zadokite priesthood cf. J. Bowman, *T.G.U.O.S.* xvi, 1957, pp. 1ff.

[4] Ezek. 44.6ff.   [5] 2 Kings 11.4, 19.

[6] Carians appear in Herodotus ii.152 as soldiers of fortune. Elsewhere we read of the royal bodyguard as consisting of Cherethites and Pelethites (2 Sam. 8.18; 15.18; 20.7). In 2 Sam. 20.23 the Hebrew has Carites in the *K^ethîbh*, but Cherethites in the *K^erê*. From these passages it is clear that David had foreign mercenaries in his bodyguard, and it would appear that this had continued after the construction of the royal palace and the Temple. The royal guards served in both palace and Temple. Cf. W. Robertson Smith, *O.T.J.C.*, 2nd edn, 1907, pp. 262f.

[7] 2 Chron. 23.2ff.   [8] Cf. Luke 1.5ff.

[9] Num. 3.6ff; 18.1ff. Cf. de Vaux, *A.I.*, p. 266: "This explains why they (sc. the Levites) were not over-anxious to return from exile; cf. 74 Levites (Ezra 2.40) as against 4289 priests (Ezra 2.36ff)."

descendants of Eleazar, or the Zadokites, and the descendants of Ithamar, with a rotation of duties.[1] The head of the Jerusalem priesthood continued to be in the line of Zadok. From all this it seems probable that the Temple priesthood was at no time composed exclusively of descendants of Aaron or Levi. The high priests were probably descended from a Jebusite priest, and many of the other priests were only reckoned to be descended from Aaron at the time of the final compromise, while the Levites were drawn from priests who had come to be reckoned as Levites because they exercised the priestly function. But once the compromise of the Priestly Code had been reached, recruitment of the priesthood or of the Levites was from strictly closed families.

Deuteronomy has little to say about the duties of the Levites whom it identifies with the priests. It is more concerned to define their dues,[2] and it defines their functions as simply to minister before the Lord.[3] The Blessing of Moses gives us more information. Here the Levites are said to have charge of the Urim and Thummim,[4] to teach God's law and judgements, and to offer incense and sacrifice.[5] The priest's rôle in sacrifice was chiefly to attend to the disposal of the blood, which was sacred and which had to be thrown against the altar or poured or drained at its base.[6] The care of the Urim and Thummim indicates that when the sacred oracle was consulted it was done by the priests, but as I have said earlier this kind of mechanical consultation fell into disuse, until the Urim and Thummim were reduced to ornaments in the High Priest's breastplate.

The teaching function of the priest was of great importance.[7]

[1] Num. 3.4; Lev. 10.6f; 1 Chron. 24.2ff.   [2] Deut. 18.3f.
[3] Deut. 18.5, 7.   [4] Deut. 33.8.   [5] Deut. 33.10.
[6] Lev. 4.34; 8.15; 9.9; Ex. 29.12; Lev. 1.5, 11; 3.2, 8, 13; Ex. 24.6; 29.16; Lev. 1.15; 5.9. Cf. G. F. Moore, in *E.B.* iv, 1907, col. 4217: "From first to last the utmost importance attaches to the disposition of the victim's blood."
[7] On the teaching function of the priest cf. A. Kuenen, *Origin and Composition of the Hexateuch*, E. Tr., 1886, pp. 177f; J. Begrich, in *B.Z.A.W.* lxvi, 1936, pp. 63ff; J. Hempel, *Das Ethos des Alten Testaments*, 2nd edn, 1964, pp. 19ff; J. Pedersen, *Israel III–IV*, 1940, pp. 160ff; G. Östborn, *Tōrā in the Old Testament*, 1945, pp. 89ff; R. de Vaux, *A.I.*, pp. 353ff. The word *tôrāh*, or authoritative direction, is sometimes traced to the Akkadian *tērtu* (for references cf. Östborn, op. cit., pp. 17ff), and the teaching function of the priest connected with the use of the

He was the depositary of sacred lore and could advise men in any ritual matter.[1] In the Priestly law the priests are charged with the task of distinguishing between the holy and the profane,[2] and Ezekiel recognizes this as one of their functions,[3] though he accuses them of neglecting it. In the early post-exilic period we read of occasions when the priests were consulted on such matters.[4] The priest was also charged with the decision whether a man had leprosy[5]—which was not the disease known as leprosy to-day[6]—or

sacred lot (so also H. W. Robinson, in *Law and Religion*, ed. by E. I. J. Rosenthal, 1938, p. 51), but this is rejected by de Vaux, who says (*A.I.*, p. 354): "The way in which the word is used and the verbs which are used with it indicate that its root is rather *yrh*, which is frequently employed in the factitive form with the meaning 'to show', 'to teach'. The *tôrāh* is, therefore, in the strict sense 'instruction' and the usual translation of this word as 'law' is not quite accurate" (cf. Begrich, loc. cit., p. 68). Cf. also Kuenen, op. cit., p. 177: "Tora primitively signified the instruction given by the priest, who pronounced in Yahwè's name, not only on cleanness and uncleanness, but also . . . on right and wrong. . . . Tora always remains the *vox propria* for the priestly decisions, especially in the administration of justice." G. E. Wright (*V.T.* iv, 1954, p. 329) argues that teaching was the function of Levites who did not serve the altar, and who are therefore to be distinguished from the Levites who exercised the priesthood. He cites 2 Chron. 17.7ff; 35.3; Neh. 8.7ff, all of which are late post-exilic passages. In the pre-exilic passages cited below the teaching function is ascribed to the priests. Cf. de Vaux, op. cit., p. 355: "From the time of the Exile onwards, the priests ceased to have the monopoly of teaching the Torah. The Levites, who by then had been taken away from strictly priestly functions, became preachers and catechists. In the end, teaching was given quite apart from worship in the synagogues, and a new class arose, of scribes and teachers of the Law. This class was open to all, priests and Levites and layfolk alike." For pre-exilic and exilic references to the teaching duty of the priests cf. Mic. 3.11; Jer. 18.18; Ezek. 7.26. Hos. 4.6 shows that one of the priest's duties was to keep alive the knowledge of God (cf. H. W. Wolff, *Gesammelte Studien*, 1964, pp. 182ff; also S. Mowinckel, *Erkenntnis Gottes bei den alttestamentlichen Profeten*, 1941). A post-exilic text which shows that the priest still retained a teaching function is Mal. 2.7.

[1] On his function also as judge cf. de Vaux, *A.I.*, pp. 153ff.
[2] Lev. 10.10.   [3] Ezek. 22.26; 44.23.
[4] Hag. 2.11ff.   [5] Lev. 14.57; Deut. 24.8.
[6] Cf. the article on Leprosy, by G. R. Driver with the help of R. G. Cochrane and H. Gordon, in Hastings' one volume *D.B.*, rev. edn, 1963, pp. 575ff; also K. P. C. A. Gramberg, *Bible Translator*, xi, 1960, pp. 10ff; J. L. Swellengrebel, ibid., pp. 69ff; E. A. Nida, ibid., pp. 80f; D. H. Wallington, ibid. xii, 1961, pp. 75ff; R. G. Cochrane, ibid., pp. 202f; S. G. Browne, *E.T.* lxxiii, 1961–2, pp. 242ff.

whether, having had it, he was cured of it. It was not as a physician that the priest functioned in this case, but as the guardian of the ritual purity of the community.[1] For ritual cleanness or uncleanness were held to be of paramount importance. Particularly when there had been contact with a corpse ritual uncleanness ensued and the ritual of the Red Heifer prescribes the means for its removal.[2]

Yet another function of the priesthood was the pronouncement of blessing.[3] In the Priestly Code we find preserved the formula of blessing[4] which is still in Christian use to-day, and it is probable that it was in use in the Temple in pre-exilic days. We should not think of the priest's function in any narrow or purely cultic way, however. He was familiar with precepts and precedents on a wide variety of matters and could advise on men's duty to God and relations with one another.

The function of the priest, therefore, went far beyond what we think of as the conduct of public worship. Indeed, so far I have said nothing at all about the public worship of the Temple, which we commonly think of almost exclusively in terms of sacrificial ritual. Of that ritual I shall speak in a later chapter. Here I would observe that there is every reason to believe that the ritual acts were accompanied by the recital of liturgical texts, which were designed to make the ritual acts the vehicle of the spiritual worship of the people.[5] J. G. S. S. Thomson observes: "That public worship in the Temple was a spiritual reality is clear from the fact that when the sanctuary was destroyed, and the exiles found themselves in Babylon, worship remained a necessity."[6] Singing and prayer were also given a place in the worship of the Temple, as well as in that of other shrines in the land,[7] and there is ample evidence that prophets functioned beside priests in the worship.[8]

---

[1] Cf. de Vaux, *A.I.*, p. 462.
[2] Num. 19.1ff. On this ritual cf. G. B. Winer, *Biblisches Realwörterbuch*, 3rd edn, ii, 1847, pp. 504ff; G. A. Simcox, in *E.B.* i, 1899, cols. 846ff; A. R. S. Kennedy, in Hastings' *D.B.* iv, 1902, pp. 207ff; G. B. Gray, *Numbers*, 1903, pp. 241ff; J. D. Eisenstein, in *J.E.* x, 1905, pp. 344f; J. A. Bewer, *J.B.L.* xxiv, 1905, pp. 41ff; H. P. Smith, *A.J.Th.*, xiii, 1909, pp. 207ff; J. Scheftelowitz, *Z.A.W.* xxxix, 1921, pp. 113ff; J. H. Greenstone, *Numbers*, 1939, pp. 200ff; W. G. Plant, in *U.J.E.* ix, 1943, pp. 95f; L. E. Toombs, in *I.D.B.* iv, 1962, pp. 18f.
[3] Cf. below, p. 210.   [4] Num. 6.24ff.   [5] Cf. below, p. 135.
[6] *N.B.D.*, 1962, p. 1340b.   [7] Cf. below, pp. 161, 172f, 179 n.
[8] Cf. below, pp. 150f.

Of all these things I shall speak in subsequent chapters. Here it must suffice to say that people came to the Temple daily for a variety of purposes. In the court surrounding the Temple men could meet and the prophets could address them.[1] Here men could offer their private prayer, as the Pharisee and the Publican did in the parable of our Lord.[2] And when men came to worship, it was not just to watch a sacrificial act but to participate in an approach to God. That the prophets condemned men because they did not really so participate means that not all entered into the reality of worship, since true worship must be free and unconstrained, the offering of the worshipping spirit and not the mere attendance at a ceremony.

There is evidence[3] that much of the pre-exilic worship was marked by rejoicing.[4] Men went to the Temple, as to the other shrines in the land, to praise God for his gifts in nature, when they assembled for the agricultural festivals. The shrines were the scene of dancing.[5] The maidens of Shiloh were dancing at the time of the Benjamite seizure of their brides,[6] and there are passages in the Psalms which clearly indicate that dancing had a place in the worship of the Temple.[7] Dancing which did not take place at any shrine could also have a religious character, as the dance of Miriam after the deliverance at the Red Sea,[8] the dance of Jephthah's daughter when she came to welcome him after his victory,[9] and the dance of David before the Ark,[10] must have had.

---

[1] Cf. Jer. 26.2.   [2] Luke 18.10.

[3] Cf. Hos. 2.11 (M.T. 13); Isa. 30.29; Ps. 149.2.

[4] This is not to say that the note of rejoicing was absent from the worship of the Second Temple. Cf. G. B. Gray, *Sacrifice in the Old Testament*, 1925, p. 322: "In the Jewish religion, in the time of our Lord, the Day of Atonement with its stress on sin and expiation, with its fasting and solemn rest and inactivity, was the supreme day of the year: yet it was but one day; within the year some twenty days of full festival joy also occurred, and some forty other days were observed as happy memorials of the works which God had wrought, especially in relatively recent times, on behalf of His people. In any estimate of Jewish religious life in the time of our Lord, these feasts should not be overlooked, nor their significance depreciated."

[5] On dancing and worship cf. *E.B.* i, 1899, cols. 999ff (unsigned); J. Millar, in Hastings' *D.B.* i, 1898, pp. 549f. Cf. also W. O. E. Oesterley, *The Sacred Dance*, 1923.

[6] Judges 21.21.   [7] Ps. 87.7; 149.3; 150.4.   [8] Ex. 15.20.

[9] Judges 11.34.   [10] 2 Sam. 6.14.

Little of all this was peculiar to the Temple, and much of it was not peculiar to Yahwism. It is probable that sabbath and Passover were specifically Yahwistic occasions, but neither of these was observed solely at the Temple through most of the pre-exilic period. Moreover, in other shrines priests sacrificed and served, though there were probably fewer of them in any other shrine than in the Temple. In other shrines men gathered for private sacrifice and consultation, or to celebrate the great festivals. The influence of the Canaanite origin of the agricultural festivals persisted in the addressing of thanksgiving to Baal, we learn from Hosea,[1] though it is probable that the people would have said that by Baal they meant Yahweh. If the books of Kings are to be trusted, some of the kings of Judah followed "the abominations of the heathen whom the Lord drave out before the children of Israel",[2] and we cannot suppose that these things were not followed in the royal shrine of the Temple. Kings who promoted the licence of the fertility cult cannot be thought to have preserved the Temple from them, and we should not idealize the Temple and its worship. Its significance lay in what it became.

Peculiar to the Temple were the royal rites of the kings of Judah, which were almost certainly specifically Yahweh rites. Of these rites we are not well informed, but some things seem to be reasonably probable, and to these we shall give attention in a later chapter.[3] In the northern kingdom the royal shrines of Bethel and Dan sought to attach to themselves something of the prestige that attached to the Jerusalem shrine, and royal rites may have been observed there. They seem to have left no separate trace, and it is improbable that they ever really rivalled those of Jerusalem. When Amos prophesied in the northern kingdom, he said, "The Lord shall roar from Zion and utter his voice from Jerusalem."[4] In the days of the Judges God's seat was still thought of as in the sacred mountain in the wilderness, and Deborah sang of the day when the Lord went forth from Seir;[5] but now he was thought to reside in Jerusalem, where his Ark was regarded as the guarantee of his presence. The northern kingdom had nothing to compare with this. Elijah, a northern prophet, went to Horeb in the wilderness to find Yahweh, when his life was no longer safe in Israel.[6] Israel had no place which was thought of as the mount of the Lord, as

---

[1] Hos. 2.8 (M.T. 10).   [2] 2 Kings 16.3; 21.2.   [3] Cf. below, pp. 190ff.
[4] Amos 1.2.   [5] Judges 5.4.   [6] 1 Kings 19.8.

Zion was. The sacredness of this site was celebrated in Psalms,[1] and in the familiar prophecy of the coming Golden Age that is duplicated in Isaiah and Micah it is to the mount of the Lord that all peoples are destined to turn in worship.[2] It is not surprising, then, that when religion was centralized, it was centralized in the Jerusalem Temple.

It seems probable that when the compilers of Deuteronomy planned their programme of reform they did not think of Jerusalem as the future central sanctuary. At that time Manasseh was on the throne and Judah could not have seemed fruitful ground for reform. The northern links of Deuteronomy have often been noted,[3] and there is some reason to think the reformers may have had Shechem in mind as a more central location.[4] They thought in terms of a sanctuary for the whole land, and since they included an account of the making of the Ark[5] they presumably expected that it would be housed in the sanctuary. But when the book was

[1] Cf. Ps. 2.6; 9.11 (M.T. 12); 48.1f (M.T. 2f.); 50.2; 76.2 (M.T. 3); 78.68; 87.2; 102.16 (M.T. 17); 122.3ff; 128.5; 132.13; 134.3.

[2] Isa. 2.2ff; Mic. 4.1ff.

[3] Cf. C. F. Burney, *Judges*, 1920, p. xlvi; A. C. Welch, *The Code of Deuteronomy*, 1924, pp. 34, 39, 76, 132, 185, 190, 219; A. Bentzen, *Die josianische Reform*, 1926, p. 86; F. Horst, *Das Privilegrecht Jahves*, 1930, p. 123; J. Hempel, *Die althebräische Literatur*, 1930–4, pp. 126, 139; L. Gautier, *Introduction à l'Ancien Testament*, 2nd edn, i, 1939, p. 139; K. Galling, in *Festschrift für Alfred Bertholet*, 1950, p. 191, and *Th.L.Z.* lxxvi, 1951, col. 138; A. Alt, *Kleine Schriften*, ii, 1953, pp. 250ff; G. E. Wright, *I.B.* ii, 1953, pp. 319, 326; H. Cazelles, in Robert and Feuillet, *Introduction à la Bible*, i, 1953, p. 371; N. K. Gottwald, *A Light to the Nations*, 1959, pp. 338, 340; F. Dumermuth, *Z.A.W.* lxx, 1958, p. 95; G. von Rad, in *I.D.B.* i, 1962, pp. 836f; H. W. Wolff, *Th.L.Z.* lxxxi, 1956, col. 93 (reprinted in *Gesammelte Studien zum Alten Testament*, 1964, pp. 248f).

[4] Cf. B. Luther, in E. Meyer, *Die Israeliten und ihre Nachbarstämme*, 1906, pp. 542ff; W. F. Albright, *F.S.A.C.*, 2nd edn, 1946, p. 241; G. A. Danell, *Studies in the Name Israel in the Old Testament*, 1946, p. 13; I. Engnell, *Symbolae Biblicae Upsalienses*, vii, 1946, pp. 21f; R. Brinker, *The Influence of Sanctuaries in Early Israel*, 1946, pp. 211f; N. Walker, *V.T.* iii, 1953, pp. 413f; E. Nielsen, *Shechem*, 1955, pp. 45, 85; cf. also R. H. Kennett, *J.T.S.* vii, 1906, pp. 493ff. A. C. Welch (*The Code of Deuteronomy*, 1924, pp. 38f, 91) thought the compiler might have had Bethel in mind, and so Oesterley and Robinson (*Introduction to the Books of the Old Testament*, 1934, p. 50); cf. J. N. Schofield, in *Essays and Studies presented to S. A. Cook*, 1950, p. 27.

[5] Deut. 10.1ff.

found, Jerusalem had a reforming king and the reformation had
already begun,[1] and since the book was found in the Temple,
where the Ark already was, it was natural that a new direction
should be given to the reformation and that Jerusalem should
step into the place of the unnamed sanctuary of Deuteronomy.

Josiah may well have carried his centralization of worship
beyond the bounds of Judah,[2] though some have denied this.[3] For
Josiah sought to reconstitute an independent kingdom, and the
northern tribes would be as eager as the southern to seize the
opportunity afforded by the collapsing Assyrian empire to recover
independence. Yet they had no royal leader of their own to be
the focus of their aspirations. The hope of independence proved
illusory, and reaction set in after the reform. Yet it had not passed
leaving nothing behind it. In post-exilic days, when the Jerusalem
Temple was rebuilt, we hear nothing of the local shrines, and the

[1] According to the account of 2 Kings 22 the repair of the Temple had
already begun when the book of the Law was found. The repair of the
Temple was probably marked by the removal of the symbols of Assyrian
suzerainty and was associated with the assumption of political independence. Deuteronomy gave direction to the reform, which had already
begun. The Chronicler dates the reform in Josiah's twelfth year (2 Chron.
34.3). This would make the reform prior to the revolt of Babylon under
Nabopolassar, and since the reform must have been associated with
revolt against Assyria, it is doubtful if it took place so early as this; cf.
A. Lods, *The Prophets and the Rise of Judaism*, E. Tr., 1937, p. 140. Cf.
also J. Bright, *History of Israel*, 1960, p. 296.

[2] Cf. 2 Kings 23.15ff, where the reform is said to have been carried to
Bethel. The Chronicler extends it as far north as Naphtali (2 Chron.
34.6).

[3] Cf. A. Loisy, *La Religion d'Israël*, 3rd edn, 1933, p. 204, where even
the extension of the reform to Bethel is said to be "de pure fantaisie";
R. H. Pfeiffer, *Introduction to the Old Testament*, 1941, p. 402, where it is
said to be "historically absurd". A. Lods (op. cit., p. 141) thinks the
extension to Bethel may not have taken place till after the fall of Nineveh,
but J. Gray (*Kings*, 1964, pp. 649f) allows the possibility that it may have
been earlier than this. Cf. M. Noth, *History of Israel*, E. Tr., 2nd edn,
1960, pp. 273ff. Some scholars have denied the historicity of the account
of Josiah's reform altogether, on the ground that it was too unpractical to
have been possible or that it is the fictitious ascription to Josiah of the
programme of Deuteronomy; cf. E. Havet, *Le Christianisme et ses origines*,
iii, 1878, pp. 32ff; L. Horst, *R.H.R.* xvii, 1888, pp. 11ff; M. Vernes,
Précis d'histoire juive, 1889, pp. 469, 795 n; G. Hölscher, *Z.A.W.* xl, 1922,
pp. 201ff, 227; F. Horst, *Z.A.W.* xli, 1923, pp. 119ff, and *Z.D.M.G.*
lxxvii, 1923, pp. 220ff; A. Loisy, op. cit., pp. 200ff.

Temple alone was the focus of the religion of Judaea. But for the growing tension between Jerusalem and Samaria, it might have been recognized as the central sanctuary for the whole country. For when the Temple was being rebuilt, the northerners desired to share in the work, but were rebuffed by the Jerusalem leaders,[1] and tension continued to mount until at last the Samaritan shrine was built and relations between Jerusalem and Samaria were broken.[2]

Nehemiah and Ezra were the architects of the isolation of Judaism. It is easy to castigate them for their narrowness, as innumerable writers have done. Yet they served their own generation, and we have entered into the heritage of their labours.[3] To use a metaphor I used many years ago, they sought to build a wall round the garden of their faith to prevent it being trampled down by the feet of strangers.[4] We should not forget that there was always a gate in the wall to admit proselytes who entered the garden to share the faith. And before we condemn Nehemiah and Ezra too severely, we should reflect that post-exilic Judaism was purged of many of the abuses of the pre-exilic age, and post-exilic Judaism provided the matrix from which Christianity was born. The law which Ezra brought to Jerusalem is commonly thought to have been the Priestly Code.[5] This does not mean that it had

[1] Ezra 4.1ff.

[2] On the relations between Samaria and Jerusalem in the post-exilic period to the final breach and the building of the Samaritan Temple, cf. *M.G.*, pp. 246ff.

[3] On Nehemiah cf. *M.G.*, pp. 211ff, 262ff, and for a more sympathetic estimate of the policy of particularism than is commonly made, cf. *I.M.W.*, 1939, pp. 39ff.

[4] Ibid., p. 50.

[5] So E. Meyer, *Entstehung des Judentums*, 1896, pp. 206ff; F. H. Woods, in Hastings' *D.B.* ii, 1899, p. 371a; J. E. Carpenter, *The Composition of the Hexateuch*, 1902, p. 265; C. Cornill, *Introduction to the Canonical Books of the Old Testament*, E. Tr., 1907, pp. 112ff; A. T. Chapman. *Introduction to the Pentateuch*, 1911, p. 185; D. C. Simpson, *Pentateuchal Criticism*, 1914, p. 148; E. Sellin, *Introduction to the Old Testament*, E. Tr., 1923, p. 85; Oesterley and Robinson, *Introduction to the Books of the Old Testament*, 1934, p. 62; H. Cazelles, *V.T.* iv, 1954, pp. 12ff. Others hold that Ezra's lawbook was the complete Pentateuch; so R. H. Kennett, *The Church of Israel*, 1933, p. 64; A. Weiser, *Introduction to the Old Testament*, E. Tr., 1961, p. 138; S. Mowinckel, *Studien zu dem Buche Ezra-Nehemia*, iii, 1965, pp. 136ff; J. M. Myers, *Ezra-Nehemiah* (Anchor Bible), 1965, p. lix. W. W. von Baudissin (*Einleitung in die Bücher des*

just been written or that no one had heard of it in Jerusalem before he came. It may well have been known,[1] but it had not been put into effect until he came, and this was the task with which he was charged. This law gave to the ritual of the Temple greater control than it had had before, and with a single controlled sanctuary it was easier to prevent the return of the abuses which had marked the shrines of pre-exilic Israel. The old fertility cult was now eradicated, and if something of the exuberance of pre-exilic worship had gone, there was a stateliness and solemnity about the ritual that turned men's thought with a deeper insistence to the problem of sin. There was much preoccupation with purely ritual and involuntary sin, a preoccupation which had its roots far back in the past. It will be remembered that before the shewbread was given to David, the priest had to be assured that David was in a state of ritual purity.[2] But the Priestly law was not indifferent to moral issues. Sin had to be confessed before it could be expiated,[3] and there is no reason to suppose that a perfunctory confession was envisaged. Where restitution could be made, it had to be made.[4] In the ritual of the Day of Atonement, so close to the spirit of post-exilic Judaism in its preoccupation with sin, the High Priest represented the community in confession and in approach to God,[5] and there is no reason to suppose that the one was more superficial than the other. If he did not truly represent them in confession he did not in his approach to God. The Priestly law embodied the Holiness Code,[6] where we find the great word "Thou shalt love thy neighbour as thyself",[7] and post-exilic Judaism cherished the book of Deuteronomy and exalted its

---

Alten Testaments, 1901, p. 194) maintains that Ezra's lawbook contained more than P. J. Morgenstern (*H.U.C.A.* x, 1935, p. 145 n) holds that the *Grundschrift* of P was composed later than the time of Ezra. R. H. Pfeiffer (*Introduction to the Old Testament*, 1941, p. 828) denies that Ezra could have brought P with him, and holds that the author of the Ezra story unhistorically believed that Ezra brought the Pentateuch, which did not then exist. W. Rudolph (*Esra and Nehemia*, 1949, p. 169) and M. Noth (*History of Israel*, E. Tr., 2nd edn. 1960, p. 336) think it impossible to define Ezra's law.

[1] A. S. Kapelrud (*A.S.T.I.*, iii, 1964, pp. 58ff) maintains that the Priestly Code was completed before 550 B.C., while R. E. Clements (*God and Temple*, 1965, p. 111) would date it *circa* 515 B.C.; S. Mowinckel (op. cit., pp. 124ff) insists that Ezra's law was not new.

[2] 1 Sam. 21.4f (M.T. 5f).   [3] Lev. 5.5.   [4] Num. 5.6f.   [5] Lev. 16.21.
[6] Lev. 17—26.   [7] Lev. 19.18.

precept "Thou shalt love the Lord thy God" to the supreme place among all the commands.[1] It took seriously the exaltation of chastity and humanity that is characteristic of Deuteronomy, and it cherished the prophetic books with all their insistence on that ethical religion which was formulated in the Decalogue. The Temple, founded by Solomon to be one among many, and to be the royal shrine of the kingdom, had become the only shrine for sacrifice and for the national rites, and the guardian of the purity of Yahwism.

[1] Deut. 6.5.

4

The Forms and Meaning of Sacrifice

In this chapter I am concerned with the forms and meaning of
Israelite sacrifice. It is not my intention to try to go back to the
beginnings of sacrifice and to ask what was believed to be its
original significance.[1] On this various theories have been pro-

[1] On sacrifice in a wider field cf. H. Hubert and M. Mauss, *L'Année
sociologique*, ii, 1898, pp. 29ff (E. Tr. by W. D. Halls, *Sacrifice: its Nature
and Function*, 1964); *E.R.E.* xi, 1920, pp. 1–39, where a number of
scholars write on sacrifice in primitive religion and in the historical
religions. Cf. also H. Lesêtre, in Vigouroux's *D.B.* v, 1912, cols. 1311ff;
O. Baumgarten, in *R.G.G.*, 1st edn, iv, 1913, cols. 956ff; A. Bertholet, in
R.G.G., 2nd edn, iv, 1930, cols. 704ff, and *J.B.L.* xlix, 1930, pp. 218ff; A.
Schimmel, in *R.G.G.*, 3rd edn, iv, 1960, cols. 1637ff; G. Lanczkowski, in
L.Th.K. vii, 1962, cols. 1166ff; A. Loisy, *Essai historique sur le sacrifice*,
1920; E. W. Hopkins, *Origins and Evolution of Religion*, 1923, pp. 151ff;
F. B. Jevons, *Introduction to the History of Religions*, 9th edn, 1927, pp.
144ff; E. B. Tylor, *Primitive Culture*, 5th edn, 1929, pp. 375ff; E. O.
James, *Origins of Sacrifice*, 2nd edn, 1937; G. van der Leeuw, *Religion, its
Essence and Manifestation*, E. Tr. by J. E. Turner, 1938, pp. 350ff. On
Semitic sacrifice, cf. W. Robertson Smith, *Religion of the Semites*, 3rd
edn, ed. by S. A. Cook, 1927; M. J. Lagrange, *Études sur les religions
sémitiques*, 1903, pp. 244ff; R. Dussaud, *Les Origines cananéennes du
sacrifice israélite*, 1921, 2nd edn, 1941; S. H. Hooke, *The Origins of Early
Semitic Ritual*, 1938, pp. 63ff; T. H. Gaster, in *Mélanges Syriens* (Dussaud
Festschrift), ii, 1939, pp. 577ff; D. M. L. Urie, *P.E.Q.* lxxxi, 1949,
pp. 67ff; A. de Guglielmo, *C.B.Q.* xvii, 1955, pp. 196ff (= O'Hara
Festschrift, pp. 76ff). On sacrifice in the Old Testament, cf. W. P.
Paterson, in *D.B.* iv, 1902, pp. 329ff; G. F. Moore, in *E.B.* iv, 1907, cols.
4183ff; C. von Orelli, in *New Schaff-Herzog Encyclopedia of Religious
Knowledge*, x, 1911, pp. 163ff; H. Gressmann, in *R.G.G.*, 1st edn, iv,
cols. 959ff; R. A. S. Macalister, in *E.R.E.* xi, pp. 36ff; O. Eissfeldt, in
R.G.G., 2nd edn, iv, cols. 711ff; A. Médebielle, in *S.D.B.* iii, 1938, cols.
48ff; R. Hentschke, in *R.G.G.*, 3rd edn, iv, cols. 1641ff; T. H. Gaster, in
I.D.B. iv, 1962, pp. 47ff; R. J. Thompson, in *N.B.D.*, 1962, pp. 1113ff;
and *Penitence and Sacrifice in Early Israel*, 1963; W. Kornfeld, in *L.Th.K*,
vii, 1962, cols. 1169ff; G. B. Gray, *Sacrifice in the Old Testament*, 1925.

pounded, and it has been argued that in its beginnings it was designed to effect communion between the worshipper and his god,[1] or that it was a gift to the god to secure his aid,[2] or food to sustain the god,[3] or that it was believed to release power through the death of the animal.[4] I am doubtful if it could be reduced to simple terms even in its origin, and it seems to me certain that all of these ideas can be found in the sacrifices of the Old Testament.[5]

A. Wendel, *Das Opfer in der israelitischen Religion*, 1927; W. O. E. Oesterley, *Sacrifices in Ancient Israel*, 1927; A. Bertholet, *J.B.L.* xlix, 1930, pp. 218ff; J. E. Coleran, *C.B.Q.* ii, 1940, pp. 130ff; R. de Vaux, *A.I.*, pp. 415ff and *Studies in Old Testament Sacrifice*, E. Tr., 1964.

[1] So W. Robertson Smith, op. cit., p. 245; F. B. Jevons, op. cit., p. 285; C. F. Burney, *Outlines of Old Testament Theology*, 3rd edn, 1930, pp. 55f.

[2] So E. B. Tylor, op. cit., p. 376; S. I. Curtiss, *Primitive Semitic Religion Today*, 1902, p. 221f; O. Baumgarten, loc. cit., col. 956. G. B. Gray (op. cit.) emphasizes the gift element in sacrifice, but recognizes also other elements (p. 11). O. Eissfeldt (loc. cit., col. 712) thinks the gift element in Israelite sacrifice tended to displace the communion element. Cf. also A. B. Davidson, *Theology of the Old Testament*, 1904, p. 315; H. W. Robinson, *J.T.S.* xliii, 1942, p. 129. On the *do-ut-des* view of sacrifice, G. van der Leeuw, *A.R.W.* xx, 1920–1, pp. 241ff. S. H. Hooke (op. cit., pp. 63ff) argues that all sacrifices are either gifts or connected with the slaying of the god and ideas arising from this, while L. Koehler (*Old Testament Theology*, E. Tr. by A. S. Todd, 1957, p. 182) finds all to be either gifts or communion sacrifices (cf. M. J. Lagrange, op. cit., pp. 244ff).

[3] So E. Westermarck, *The Origin and Development of Moral Ideas*, ii, 1908, p. 611; W. Eichrodt, *Theology of the Old Testament*, E. Tr., i, 1961, pp. 141f; R. H. Pfeiffer, *Religion in the Old Testament*, 1941, p. 35.

[4] So E. O. James, op. cit., p. 256. Cf. R. Dussaud, op. cit., p. 27; A. Bertholet, in *R.G.G.*, 2nd edn, iv, col. 704; H. H. Gowen, *History of Religion*, 1934, p. 64. Hubert and Mauss (loc. cit., pp. 41f, 133; E. Tr., pp. 11ff, 97) approach this view in saying that by the death of the victim sacrifice establishes communication and achieves desired objects. H. Lesêtre (loc. cit., col. 1315) emphasizes the idea of substitution in sacrifice.

[5] Cf. A. Bertholet, loc. cit., col. 704; A. Loisy, op. cit., p. 11; E. W. Hopkins, op. cit., pp. 151ff; A. Wendel, op. cit., pp. 32ff; W. O. E. Oesterley, op. cit., pp. 11ff; G. van der Leeuw, op. cit., pp. 350ff; J. Pedersen, *Israel III–IV*, 1940, pp. 299ff; F. F. Hvidberg, *Den israelitiske Religions Historie*, 1943, pp. 91f; R. Herrmann, in *Calwer Bibellexikon*, 5th edn, 1959, col. 968; A. Schimmel, loc. cit., cols. 1637ff; W. Kornfeld, loc. cit., cols. 1169ff. Cf. R. de Vaux, *A.I.*, p. 451: "Sacrifice is one act with many aspects, and we must beware of simple explanations"; T. H. Gaster, in *I.D.B.* iv, p. 147b: "All monogenetic theories of the origin of sacrifice

Yet, as I shall say, I do not think that all of them together give an adequate interpretation of Israelite sacrifice, for the ritual was believed to be effective only when it was the organ of the spirit. It is true that many in Israel thought its efficacy lay in the due performance of the ritual act, and there were sacrifices which encouraged such a notion. But it is also true that the efficacy of the ritual act was believed to depend on its being the expression of the spirit of the offerer. But this is to anticipate.

That Israel was not alone in having a sacrificial cultus does not need to be argued. Animal sacrifice was widespread and ancient. The Bible itself ascribes to it an antiquity as great as that of the human race, for it tells of the sacrifices of Cain and Abel.[1] It tells us of sacrifices by the patriarchs,[2] and of sacrifices by Israel's neighbours. Balaam offered sacrifices on seven altars.[3] The priests of the Tyrian Baal called on their god to send fire to consume their sacrifice on Mount Carmel.[4] The king of Moab offered his son in sacrifice to weight his appeal to his god for help.[5] Ahaz saw a sacrificial altar in Damascus and had one like it made in the Temple in Jerusalem.[6] There was nothing unique in Israel's practising sacrifice, and we cannot suppose that it was first prescribed by God to Moses.

The older Israelite codes and the pre-exilic history give us little information about the details of sacrifice, but take it for granted. Most of the sacrificial law of the Pentateuch is found in the Priestly Code, which did not reach its present form until the post-exilic age. That Code continued and developed older forms of sacrifice, and perhaps added new forms. We can neither take it for granted that everything in that Code is brand new, nor that everything was ancient. That there was development in the

may be safely discountenanced from the start"; A. Wendel, *Das Opfer in der altisraelitischen Religion*, 1927, p. 215: "Fast jedes Opfer ist ein Komplex, oder, besser gesagt, ein Knotenpunkt von Ideen und aus ihnen sich ergebender Handlungen"; F. L. Moriarty, *The Way*, v, 1965, p. 97: "In the Old Testament we are confronted with a very elaborate system of sacrifices; but it is impossible to find anything like a unified or coherent theory of sacrifice." C. von Orelli (loc. cit., p. 163b), oversimplifies by saying: "The real solution of the theory of sacrifice, the origin of which is prehistoric, must be sought in the childlike dependence of man upon the gods."

[1] Gen. 4.3ff.   [2] Cf. above, pp. 22f.   [3] Num. 23.1ff, 14, 29f.
[4] 1 Kings 18.26ff.   [5] 2 Kings 3.27.   [6] 2 Kings 16.10ff.

ritual of sacrifice over the period covered by the Old Testament
is clearly indicated in the Bible itself. In the time of Eli we are told
that it was the custom of the priest to cast a flesh-hook into the
vessel in which the flesh of the sacrifice was seething, and to have
as his portion whatever it brought up.[1] But the sons of Eli caused
great offence by demanding raw flesh, and by demanding it before
the burning of the fat.[2] It is commonly thought that both statements refer to innovations by the sons of Eli, and that the casting
of the flesh-hook was their encroachment on the offerer's right
to choose what portions should go to the priests.[3] But it is hard
to see how the demand for raw flesh could be squared with the
casting of a flesh-hook into meat that was already seething,[4] and
it seems to me that the passage means that the established custom
was to cast the flesh-hook into the pot, and that the offence of
Eli's sons lay in their demand for raw flesh. Later law specifies
the portions which the priests should have, and it would appear
that they were received in a raw state. In the law of Deuteronomy
the priestly dues are defined as the shoulder, the two cheeks, and
the maw,[5] whereas in the Priestly Code they are stated to be the
breast and the right thigh.[6]

Yet though we know there was development, we are not sufficiently well informed to write a detailed history of sacrifice in
Israel, and we are often dependent on the Priestly Code as our only
source of knowledge. In an earlier chapter I have said that while
the sacrifice of the Passover was something that Israel brought
with her into Canaan, she probably took over the agricultural
festivals and their observance from the Canaanites after the
Settlement.[7] The view has been advanced that Israel's sacrificial
ritual was largely taken over from the Canaanites,[8] though it is

---

[1] 1 Sam. 2.13f.   [2] 1 Sam. 2.15ff.

[3] So W. Nowack, *Die Bücher Samuelis*, 1902, p. 11; A. R. S. Kennedy,
Samuel, p. 46; H. P. Smith, *Samuel*, 1912, p. 18; S. R. Driver, *Samuel*,
2nd edn, 1913, p. 29; K. A. Leimbach, *Samuel*, 1936, pp. 27f; A. Méde-
bielle, in *La Sainte Bible*, ed. by L. Pirot and A. Clamer, iii, 1949, p. 358;
M. Rehm, in *Echt. B.*, *Altes Testament*, ii, 1956, p. 18; H. W. Hertzberg,
Samuel, E. Tr. by J. S. Bowden, 1964, p. 35.

[4] Cf. R. J. Thompson, *Penitence and Sacrifice in Early Israel*, 1963,
p. 99.

[5] Deut. 18.3.   [6] Lev. 7.34.   [7] Cf. above, p. 88.

[8] Cf. R. Dussaud, *Les Origines cananéennes du sacrifice israélite*, 1941;
J. Pedersen, *Israel III–IV*, 1940, p. 317; J. P. Hyatt, *Prophetic Religion*,
1947, p. 128; T. C. Vriezen, *Outline of Old Testament Theology*, E. Tr. by

recognized that the Passover was an exception.[1] While I have little doubt that the Israelites were much influenced by Canaanite practice, I find it difficult to believe that they practised no sacrifice but the Passover prior to their entry into Palestine.[2]

It is true that Amos and Jeremiah are commonly held to provide evidence that sacrifice was not offered in the Wilderness,[3] but I am not persuaded that this is the true interpretation of their words.[4] De Vaux, who a few years ago held that the evidence "does not justify the conclusion that Israel took all its ritual for sacrifices from Canaan",[5] has more recently suggested that in the pre-Settlement period the Israelites would have known only the Passover type of sacrifice, and that they borrowed the other forms after they gained possession of Canaan.[6] But the Passover was

S. Neuijen, 1958, pp. 27ff; G. von Rad, *Old Testament Theology*, E. Tr. by D. M. G. Stalker, i, 1962, p. 262. For a wider view of the assimilation of Old Testament religion and Canaanite religion cf. I. Engnell, *Gamla Testamentet*, i, p. 136, and *S.B.U.* i, 1948, col. 673, and G. W. Anderson's reply, *O.T.M.S.*, 1951, pp. 288f.

[1] Cf. R. Dussaud, op. cit., p. 207; J. Pedersen, op. cit., pp. 317, 382, 400f.

[2] Cf. A. Lods, *Israel*, E. Tr., 1932, p. 281, and *R.H.P.R.* viii, pp. 405ff.

[3] Amos 5.25; Jer. 7.22.

[4] Cf. *B.J.R.L.* xxix, 1946, pp. 340ff, where I discuss these passages; also my discussion with C. J. Cadoux (*E.T.* lviii, 1946–7, pp. 43ff) in *E.T.* lviii, 1946–7, pp. 69ff, with N. H. Snaith (*E.T.* lviii, 1946–7, pp. 152f) in *E.T.* lviii, 1946–7, pp. 305ff, and with R. Dobbie (*E.T.* lxx, 1958–9, pp. 299ff) in *E.T.* lxx, 1958–9, pp. 341f. Cf. also *M.Q.*, 1963, pp. 73f.

[5] *A.I.*, p. 440.

[6] *Studies in Old Testament Sacrifice*, 1964, pp. 19f. In *A.I.*, p. 428, de Vaux maintained that Amos 5.25 and Jer. 7.22 were "directed, not against the cult itself, but against the external and material cult which was practised by their contemporaries"; but in *Studies in Old Testament Sacrifice*, p. 20, he withdraws this and finds instead "a clear reflection . . . of the fact that the Israelites in the desert were not yet acquainted with holocausts and communion sacrifices". This would involve the rejection of traditions much older than the time of Amos and Jeremiah, and is against all probability as well as against the earlier Biblical accounts. It would be surprising if Israel, alone of the peoples of the ancient Near Eastern world, had practised no sacrifice but the Passover. H. W. Robinson (*Redemption and Revelation*, 1942, p. 249) believed the burnt offering was borrowed by Israel from the Canaanites, whereas the peace offering was offered in the pre-Settlement period. V. Maag (*Text, Wortschatz und Begriffswelt des Buches Amos*, 1951, pp. 221f) thinks Amos relied on a lost —and unreliable—source, different from J and E.

not a type of sacrifice. It was a specific sacrifice offered on a particular night of the year. Moreover, the words of Amos and Jeremiah can give no support for this idea. Amos spoke of *zebhāḥîm* and *minḥāh*, while Jeremiah spoke of *'ōlāh* and *zebhaḥ*. Since the Passover was called a *zebhaḥ* in the Ritual Decalogue,[1] which is commonly regarded as the oldest Decalogue and which I have argued is pre-Mosaic in its origin,[2] it cannot be excluded from the sayings of Amos and Jeremiah,[3] and if their words are appealed to as evidence, they are equally evidence against the antiquity of the Passover in Israel.

Moreover, the stories of the patriarchs in our oldest sources represent them as offering sacrifice,[4] and there is no reason to doubt that they did, and as little reason to doubt that the practice of sacrifice continued through the intervening years. It is impossible to suppose that their sacrifices were of a Passover type. In treating of the Passover, de Vaux argues that its original significance was as a means of warding off danger from the flocks.[5] We cannot suppose that the sacrifices attributed to the patriarchs had any such apotropaic purpose, or that they were offered in the night, or at a particular time of the year. Similarly, the covenant sacrifice in the Wilderness[6] has nothing in common with a Passover sacrifice. De Vaux is therefore compelled to doubt whether our records can be trusted, and thinks they describe in the terms of their authors' days the sacrifices which they attributed to their ancestors.[7] A theory seems insufficient evidence on which to dismiss these accounts, and I think de Vaux himself points the way to a better explanation of the evidence. To this we shall come. Here I would simply say that while I recognize Canaanite influence on Israelite ritual in the post-Settlement period, I do not trace all but the Passover to that influence.[8] Canaanite influence would be most felt in the period that immediately followed the Settlement. But the developments that followed need not all be attributed to that influence.

[1] Ex. 34.25.   [2] Cf. *M.G.*, pp. 7ff, 18.

[3] De Vaux would restrict the word *zebhaḥ* here, so as to exclude the Passover.

[4] Cf. above, pp. 22f.   [5] Op. cit., pp. 17f.

[6] Cf. above, p. 52.   [7] Op. cit., p. 19.

[8] Cf. *M.Q.*, p. 75 n: "While Israel doubtless brought some sacrificial ritual with her when she entered Canaan, she borrowed much from the Canaanites for its development in the post-Settlement period."

That the Passover was unlike other sacrifices is undeniable. Moses asked Pharaoh to let the Israelites go into the Wilderness to offer sacrifice,[1] and it is generally believed, though this is far from certain,[2] that by this the Passover was meant. When Pharaoh refused to let the people go, the Passover was sacrificed in Egypt[3] and became the occasion of the Exodus. In the account of that Passover there is no mention of any altar, and consequently no mention of the disposal of blood and fat on the altar. It would appear that each household killed its own animal and blood was sprinkled on the doorposts and lintels of their houses, while the entire animal had to be roasted and consumed before dawn, save for such parts as could not be eaten, and these had to be burned with fire before daybreak. In the Ritual Decalogue we read: "Thou shalt not offer the blood of my sacrifice with leavened bread",[4] and this is understood to refer to the Passover. In Ex. 12.34, which is assigned to the J document, we are told that when the Israelites left Egypt after the slaughter of the Egyptian firstborn at midnight, they took their dough with them before it was leavened, while in Ex. 12.8, which is assigned to the Priestly Code, the instruction is given in advance that the Passover should be eaten with unleavened bread and bitter herbs. While there are obvious differences here, all agree in associating unleavened bread with the Passover, and this association must have made easier the combination of the Passover with the once separate Feast of Unleavened Bread at a later date.[5]

Sacrifices similar in some respects to the Passover are known among Arabian tribes,[6] and it is probable, as I have said, that in origin this was a nomadic springtime festival to ward off evil from flock and home. We have no idea how the Passover was observed in the post-Settlement period. The Chronicler tells us that in the days of Hezekiah Passover was celebrated in Jerusalem,[7] and since

---

[1] Ex. 5.8.

[2] Cf. A. C. Welch, *Prophet and Priest in Old Israel*, 1936, p. 39.

[3] Ex. 12.1ff.   [4] Ex. 34.25.

[5] De Vaux (*Studies in Old Testament Sacrifice*, pp. 10f) notes the essential difference between the significance of Unleavened Bread at Passover and at the feast of Unleavened Bread, but thinks the fusion of the two festivals could have been stimulated by this link.

[6] Cf. R. de Vaux, op. cit., pp. 15ff.   [7] 2 Chron. 30.

Hezekiah attempted to centralize worship in Jerusalem,[1] it is possible that this was done. But in view of the fact that this is not mentioned in the account of Hezekiah's reign in the book of Kings, and the further fact that we are told that Josiah's Passover was unlike any that had preceded it,[2] it must remain doubtful.[3] Throughout the intervening period since the Settlement, Passover must have been observed as a home festival wherever men lived. In that case the animals must have been taken to the local shrine to be slaughtered, since in that period all slaughter was sacrifice. It was laid down by Deuteronomy that the Passover must be eaten at the place where the central sanctuary was,[4] and therefore implied that it must be slain at the central sanctuary, and the fat and the blood would be disposed of at the altar, though this is not stated. What is stated is the meaning of the sacrifice. Any meaning it may have had in pre-Mosaic days, either in Israel or elsewhere, is superseded by its significance as a memorial of the Exodus. This memorial character is stated in Deuteronomy,[5] and in the book of Exodus we have a brief liturgical passage to be used at the Passover, emphasizing the same memorial character.[6] This is also assigned to the Deuteronomist, but there is no reason to suppose that that character was first given to it by the Deuteronomist. The connection of the Passover in Egypt with the deliverance from Egypt would sufficiently stamp the festival with the memory of that deliverance, even though the words of the liturgy for its celebration come from the Deuteronomic school. By its reminder of the deliverance it called for renewed gratitude to God and

---

[1] Hezekiah's reform, save for the destruction of the Brazen Serpent, has been denied historicity by a number of scholars, including J. Wellhausen (*Prolegomena to the History of Israel*, E. Tr., 1885, p. 25), B. Stade (*G.V.I.* i, 1889, p. 607), T. K. Cheyne (in *E.B.* ii, 1901, cols. 2058f), G. Hölscher (*Die Profeten*, 1914, pp. 165, 261, and *Geschichte der israelitischen und jüdischen Religion*, 1922, p. 99), and A. Lods (*The Prophets and the Rise of Judaism*, E. Tr. by S. H. Hooke, 1937, p. 115). It is, however, accepted by the following, among others: J. A. McClymont (in Hastings' *D.B.* ii, 1899, p. 377a), W. R. Smith (*The Prophets of Israel*, 2nd edn, 1912, pp. 361ff), E. Frisch (in *Studies in Jewish Literature* (Kohler Festschrift), 1913, pp. 117ff), R. Kittel (*G.V.I.* ii, 7th edn, 1925, pp. 373ff), T. H. Robinson (*History of Israel*, i, 1932, pp. 392ff), H. B. MacLean (in *I.D.B.* ii, 1962, pp. 598f). For my defence of its historicity cf. *M.G.*, pp. 126ff.

[2] 2 Kings 23.22; 2 Chron. 35.18f. [3] Cf. above, pp. 89f n.
[4] Deut. 16.2. [5] Deut. 16.3. [6] Ex. 12.25ff.

renewed loyalty to the Covenant which followed the deliverance. Many might celebrate the Passover without bringing gratitude and loyalty, just as many to-day celebrate Christmas with no thought of its message and with no response to it in their hearts. But the practice of the superficial is no true guide to the significance intended by an observance.

We have found two other kinds of sacrifices mentioned as offered in the period before the erection of the Temple, and both continued to be offered throughout the whole of the Old Testament period. These are the whole burnt offering and the so-called "peace offering".[1] The former figures relatively rarely in the early period, but it appears to have predominated over the latter in the later period.[2] De Vaux is of the opinion that this was due to the centralization of the cultus and the fact that the increasing frequency of the public sacrifices tended to make individual and family sacrifices fall into the background and become less frequent.[3] It was inevitable that the centralization of the cultus should reduce the number of individual and family sacrifices, since in pre-Deuteronomic days, when all slaughter was sacrifice, the local shrine would be resorted to on occasions that would not justify a journey to Jerusalem, and when Deuteronomy provided for non-sacrificial slaughter for food this would no longer be necessary.[4] This is not to say that the Temple in Jerusalem did not continue to be the daily scene of private and family sacrifices, and the relative infrequency of our records of such sacrifices is no evidence that they were in fact relatively infrequent. Our records for the period of the monarchy after the building of the Temple and for the post-exilic period are not marked by the same wealth of personal detail as our earlier records, and the interest of the compilers of our accounts was more largely centred on national events. Individual sacrifices figure largely in the Priestly law, and there is every reason to believe that the Temple was constantly resorted to for such sacrifices.

---

[1] Cf. above, p. 52.

[2] Cf. de Vaux, *Studies in Old Testament Sacrifice*, pp. 33ff, where the references to the burnt offering in texts relating to the early period are given, while he states that the "peace offering" is mentioned forty-seven times in the historical books from Joshua to Kings (pp. 34f).

[3] Ibid., p. 36.   [4] Deut. 12.15, 21ff.

The whole burnt offering is sometimes called the '*ôlāh*,[1] a name which indicates that it "went up" in smoke to God, and sometimes the *kālîl*, to indicate that it was "wholly" consumed on the altar. A further term, which is common in the Priestly Code but rare elsewhere, is '*ishsheh*, which indicates that it was consumed by "fire".[2] Here the offerer slaughtered the victim, skinned it and cut it into pieces, according to the Priestly Code,[3] and this seems to have been the practice in the days of Herod's Temple,[4] though Ezekiel in his sketch of the restored community assigned this task to the Levites.[5] The disposal of the blood and the laying of the fat and of the pieces of the animal on the altar was the duty of the priest,[6] and we cannot doubt that this was always the case in the Temple from its consecration. The purpose of the whole burnt offering was probably originally to express homage to God and to win his favour by a costly gift.[7] The Priestly Code describes it as a "pleasing odour" to the Lord,[8] and this is the same expression as is used in Genesis of the whole burnt offering which Noah is said to have offered after the Flood.[9] It is characteristic of the

[1] On the '*ôlāh* cf. W. B. Stevenson, in *Festschrift für Alfred Bertholet*, 1950, pp. 489ff.

[2] This is the usual view. But H. Cazelles (*Lévitique*, 2nd edn, 1958, p. 13; *Deutéronome*, 2nd edn, 1958, p. 82) connects it with the Sumerian EŠ =food. Cf. W. B. Stevenson, in *Festschrift für Alfred Bertholet*, 1950, p. 488. G. B. Gray (*Sacrifice in the Old Testament*, 1925, pp. 9ff) allows the possibility that the word originally came from a root meaning "to be friendly", but says that if it ever had this meaning it lost it and attracted to itself a connection with fire.

[3] Lev. 1.5ff. The same procedure appears to be laid down for the "peace offering" in Lev. 3.2.

[4] Cf. Mishnah, *Zebaḥim* iii.1 (H. Danby, *The Mishnah*, 1933, p. 471), where this rule appears to apply to all sacrificial slaughter, and not merely to the whole burnt offering.

[5] Ezek. 44.11. In 2 Chron. 29.22, 24 the victims are said to have been slaughtered by the priests, but flayed by the priests and Levites (v. 34), the latter being called on for help as the number of victims was too great for the priests to deal with. In the account of Josiah's Passover, the Chronicler says the Levites both slaughtered the animals and flayed them, the priests disposing of the blood (2 Chron. 35.11). On these passages cf. J. Hänel, *Z.A.W.* lv, 1937, pp. 46ff.

[6] Lev. 4.7, 18, 25, 30, 34; 9.9, etc., and Lev. 1.8f, 12f; 3.3ff, 9ff; 4.26, 35, etc.

[7] Cf. de Vaux, op. cit., p. 36.   [8] Lev. 1.9, 13, 17, etc.

[9] Gen. 8.21.

Priestly Code, with that emphasis on sin which we have already noted, to give to the whole burnt offering an expiatory value.[1] The Priestly Code requires the sacrifice of a whole burnt offering twice a day as a public offering, once in the morning and once in the evening.[2] Ezekiel mentions only a daily morning burnt offering,[3] and in the account of sacrifice in the time of Ahaz only the morning burnt offering is referred to.[4] Before we conclude that the doubling of this offering was an innovation of the Priestly Code,[5] we should note that in the account of Ahaz there is reference also to the evening *minḥāh*. This term in exilic and post-exilic usage always denotes a cereal offering, but there is some evidence that earlier it was used for an animal offering.[6] It is used of Abel's animal sacrifice,[7] and in a number of other passages it is possible or probable that it has this meaning.[8] In the account of Elijah's sacrifice on Mount Carmel it is stated that the prophet prepared

---

[1] Lev. 1.4.   [2] Ex. 29.38ff; Num. 28.2ff.
[3] Ezek. 46.13.   [4] 2 Kings 16.15.
[5] Cf. S. R. Driver, *Exodus*, 1911, p. 326; W. O. E. Oesterley, *Sacrifices in Ancient Israel*, p. 221; R. de Vaux, *A.I.*, p. 469.
[6] Cf. G. B. Gray, *Sacrifice in the Old Testament*, p. 398: "In early Hebrew usage . . . the term *minḥāh*, which later (in P) became a technical term for cereal offerings only, is used comprehensively of all sacred offerings." On the meaning of the term *minḥāh*, cf. ibid., pp. 13ff. N. H. Snaith (*V.T.* vii, 1957, pp. 314ff) maintains that "at all times *minḥāh* must strictly have been 'a gift of grain (cereal)', but that, since the word originally meant 'tribute, gift' it could be used loosely in a wider sense". This presupposes a strange development: that the word originally meant a gift of grain then came to be used more widely to include animal sacrifice, but then in the Priestly Code reverted to its stricter use and was limited to cereal offerings. It seems more natural to follow the usual view that the word was originally used more widely of offerings of animal or grain and then became restricted to cereal offerings. Since it is clearly known that in late usage it was restricted, it is a little odd to suppose that it began with this usage and then deviated and then returned. In the earliest document of the Pentateuch the wider use is found. R. J. Thompson (*Penitence and Sacrifice in Early Israel*, 1963, p. 50 n) rejects the view of Snaith.
[7] Gen. 4.2ff. Here the term *minḥāh* is used of Cain's vegetable offering and of Abel's animal offering. Snaith (loc. cit., p. 316) says the word here may have the general sense of "tribute, present", but this cannot affect the fact that it refers to Abel's offering as well as to Cain's.
[8] Cf. 1 Sam. 2.17, where the context refers only to animal offerings. Other passages where the reference is probably or possibly to animal offerings are given in *B.D.B.*, p. 588a.

his sacrifice at the time of the offering up of the *minḥāh*.[1] This would seem to imply that in northern Israel at this time there was an evening animal sacrifice,[2] though the time may have been earlier than that prescribed in the Priestly law.[3] We must therefore leave open the possibility that the daily offering, or *tāmîdh*, was sacrificed twice daily in pre-exilic times. According to the Priestly Law it was accompanied by a *minḥāh*, which here must mean a cereal offering, and also by drink offerings on both occasions.[4] On sabbaths the daily offerings are doubled in the Priestly law, and on other occasions they were increased.

The "peace offerings" are sometimes called *shelāmîm*, a term which would seem to be connected with the root from which *shālôm*, "peace" or "well-being", was derived, but the *piʿēl* of the verb was used for the sense of repaying debts or vows. Koehler connects the sense of *shelāmîm* with this idea, and finds it to express the sense of being quits.[5] It is doubtful if this covers all the cases. Pedersen calls them "covenant offerings".[6] This would seem well to define the character of the offerings made at the sacred mount at the time of the conclusion of the Covenant,[7] but

[1] I Kings 18.29.

[2] As Elijah was offering an animal sacrifice it would be more relevant to note the synchronism with the evening animal sacrifice.

[3] According to Ex. 29.41; Num. 28.4, the evening offering was made "between the two evenings". The meaning of this phrase is uncertain and much discussed; cf. S. R. Driver, *Exodus*, 1911, pp. 89f. According to Josephus (*Ant.* XIV. iv. 3 (65)) the evening sacrifice was offered at the ninth hour, and according to the Mishnah, *Pesaḥim* v.1 (cf. H. Danby, *The Mishnah*, p. 141), it was normally slaughtered at a half after the eighth hour and offered at a half after the ninth hour. This would be near the time when Elijah's sacrifice was made, in view of all that had to happen afterwards.

[4] Ex. 29.40f; Num. 28.5ff.

[5] Cf. *Old Testament Theology*, E. Tr., p. 188. W. P. Paterson (in Hastings' *D.B.* iv, 1902, p. 333a) is uncertain whether the term denotes that friendly relations existed or whether it implied estrangement and the offering of restitution. On the *shelāmîm* cf. R. Schmid, *Das Bundesopfer in Israel*, 1964. Cf. also J. H. Kurtz, *Sacrificial Worship of the Old Testament*, E. Tr. by J. Martin, 1863, pp. 251ff.

[6] Cf. *Israel III–IV*, 1940, p. 335. So also R. Schmid, *Das Bundesopfer in Israel*, 1964 (on which cf. D. Gill, *Biblica*, xlvii, 1966, pp. 255ff), and H. Graf Reventlow, *Th.L.Z.* xci, 1966, cols. 497ff). A. Haldar (*Associations of Cult Prophets among the Ancient Semites*, 1945, p. 212) thinks they were divinatory sacrifices. This is not very probable.

[7] Ex. 24.4ff.

less certainly to cover all the cases of these sacrifices. It seems to me more likely that this term expressed the idea that these sacrifices were for the maintenance or restoration of good relations with God. This would seem to connect well with the sense of "peace" or "well-being", and the recognition that man's well-being rested on right relations with God.

Sometimes we find these sacrifices referred to under the term *zᵉbhāhîm*, a general term for sacrifices, which merely indicates that they are slaughtered, and therefore in the days when all slaughter was sacrifice it acquired the meaning of "sacrifice". Sometimes we find a combination of the two terms, *zebhah shᵉlāmîm*.[1] In the Holiness Code and the Priestly Code these offerings were made to include three varieties, the thank offering, the offering in fulfilment of a vow, and the freewill offering.[2] The thank offering was an expression of gratitude to God for mercies received. The votive offering was the fulfilment of a conditional promise which had been made and whose condition had been fulfilled. Both were the expression of some degree of moral obligation. The freewill offering would seem to be the spontaneous expression of the devotion of the offerer.[3] All would seem to fall within the general idea which I have suggested. Every obligation to God, whether voluntarily undertaken or not, must be acknowledged, if right relations were to be maintained, and the freewill offering as the expression of the heart's devotion was designed to ensure right relations and therefore well-being.

In these sacrifices the blood was disposed of against the altar and the fat was burned on the altar,[4] part of the flesh became the due of the priests, and part was eaten by the offerer with his

---

[1] On the interchangeability of the terms *shᵉlāmîm*, *zebhah*, *zebhah shᵉlāmîm*, and *zebhah*, cf. W. B. Stevenson, in *Festschrift für Alfred Bertholet*, 1950, pp. 492f.

[2] Lev. 22.21ff, 29f (H); Lev. 7.11ff (P). Cf. also Lev. 3 for the ritual of the "peace offering".

[3] Cf. W. P. Paterson (loc. cit., p. 338a): "As to the distinction of the three varieties, the most satisfactory explanation is that which interprets the thank-offering as a response to experienced acts of Divine goodness, while the votive offering and the free-will offering are connected with expectation of benefit and supplicatory prayer. The first, in short, was contemplated only after blessings received while the last two were decided on when some special blessing was still awaited at the hand of God."

[4] Lev. 3.2ff.

family and guests.[1] They are therefore called by some "communion offerings"[2] or "shared offerings".[3] This describes certain aspects of their character, but does not explain their name. For they led to a meal, which the offerer might be said to share with God. De Vaux aptly cites[4] 1 Cor. 10.18: "Have not they which eat the sacrifices communion with the altar?"

We need not here discuss whether these offerings were conceived of as shared with God in the sense that God was thought to partake of the food.[5] It is probable that such an idea was once held, and the fact that cereal offerings accompanied the animal sacrifice lends some colour to such an idea.[6] But if so, there is no evidence that it was held within the historical period of Israel's life. After carefully considering this question de Vaux concludes that the blood and the fat go to the altar, the one to be cast against it and the other to be consumed by fire upon it, because these belong exclusively to God, and not as food for him. They must

[1] Lev. 7.11ff.

[2] So de Vaux, *Studies in Old Testament Sacrifice*, p. 31.

[3] The new Jewish translation calls them "sacrifices of well-being" (cf. *The Torah*, 1962, p. 181). Cf. above, p. 122.

[4] Op. cit., p. 38.

[5] Cf. *B.D.B.*, p. 257a: "The common and most ancient sacrifice, whose essential rite was eating the flesh of the victim at a feast in which the god of the clan shared by receiving the blood and fat pieces." Cf. W. R. Smith, *Religion of the Semites*, 3rd edn, 1927, p. 345: "Throughout the Semitic field, the fundamental idea of sacrifice is not that of a sacred tribute, but of communion between the god and his worshippers by joint participation in the living flesh and blood of a sacred victim"; also W. O. E. Oesterley, *Sacrifices in Ancient Israel*, p. 173: "Both Yahweh and His worshippers partake of the same sacrificial victim." For a criticism of this view cf. N. H. Snaith, *V.T.* vii, 1957, pp. 308ff.

[6] Cf. also the references to the altar as the table of Yahweh (Ezek. 44.16; Mal. 1.12), or to the food of Yahweh (Lev. 3.11; 21.6, 8; 22.25; Num. 28.2). W. Eichrodt (*Theology of the Old Testament*, E. Tr., i, p. 141f) says: "The most primitive attitude is certainly that which sees the sacrifice as the means by which the deity is provided with nourishment and renewed strength. . . . An examination of the ritual and language of Israelite sacrifice with this in mind reveals unmistakable traces of this conception." On the other hand de Vaux points out (*Studies in Old Testament Sacrifice*, p. 40) that the expressions "food of Yahweh" and "table of Yahweh" are first introduced during the Exile and in a Babylonian environment and says that "they simply bear witness to the Yahwistic religion's power of assimilation".

not be eaten by man because they are too sacred.[1] Similarly, James Barr says: "It is probably too crude and one-sided an interpretation to say that the worshippers were sharing a common meal with the deity."[2] He notes that in Deuteronomy we find the phrase: "Ye shall eat before the Lord your God",[3] not with him. If God were thought of as sharing the meal, we should expect him to have some of the best cuts.

These two varieties of sacrifice appear to have been found among the Canaanites.[4] De Vaux shows that while the Passover can be paralleled from Arabian sources, neither the whole burnt offering nor the peace offering seems to be paralleled there.[5] On the other hand, there is evidence that these types of sacrifice were known at Ugarit[6] and at the Phoenician colony of Carthage,[7] though the terminology is not the same as in the Old Testament, and it is on this ground that he thinks the Israelites borrowed these sacrifices from the Canaanites after they conquered the land.[8] But he shows that similar types of sacrifice were found in Greece,[9] and he argues that Canaanites and Greeks borrowed them from a pre-Semitic civilization.[10] This must have been very

---

[1] Cf. N. H. Snaith, V.T. vii, 1957, p. 312: "He [sc. God] gets all the fat, He gets all the blood. He gets all this because it is His right, and He gets it whatever the animal and whatever the intention of the rite. . . . God therefore does not eat the fat of the zebhaḥ because He shares the meal. He gets it because it is the fat." Similarly de Vaux, op. cit., p. 42: "The reason for the pouring out of the blood and the burning of the fat on the altar is not that Yahweh feeds on them, but that the blood and fat belong to Yahweh alone."

[2] Hastings' one volume D.B., rev. edn, 1963, p. 870b.

[3] Deut. 12.7.

[4] Cf. de Vaux, op. cit., pp. 44ff. On the 'ōlāh and the zebhaḥ cf. W. B. Stevenson, in Festschrift für Alfred Bertholet, 1950, pp. 488ff; H. J. Kraus, Worship in Israel, E. Tr., 1966, pp. 113ff; L. Rost, Das kleine Credo und andere Studien zum Alten Testament, 1965, pp. 112ff.

[5] Op. cit., pp. 43f.

[6] Cf. T. H. Gaster, in Mélanges Syriens (Dussaud Festschrift), ii, 1939, pp. 577ff; R. Dussaud, Les Origines cananéennes du sacrifice israélite, 2nd edn, 1941, pp. 326ff; D. M. L. Urie, P.E.Q. lxxxi, 1949, pp. 67ff; J. Gray, Z.A.W. lxii, 1950, pp. 207ff; A. de Guglielmo, C.B.Q. xvii, 1955, pp. 196ff (= O'Hara Festschrift, pp. 76ff); N. H. Snaith, V.T. vii, 1957, pp. 313f.

[7] Cf. de Vaux, op. cit., pp. 45f; also S. Langdon, J.B.L. xxiii, 1904, pp. 79ff; R. Dussaud, op. cit., pp. 134ff, 320ff; D. M. L. Urie, loc. cit., pp. 67ff.

[8] Cf. above, p. 114.   [9] Op. cit., pp. 48ff.   [10] Ibid., p. 49.

ancient, and there can be no antecedent reason why the patriarchs could not have adopted them long before the Settlement. The Kenites could equally well have adopted them, and there is nothing necessarily unhistorical in the representation of Jethro as offering such sacrifices.[1] De Vaux finds significance in the fact that the character of a meal shared with the deity, which belonged to the Canaanite and the Greek rite, was obscured in Israel by the fact that no lean meat was burned on the altar.[2] It is unlikely that in the period following the Settlement, when we know that syncretism with Canaanite religion took place, the Israelites imposed this difference on rites which they then took over, and it is more likely that where the Israelite rite differed from the Canaanite they brought the difference with them.

In the Priestly law we meet with two terms in connection with these offerings, used to describe the portions that went to the priests. These are *tenûphāh*[3] and *terûmāh*.[4] The former is rendered "wave offering" by the R.V. and the latter "heave offering".[5] These do not seem very relevant renderings, for the whole body of the Levites are said elsewhere to be a *tenûphāh*,[6] and it is unlikely that they were "waved". G. R. Driver has therefore suggested a different derivation for the word *tenûphāh*, which would yield the sense "something additional", "special contribution".[7] He holds that *tenûphāh* and *terûmāh* were indistinguishable in sense. N. H. Snaith gives to both words the sense of "something lifted off", but distinguishes between them on the basis of Lev. 7.30, 33, so that the first means the portion which went to the priests as a whole, and the second means that which went to the officiating priest as his personal portion.[8]

In the Priestly Code we find two other sacrifices,[9] the sin

---

[1] Ex. 18.12.   [2] Op. cit., p. 50.

[3] Ex. 29.26f; Lev. 7.34; Num. 18.11, etc.

[4] Ex. 29.27; Lev. 7.34; Num. 6.20, etc.

[5] R.S.V. renders "wave offering" and "priests' portion" (the latter with variations). On these two terms cf. A. Vincent, in *Mélanges Syriens* (Dussaud Festschrift), i, 1939, pp. 267ff.

[6] Num. 8.11, 13, 15, 21.   [7] Cf. *J.S.S.* i, 1956, pp. 100ff.

[8] Cf. *V.T.* vii, 1957, p. 311; *E.T.* lxxiv, 1962–3, p. 127b. R. de Vaux (*A.I.*, p. 435) suggests that both terms may have been borrowed from Babylonian juridical, but not liturgical, language.

[9] On these two sacrifices cf. P. Saydon, *C.B.Q.* viii, 1946, pp. 393ff; N. H. Snaith, *V.T.* xv, 1965, pp. 73ff. See also A. Vincent, in *Mélanges Syriens* (Dussaud Festschrift), i, 1939, pp. 267ff.

offering[1] and the guilt offering.[2] Here we find that deeper concern for sin[3] which marks the Priestly Law reflected, though it is improbable that these were entirely post-exilic creations. The term for guilt offering, *'āshām*, is found in pre-exilic writings, though it is not used for an animal sacrifice. It is used for the golden symbols which accompanied the Ark when it was returned by the Philistines.[4] It is also used of a payment made to the priests.[5] Elsewhere it is used for guilt, where there is no reference to any guilt offering, just as the term *ḥaṭṭā'th*, sin offering, is often used for sin, where there is no reference to a sacrifice.[6] But the fact that in the law of Lev. 5.1–9 it is impossible to distinguish between the *ḥaṭṭā'th* and the *'āshām* suggests that they were really older sacrifices, which were once quite distinct, but whose distinction had become blurred.[7] In Isaiah 53, which almost certainly comes from a prophet of the exilic period, and therefore earlier than the Priestly Law,[8] the Servant is said to be an

---

[1] Lev. 4.24f; Num. 6.14, and frequently. On the sin offering, cf. L. Moraldi, *Espiazione sacrificale e riti espiatori*, 1956, pp. 133ff.

[2] Lev. 5.6f; Num. 6.12, etc. On the guilt offering, cf. L. Moraldi, op. cit., pp. 159ff; also L. Morris, *Evangelical Quarterly*, xxx, 1958, pp. 196ff.

[3] S. Herner (*Sühne und Vergebung in Israel*, 1942, p. 105) notes that the idea of expiation is very rare in the Psalms. This is consistent with the pre-exilic dating of large numbers of the Psalms today, as against the earlier location of most in the post-exilic age (cf. below, pp. 176f). It is not to say that the consciousness of sin was unknown in pre-exilic days, but only that the emphasis on the ritual means of dealing with sin appears to have been much increased in post-exilic days. Much of the "sin" so dealt with was purely ritual "sin" and not moral delinquency (cf. pp. 102f above), and A. C. Welch (*The Psalter*, 1926, pp. 107f) notes that this is a very primitive conception of sin, which must have been ancient in Israel; but it was not wholly ritual "sin", and in the solemn ritual of the Day of Atonement, in particular, there seems to have been a deeper emphasis on sin than we find in earlier days. G. Nagel (in *Vocabulary of the Bible*, ed. by J. J. von Allmen, E. Tr., 1958, p. 378b) thinks it was under the influence of the prophets that the sense of sin was enormously increased.

[4] 1 Sam. 6.3, 4, 8, 17.   [5] 2 Kings 12.16 (M.T. 17).

[6] Gen. 4.7; 31.36; and frequently.

[7] G. A. Barton (*J.B.L.* xlvi, 1927, p. 82) thought both terms denoted a single sacrifice, which was first called *'āshām* and later *ḥaṭṭā'th*.

[8] M. Noth (*Leviticus*, E. Tr. by J. E. Anderson, 1965, p. 5a) is of the opinion that the word *'āshām* became specialized as a cultic technical term in two different and independent senses, one meaning "atonement"

'āshām.[1] The whole thought of this passage is sacrificial,[2] and the Servant, who is described as an unblemished man, effects for others deliverance from sin by his death. This passage seems to me to provide strong evidence for *'āshām* as a sacrificial term older than the Priestly Code.[3]

In the sin offering the fat was always burned on the altar,[4] but the blood and the flesh were differently treated according to whether the offering was on behalf of a lay individual, on the one hand, or on behalf of a priest or of the whole community, on the other. In the former case some of the blood was smeared with the finger on the horns of the altar of sacrifice and the rest was poured at its base;[5] in the latter case there was a sevenfold sprinkling of blood before the division which separated off the inner sanctuary, some was smeared on the horns of the altar of incense, and the for "false dealing" and the other meaning "guilt offering" for the purpose of ritual cleansing, and that the course followed by the guilt offering was assimilated to that of the sin offering.

[1] Isa. 53.10. W. O. E. Oesterley (*Sacrifices in Ancient Israel*, 1937, pp. 76, 232, 237f, 287) would remove the word *'āshām* from this verse, on the ground that it is out of keeping with the context. That there is corruption in the verse is generally agreed (cf. *U.B.*, 1953, p. 55 n; C. R. North, *The Suffering Servant in Deutero-Isaiah*, 2nd edn, 1956, p. 126), though T. H. Gaster (in *I.D.B.* iv, 1962, p. 152b) emphatically rejects all emendation of it. There is in any case no reason to question the word *'āshām*.

[2] Cf. *U.B.*, pp. 55f; also J. Skinner, *Isaiah xl–lxvi*, rev. edn, 1917, p. 147: "The difficulty does not lie in the analogy of the guilt-offering, for this probably signifies nothing more than has been already expressed in plain words."

[3] It was earlier held that the word *ašm* or *aṭm* in the Ras Shamra texts was a sacrificial term corresponding to *'āshām* (cf. P. Dhorme, *R.B.* xl, 1931, p. 53; J. W. Jack, *The Ras Shamra Tablets*, 1935, p. 30; W. O. E. Oesterley, op. cit., p. 76; A. Vincent, *La Religion des judéo-araméens d'Éléphantine*, 1937, p. 157; S. H. Hooke, *The Origins of Early Semitic Ritual*, 1938, p. 66; T. H. Gaster, in *Mélanges Syriens*, ii, 1939, p. 578; R. Dussaud, *Les Origines cananéennes du sacrifice israélite*, 2nd edn, 1941, pp. 327f; C. H. Gordon, *Ugaritic Handbook*, 1947, p. 46; W. F. Albright, *A.R.I.*, 3rd edn, 1953, p. 61; C. F. Pfeiffer, *Ras Shamra and the Bible*, 1962, p. 57). This is now rejected (cf. Gordon, ibid., p. 217; D. M. L. Urie, *P.E.Q.* lxxxi, 1949, p. 72; J. Gray, *Z.A.W.* lxii, 1950, pp. 210f, and *The Legacy of Canaan* (S.V.T. v), 1957, pp. 144f; T. H. Gaster, in *I.D.B.* iv, 1962, p. 152b; R. de Vaux, *Studies in Old Testament Sacrifice*, p. 111).

[4] Lev. 4.8ff, 18, 26, 31, 35.

[5] Lev. 4.25, 30, 34. On the sacrificial blood cf. J. E. Steinmueller, *Biblica*, xl, 1959, pp. 556ff.

rest was poured at the base of the altar of sacrifice.[1] As the altar of sacrifice stood outside the Temple proper, in the court, this means that in the case of a lay individual none of the blood was carried into the Temple proper, whereas in the other case some was taken there. In the case of a lay individual, the flesh went entirely to the priests, but in the case of a priest or of the community, none went to the altar or to the priests, but all was taken outside the sanctuary and burned.[2]

In the guilt offering the blood is thrown against the altar and not poured at its base.[3] The fat of the victim is burned on the altar[4] and the flesh is eaten by the priests.[5] The ritual is therefore very similar to that of the sin offering for a lay individual, except in the disposal of the blood. But with the guilt offering something more than the animal sacrifice is always involved. There must always be some payment in addition.[6] Hence de Vaux calls it a reparation sacrifice[7] and Snaith a compensation offering.[8] Where the property or rights of another have been infringed, compensation amounting to the value of the injury plus one fifth must be paid. It is clear that there must have been some distinction between the sin offering and the guilt offering, since they involved diverse rituals, but it is extremely difficult to distinguish between them in our present texts, and some scholars give up all attempts to do so,[9] while those who do attempt it reach quite different conclusions.[10]

[1] Lev. 4.6f, 17f.   [2] Lev. 4.9ff, 21.   [3] Lev. 7.2.
[4] Lev. 7.4f.   [5] Lev. 7.8.   [6] Lev. 5.16.
[7] Cf. *Studies in Old Testament Sacrifice*, p. 98.
[8] Cf. Manson's *Companion to the Bible*, 2nd edn, p. 531; *V.T.* xv, 1965, p. 80.
[9] Cf. L. Aubert, in Westphal's *Dictionnaire encyclopédique de la Bible*, ii, 1935, p. 605a; J. Pedersen, *Israel III–IV*, 1940, pp. 372f; R. de Vaux, *Studies in Old Testament Sacrifice*, 1964, pp. 100ff; Š. Porúbčan, *Sin in the Old Testament*, 1963, pp. 334ff. L. Koehler (*Old Testament Theology*, E. Tr., p. 189) holds, rightly in the present writer's view, that the two types of sacrifices have lost what original distinction they may have had.
[10] For a full survey of older views cf. J. H. Kurtz, *Sacrificial Worship of the Old Testament*, E. Tr. by J. Martin, 1863, pp. 189–213. W. P. Paterson (in Hastings' *D.B.* iv, 1902, p. 338) notes the suggestions (a) that the sin offering was for sins of omission and the guilt offering for sins of commission, (b) that the sin offering was to avert punishment and the guilt offering to appease the conscience, and (c) that the sin offering was for open sins and the guilt offering for secret sins (cf. Josephus, *Ant.* III. ix. 3 (230–2)).

By some the sin offering is thought to have been called for only by involuntary acts, while the guilt offering would be called for by voluntary or involuntary acts which involved some assessable injury.[1] This is difficult to press, however. For after childbirth a woman was required to make a sin offering.[2] This could hardly be thought of as involuntary.[3] In the case of a cleansed leper[4] and in

[1] Cf. A. Vincent, *La Religion des judéo-araméens d'Éléphantine*, 1937, p. 156. P. R. Saydon (*C.B.Q.* viii, 1946, pp. 393ff) contrasts them as sins into which a man falls more or less consciously through frailty and sins into which he falls unintentionally or through ignorance. It is hard to see how the sin of Lev. 19.20f could fit into this. Many scholars emphasize the element of reparation as the distinguishing feature of the *'āshām*. Thus L. Moraldi (*Rivista Biblica*, ix, 1961, pp. 294f; cf. *Espiazione sacrificale e riti espiatori*, 1956, pp. 159ff) holds that the one involves expiation and the other reparation. Similarly Paterson (loc. cit.) says the sin offering was for the cases where reparation could be made (cf. G. B. Gray, *Sacrifice in the Old Testament*, 1925, p. 58). Against this T. H. Gaster (in *I.D.B.* iv, 1962, p. 152) maintains that the sin offering and the guilt offering were utterly distinct, but says the latter was not a vehicle of rehabilitation but a fine. Of other views a few may be mentioned. R. Dussaud (*Les Origines cananéennes du sacrifice israélite*, 2nd edn, 1941, p. 350) holds that the sin offering was for a simple breach of ritual, while the guilt offering was called for where there had been the infringement of the rights of others. G. F. Moore (in *E.B.* iv, 1903, cols. 4203f) says the guilt offering was limited to cases involving the unlawful appropriation of another's property (cf. A. Médebielle, in *S.D.B.* iii, 1938, cols. 60f, where the guilt offering is said to be required where there has been the infringement of the property rights of God or man; cf. also A. R. S. Kennedy, in Hastings' one volume *D.B.*, 1909, p. 816b, and J. Heuschen, in *Dictionnaire encyclopédique de la Bible*, 1960, col. 1646). H. Cazelles (*Lévitique*, 2nd edn, 1958, p. 12) distinguishes the sin offering as the infringement of the rights of man from the guilt offering as the infringement of the rights of God. R. J. Thompson, on the other hand, says (in *N.B.D.*, 1962, p. 1120b) that sins against the neighbour are more prominent in the *'āshām* and those against God in the *ḥaṭṭā'th*. H. C. Thomson (*T.G.U.O.S.* xiv, 1953, pp. 20ff) maintains that the *'āshām* "is concerned with deliberate offences as well as sins of ignorance, with sins against God as well as against man, and with cases where a life seems to be forfeit because of guilt or ritual error. It is to some extent substitutionary and expiatory as well as compensatory, and is offered both by individuals and also by the people or their representative."

[2] Lev. 12.6, 8.

[3] This alone is sufficient to disprove the statement of G. Nagel, in *Vocabulary of the Bible*, ed. by J. J. von Allmen, 1958, p. 379b: "It is of course entirely a question of unwitting faults."

[4] Lev. 14.1–32.

that of a Nazirite[1] who has contracted impurity both a sin offering and a guilt offering were prescribed. It is very difficult to see how assessable injury was involved in either of these cases.

It is undeniable that "sin" is given a purely ritual meaning where the sin is unavoidable and involuntary, and equally in such a case as childbirth. For there was no breach of any moral law in such cases. Children were highly valued in Israel as God's gifts, and in a passage which stands in the Priestly document we are told that God's first command to man was to be fruitful and multiply.[2] The sin offering after childbirth was not for the removal of any moral lapse, therefore, but purely to fit the mother ritually to take her place in the community of God's people once more. The "sin" of the leper was probably similarly ritual. His offerings were not the means of removing any supposed sin which had caused the leprosy, since they were not offered until he had been cleansed, and therefore until any such supposed sin had been forgiven.

Such a conception of "sin" is very ancient, yet it persists in the latest strands of Israelite law and is very prominent there. While we may allow that the purpose of those who framed that law was to foster a sense of horror at even the slightest thing that could be displeasing to God, we must equally recognize the danger of confusing the ritual and the moral. Where "sin" was unwitting or unconscious or wholly ritual there could not be any true repentance, and the ritual cleansing could only be thought of as automatic. This could only tend to make men think of all sacrificial acts as automatic in their effects. This was the attitude which the great pre-exilic prophets condemned, and it was equally far from the mind of the framers of the Priestly law.

It has long been a widespread view that the eighth- and seventh-century prophets were inflexibly opposed to the whole sacrificial cultus.[3] It is quite clear that they were inflexibly opposed to what

---

[1] Num. 6.9ff.   [2] Gen. 1.28.

[3] Cf. J. Wellhausen, *Prolegomena to the History of Israel*, E. Tr., 1885, p. 423; E. Kautzsch, in Hastings' *D.B.* v, 1904, p. 686b; J. A. Bewer, *The Literature of the Old Testament*, 1922, p. 267; J. Skinner, *Prophecy and Religion*, 1922, p. 181; C. R. North, *E.T.* xlvii, 1935–6, p. 252b; E. A. Leslie, *Old Testament Religion*, 1936, pp. 170f; Oesterley and Robinson, *Hebrew Religion*, 1937, p. 232; P. Volz, *Prophetengestalten des Alten Testaments*, 1938, p. 19, and *Z.S.T.* xiv, 1937, pp. 63ff; S. Herner, *Sühne und Vergebung in Israel*, 1942, pp. 30f; L. Waterman, *Religion faces the*

they saw around them, but a growing number of scholars to-day would say that what they condemned was the hollowness of the sacrifices of their day rather than the cultus *per se*.[1] They saw men offering splendid sacrifices yet violating the law of God in their lives, and condemned the worship because it was not the expression of the real spirit of the worshippers. To honour God in word but not in deed was not to honour him at all, and he who penetrated to the hearts of men must repudiate their meaningless worship. For such a view I have argued elsewhere,[2] and I cannot repeat that here.

What must relevantly be repeated here is that where any moral offence had been committed, the framers of the law did not suppose that the ritual act could have meaning unless it were the organ of the spirit of the worshipper, and therefore accompanied by his true repentance and the making of amends where this was possible. He who offered a sin offering or a guilt offering was required to confess his offence. The Law says: "It shall be, when he shall be guilty in one of these things, that he shall confess that

World Crisis, 1943, pp. 56, 68; J. P. Hyatt, *Prophetic Religion*, 1947, p. 127; I. G. Matthews, *The Religious Pilgrimage of Israel*, 1947, p. 128; V. Maag, *Text, Wortschatz und Begriffswelt des Buches Amos*, 1951, pp. 225f; L. Koehler, *Old Testament Theology*, E. Tr., 1957, pp. 181ff.

[1] Cf. A. C. Welch, *Prophet and Priest in Old Israel*, 1936, pp. 17f; W. O. E. Oesterley, *Sacrifices in Ancient Israel*, 1937, pp. 208, 213; J. M. Powis Smith, *The Prophets and their Times*, 2nd edn, rev. by W. A. Irwin, 1941, p. 62; H. W. Robinson, *J.T.S.* xliii, 1942, p. 137, *Redemption and Revelation*, 1942, p. 250, and *Inspiration and Revelation in the Old Testament*, 1946, p. 226; J. E. Coleran, *Theological Studies*, v, 1944, pp. 437f; P. S. Minear, *Eyes of Faith*, 1946, p. 22; J. Paterson, *The Goodly Fellowship of the Prophets*, 1948, p. 27; N. W. Porteous, *E.T.* lxii, 1950–1, pp. 4ff (cf. in *Tradition and Situation* (Weiser Festschrift), 1963, pp. 93ff); T. C. Chary, *Les Prophètes et le Culte*, 1957, pp. 284ff; B. W. Anderson, *Understanding the Old Testament*, 1957, pp. 460f; R. Martin-Achard, in *Vocabulary of the Bible*, ed. by J. J. von Allmen, E. Tr., 1958, p. 473a; E. Jacob, *Theology of the Old Testament*, E. Tr. by A. W. Heathcote and P. J. Allcock, 1958, p. 176, and *R.H.P.R.* xxxix, 1959, p. 294; P. van Imschoot, in *Dictionnaire encyclopédique de la Bible*, 1960, cols. 1640f; R. de Vaux, *A.I.*, p. 384; W. Eichrodt, *Theology of the Old Testament*, E. Tr., i, 1961, pp. 364f; C. Hauret, in *Vocabulaire de Théologie biblique*, ed. by X. Léon-Dufour, 1962, col. 971; E. Würthwein in *Tradition und Situation* (Weiser Festschrift), 1963, pp. 115ff; R. E. Clements, *Prophecy and Covenant*, 1965, pp. 95, 100.

[2] Cf. *B.J.R.L.* xxix, 1945–6, pp. 326ff; *B.J.R.L.* xxxiii, 1950–1, pp. 74ff (reprinted in *M.G.*, 1963, pp. 67ff); *U.B.*, 1953, pp. 30ff.

wherein he hath sinned; and he shall bring his forfeit unto the
Lord for his sin which he hath sinned . . . and the priest shall
make atonement for him as concerning his sin."[1] Or again:
"When a man or woman shall commit any sin that men commit . . .
then they shall confess their sin which they have done; and he
shall make restitution for his guilt in full, and add unto it the fifth
part thereof, and give it unto him in respect of whom he hath been
guilty."[2] When the High Priest offered the sacrifice on the Day
of Atonement he made confession of the sin of the community as
its representative before he offered the sacrifice for its forgiveness.[3] When any man offered a burnt offering or a peace offering,
he laid his hand upon the head of the animal[4] to symbolize his
identification of himself with it,[5] so that its death might symbolize
the removal of whatever stood between him and God, or his
surrender of himself to God in gratitude and loyalty.

We have no right to suppose that to the framers of the law these
were meaningless forms, whose validity derived merely from the
act and not from the spirit. We should ask how these laws of post-
exilic Judaism were understood in the Judaism of that and later
ages. In Proverbs we read: "The sacrifice of the wicked is an
abomination to the Lord."[6] This does not suggest that it was
thought to have automatic power. Ben Sira said: "The sacrifice of
an unrighteous man is a mockery, and the offerings of the wicked
are not acceptable."[7] In the Mishnah tractate on the Day of

[1] Lev. 5.5f.   [2] Num. 5.6f.
[3] Lev. 16.21.   [4] Lev. 1.4; 3.2, 8, 13, etc.
[5] Cf. J. Pedersen, *Israel III–IV*, 1940, p. 366: "By this act he establishes
the fact that the animal is his property. It belongs to his sphere, and when
it is sanctified, the sanctification primarily affects him"; H. W. Robinson,
J.T.S. xliii, 1942, p. 130: "The natural meaning of the laying of hands on
the sacrifice is the closer identification of the offerer with his offering."
[6] Prov. 21.27. In Prov. 15.8 we find this saying repeated, but with a
different parallel line: "The sacrifice of the wicked is an abomination to
the Lord: But the prayer of the upright is his delight." That the spirit is
more important than the act of worship is here unmistakably declared.
[7] Sir. 34.18 (31.21f). R.V. renders "He that sacrificeth of a thing
wrongfully gotten, his offering is made in mockery; and the mockeries of
wicked men are not well-pleasing"; R.S.V. "If one sacrifices from what
has been wrongfully obtained, the offering is blemished; the gifts of the
lawless are not acceptable." The Syriac version has "The sacrifices of the
unrighteous are unrighteous, and the offerings of the wicked are not
acceptable." The rendering given above in part follows this (cf. now the
text of J. Ziegler, *Sapientia Jesu Filii Sirach*, 1965, p. 285). Box and

Atonement we read: "If a man say, I will sin and repent, I will sin again and repent, he will be given no chance to repent. If he say, I will sin and the Day of Atonement will clear me, the Day of Atonement will effect no atonement."[1] Here it is specifically stated that deliberate, premeditated sin cannot be cleared by any sacrifice. This is in full accord with what we find in the Law, where it is said that high-handed sins could not be cleansed by any sacrifice.[2] This does not merely refer to acts knowingly committed, for many acts knowingly committed were provided for in the Law. This means acts committed of set purpose, knowingly and defiantly committed, as distinct from sins committed in moments of weakness.[3] Where provision was made for cleansing by sacrifice, repentance was equally a requirement. In the Talmud we read: "Sin offering and guilt offering and death and the Day of Atonement all put together do not effect atonement without repentance."[4]

That repentance is of greater importance than sacrifice is shown by the fact that in cases for which no sacrifice was prescribed true repentance might lead to forgiveness. No sacrifices are prescribed for such sins as murder or adultery. David, who was guilty of adultery with Bathsheba and of the death of Uriah, was rebuked by Nathan and his conscience was touched into genuine repentance.[5] And Nathan said: "The Lord also hath put away thy sin."[6] No act of sacrifice is recorded; for none was relevant. The spirit is of more importance than any ritual act. This was stated in an utterance ascribed to Samuel: "Hath the Lord as great delight in burnt offerings and sacrifices as in obeying the voice of the Lord? Behold, to obey is better than sacrifice, and to hearken than

Oesterley (in Charles's *Apocrypha and Pseudepigrapha*, i, 1913, p. 435) render: "The sacrifice of the unrighteous man is a mocking offering; and unacceptable are the oblations of the godless."

[1] *Yoma* viii.9. Cf. H. Danby, *The Mishnah*, 1933, p. 172.
[2] Num. 15.30f.
[3] Cf. *M.Q.*, 1963, p. 94: "It is a distinction between sins which a man commits through ignorance or through weakness, or willy-nilly, and those which he commits because they are the expression of his real nature, arising out of the essential purpose of his heart." Cf. also A. B. Davidson, *The Theology of the Old Testament*, 1904, pp. 315f; A. Médebielle, in *S.D.B.* iii, 1938, col. 74. G. Nagel (in *Vocabulary of the Bible*, ed. by J. J. von Allmen, 1958, p. 379b) identifies high-handed sins with voluntary sins.
[4] Tosephta, *Yoma* v.9 (ed. M. S. Zuckermandel, 2nd edn, 1937, p. 190).
[5] 2 Sam. 12.13.   [6] Ibid.

the fat of rams."[1] The religion which from the days of Moses was an ethical religion, concerned not alone for the act but for the spirit which lay behind it, continued to be an ethical religion and to be concerned for the spirit. However this may have been forgotten in popular religion, which was admittedly so much contaminated by Canaanite influence, the true religion of Yahwism never lost this character, and there were always voices recalling men to the inner principles of their faith.[2]

It is probable that the ritual acts were accompanied by the recital of liturgical texts which explained the meaning of the acts,[3] and these would enable all sensitive spirits to enter into the meaning of the acts and make them the vehicle of their spirit. As A. C. Welch pointed out many years ago, a ritual act might be substantially repeated but given a new significance by a new liturgical text.[4] We have already noted a liturgical text which gave a new meaning to the Passover ritual.[5] In Yahweh worship the liturgical texts would relate the act to the God of Israel, and whatever corruptions may have invaded the Jerusalem Temple, it always continued to be a Yahweh shrine, and doubtless used liturgical texts which invoked his name. In Deut. 26.1ff we have a liturgical text for use when firstfruits were brought to the sanctuary, and this was designed to make the bringing of the firstfruits a genuine sacrament and to call forth from the worshipper the spirit of gratitude and consecration of himself which the firstfruits themselves symbolized.[6] Here we may pause to note

---

[1] 1 Sam. 15.22. Cf. Eccles. 5.1.
[2] Cf. A. B. Davidson, *The Theology of the Old Testament*, 1904, p. 315: "It (i.e. sacrifice) is an institution provided of God for sins committed *within* the covenant." Cf. also G. Nagel, in *Vocabulary of the Bible*, ed. by J. J. von Allmen, 1956, p. 379b; R. J. Thompson, *Sacrifice and Penitence in Early Israel*, 1963, p. 9.
[3] That liturgical texts accompanied the sacrifice in the Chronicler's day would seem to be apparent from 2 Chron. 29.27ff.
[4] Cf. *Prophet and Priest in Old Israel*, 1936, pp. 112ff.
[5] Cf. above, p. 118.
[6] Cf. Welch, op. cit., pp. 112, 116ff. On this passage cf. G. von Rad, *The Problem of the Hexateuch and Other Essays*, E.Tr., pp. 3ff; H. Cazelles, *R.B.* lv, 1948, pp. 54ff; A. Weiser, *Introduction to the Old Testament*, E. Tr., pp. 83ff; L. Rost, *Das kleine Credo und andere Studien*, 1965, pp. 11ff; H. B. Huffmon, *C.B.Q.* xxvii, 1965, pp. 101ff. For a criticism of the view of von Rad cf. T. C. Vriezen, in *Studies on the Psalms*, 1963, pp. 5ff.

that not all the ritual of the Temple was concerned with animal sacrifice and its cereal accompaniments. These firstfruits[1] were brought to God because they were recognized to be his. They were not the worshipper's gifts to God. The fruits of the earth were acknowledged to be God's gifts to man, and they were only rightly to be enjoyed by man when he had first brought to God what God ordained should be brought.[2]

Other non-sacrificial offerings were tithes and freewill offerings of substance. There is no law of tithes in the pre-Deuteronomic law, though in Genesis we read that Abraham paid tithes of his spoil from the battle to Melchizedek[3] and that Jacob at Bethel pledged himself to pay tithes to God if he returned in peace.[4] According to the law of Deuteronomy the tithe was to be brought to the central sanctuary, and there to be enjoyed by those who brought it or dispensed in charity, especially to the Levite.[5] According to the Priestly Law it was to be paid to the Levites, who in their turn paid a tenth of it to the priests.[6] The freewill offerings of substance that were brought to the Temple appear to have been enjoyed by its priesthood at one time, but from the time of Joash they were devoted to the repair of the Temple.[7] They were placed in a chest, which could only be opened by the priests in the presence of the king's officers. At the time of the repair of the Temple in the reign of Josiah this arrangement was still in force.[8]

To what extent liturgical texts were used to accompany the sacrificial rites of the Temple can only be conjectured, but it is widely thought that in the Psalter there are preserved texts which were so used.[9] This view seems to me to be highly

---

[1] On firstfruits cf. O. Eissfeldt, *Erstlinge und Zehnten im Alten Testament*, 1917.

[2] Cf. J. Pedersen, *Israel III–IV*, 1940, p. 304: "He acquires the full right to use the crops when he has given Yahweh his share."

[3] Gen. 14.20. R. H. Smith (*Z.A.W.* lxxvii, 1965, p. 134) suggests improbably that in the original form of the story Abraham was the aggressor against Melchizedek, and it was the latter who paid tithes to Abraham.

[4] Gen. 28.22.   [5] Deut. 14.22–9.   [6] Num. 18.21–32.

[7] Cf. 2 Kings 12.4ff (M.T. 5ff).   [8] 2 Kings 22.3ff.

[9] In a paper published in *Theologisch Tijdschrift* in 1919 (pp. 95ff) and reissued in *Semietische Studiën uit de nalatenschap van A. J. Wensinck*, 1941, pp. 51ff, A. J. Wensinck put forward this view; cf. p. 57 (*Theologisch Tijdschrift*, p. 102): "My thesis is that, for the greater part, the Psalms are spoken rhythmic illustrations of the acts of worship; just as

probable,[1] and it is the view which I am presenting in this book. More than forty years ago Mowinckel propounded the view that the psalms were such liturgical texts and that they were essential to the ritual in the sense that unless the right text accompanied the rite it was invalid.[2] Many of them, he thought, were designed to break magical spells which the worshipper believed to have been cast on him by his enemies.[3] A. C. Welch related them more closely to the known liturgical texts already mentioned, and thought they were designed to help the worshipper to enter into the meaning of the ritual act, and so to make the act his act of worship in a meaningful way.[4] He suggested that Psalm 114 was a hymn for Passover, which might have been chanted in the Temple when the lambs were being slaughtered by the priests or sung in the home when the lamb was eaten,[5] and that the penitential psalms may have accompanied offerings for the expiation of sin.[6] More than twenty years ago I wrote that "I can think of nothing more

the musical part of the Catholic Mass is an illustration and a rhythmization of the ritual acts." In 1922 J. P. Peters (*The Psalms as Liturgies*) argued for the view that the Psalms were liturgical texts composed to accompany the ritual of the sanctuary. In the same year J. M. Powis Smith (*J.R.* ii, 1922, pp. 58ff) presented a similar view, arguing that the Psalms provided a "rhythmization of the acts of the ritual", and that they were sung to accompany the sacrifices.

[1] In *B.J.R.L.* xxix, 1945–6, p. 29, I wrote: "I think it is truer to say that particular psalms accompanied particular ritual acts, as both the necessary accompaniment and interpretation of the rite, . . . in order that the psalm might evoke the appropriate spirit from the worshipper, and so make the rite in a very real sense the organ of his worship."

[2] Cf. *Psalmenstudien I–VI*, 1921–4. In *Psalmenstudien III*, 1923, he argued for the association of cultic prophets with the priests in the utterance of these ritual texts. On the use of the Psalms in the cult, cf. also A. Weiser, *Festschrift für Alfred Bertholet*, 1950, pp. 513ff (reprinted in *Glaube und Geschichte im Alten Testament*, 1961, pp. 303ff). Cf. H. Bückers, *Biblica*, xxxii, 1951, pp. 401ff.

[3] Cf. *Psalmenstudien I*, 1921. Cf. below, pp. 182f.

[4] Cf. *The Psalter in Life, Worship and History*, 1926; also *Prophet and Priest in Old Israel*, 1936, pp. 131ff. Cf. also N. W. Porteous, *Interpretation*, iii, 1949, pp. 404f. In 1913 H. W. Robinson (*Religious Ideas of the Old Testament*, p. 150), without suggesting that the Psalms were used to accompany ritual acts, said: "No just view of Jewish religion can be gained by any one who does not see the Psalter written, so to speak, in parallel columns with the Book of Leviticus." Cf. in Manson's *Companion to the Bible*, 1939, p. 304.

[5] Cf. *Prophet and Priest in Old Israel*, p. 132.   [6] Ibid., p. 133.

appropriate or more effective than Psalm 51 to make the worshipper realize that his offering was of less significance than the spirit in which he brought it, or to call forth from him that spirit of penitence which would make the cry of his offering the genuine cry of his heart, that his offering might be at once the organ of his approach to God, and of God's approach in grace to him".[1] I shall return to a fuller consideration of the Psalms in a later chapter. But it is necessary to say so much here, that we may guard against the thought of the worship of the Temple as being wholly and necessarily and designedly an arid agglomeration of ceremonies, in which all that mattered was the ritual act. To quote Welch again: "The significance of the cult, according to these hymns, rested, not on the rite *per se*, but on the character of Him who had commanded it, and on the attitude of those who fulfilled it."[2]

This seems to me of great importance for the understanding of the Old Testament as a whole. Many of the older treatments held the pre-exilic prophets to be creative exponents of spiritual religion, who had no use for the Temple or its ritual, and who would gladly have seen religion stripped of all its forms. On the other hand, they regarded the Law, and especially in its formulation in the Priestly Code, to be the embodiment of all that the prophets abhorred.[3] The Psalter was left as an erratic block, not very clearly related to either of the others.[4] On this view it is hard to see who could have brought the whole together to form the Old Testament. It had to press certain passages in the Law and the Prophets and pass lightly over others. That there were differences of emphasis in Law and Prophets is both undeniable and

[1] Cf. *B.J.R.L.* xxix, 1945–6, pp. 29f.

[2] Cf. *Prophet and Priest in Old Israel*, p. 133.

[3] Cf. P. Volz, *Prophetengestalten des Alten Testaments*, 1938, p. 19 (cited above, p. 2); E. Kautzsch, in Hastings' *D.B.* v, 1904, p. 723a: "The gulf between the religion of the Prophets and that of the Priests' Code has been described as one that cannot be bridged. That there is, in fact, a deep gulf between the two, and that this shows itself in P in the shape of a falling away from the pure level reached by the Prophets, are truths that need be denied all the less, seeing that the teaching of Jesus certainly attached itself to the prophets, and would have the Law interpreted only in their sense and spirit."

[4] Kautzsch (ibid., p. 686b) thinks that the Psalms which reflect the prophetic view only found their way into the collection by being given a forced interpretation.

natural, since they were designed for such different purposes. But that they were fundamentally at cross-purposes fails to explain their collection in a single Canon. The understanding of the Psalter as a collection of liturgical texts which were used to accompany the ritual acts of Temple worship seems to me to provide a valuable link between the Law and the Prophets. As S. Terrien observes: "Alone in the Bible, the psalmists have succeeded in unifying the prophetic and the priestly approaches to religion."[1] N. W. Porteous well says: "It must never be forgotten that the clue to the meaning of what Israel did in her religious practice is to be found reflected in the Psalter. It is quite unlikely that these ancient Hebrew hymns which have inspired so much that is best in Christian worship should have originally, many of them, been composed to accompany a ritual which did not represent a genuine synthesis of the religious and the ethical. To suppose anything else is to suppose that the Psalms were fundamentally irrelevant to the ritual setting to which they originally belonged. In other words, the evidence of the Psalter must be allowed to qualify the evidence of the prophets."[2]

With all this, we must fully recognize that the worship of the Temple was believed to have potency.[3] Blessings and curses were believed to have a potency far greater than we should to-day attribute to them.[4] Once spoken, they were believed to have a power to work for their own fulfilment, and once they had been

[1] Cf. *The Psalms and their Meaning for Today*, 1952, p. 269. Cf. S. Mowinckel, in *I.D.B.* iii, 1962, p. 142: "The religion of the Psalms is the spiritual background of the prophets, who always stood in close connection with the Temple and the cult."

[2] Cf. *Interpretation*, iii, 1949, pp. 404f.

[3] Cf. A. S. Herbert, *Worship in Ancient Israel*, 1959, p. 23: "It is perhaps significant that the Holiness Code with its emphasis on the ritual of the Temple includes the statements of Yahweh's ritual and moral requirements in chapter 26. Yet granted the right spirit, the sacrifice was believed to be effective."

[4] Cf. J. Pedersen, *Israel I–II*, 1926, p. 200: "The act of blessing another means to communicate to him strength of soul, but one can communicate to him only of the strength one has in oneself. He who blesses another gives him something of his own soul"; p. 441: "Just as a man may utter the blessing into the soul of another, thus he can also utter the curse into it. . . . The power of the curse is not *per se* implied in the wish or the word. It lies in the mysterious power of the souls to react upon each other." Cf. also S. Mowinckel, *Psalmenstudien V*, 1924. On the curse cf. H. C. Brichto, *The Problem of "Curse" in the Hebrew Bible*, 1963.

uttered, they had gone beyond the control of those who uttered them. When Isaac had been tricked into pronouncing on Jacob the blessing he had designed for Esau, he could not call it back.[1] Similarly, the words of the prophets were believed to have power in themselves to work for their fulfilment.[2] This power they possessed, not in virtue of having been spoken by the prophets, but in virtue of the fact that their source was God. It is true that many of the prophets are charged with speaking words which have no deeper source than their own hearts,[3] and Micaiah declared that Zedekiah the son of Chenaanah spoke words which were put into his mouth by a lying spirit.[4] But this does not alter the fact that true prophecy was believed to be inspired by God. That was why those we recognize as true prophets so strongly denounced the false prophets. It was impossible for the hearer to distinguish the true prophecy from the false, and hence men were deceived into ascribing potency to what really lacked it.[5]

In the same way, the ritual act, when it was all that it should be, that is, when it was correct not only in its form but in the spirit that was brought to it by the worshipper, was believed to be potent. It was charged with a power which derived from God, and it was believed to have that power because God had so ordained. It could not be wrested from God by one whose heart was far from him; but it could be claimed by one who approached him in the right spirit. Wheeler Robinson wrote: "That the personal act of sacrifice was generally regarded as doing something, i.e. as efficacious, hardly needs demonstration. This is implied, on the one hand, in the detailed attention given to sacrifice in the Old Testament. This would be meaningless unless

[1] Gen. 27.37.

[2] Cf. Isa. 45.23; 55.10ff. Cf. T. C. Vriezen, *Outline of Old Testament Theology*, E. Tr., p. 94: "We must keep in mind that the term *dabar* in Hebrew is much more dynamic and concrete than its Western equivalent *word. Dabar* is something concrete, living, it *comes to* the prophets." Cf. also G. von Rad, *Old Testament Theology*, E. Tr., ii, 1965, pp. 80ff.

[3] Cf. Jer. 14.14; 23.32.

[4] 1 Kings 22.20ff.

[5] Cf. A. Lods, *The Prophets and the Rise of Judaism*, E. Tr. by S. H. Hooke, 1938, p. 59: "The great prophets knew of no exterior sign by which the genuinely inspired of Yahweh could be distinguished"; J. Skinner, *Prophecy and Religion*, 1922, p. 188: "In externals there was nothing to distinguish the one kind of prophet from the other."

sacrifices were meaningful, to a degree far beyond a figurative and merely declaratory symbolism."[1]

This was probably particularly true in the case of involuntary and unwitting sins, where there could be no real penitence and the duly performed ritual would be thought to have potency in itself.[2] Where there was a consciousness of wrong done, and the confession sprang from a sense of guilt and of penitence, the sacrifice would again be thought to be potent. In the case of a thank offering it could hardly be thought to do anything for the worshipper, since there was nothing to be done. He was expressing his gratitude to God for what he, God, had done. Where the worshipper came with a plea, the sacrifice was believed to have potency as the expression of the earnestness of his desire for right relations with God and therefore for God's blessing; but he was never encouraged by the true leaders of Israel's religion to think that he was entitled to what he asked for. God was not to be coerced by magic,[3] and the note of pleading in the psalms of petition sufficiently indicates that the worshipper was not encouraged to think he was entitled to command God's gifts.

The view of sacrifice which I have here presented seems to me to make sense of the teaching of the Old Testament. It does not seek to minimize the danger of the elevation of the inadvertent ritual incurrence of impurity to the level of "sin", or to forget that the effect of this on insensitive souls could be to reduce the level of real sin, in the sense of disobedience to the will of God in life and the denial of the brotherhood which should bind all God's people together, to the level of the involuntary and the trivial.[4]

[1] Cf. *J.T.S.* xliii, 1942, p. 131.

[2] Cf. *M.Q.*, p. 98: "It must be recognized that there was peril in the Law's emphasis on unwitting sin and provision of sacrifices for its cleansing, since it is undeniable that unwitting sin could mean, and often did mean, sins committed in ignorance or involuntarily, and especially ritual rather than moral offences. . . . Hence, the evils against which the prophets had protested were not wholly guarded against, and while at its best Judaism was spiritually sensitive, at its worst it became a mere externalism."

[3] Cf. H. W. Robinson, *J.T.S.* xliii, 1942, p. 132: "Magic constrains the unseen; religion means surrender to it."

[4] In some of the Mishnah tractates we find this concern for the technical and the trivial, and in the New Testament the scribes and Pharisees are condemned for their preoccupation with such things. Cf. J. Klausner, *Jesus of Nazareth*, E. Tr. by H. Danby, 1925, p. 216: "The

But it recognizes that the purpose of the ritual with its accompanying liturgy was to foster penitence, thanksgiving, adoration, devotion, and humble surrender and consecration to God, and it brings the Law, the Prophets, and the Psalms together into a natural synthesis.[1] R. J. Thompson says, in words to which I can subscribe: "While not accepting the view, on the one hand, that the efficacy of sacrifice was limited to inadvertent sins, which were no real sins at all, or, on the other, that the prophets and pious psalmists saw no value in sacrifice whatsoever, it remains true that the cult was liable to abuse, when the inward tie between worshipper and means of worship was loosed, and prophetic religion became necessary to emphasize the priority of a personal relation to God. It is no accident, however, that when priestly and prophetic religion meet in the figure of the Servant of the Lord in Isaiah 53 the highest point of Old Testament religion is reached, as all that is valuable in cult is taken up into a person, who both makes a sacrificial atonement and calls for the love and personal allegiance of the human heart."[2] It would fall outside my subject to speak of the Servant here, since the guilt-offering of the Servant did not lie within the Temple or fall within the Old Testament cultus, though I have elsewhere underlined the significance of that passage as bringing Law and Prophets together in a synthesis which pointed to the transcendence of both in a sacrifice which should supersede all the sacrifices of the cultus and be more widely efficacious than any of them, and which should once more offer its power only to those who made it the organ of their

casuistry and immense theoretical care devoted to every one of the slightest religious ordinances left them open to the misconception that the ceremonial laws were the main principle and the ethical laws only secondary." To be fair to Pharisaism its aim was to exalt the trivial to the level of the important. Cf. the saying of Rabbi Judah the Prince (*Pirke Aboth* ii.1, in H. Danby's translation of *The Mishnah*, 1933, p. 447): "Be heedful of a light precept as of a weighty one." But inevitably the exaltation of the trivial to the level of the important could lead to the equation of trivial and important and therefore to the idea that the important was only trivial.

[1] Cf. E. Hammershaimb, *Some Aspects of Old Testament Prophecy*, 1966, p. 66; cf. also p. 35: "The chief deficiency of the older method [of the study of the Psalms] lay in its failure to recognize that many—I will not say all—of the psalms gained in meaning when one endeavoured to see them in connection with the services held in the pre-exilic temple."

[2] Cf. *N.B.D.*, 1962, p. 1122a.

approach to God.[1] It is in this last respect that it brings support to the view of sacrifice which I have presented. For the efficacy of the sacrifice of the Servant was only for those who brought to it their penitence and made it the organ of their approach to God, saying: "He was wounded for our transgressions, he was bruised for our iniquities: the chastisement of our peace was upon him; and with his stripes we are healed."[2] It is not thought of as automatically effective, independently of the spirit of those to whom it brought blessing. It must be the organ of the approach of men to God in the sincerity of their confession before it could be the organ of God's approach to them in delivering them from their iniquity and in restoring them to righteousness. In the sacrifices of the Temple I find a similar requirement for them to be the organ of the spirit of the offerer before they can be the organ of God's blessing upon him.

[1] Cf. *U.B.*, 1953, pp. 54ff, 104ff; *M.Q.*, 1963, pp. 100ff.
[2] Isa. 53.5.

5

The Prophets and the Cult

Few subjects of Old Testament study have undergone greater change in the present century than that of the Old Testament prophets. It was once the fashion to concentrate attention on the major prophets of whom we have records, and to treat them as preachers of righteousness who had little or no interest in the cult until post-exilic days, when a lesser breed of prophets arose, with an interest in the Temple and its sacrifices.[1] It was recognized that there were other prophets, the false prophets,[2] but these were largely left on one side. There was the recognition that prophecy was not confined to Israel, but was also found in the surrounding area, as the story of Wen-Amon[3] and the account of the prophets of Baal with whom Elijah contended showed.[4]

To-day all this is changed. We have more knowledge of prophecy outside Israel,[5] and a closer study of the greater figures of

---

[1] R. E. Clements (*Prophecy and Covenant*, 1965, p. 15) well observes that writers of this school did the prophets a disservice by claiming too much for them.

[2] On the false prophets cf. G. von Rad, *Z.A.W.* li, 1933, pp. 109ff; K. Harms, *Die falschen Propheten*, 1947; G. Quell, *Wahre und falsche Propheten*, 1952; E. Osswald, *Falsche Prophetie im Alten Testament*, 1962.

[3] Cf. *A.N.E.T.*, pp. 25ff.   [4] 1 Kings 18.20ff.

[5] Cf. A. Lods, in *Studies in Old Testament Prophecy*, (T. H. Robinson Festschrift), 1950, pp. 103ff; M. Noth, *B.J.R.L.* xxxii, 1949–50, pp. 194–206, and *Geschichte und Gotteswort im Alten Testament*, 1950 (reprinted in *Gesammelte Studien*, 1957, pp. 230ff); F. M. Th. de Liagre Böhl, *Ned.T.T.* iv, 1949–50, pp. 82ff, and *Opera Minora*, 1953, pp. 63ff, W. von Soden, *W.O.* i, 1947–52, pp. 397ff; H. Schmökel, *Th.L.Z.* lxxvi, 1950, cols. 54ff; N. H. Ridderbos, *Israëls Profetie en "Profetie" buiten Israël*, 1955; and A. Malamat, *Eretz-Israel*, iv, 1956, pp. 74ff, v, 1958, pp. 67ff. H. M. Orlinsky (*Oriens Antiquus*, iv, 1965, p. 170) says: "It is divination, and not prophecy, that finds its parallels in the Mari and other social structures and documents in the Fertile Crescent of old."

pre-exilic prophecy has softened the sharpness of the contrast between prophet and priest which older scholars maintained. This does not mean any lessening of appreciation of the great prophets of the eighth and seventh centuries B.C. or of their contribution to the development of Israelite religion. They were once regarded as the originators of all that was good in the faith of Israel, and were held to be the creators of ethical monotheism[1] and the source of the Decalogue.[2] Moses was denied any prophetic character, despite the fact that our oldest sources describe him as a prophet,[3] and despite the fact that if the prophet is rightly defined as the spokesman of God, no Old Testament character better deserves the title, if our surviving accounts are to be relied on. I have already said that while I recognize that much of the detailed legislation which is attributed to Moses is a later formulation, I am persuaded that fundamentally the story that he led Israel out of Egypt and mediated to his people the Covenant, is to be relied on; and that there is every reason to credit the record that he established Yahwism in Israel as an ethical religion and that he gave to the people the Ethical Decalogue. The great prophets are thus denied some of the originality that was once ascribed to them. But in recalling men to the true principles of their faith, and in declaring the meaning of Covenant and ethical religion in terms of contemporary conditions, they shine with undiminished lustre, and their contribution to the development of Israelite religion was of the first importance.

In all of this a large number of Old Testament scholars would to-day concur. Much of it does not directly concern our subject here, since we are not so much thinking of the attitude of the

[1] Cf. R. H. Pfeiffer, *J.B.L.* xlvi, 1927, p. 194, and *Religion in the Old Testament*, 1961, p. 116; A. Lods, *Israel from its Beginnings to the Middle of the Eighth Century*, E. Tr. by S. H. Hooke, 1932, p. 257; I. G. Matthews, *The Religious Pilgrimage of Israel*, 1947, p. 129.

[2] Cf. A. Kuenen, *The Origin and Composition of the Hexateuch*, E. Tr. by P. H. Wicksteed, 1886, pp. 244f; J. Wellhausen, *Israelitische und jüdische Geschichte*, 2nd edn, 1895, p. 128; J. C. Matthes, *Z.A.W.* xxiv, 1904, pp. 17ff; C. H. Cornill, *Introduction to the Canonical Books of the Old Testament*, E. Tr. by G. H. Box, 1907, pp. 81ff; H. P. Smith, *The Religion of Israel*, 1914, p. 187; W. Nowack, in *Abhandlungen zur semitischen Religionskunde* (Baudissin Festschrift), 1918, pp. 381ff; A. Lods, op. cit., pp. 315f; J. Morgenstern, *U.J.E.* iii, 1941, p. 510.

[3] Num. 12.6ff (E); Deut. 18.15; 34.10; Hos. 12.13 (M.T. 14). Cf. above, pp. 69f.

prophets to the cultus as the place of prophets in the cultus. With both of these questions I have dealt elsewhere,[1] but it is necessary to return to the second of them in any study of Israelite worship to-day.

I would begin with a warning against any over-simplification of the question. When I was still a student Hölscher's book *Die Profeten*[2] was published, and I purchased my copy shortly after it appeared. Its emphasis on the ecstatic element in prophecy[3] exercised a great influence on scholarship, and before long it was being pressed to greater extremes than Hölscher himself had proposed. Ecstasy was declared to be of the essence of prophecy,[4] or to belong to all types of prophecy,[5] or to characterize every prophetic utterance,[6] though Hölscher himself had said that with Amos all excited behaviour had given place to clear spiritualization.[7] Some writers distinguished between the ecstatic prophets and the non-ecstatic, and equated the former with the false prophets and the latter with the true.[8] But they will not fit into this neat division, any more than into others which scholars have sought to impose on them.[9]

Some have divided the prophets into prophets of weal and prophets of woe, and have regarded the former as the false

---

[1] On the first cf. *Melilah*, i, 1944, pp. 185ff; *B.J.R.L.* xxix, 1945–6, pp. 326ff; ibid. xxxiii, 1950–1, pp. 74ff (reprinted in *M.Q.*, 1963, pp. 67ff); *U.B.*, 1953, pp. 30ff. On the second cf. *J.S.S.* i, 1956, pp. 338ff (reprinted in *M.Q.*, pp. 111ff).

[2] 1914.

[3] Hölscher (op. cit., pp. 140ff) argued that ecstasy came into Israel from the Canaanites (cf. A. Jepsen, *Nabi*, 1934, pp. 143ff), and that it only flourished in a mixed culture. For a criticism of this view cf. J. Lindblom, in *Von Ugarit nach Qumran* (Eissfeldt Festschrift), 1957, pp. 89ff and *Prophecy in Ancient Israel*, 1962, pp. 97ff.

[4] Cf. W. Jacobi, *Die Ekstase der alttestamentlichen Propheten*, 1920, p. 4.

[5] Cf. H. Gunkel, *Exp.*, 9th series, i, 1924, p. 358.

[6] Cf. T. H. Robinson, *Prophecy and the Prophets in Ancient Israel*, 1923, pp. 39ff; *Z.A.W.* xlv, 1927, p. 4; *E.T.* xlvi, 1934–5, p. 43.

[7] Cf. *Die Profeten*, p. 197.

[8] Cf. S. Mowinckel, *J.B.L.* liii, 1934, pp. 199ff, lvi, 1937, pp. 261ff (earlier Mowinckel had held that Isaiah instructed his disciples in the technique of ecstasy; cf. *Profeten Jesaja*, 1916, p. 19); H. T. Obbink, *H.U.C.A.* xiv, 1939, pp. 23ff.

[9] Cf. *H.T.R.* xxxviii, 1945, pp. 1ff (reprinted in *S.L.*, 2nd edn, 1965, pp. 95ff).

prophets and the latter as the true.[1] It is true that Jeremiah denounces the prophets who cried Peace, Peace, when there was no peace,[2] and that the note of warning characterizes much of the prophecy preserved in the Old Testament. Yet this simple division breaks down immediately when we remember that Isaiah prophesied the deliverance of Jerusalem[3] no less than the folly of opposing Assyria.[4]

Yet another simple division was that between the *nābhî*,[5] or ecstatic prophet, and the *rō'eh* or *ḥōzeh*, the seer. Here we were told that the former functioned spontaneously, while the latter worked to order.[6] When Samuel was consulted by Saul for a small fee he is described as a *rō'eh*, or seer.[7] But in the same narrative we read that Samuel functioned spontaneously when he encouraged Saul to take the lead and deliver Israel.[8] Similarly

---

[1] Cf. B. Baentsch, *Z.W.Th.* l, 1908, p. 464; H. Gressmann, *Der Messias*, 1929, pp. 77ff; H. Gunkel, in *R.G.G.*, 2nd edn, iv, 1930, cols. 1543f; F. Weinrich, *Der religiös-utopische Charakter der "prophetischen Politik"*, 1932, pp. 24ff; S. Mowinckel, *J.B.L.* liii, 1934, p. 217.

[2] Jer. 6.14; 8.11.   [3] Isa. 36.6ff; 37.21ff.   [4] Isa. 20.1–6; 30.1–5.

[5] W. F. Albright (*F.S.A.C.*, 2nd edn, 1946, pp. 231f) has maintained that *nābhî'* is connected with Akkadian *nabû*, "call", "announce" (cf. Arabic *naba'a*, "announce"), and means "one who is called [by God]" (cf. H. Torczyner, *Z.D.M.G.* lxxxv, 1931, p. 322; J. Lindblom, *Prophecy in Ancient Israel*, 1962, p. 102). Others prefer to take it in the active sense "one who announces" (so W. Eichrodt, *Theology of the Old Testament*, E. Tr. by J. A. Baker, *i*, 1961, p. 312; R. E. Clements, *Prophecy and Covenant*, 1965, p. 33 n; cf. E. König, *Hebräisches und aramäisches Wörterbuch zum Alten Testament*, 1936 edn, p. 260b). An older view connected it with the root *nābha'*, "bubble forth" (so W. Gesenius, *Thesaurus Linguae Hebraeae et Chaldaeae Veteris Testamenti*, II ii, 1840, p. 838a), but this is very improbable. J. A. Bewer (*A.J.S.L.* xviii, 1901–2, p. 120) connected it with Akkadian *nabû*, "tear away", and thought the *nābhî'* was "one who is carried away by a supernatural power", while N. Walker (*Z.A.W.* lxxiii, 1961, pp. 99f) advanced the unlikely suggestion that the word is of Egyptian derivation and meant "[God]-honoured one". On the derivation of the word cf. the full note by Johnson, *The Cultic Prophet in Ancient Israel*, 2nd edn, 1962, pp. 24f n, and on the function of the *nābhî'* cf. *S.L.*, 2nd edn, 1965, pp. 97ff. Cf. also the articles by R. Rendtorff in *Th.W.B.* vi, 1959, pp. 781ff, and by H. W. Wolff, *Gesammelte Studien zum Alten Testament*, 1964, pp. 206ff.

[6] Cf. Hölscher, *Die Profeten*, pp. 125f; A. Causse, *Les plus vieux chants de la Bible*, 1926, p. 214 n; T. H. Robinson, *Exp.*, 8th series, xxi, 1921, p. 220.

[7] 1 Sam. 9.11.   [8] 1 Sam. 10.1ff.

Ahijah functioned spontaneously when he encouraged Jeroboam to divide the kingdom,[1] but later the wife of Jeroboam carried a gift to him when she went to consult him as to whether their child would recover, exactly after the pattern of Saul's consultation of Samuel, though in the event Ahijah delivered a spontaneous message to the wife of Jeroboam, as Samuel had done to Saul.[2]

In truth, all these simple schemes break down, and it is wiser to recognize that there were many varieties of prophet in Israel.[3] What they all had in common was the claim to deliver a word of God. Samuel, the seer, is at the shrine of Ramah when Saul consults him, and he is presiding at a sacred feast there.[4] Ahijah is probably at his own house in Shiloh when Jeroboam's wife consults him, since it is almost certain that the shrine of Shiloh was destroyed by the Philistines when the Ark was taken,[5] and the site of Shiloh was marked by nothing more than a small settlement for long thereafter. Amos prophesied in the shrine of Bethel,[6] and Jeremiah in the Jerusalem Temple.[7] When Ahijah incited Jeroboam to seize the throne he was in the field,[8] and Isaiah delivered the Immanuel prophecy to Ahaz by the conduit that brought water into Jerusalem.[9] Jehu was anointed by a prophet in a military camp during a campaign.[10] Gad, who is described as David's seer,[11] was attached to the court. Nathan was sent to David, either by the wayside or in his house, and delivered to him a never-to-be-forgotten word of the Lord,[12] and Elijah met Ahab by Naboth's vineyard,[13] while another unnamed prophet delivered his rebuke to Ahab when he waylaid him after a battle.[14] Elisha was consulted by Naaman in his own home,[15] and was visited and consulted by Jehoram and Jehoshaphat during their campaign against Moab.[16] We read of large companies of court prophets, such as the 400 at Ahab's court when Micaiah confronted Zedekiah the son of Chenaanah,[17] or the 450 Baal prophets

---

[1] 1 Kings 11.29ff.   [2] 1 Kings 14.1ff.

[3] Cf. G. von Rad, *Old Testament Theology*, E. Tr., ii, 1965, p. 7: "We can be perfectly sure that, if the sources use a number of different terms for prophet, this indicates in the last analysis that there were different kinds of prophets and different kinds of prophecy."

[4] 1 Sam. 9.13, 23f.   [5] Cf. above, p. 64, n 3.
[6] Amos 7.10ff.   [7] Jer. 7.1ff; 26.1ff.   [8] 1 Kings 11.29.
[9] Isa. 7.3.   [10] 2 Kings 9.1ff.   [11] 2 Sam. 24.11.
[12] 2 Sam. 12.1.   [13] 1 Kings 21.17f.   [14] 1 Kings 20.38.
[15] 2 Kings 5.9.   [16] 2 Kings 3.12.   [17] 1 Kings 22.6.

who were maintained at Jezebel's expense.[1] Saul met a company of prophets below Gibeah,[2] and it is clear that they were functioning as prophets at the time. When Saul went to take Samuel and was himself seized with ecstatic frenzy, Samuel was in Ramah with a company of prophets.[3] We read of prophetic communities at Bethel,[4] Jericho,[5] and Gilgal.[6] From this it is apparent that the seer could function in shrine or in court or in home, and that the *nābhī'* could function in companies in the neighbourhood of shrines or at court, or singly at home or by the wayside or in the Temple or in the Bethel shrine. No simple pattern can be imposed on all these incidents, and as little can we divide them into two groups, each with its own clearly marked character. All the prophets were men of God, delivering God's word to men in different ways. But that having been said, they can be divided into no two classes, but into many.

In none of these cases is there any reason to suppose that the seer or prophet functioned as an official of any shrine, save that Samuel's presiding at the sacred meal at Ramah, evidently in a position of some authority, would suggest that he had some official standing there. But Samuel seems to have filled the functions of a priest as well as a prophet, since we read of his sacrificing at more than one shrine.[7] Elijah, too, sacrificed on the altar which he erected, or re-erected, on Mount Carmel.[8] It has been suggested that Jeremiah and Ezekiel were both priests and prophets,[9]

---

[1] I Kings 18.19.   [2] I Sam. 10.5, 10.   [3] I Sam. 19.18ff.
[4] 2 Kings 2.3.   [5] 2 Kings 2.5.   [6] 2 Kings 4.38.
[7] I Sam. 7.9 (Mizpah); 11.15 (Gilgal).   [8] I Kings 18.30ff.
[9] Cf. S. Mowinckel, *Psalmenstudien III*, 1923, p. 17 (in *The Psalms in Israel's Worship*, ii, 1962, p. 55 this is modified to the statement that they were both members of priestly families). A. Haldar (*Associations of Cult Prophets among the Ancient Semites*, 1945, p. 112) says that Jeremiah is "clearly" described as a member of the Temple staff (cf. also p. 121). On the other hand T. J. Meek (*Exp.*, 8th series, xxv, 1923, pp. 215ff) and J. P. Hyatt (*J.B.L.* lix, 1940, p. 511) deny that he was of a priestly family at all. If Ezekiel exercised priestly functions it must have been in Jerusalem, whereas his call to be a prophet is said to have come in Babylonia, where he could no longer exercise priestly functions. He does not, therefore, appear to have exercised priestly and prophetic functions at the same time. His interest in the priesthood and the cult is clear from Ezek. 40—8. On the question how far he may be thought to be the author of these chapters, and how far the statement that his prophetic ministry was exercised in Babylonia may be accepted cf. *M.G.*, 1963, pp. 169ff.

since it is known that both came of priestly families.[1] But there is no evidence that either exercised the functions of a priest. By many scholars[2] Jeremiah is believed to have been a descendant of the Abiathar whom Solomon cashiered,[3] since Abiathar is said to have retired to his patrimony in Anathoth and Jeremiah came from Anathoth. While there is no strong evidential value in this—which would automatically have excluded him from priestly service in the Temple if it could be established—we are equally without any hint that he ever served as priest. Similarly with Ezekiel, who, according to our Biblical information, exercised his prophetic ministry in Babylon, where there was no Yahweh shrine at which he could have served.

There are, however, some passages where priests and prophets are mentioned together as though they both functioned in the service of the Temple. In the book of Jeremiah we read: "The prophets prophesy falsely, and the priests bear rule at their direction."[4] For the rendering of the last phrase I follow R.S.V., and it is supported by the clear meaning of other passages, where

---

[1] Jer. 1.1 says that Jeremiah was of the priests that were in Anathoth, and Ezek. 1.3 says Ezekiel was a priest.

[2] With varying degrees of assurance this is held by the following: A. B. Davidson, in Hastings' *D.B.* ii, 1899, p. 569b; B. Duhm (*Jeremia*, 1901, pp. 2f; A. S. Peake, *Jeremiah*, i, p. 3; V. Ryssel, in *J.E.* vii, 1907, p. 96a; R. Liechtenhan, *Jeremia* (Religionsgeschichtliche Volksbücher), 1909, p. 6; A. W. Streane, *Jeremiah and Lamentations*, 1913, p. x n. 8; H. W. Robinson, in Peake's *Commentary on the Bible*, 1920, p. 474; J. Skinner, *Prophecy and Religion*, 1932, p. 19; C. F. Kent, *The Growth and Contents of the Old Testament*, 1926, pp. 116f; E. Bruston, in Westphal's *Dictionnaire encyclopédique de la Bible*, i, 1932, p. 603b; A. Condamin, *Le Livre de Jérémie*, 1936, p. v; A. Lods, *Histoire de la littérature hébraïque et juive*, 1950, p. 405; R. Augé, *Jeremias*, 1950, p. 13 n; J. Steinmann, *Le prophète Jérémie*, 1952, p. 23; A. Penna, *Geremia*, 1952, p. 5; E. A. Leslie, *Jeremiah*, 1954, p. 20; B. Mariani, *Introductio in libros sacros Veteris Testamenti*, 1955, p. 357 n; B. N. Wambacq, *Jeremias*, 1957, p. 27; B. W. Anderson, *Understanding the Old Testament*, 1957, p. 300; W. Rudolph, *Jeremia*, 2nd edn, 1958, p. 2; A. Gelin, *Jérémie, Lamentations, Baruch*, 2nd edn, 1959, p. 9; H. Wildberger, in *R.G.G.*, 3rd edn, iii, 1959, col. 581; J. T. Nelis, in *Dictionnaire encyclopédique de la Bible*, 1960, col. 919; J. Muilenburg, in *I.D.B.* ii, 1962, p. 825a; J. Paterson, in Peake's *Commentary on the Bible*, 2nd edn, 1962, p. 541b; J. Bright, *Jeremiah*, 1965, pp. lxxxviif.

[3] 1 Kings 2.26f.

[4] Jer. 5.31. R.V. has "by their means".

the phrase occurs.[1] A. R. Johnson regards this as evidence that the priests were subordinate to the prophets.[2] If this really is so, it is surprising, for later we read how from Babylon Shemaiah wrote to Zephaniah, the chief priest, rebuking him for not controlling Jeremiah and putting him in the stocks.[3] Our concern now, however, is not with the relative position and authority of priest and prophet, but merely with the recognition that they are represented as colleagues in the service of the Temple. In another passage Jeremiah says: "Both prophet and priest are profane; yea, in my house have I found their wickedness, saith the Lord."[4] Again, in Lamentations we read: "Shall the priest and the prophet be slain in the sanctuary of the Lord?"[5] Priest and prophet are mentioned together in a passage in Isaiah, where, however, there is no direct mention of the Temple: "The priest and the prophet have erred (R.S.V. reel) through strong drink."[6] It is more relevant to note that we read of the sons of a "man of God"—which is a common term for a prophet[7]—having a room in the Temple,[8] and after Jeremiah had uttered his Temple address, predicting the destruction of the Temple if men did not amend their ways, the priests and the prophets who had heard it laid hold of him and reported what he had said to the princes.[9] This would all seem to imply that the prophets had some official standing in the Temple. We may also note that when the Shunammite woman was going

[1] In Jer. 33.13; 1 Chron. 25.2, 3, 6; 2 Chron. 23.18; 26.13 R.V. renders the same phrase "under the hands of" and in Ezra 3.10 "after the order of". In the first of these passages R.S.V. has "under the hands of", in the next four "under the direction of", in the next "under command of", and in the last "according to the directions of".

[2] Cf. *The Cultic Prophet in Ancient Israel*, 2nd edn, 1962, pp. 63f.

[3] Jer. 29.24ff. Johnson understands this passage in a general sense (ibid., pp. 62f), and takes it to mean that there was a priest attached to the Jerusalem Temple whose duty it was to keep a check on any wild behaviour, and not merely on prophetic behaviour. But if his powers included the control of the prophets, it would seem that he had authority over them, as Hölscher (*Die Profeten*, p. 143) held (cf. also S. Mowinckel, *The Psalms in Israel's Worship*, E. Tr. by D. R. Ap-Thomas, ii, 1962, p. 56).

[4] Jer. 23.11.   [5] Lam. 2.20.   [6] Isa. 28.7.

[7] Cf. 1 Sam. 9.6ff; 1 Kings 13.11, 18; 2 Kings 5.8.

[8] Jer. 35.4. W. McKane (*Prophets and Wise Men*, 1965, p. 122) conjectures that this room is the same as that mentioned in Jer. 36.10, where Baruch read Jeremiah's Roll, and that it provided a kind of pulpit from which one could address the assembled people in the court.

[9] Jer. 26.7ff.

to Elisha on the death of her son, her husband asked why she should go to consult the prophet on a day that was neither new moon nor sabbath.[1] This would suggest that on days of special cultic observance it was common to consult prophets. Professor Johnson finds significance in the fact that Elisha was to be visited on Mount Carmel,[2] and regards this as sufficient to prove that he had some sort of connection with the formal worship of Yahweh.[3] That there had been a Yahweh sanctuary on Mount Carmel is indicated by the story of Elijah's contest with the prophets of Baal, where we are told that the altar had been broken down but was restored by Elijah,[4] and it is possible that the sanctuary was restored to use from that time, though we have to remember that in the account of Elijah's contest we are told that the fire from heaven consumed the stones of the altar.[5] Montgomery thought Carmel may have been a well-known pilgrimage objective of pious men,[6] and John Gray thinks there may have been a prophetic community there and that Elisha may have paid them periodic visits,[7] while Lindblom thinks Elisha functioned at the restored sanctuary on Carmel.[8] While we must beware of reading too much into the reference to Mount Carmel, it is clear that prophets had associations with shrines and sacred days, and especially that they had associations with the Jerusalem Temple. The view has therefor been advanced that there were cultic prophets, with a defined place in the cultus of the Temple,[9] and this view has found a growing following among scholars.[10] H. J. Kraus, indeed, goes so

---

[1] 2 Kings 4.23.   [2] 2 Kings 4.25.

[3] Cf. *The Cultic Prophet in Ancient Israel*, 2nd edn, p. 26. Against this A. González Núñez (*Profetas, Sacerdotes y Reyes en el Antiguo Israel*, 1962, p. 276) denies that Elisha was a cultic specialist consecrated to the service of the sanctuary on Carmel.

[4] 1 Kings 18.30.   [5] 1 Kings 18.38.   [6] Cf. *Kings*, 1951, p. 356.

[7] Cf. *I and II Kings*, 1964, p. 417.

[8] Cf. *Prophecy in Ancient Israel*, 1962, p. 79.

[9] First briefly by G. Hölscher and then more fully by S. Mowinckel and A. R. Johnson; for references see below, p. 154.

[10] Cf. A. Causse, *R.H.P.R.* vi, 1926, pp. 1ff; H. Junker, *Prophet und Seher in Israel*, 1927; G. von Rad, *Z.A.W.* li, 1933, pp. 109ff; A. Jepsen, *Nabi*, 1934, pp. 191ff; Graham and May, *Culture and Conscience*, 1936, pp. 170, 217; A. C. Welch, *Prophet and Priest in Old Israel*, 1936, pp. 75 n, 130f n, and *Kings and Prophets of Israel*, 1952, p. 184; J. Pedersen, *Israel III–IV*, 1940, pp. 115ff; R. B. Y. Scott, *The Relevance of the Prophets*, 1944, pp. 42f; A. Haldar, *Associations of Cult Prophets among the*

far as to say there is no longer any question that cultic prophets played an important rôle in Israel.[1] This is perhaps going too far, since there are still scholars who question it.[2] I would prefer to say that it is probable that there were such prophets, and that the attention given to this subject has brought new meaning to much in the Old Testament.

Ancient Semites, 1945, pp. 90ff; I. Engnell, *S.E.Å.* xli, 1947, pp. 114ff; J. P. Hyatt, *Prophetic Religion*, 1947, p. 57; E. Würthwein, *Z.A.W.* lxii, 1950, pp. 10ff, and *Z.Th.K.* xlix, 1950, pp. 1ff (cf. F. Hesse, *Z.A.W.* lxv, 1953, pp. 45ff); N. W. Porteous, *E.T.* lxii, 1950–1, p. 7; A. S. Kapelrud, *St.Th.* iv, 1951–2, pp. 5ff; O. Plöger, *Z.A.W.* lxiii, 1951, pp. 174ff; B. W. Anderson, *Understanding the Old Testament*, 1957, p. 460; R. Hentschke, *Die Stellung der vorexilischen Schriftpropheten zum Kultus*, 1957; G. von Rad, *Old Testament Theology*, E. Tr. by D. M. G. Stalker, i, 1962, p. 97, ii, 1965, pp. 51ff; G. W. Anderson, in Peake's *Commentary on the Bible*, 2nd edn, 1962, p. 164b; H. Ringgren, *Israelitische Religion*, 1963, pp. 194ff; W. Harrelson, *Interpreting the Old Testament*, 1964, p. 317. W. Eichrodt (*Theology of the Old Testament*, i, E. Tr. by J. A. Baker, 1961, p. 333) allows a degenerate form of cultic prophecy by prophets who deserted to the guardians of the popular faith.

¹ Cf. *Worship in Israel*, E. Tr., p. 101 (cf. *Gottesdienst in Israel*, 1954, p. 110). Cf. B. D. Napier, in *I.D.B.* iii, 1962, p. 900b: "The function of Old Testament prophetism in association with the cultus as institutionalized at sanctuary or court is not in question. The real question has to do with the extent of this association and the possibility that we actually have traces in the canonical Old Testament of the work of such cultic *nebhî'îm*." J. Lindblom, op. cit., p. 80 says: "There can be little doubt that prophets belonged to the permanent staff of the Jerusalem temple."

² Cf. J. Begrich, *Einleitung in die Psalmen*, 1933, pp. 370ff; B. D. Eerdmans, *The Religion of Israel*, 1947, p. 141; A. Robert, in *Miscellanea Biblica B. Ubach*, 1953, p. 12; G. Quell, *Th.L.Z.* lxxxi, 1956, cols. 401ff; K. Roubos, *Profetie en Cultus in Israël*, 1956; T. C. Vriezen, *An Outline of Old Testament Theology*, E. Tr., 1958, p. 261; W. Eichrodt, *Theology of the Old Testament*, i, E. Tr. by J. A. Baker, 1961, pp. 313f (cf. A. R. Johnson, *The Cultic Prophet in Ancient Israel*, 2nd edn, pp. 22f n); R. de Vaux, *A.I.* pp. 384ff (cf. Johnson, op. cit., p. 74 n); J. A. Motyer, in *N.B.D.*, 1962, pp. 1042f; W. C. Klein, in Hastings' one volume *D.B.*, rev. edn, 1963, pp. 801f. A. González Núñez (*Profetas, Sacerdotes y Reyes en el Antiguo Israel*, 1962, p. 82) thinks there is insufficient evidence to assign to the prophets a determinate function in the cult. Mowinckel expresses astonishment that M. Schmidt (*Prophet und Tempel*, 1948) can devote a whole book to the theme of prophet and Temple without even touching on the question of the relation of the prophets to the Temple and cult. On the question of prophets and the cult, cf. the cautious statement of J. Lindblom, *Prophecy in Ancient Israel*, 1962, pp. 78ff (cf. *Festschrift für Alfred Bertholet*, 1950, pp. 327ff).

It was Hölscher who first suggested that prophets belonged to the cultic staff of Israelite shrines.[1] He thought this went back to the Canaanite Baal cult, in which ecstatic prophets served beside the priests in the shrines. The subject was greatly developed by Mowinckel in his *Psalmenstudien* in 1923,[2] and it is to him that we owe the wide interest in the subject we find to-day. He has presented his views more recently in revised form in Swedish in *Offersang og Sangoffer*,[3] which has now appeared in English in a further revised form.[4] Meanwhile A. R. Johnson had devoted attention to this subject, and after a preliminary article[5] had issued a monograph which had wide influence in English-speaking circles,[6] and which has now been reissued in revised form.[7]

As always when some new avenue of study is opened, some scholars wish to push it to extremes.[8] At the beginning of the century the Pan-Babylonian school greatly exaggerated Babylonian influence on Israel, and when the Ras Shamra texts first came to light the influence of Ugarit on Israel was seen to excess by some scholars. Again, when Hurrian studies became established through archaeological finds the view was expressed that we needed barriers against a Hurrian invasion,[9] and the finding of the Dead Sea Scrolls led to excessive claims of their influence on nascent Christianity and the New Testament.[10] Similarly, some

---

[1] Cf. *Die Profeten*, 1914, p. 143. It is to be noted that Hölscher distinguished between the cultic prophets and the canonical prophets (so also G. von Rad, *Old Testament Theology*, E. Tr., ii, 1965, pp. 52, 55). Some of his successors have blurred any distinction between them, while others have carefully guarded against drawing any conclusions for all the prophets from the recognition of cultic prophets. On the other hand, some of the writers on the other side have attributed to the proponents of the theory of cultic prophets the view that all prophets were cultic prophets. The issues are only confused when on either side conclusions that outrun the evidence are drawn.

[2] *Psalmenstudien III*, 1923.   [3] 1951.

[4] *The Psalms in Israel's Worship*, E. Tr. by D. R. Ap-Thomas, ii, 1962.

[5] Cf. *E.T.* xlvii, 1935–6, pp. 312ff.

[6] *The Cultic Prophet in Ancient Israel*, 1944.   [7] 2nd edn, 1962.

[8] Cf. N. W. Porteous, *Interpretation*, iii, 1949, p. 402.

[9] Cf. R. de Vaux, *R.B.* xlviii, 1939, p. 621 n.

[10] For an assessment of these cf. the present writer's *The Dead Sea Scrolls and the New Testament*, 2nd edn, 1964, and *M.Q.*, 1963, pp. 239ff.

scholars have seen cultic prophets everywhere.[1] The inevitable result is that others react strongly against the new emphases. One of those who have pressed cult prophecy to extremes is the Swedish scholar, A. Haldar, who saw all Old Testament prophecy in terms of the Babylonian *bārū* and *maḥḥū* guilds of diviners.[2] That divination was one function of Israelite prophecy is clear from the Old Testament. For Micah says: "The prophets divine for money",[3] and Jeremiah says of the prophets: "They prophesy unto you a lying vision, and divination, and a thing of nought, and the deceit of their own heart."[4] Ezekiel similarly says: "Mine hand shall be against the prophets that see vanity, and that divine lies."[5] But these passages would seem to imply that the prophets whose words I have quoted condemned divinatory practice, as divination is condemned elsewhere in the Old Testament.[6] It is therefore surprising to find Haldar equating Old Testament prophecy as a whole with Babylonian divination.[7]

The question whether any parts of the prophetic books of the Old Testament can be regarded as coming from cultic prophets is one to which we shall come. Johnson specifically refrains from dealing with that question in his monograph.[8] Haldar, however, is less cautious. In discussing Haldar's work Eissfeldt says: "The question whether the writing prophets belonged to the cultic associations is answered with an emphatic affirmative, and it is plainly laid down that no more difference is to be made between the writing prophets and their predecessors in this respect than in any other."[9] Such a conclusion would demand far more evidence than is provided.

The *bārū* was one who divined by technical means, while the *maḥḥū* received his oracle in a state of ecstasy. The former is

---

[1] Cf. N. H. Snaith, in Manson's *Companion to the Bible*, 2nd edn, 1963, p. 535: "Haldar . . . sees cultic officials, cultic ceremonies everywhere, and almost every passage of psalm and many passages of Scriptures speak 'plainly' and 'obviously' of these things."

[2] *Associations of Cult Prophets among the Ancient Semites*, 1945.

[3] Mic. 3.11; cf. Isa. 3.2. [4] Jer. 14.14; cf. 27.9; 29.8.

[5] Ezek. 13.9; cf. 13.6 and 22.28.

[6] Lev. 19.26; Deut. 18.10; 1 Sam. 15.23; 28.3; 2 Kings 17.17; 21.6.

[7] N. W. Porteous (*Interpretation*, iii, 1949, p. 402) says: "Here we are right back in the jungle of primitive superstition out of which Israel was the first to hack a way."

[8] Cf. 2nd edn, p. v. [9] *O.T.M.S.*, 1951, pp. 123f.

therefore identified by Haldar with the seer and the latter with the *nābhî*'.[1] The name *bārū* corresponds in meaning to the Hebrew *rō'eh*, or seer, and the *bārū* was one who was able to give information about the future. He secured this information by studying the entrails of animals slain for sacrifice, or by watching the flight of birds, or from the stars, and such-like technical means.[2] In view of the references to divining prophets in the Old Testament, we cannot exclude the possibility that some of them pursued means comparable with those of the *bārū* diviners. Nor can we be surprised to find ecstatics in Babylon and Israel, since it has long been recognized that ecstatic prophecy was found outside Israel as well as in.[3] What is not established is that all Israelite prophecy falls within the categories of the *bārū* and the *maḫḫū* types of divination. Mowinckel observes: "Haldar's treatment of the cultic prophets of Israel is not very satisfactory, as it has been much too highly adapted to the corresponding Babylonian phenomena, and does not give sufficient consideration to the peculiarities of Israelite religion."[4] Israelite prophecy as it appears in the Bible is much too varied a phenomenon to be forced into the straitjacket of these Babylonian categories, and their division into the two groups of seer and ecstatic is no more satisfactory than the other simple divisions which we have noted.

It is to be observed, however, that Haldar's distinction between the *nābhî*' and the *rō'eh* is not quite the same as the one at which we have looked. That proposed to distinguish between them as spontaneous or as working to order, whereas Haldar distinguishes between them as working through ecstasy or by a divinatory technique. He says the *rō'eh* and the *nābhî*' in the Old Testament are obviously quite different from one another.[5] To the careful student of the Old Testament this is not really obvious, and while it is likely that they were once distinct, the distinction had been lost. The well-known verse in 1 Sam. 9.9 does not help very much, and it has been very diversely interpreted. It says: "He that is now called a Prophet was beforetime called a Seer." This does not

---

[1] Op. cit., p. 124.   [2] Cf. Haldar, ibid., pp. 6f.   [3] Cf. above, p. 144.
[4] *The Psalms in Israel's Worship*, E. Tr., ii, p. 56 n.
[5] Op. cit., p. 124. H. M. Orlinsky (*Oriens Antiquus*, iv, 1965, pp. 153ff) distinguishes between the seer and the prophet, holding that the former commonly belonged to a guild associated with a holy place, engaging in activities largely coinciding with that of the priests, while the latter was individualistic and dealt in words, not deeds.

distinguish between them, but appears to say that "prophet" is a later name for a "seer". Yet we find the term "seer"[1] used in later passages,[2] and sometimes the same person is called a seer and a prophet.[3] It would appear to be probable, therefore, that there was a blurring of any difference that once existed between the *nābhî'* and the *rō'eh*, and that *nābhî'* had come to be used normally without discrimination.

The recognition that some prophets may have had a defined place in the cultus of Israel does not justify us in supposing that all prophets had such a place, especially in view of the inner divisions among the prophets. That prophecy did not function solely in the cultus is certain, since we have noted many instances of prophetic activity where no cultic ceremony could have figured. Even where a prophet functions within the precincts of a shrine, we cannot immediately assume that it was as a participant in some official activity.

Amos prophesied in the shrine of Bethel,[4] but he does not appear to have been a member of the staff of that shrine, and I find it very hard to think of him as a cultic prophet.[5] Yet not a few writers have turned him into one. One scholar has held him to have

[1] Sometimes the word used is *rō'eh* and sometimes the synonymous *ḥōzeh*. M. Jastrow (*J.B.L.* xxviii, 1909, pp. 42ff) and J. Hänel (*Das Erkennen Gottes bei den Schriftpropheten*, 1923, pp. 7ff) distinguish between these terms, but it is improbable that any distinction is to be drawn; cf. M. A. van den Oudenrijn, *Biblica*, vi, 1925, pp. 294ff, 406ff, and J. Lindblom, *Die literarische Gattung der prophetischen Literatur*, 1924, p. 39 n. It is probable, as van den Oudenrijn suggests (pp. 304f) that *ḥōzeh* is of Aramaic origin and *rō'eh* of Arabic origin. A. R. Johnson (*The Cultic Prophet in Ancient Israel*, 2nd edn, 1962, p. 12) thinks there was a slight difference between the two words, but says it may not be pressed (p. 14).

[2] Cf. Isa. 30.10 and 2 Chron. 16.7 (*rō'eh*); 2 Sam. 24.11; 2 Kings 17.13; 1 Chron. 21.9; 25.5; 29.29; 2 Chron. 9.29; 12.15; 19.2; 29.25, 30; 33.18; 35.15; Isa. 29.10; 30.10, Amos 7.12; Mic. 3.7 (*ḥōzeh*). Here it may be noted that the Chronicler describes Hanani as a *rō'eh* (2 Chron. 16.7), but speaks of Jehu the son of Hanani the *ḥōzeh* (2 Chron. 19.2).

[3] Cf. 2 Sam. 24.11, where Gad is called a *nābhî'* (cf. 1 Sam. 22.5) and a *ḥōzeh* (cf. 1 Chron. 21.9; 29.29; 2 Chron. 29.25); 2 Chron. 13.22, where Iddo is called a *nābhî'*, and 2 Chron. 9.29; 12.15, where he is called a *ḥōzeh*; also 1 Kings 16.7, 12, where Jehu, mentioned in the preceding note, is called a *nābhî'*.

[4] Amos 7.10ff.

[5] H. W. Wolff (*Amos' geistige Heimat*, 1964, pp. 1ff) rejects the view that Amos is a cultic prophet.

been a liver-diviner,[1] while others have argued that since he is called a *nōkēdh* he must have been a cultic official, on the ground that in a Ras Shamra text the same word is used of a priest.[2] But we cannot be certain that the area of meaning of a word was identical in Ugarit and Israel, and since Mesha, the king of Moab, is said to have been a *nōkēdh*,[3] where the word clearly means a sheep-farmer,[4] there is the less reason to make Amos into a cultic official.[5] In the passage which describes Amos' interview with Amaziah, the priest of the Bethel shrine, Amos is described as a *bôkēr*.[6] Some scholars regard this as an error for *nōkēdh*,[7] while Haldar simply states that it shows him to have been a member of a cultic staff.[8] Here Mowinckel would seem to offer some support for the view. For in Ps. 5.3 (M.T. 4), where R.S.V. renders "O Lord, in the morning thou dost hear my voice; in the morning I prepare a sacrifice for thee, and watch", he reads the word *bōḳer*, morning, as *bōḳēr*, and claims that there is a reference to sacrificing for omens, and in Ps. 27.4, where R.S.V. has "One thing have I asked of the Lord, that will I seek after", he takes the word *biḳḳēr*, "seek", to mean "find out [the tokens]", or "take

---

[1] Cf. M.Bič, *V.T.* i, 1951, pp. 293ff (against this cf. A. Murtonen, *V.T.* ii, 1952, pp. 170ff).

[2] Cf. I. Engnell, *Studies in Divine Kingship in the Ancient Near East,* 1943, p. 87, and in *S.B.U.* i, 1948, cols. 59f; A. Haldar, op. cit., pp. 79 n, 112; A. S. Kapelrud, *Central Ideas in Amos,* 2nd edn, 1961, pp. 5ff. Against this cf. K. Roubos, op. cit., pp. 4ff. Cf. also G. A. Danell, *S.E.Å.* xvi, 1951, pp. 7ff. Among others who have held Amos to have been a cultic prophet may be noted E. Würthwein (*Z.A.W.* lxii, 1950, p. 18) and J. Lindblom (*Prophecy in Ancient Israel,* 1962, p. 209).

[3] 2 Kings 3.4.

[4] Cf. what I have written in *Th.L.Z.* lxxxviii, 1963, cols. 112f.

[5] J. J. Glück (*V.T.* xiii, 1963, pp. 144f) argues that *nōkēdh* means "shepherd", and that philologically it is akin to *nāghîdh*, which means "leader".

[6] Amos 7.14 (E.V. herdsman).

[7] So W. Nowack, *Die Kleinen Propheten,* 1897, p. 151; K. Marti, *Das Dodekapropheton,* 1904, p. 213; E. A. Edgehill, *The Book of Amos,* 1914, p. 78; E. Sellin, *Das Zwölfprophetenbuch,* 2nd edn, 1929, p. 253; R. S. Cripps, *The Book of Amos,* 1929, p. 234; T. H. Robinson, *Die zwölf kleinen Propheten,* 1938, p. 98; J. Morgenstern, *Amos Studies,* 1941, pp. 19f; V. Maag, *Text, Wortschatz und Begriffswelt des Buches Amos,* 1951, p. 50; D. Deden, *De kleine Profeten,* i, 1953, p. 156. J. Lindblom (*Prophecy in Ancient Israel,* 1962, pp. 182f n) sees no reason for this.

[8] Op. cit., p. 112.

omens".[1] I am not persuaded that there is any reference to divination in either of these passages.

Lindblom thinks that Amaziah regarded Amos as a professional cultic prophet because, though not belonging to a professional cultic association, Amos had attached himself to the cultic personnel of the Bethel sanctuary, and when Amos repudiates the title of prophet, Lindblom thinks he was merely repudiating the suggestion that he was really a cultic prophet.[2] This is a very far cry from the once favoured view that Amos objected to the whole cultus, root and branch.

For myself, I see no reason to think of Amos as in any sense a cultic prophet on the ground of the incident at Bethel any more than to think of Jeremiah as a cultic prophet because he figured in a Temple incident.[3] Here again Haldar says that he obviously belonged to the Temple staff,[4] where, as so often in Haldar's work, the word "obviously" is a substitute for any solid argument. Jesus taught in the Temple,[5] but it is impossible to think of him as being a member of the Temple staff. If the term "cultic prophet" is to be given any meaning, it must denote a person who took some defined part in the official services of the shrine, and not merely a person who spoke to groups of people in the Temple court. When Jeremiah sent Baruch into the Temple to read the roll of his prophecies,[6] we cannot suppose that Baruch was a cultic prophet who read the roll in the course of some Temple service. We are told that he read it in the ears of all the people, but that he read it in the chamber of Gemariah the son of Shaphan at the entry of the new gate of the Temple.[7] Much went on in the Temple besides sacrifice and its accompanying ritual. Prophets

[1] Cf. *Psalmenstudien I*, 1922, p. 146; *The Psalms in Israel's Worship*, E. Tr., p. 54.
[2] Cf. *Prophecy in Ancient Israel*, pp. 182ff. On the vexed question whether Amos is repudiating the title of prophet cf. my paper in *Festschrift Otto Eissfeldt*, 1947, pp. 191ff, and *S.L.*, 2nd edn, 1965, pp. 120f, and the literature cited there. G. R. Driver (*E.T.* lxvii, 1955–6, pp. 91f) has argued that so far from denying that he is, or was, a prophet, Amos is indignantly affirming that he is a prophet (cf. J. MacCormack, ibid., p. 318; P. R. Ackroyd, *E.T.* lviii, 1956–7, p. 94; E. Vogt, ibid., pp. 301f; G. R. Driver, ibid., p. 302).
[3] Jer. 7.1ff; 26.1ff. [4] Op. cit., p. 121.
[5] Matt. 21.23ff; Mark 11.27ff; Luke 20.1ff; Mark 12.35; Luke 19.47; 21.37f; Matt. 26.55; Mark 14.49; Luke 22.53; John 8.20; 18.20.
[6] Jer. 36.1ff. [7] Jer. 36.10.

were sacred persons, and it was not unnatural that they should visit shrines or that they should take the opportunity of delivering the word of God to the people who congregated there. Moreover, Jeremiah functioned as a prophet, and just as truly as a prophet, outside the Temple. He went to the house of the potter and there found inspiration to deliver a message.[1] He was stirred by the sight of two baskets of figs of very different quality to utter an oracle.[2] He was privately sent for by King Zedekiah to give advice,[3] as other prophets and seers had been consulted by kings.[4] None of this can be held to have made him a cultic prophet in the sense of a Temple functionary.

In the previous chapter I referred to the view that the Psalter contains texts which were liturgically used to accompany the sacrificial acts, both for the interpretation of the acts to the worshipper and to lift him into the act so that in a real sense it might be his.[5] S. H. Hooke, in his essay in the volume *Myth and Ritual*, wrote: "In general the spoken part of a ritual consists of a description of what is being done, it is the story which the ritual enacts. The original myth, inseparable in the first instance from its ritual, embodied in more or less symbolic fashion the original situation which is seasonally re-enacted in the ritual."[6] This goes beyond what I am dealing with now to what we shall consider in the next chapter. But it also includes within its use of the word "myth" the liturgical text that interpreted the ritual act.[7] Relevant to this is what A. C. Welch wrote: "A parallel may be drawn between their action (i.e. the action of the religious leaders of Israel) and the attitude of the Presbyterian Communion, which has always held firmly by an approach to God ministered through word and sacrament, not through sacrament alone, nor through the

[1] Jer. 18.1ff.   [2] Jer. 24.1ff.   [3] Jer. 38.14ff.

[4] Cf. 1 Kings 22.9ff; Isa. 37.2ff.

[5] Cf. N. W. Porteous, in *Tradition and Situation* (Weiser Festschrift), 1963, p. 105: "Actualization is never complete until the act of God is matched by the responsive act of man."

[6] *Myth and Ritual*, 1933, p. 3. Cf. H. J. Hermisson, *Sprache und Ritus im altisraelitischen Kult*, 1965, pp. 127ff.

[7] Cf. B. S. Childs, *Memory and Tradition in Israel*, 1962, p. 81: "Of fundamental importance is the relation of cult to myth. The cult has as its function the renewing of the structure of the world by re-enacting the sacred drama of the myth. In this dramatic recapitulation the content of the myth is renewed, and the participants of the cultic rite experience its elemental power."

word alone, but through the combination of the two. The sacrament must have a specifically Christian intention, or it is empty; the word must issue in an act of worship, or it is incomplete."[1] It was when Mowinckel studied the Psalter in the light of the evidence that prophets had a defined place in the worship of the Temple that he was able to give some content to the office of the cultic prophet. He says: "With the organized temple prophets inspiration is rather what we should call an official, occupational inspiration, a permanent charismatic equipment belonging to the office itself."[2] He therefore propounds the view that at a certain point in the ritual the prophet announced Yahweh's answer to the prayer.[3] He leaves open the possibility that this might have been done by the priest, though he thinks it more probable that it was done by the prophet.[4] He thinks the substance of the answer was prescribed in the ritual, but that its expression may have been left to the prophetic inspiration of the moment, though here again he thinks that the wording of the promise might have been prescribed by the ritual.[5] On other occasions, Mowinckel thinks, the prophets may have served as the representatives of the worshippers in voicing their prayers.[6]

Of this there is nothing that can be termed proof. But it is undeniable that there are passages in the psalms which have the form of prophetic oracles, and Gunkel and Begrich ascribed these passages to the non-cultic prophets.[7] The view that they derive from cultic prophets with a defined place in the cultus seems more probable[8] and better comports with the evidence, at which we shall look,[9] that the Temple singers of the Chronicler's time had developed out of a class of prophets. It cannot be denied that this interpretation of the Psalter has transformed and enriched

---

[1] *Prophet and Priest in Old Israel*, 1936, p. 111. Cf. also *The Psalter*, 1926, pp. 70f, where Welch says: "This liturgy accompanied the *opus operatum* of the offering and was regarded as being of equal importance with the rite with which it was connected. . . . To utter the wrong form of words was as dangerous or futile as to sacrifice in a wrong way."

[2] *The Psalms in Israel's Worship*, ii, p. 57.   [3] Ibid.

[4] Ibid., p. 58.   [5] Ibid., p. 57.   [6] Ibid., pp. 60f.

[7] Cf. *Einleitung in die Psalmen*, 1933, pp. 375ff.

[8] R. E. Clements (*Prophecy and Covenant*, 1965, p. 21) goes so far as to say: "Some psalms were certainly composed by these prophetic temple personnel."

[9] Cf. below, pp. 171ff.

the study of this book of the Bible and, while not all of Mowinckel's views on the Psalms have won general acceptance, few would fail to pay tribute to what a Swiss scholar described as his "creative imagination",[1] or deny his contribution to that binding of the Prophets and the Law together through the Psalms, which I have already mentioned.[2]

It is possible here to give but a few illustrations of the prophetic words which Mowinckel finds in the Psalter. Psalm 27 is a plea for help, but its closing verse is a message to the suppliant: "Wait on the Lord: be strong, and let thine heart take courage; yea, wait thou on the Lord."[3] Here there would seem to be some clear change of speaker. Similarly, in Psalm 12 the opening is a plea, and then in verse 5 comes the response: "For the spoiling of the poor, for the sighing of the needy, now will I arise, saith the Lord; I will set him in safety at whom they puff."[4] In the following verses Mowinckel finds the thanksgiving of the suppliant for the answer he has received.[5]

N. W. Porteous thinks it improbable that the cultic prophets would be given two different rôles in the worship, one to act as the spokesmen of the lay element and the other to act as God's spokesmen to them.[6] I can see no difficulty here.[7] One prophet could

---

[1] Cf. L. Aubert, *R.Th.Ph.*, N.S. xv, 1925, p. 212. A. Lods (*R.H.R.* xci, 1925, p. 16) observes: "Ceux même qui en repoussent les conclusions rendent hommage à la vigueur de pensée du savant norvégien, à la nouveauté de ses aperçus, à la puissance de certains de ses arguments, à l'ingéniosité des autres et à l'intrépidité de sa logique'.

[2] Cf. above, pp. 138f.   [3] Ps. 27.14. Cf. Mowinckel, op. cit., ii, pp. 59f.

[4] Cf. Mowinckel, op. cit., p. 60. Mowinckel understands the last words to mean "who has been blown upon" and then interprets these words in terms of witchcraft. This is in harmony with his finding much reference to witchcraft in the Psalter, and interpreting the phrase "workers of iniquity" as those who are presumed to have put a spell on the speaker. This is one of the views of Mowinckel that has been much criticized, and one which the present writer does not follow. In the present passage the contempt of men is a fully intelligible and relevant thought, without importing witchcraft.

[5] Ibid. H. Schmidt (*Z.A.W.* xl, 1922, pp. 1ff) finds frequent changes of speaker in Ps. 118, though he assigns the parts to the priest, the various offerers of sacrifice, and the congregation.

[6] Cf. *E.T.* lxii, 1950–1, p. 8.

[7] Cf. A. R. Johnson, *E.T.* xlvii, 1935–6, p. 316a: "It was part of his (i.e. the prophet's) function to offer prayer as well as to give the divine response or oracle" (also *The Cultic Prophet in Ancient Israel*, 2nd edn, p. 60).

voice the cry of the worshipper and another could voice the response to the cry, just as antiphonal choirs can respond to one another.[1] For the prophet was not only the man who brought the word of God to man. He was also the spokesman of man to God, and as intercessor he figures frequently in the Old Testament.[2] In Genesis Abraham is said to be a prophet whose intercession for Abimelech might be expected to have special power.[3] The prophet Samuel is besought to pray for the people,[4] and replies: "God forbid that I should sin against the Lord in ceasing to pray for you."[5] Jeremiah refers to Moses[6] and Samuel as pre-eminent in intercessory power.[7] Zedekiah asks Jeremiah to pray for him to the Lord.[8] There would be nothing surprising in the prophet's voicing the prayer of the people or in declaring the oracle of God in answer to the prayer. As Johnson says: "It must be borne in mind that the offering of prayer was as much a part of the prophetic function as the giving of the divine response or oracle; and so it may well be that, in addition to the oracular sections, some of the prayers (and, indeed, liturgical compositions in general) within the Psalter were the work of these cultic prophets."[9] If the cultic prophet functioned in the worship in the utterance of any of the liturgies that accompanied the acts of worship, I can see no reason why he should not have uttered them all. If their utterances were once the expression of the inspiration of the moment, there would inevitably be a tendency to repeat the more successful ones, or even to use carefully prepared

---

[1] A. W. Streane (in Hastings' one volume *D.B.*, 1909, p. 637a) noted that Pss. 13, 20, 38, 68, 89, among others, were antiphonal.

[2] Cf. A. S. Herbert, *B.Q.* xiii, 1949, pp. 76ff; also G. von Rad, *Z.A.W.* li, 1933, pp. 114f, and *Old Testament Theology*, E. Tr., ii, 1965, pp. 51ff; A. Jepsen, *Nabi*, 1934, pp. 100f; J. Hempel, *Gott und Mensch im Alten Testament*, 2nd edn, 1936, pp. 126f; N. Johansson, *Parakletoi*, 1940, pp. 3ff; P. A. H. de Boer, *O.T.S.* iii, 1943, pp. 157ff; F. Hesse, *Die Fürbitte im Alten Testament*, 1949, pp. 39ff; E. Würthwein, *Z.A.W.* lxii, 1949–50, p. 27; A. R. Johnson, *The Cultic Prophet in Ancient Israel*, 2nd edn, pp. 58f, 75; Mowinckel, op. cit., i, p. 79, ii, p. 63. H. W. Hertzberg (in *Tradition und Situation* (Weiser Festschrift), 1963, pp. 63ff) denies that intercession was any function of the prophet's office.

[3] Gen. 20.7.   [4] 1 Sam. 12.19.   [5] 1 Sam. 12.23.

[6] For the intercessory prayers of Moses, cf. Ex. 32.11ff, 31f; 33.12ff; 34.9; Num. 11.11ff; 14.13ff; 21.7; Deut. 9.18ff; 10.10.

[7] Jer. 15.1.   [8] Jer. 37.3.   [9] Cf. *E.T.* xlvii, 1935–6, p. 317a.

compositions, and the liturgy would tend to develop stereotyped forms.

To continue with some further illustrations of possible liturgies which cultic prophets may have uttered in the Temple. Variety of occasion would mean variety of pattern. Psalm 20 opens with an oracle of promise, to which the first part of verse 5 (M.T. 6) is the response in confidence and hope, while the last line breaks in with a renewed word of hope and promise: "The Lord fulfil all thy petitions", followed by the renewal of the confidence and resolve of the worshippers.[1] Psalm 86 consists wholly of petition by one who was in sore trouble,[2] while Psalm 6, though it is all uttered in the name of the suppliant, changes its mood in the last section from misery to assurance that the plea has been heard and will be answered.[3]

Some psalms, which may have accompanied public sacrifices, perhaps on special occasions, are preserved in the Psalter. Thus, Psalm 85 begins by recalling God's past mercies and proceeds to cry for renewed help, and then continues: "I will hear what the Lord God will speak." Then comes the word from God, promising peace and salvation.[4] Psalm 95 opens with confidence in God and his power, but the word that follows brings rebuke in the form of a reminder of Israel's response to God's mercy in the wilderness

---

[1] On this type of psalm cf. Mowinckel, op. cit., i, p. 219. This psalm was probably used when the king set forth to meet his enemies in battle (cf. Gunkel and Begrich, *Einleitung in die Psalmen*, 1933, p. 142; A. R. Johnson, in *O.T.M.S.*, p. 179; Mowinckel, op. cit., i, pp. 69f). H. Schmidt (*Die Thronfahrt Jahves*, 1927, p. 39) thinks it rather belongs to the celebration of the annual festival.

[2] Johnson (in *O.T.M.S.*, p. 170) notes the "marked rise and fall in the psalmist's mood, as at one moment he gives expression to such an assurance (i.e. of being heard) only to sink back awhile into renewed lamentation and supplication before reaching a final conviction that his prayer will indeed be heard and accepted".

[3] Here the sufferer seems to be afflicted by bodily sickness (cf. Johnson, in *O.T.M.S.*, p. 170; Mowinckel, op. cit., ii, p. 1). From the fact that in his assurance the psalmist triumphantly turns on the "evil-doers", Mowinckel concludes that he associates his illness with their activity (p. 6).

[4] Mowinckel (op. cit., ii, p. 61) says: "Here the forms of free extempore prophetic inspiration have been transferred to the cultic oracle and combined with the announcement of promises, which perhaps made up a permanent part of the ritual with regard to both substance and form." He locates the use of the psalm in the festival cult (p. 63).

days.[1] The cultic prophets, if these psalms are rightly attributed to them, did not always speak smooth and comforting words. Psalm 50 is charged with a characteristically prophetic message, emphasizing that obedience is better than sacrifice, and declaring that the abundance of victims on the altar cannot atone for men in a society that tolerates theft, adultery, and slander. Yet it is not anti-cultic, since it calls on men to offer sacrifices, but to consider in their hearts the corollaries of sacrifice in the quality of their life.[2]

These few examples must suffice. In the next chapter we shall look at psalms in which the royal rites at the great festivals are believed to be reflected. It has been suggested that the cultic prophets are to be identified with the false prophets,[3] but if their function was in any way such as Mowinckel and Johnson conceive it, this cannot be right. For here are messages which were not unworthy of the greater prophets. If this linking of the psalms with the cultic prophets is wrong, then we have no clue to the kind of activities in which these prophets engaged.

It is clear from the Old Testament that it was very difficult for ordinary people to distinguish between true and false prophets. Deuteronomy offers two tests,[4] but neither of them is very

[1] Johnson (*Sacral Kingship in Ancient Israel*, 1955, p. 61) says the first part of this psalm, "with its characteristic emphasis upon Yahweh's universal Kingship and His power in Creation, is mainly a legacy from Canaanite mythology, while the second part, with its emphasis upon the lesson in obedience which is to be drawn from the history of the Wandering, is based upon the Hebrew traditions concerning the great events of the Exodus; and, all in all, we have good reason to believe that both together formed an important element in the liturgy of the great autumnal festival as celebrated in Jerusalem during the period of the monarchy".

[2] Cf. Mowinckel, op. cit., ii, p. 70: "All through it has the form of a prophetic word, the severe lecture and admonition of a prophet with the emphasis on the commandments and with a conditional promise attached to it. Its cultic basis is the idea of epiphany, of renewal of the covenant, the emphasis on the commandments as commandments of the covenant and conditions of the promise, and finally the prophetic promise as a permanent element of the festal cult's new year. The whole psalm is cast in the mould of prophetic speech, with a hymnal description of the glory of theophany for an introduction."

[3] So J. Jocz, *The Spiritual History of Israel*, 1961, p. 69 n. Against such a view cf. J. Lindblom, *Prophecy in Ancient Israel*, 1962, p. 215; J. H. Eaton, *Obadiah, Nahum, Habakkuk and Zephaniah*, 1961, p. 26.

[4] Deut. 13.1ff; 18.22.

satisfactory. One is that the prophet whose word does not come true is a false prophet. This glimpse of the obvious could not be very helpful to people at the moment of a prophetic utterance. The other is that the prophet who draws men away from Israel's God is a false prophet. But the false prophet spoke in the name of Yahweh, and cultic prophets who served in the Temple must be presumed to have so spoken. If the division between true prophets and false had been so simple as one between non-cultic prophets and cultic, it should have been possible to indicate it more simply. It is unwise to assume that all non-cultic prophecy was true or that all cultic prophecy was false. All these simple divisions break down in practice.[1]

Micaiah and Zedekiah[2] were clearly not thought of as prophets of a different kind, but prophets who delivered different messages. Jeremiah and Hananiah[3] were distinguished by the content of their prophecies rather than by any difference in their prophetic office. When Jeremiah denounces the prophets of his day, it is because they speak words which arise from no deeper source than their own hearts,[4] or because they borrow oracles from one another,[5] or because they pander to the popular mood,[6] or because their own life does not reflect the will of God that their oracles should proclaim.[7] There were doubtless good prophets and bad, true prophets and false, within the ranks of both cultic and non-cultic prophets, and the false were the mere technicians, who had not stood in the council of God and who were not the purveyors of his word.[8] As Lindblom says: "The marks by which one could recognize a true or false prophet cannot be expressed in a formula."[9]

I have said that I am not wholly persuaded that the utterances of the cultic prophets, whether prayer or oracle, were always spontaneous. On this Mowinckel is not quite decided.[10] In a liturgy designed to accompany a ritual act whose character was known beforehand, there would be no reason why it should not

---

[1] Cf. E. Auerbach, *Die Prophetie*, 1920, p. 19: "Die Unterscheidung des wahren und falschen Propheten ist nicht immer so einfach wie in dem Falle des Deuteronomiums."

[2] 1 Kings 22.9ff.   [3] Jer. 28.1ff.   [4] Jer. 14.14; 23.16, 26.
[5] Jer. 23.30.   [6] Jer. 6.14f; 8.10f.   [7] Jer. 23.14.
[8] Jer. 23.18, 28.   [9] Cf. *Prophecy in Ancient Israel*, 1962, p. 215.
[10] Op. cit., ii, p. 57.

be prepared beforehand, or repeated on other occasions, and Mowinckel suggests that the repetition of passages in the Psalter, as in Psalms 60 and 108, points to this.[1] Here, once more, we are warned that we should not impose any single pattern on the Old Testament prophets. Oracles which delivered an *ad hoc* message from God on the political and social conditions of the time might be expected to have a spontaneous and individual character. Liturgical forms addressed to situations which by their very nature must recur again and again would not need to have the same character. But if they were genuine prophetic utterances, they should alike stem from Israel's faith and declare the will of God. They should not be content with any mere formal observance of ritual acts, but should be designed to lift men to present themselves before God in spirit and in truth. And the Psalter would not continue still to be used in worship unless this were the dominant character of the psalms it contains.

As against the idea that the cultic prophets were the false prophets, some writers have sought to include some of the greater prophets in their ranks, and to find cultic liturgies preserved in the canonical books. I have already said that I cannot accept the view that Amos and Jeremiah were cultic prophets.[2] In general I am persuaded that T. J. Meek is right when he says: "It is questionable whether many of the canonical prophets were cult officials."[3] We cannot rule out *a priori*, however, that any cultic liturgies have been preserved in the prophetic Canon. I have referred earlier to liturgies for festivals which are preserved in the Pentateuch.[4] We cannot therefore maintain that the rest have all been preserved in the Psalter.

Mowinckel suggested that Joel and Habakkuk were Temple prophets, since their books contain passages in the form of the psalms as well as prophetic utterances.[5] So far as Habakkuk is

---

[1] Op. cit., ii, p. 59. [2] Cf. above, p. 159.

[3] Cf. *Hebrew Origins*, 2nd edn, 1950, pp. 178f. He adds (p. 179 n) that "it is striking to note how many of the most recent commentaries on the canonical prophets take the ground that they were cult functionaries."

[4] Cf. above, pp. 89, 118, 135.

[5] *Psalmenstudien III*, 1923, pp. 27ff. Cf. *Jesaja-disiplene*, 1926, p. 61. W. F. Albright (*A.R.I.*, p. 210, and in *Studies in Old Testament Prophecy* (T. H. Robinson Festschrift), 1950, p. 9 n) holds that Habakkuk was a Temple musician as well as a prophet.

concerned, Balla argued that this was a liturgy[1] and Humbert developed the view,[2] and Lindblom says that Habakkuk was certainly a cultic prophet at the Jerusalem Temple.[3] Here J. H. Eaton[4] and R. Hentschke[5] agree in the view that he was a cultic prophet. E. Nielsen is a little more cautious in arguing that the book was either a liturgy for cultic use or an imitation of such a liturgy.[6] So far as Joel is concerned, Mowinckel is himself more cautious now, and says that the book of Joel gives evidence of strong influence from the forms of psalm and cultic liturgy.[7] Kapelrud argued that it was built up in the way of a liturgy, though he did not suggest that it was actually used in the Temple.[8]

[1] Cf. *R.G.G.*, 2nd edn, ii, 1928, cols. 1556f. E. Sellin (*Einleitung in das Alte Testament*, 7th edn, 1935, p. 119) followed this view. Cf. also A. Weiser, *Introduction to the Old Testament*, E. Tr. by D. M. Barton, 1961, pp. 261f.

[2] Cf. *Problèmes du livre d'Habacuc*, 1944, pp. 296ff (cf. *R.G.G.*, 3rd edn, iii, 1959, cols. 3f). Cf. also I. Engnell, in *S.B.U.* i, 1948, cols. 769ff. T. C. Vriezen (*An Outline of Old Testament Theology*, E. Tr., 1958, p. 63) says that Habakkuk "apparently contains a prophecy by a cultic prophet" (cf. p. 251: "Habakkuk is, probably not incorrectly, taken to be a temple-prophet"). R. de Vaux (*A.I.*, 1961, p. 385) thinks Habakkuk (and Nahum) may be imitations of liturgical works. J. P. Hyatt (in Peake's *Commentary on the Bible*, 2nd edn, 1962, p. 637a) rejects this view. M. Delcor (in *La Sainte Bible*, ed. by L. Pirot and A. Clamer, viii, Part 1, 1964, p. 391) says there are insufficient reasons for Humbert's view.

[3] Cf. *Prophecy in Ancient Israel*, p. 254 (cf. also p. 208). Cf. also O. Eissfeldt, *The Old Testament: an Introduction*, E. Tr., 1965, pp. 420ff; G. Fohrer, in Sellin-Fohrer, *Einleitung in das Alte Testament*, 10th edn, 1965, p. 500.

[4] Cf. *Obadiah, Nahum, Habakkuk, Zephaniah*, 1961, p. 82.

[5] Cf. *Die Stellung der vorexilischen Schriftpropheten zum Kultus*, 1957, p. 173.

[6] Cf. *St.Th.* vi, 1953, p. 59.

[7] Cf. *The Psalms in Israel's Worship*, ii, p. 93. Cf. also C. A. Keller, *Osée, Joël, Amos, Abdias, Jonas*, 1965, p. 105, Similarly Mowinckel now says that Habakkuk gives evidence of liturgical influence (ibid.), but he says that Habakkuk was undoubtedly a Temple prophet (p. 61) and holds that the Psalm of Habakkuk was probably composed as the prophetical part of an actual Temple liturgy (p. 147, and *Th.Z.* ix, 1953, pp. 1ff). On the Psalm of Habakkuk cf. also W. F. Albright, in *Studies in Old Testament Prophecy* (T. H. Robinson Festschrift), 1950, pp. 1ff; J. H. Eaton, *Z.A.W.* lxxvi, 1964, pp. 144ff.

[8] Cf. *Joel Studies*, 1948, p. 9 (cf. A. Weiser, op. cit., p. 239). T. H. Robinson (*Die zwölf kleinen Propheten*, 1938, p. 63) held Joel 2.12–14 to be a fragment of a penitential liturgy and 2.19 to be taken from a liturgical text.

THE PROPHETS AND THE CULT

Others have gone farther. Engnell describes it as a cultic liturgy,[1] and Hentschke says Joel was a cultic prophet,[2] as also does Lindblom,[3] though he denies to Joel a few verses of the book.[4] So far as the book of Nahum is concerned, Humbert advanced the view that it was a cultic liturgy, written to be used for the celebration of the fall of Nineveh,[5] and Mowinckel now adheres to the view that Nahum was a Temple prophet.[6] Here once more Eaton[7] and Hentschke agree.[8] G. Gerleman finds the book of Zephaniah to be a cultic liturgy,[9] and Eaton also believes that Zephaniah was a Temple prophet,[10] and for good measure so regards Obadiah also.[11] Gunkel held Isaiah 33 to be a cultic liturgy,[12] and also the closing verses of the book of Micah.[13]

Engnell argued that the section of Isaiah commonly called the Isaiah Apocalypse, consisting of chapters 24 to 27,[14] and the whole of Deutero-Isaiah were modelled on cultic prophecy.[15] It is to be clearly recognized, however, that by this he does not mean that

---

[1] Cf. *S.B.U.* i, 1948, cols. 1075ff (cf. Kapelrud, *Joel Studies*, pp. 193ff).

[2] Op. cit., p. 173. So also Fohrer, op. cit., p. 471.

[3] Cf. *Prophecy in Ancient Israel*, p. 277. But Lindblom denies that the book is a liturgy or modelled on a liturgy.

[4] 3.4–8 (M.T. 4.4–8).

[5] Cf. *Z.A.W.* xliv, 1926, pp. 266ff; *A.f.O.* v, 1928–9, pp. 14ff; *R.H.P.R.* xii, 1932, pp. 1ff. So also E. Sellin (*Einleitung in das Alte Testament*, 7th edn, 1935, pp. 116f) and T. C. Vriezen (*An Outline of Old Testament Theology*, E. Tr., pp. 63, 251). This view is rejected by Weiser (op. cit., p. 258) and Eissfeldt (*Old Testament Introduction*, E. Tr. by P. R. Ackroyd, 1965, p. 415), and also by A. Haldar (*Studies in the Book of Nahum*, 1947, pp. 3ff; cf. *S.B.U.* ii, 1952, cols. 417ff), and E. Osswald (*R.G.G.*, 3rd edn, iv, 1960, col. 1297). M. Delcor (op. cit., pp. 364f) again rejects the view that the book of Nahum is a cultic liturgy.

[6] Op. cit., p. 93. So also Lindblom (op. cit., pp. 208f, 253) and Fohrer (op. cit., pp. 494f).

[7] Op. cit., pp. 53f.   [8] Op. cit., p. 173.

[9] Cf. *Zephanja textkritisch und literarisch untersucht*, 1942, pp. 100ff.

[10] Op. cit., p. 122.

[11] Ibid., p. 35; cf. Fohrer, op. cit., p. 483: "Er war vielleicht ein Kultprophet." Lindblom (op. cit., pp. 208f, 274) would add Malachi.

[12] Cf. *Z.A.W.* xlii, 1924, pp. 177ff.

[13] Cf. *What Remains of the Old Testament*, E. Tr. by A. K. Dallas, 1928, pp. 115ff. Cf. also A. S. Kapelrud, in *S.B.U.* ii, 1952, cols. 278f.

[14] Cf. *S.B.U.* i, 1948, col. 1031.

[15] Cf. *B.J.R.L.* xxxi, 1948, p. 64. K. Elliger (*Die Einheit des Tritojesaja*, 1928, pp. 15ff, 24ff, 29ff) maintains that there are liturgical passages in Trito-Isaiah (59.1–4, 9–18; 61; 62; 63.7—64.11).

Deutero-Isaiah was written for liturgical use, but that it is of the same literary type as prophetic liturgy. Here Mowinckel says: "Several indications suggest that Deutero-Isaiah, who so often clothes his prophecies in the form of the cultic psalm and the cultic ritual, has also several times used the salvation oracle of temple prophet or priest, as a style pattern of the promise."[1]

It will be seen that there is an increasing tendency to find cultic liturgies or imitations of such liturgies in the prophetical books. My own attitude here is one of great caution. We cannot rule out the possibility that the work of any cultic prophet has been preserved in the prophetic Canon,[2] and I think the strongest case is made out for the book of Nahum.[3] So far as the imitation of liturgical forms is concerned, I see no reason why the prophets should not have imitated such forms. If Isaiah could model the Song of the Vine[4] on a vintage song, yet use it for a purpose quite other than any purpose which can be presumed for a vintage song, I do not think it impossible that prophets could have modelled their utterances on liturgical compositions. But by and large I am persuaded that the oracles of the canonical prophets were not uttered as accompaniments of ritual acts, but were designed to warn their contemporaries of the dangers of the policies of their day and to call them to a deeper understanding of the ethical demands of their faith.

Finally, we must turn to the question of the disappearance of

---

[1] Op. cit., ii, p. 59.

[2] I. Hylander (*Le Monde oriental*, xxv, 1931, pp. 64f; cf. the critical comment of Lindblom, op. cit., p. 208 n), Mowinckel (*Profeten Jesaja*, 1925, p. 16; *J.B.L.* liii, 1934, p. 210), A. Haldar (*Associations of Cult Prophets among the Ancient Semites*, 1945, p. 121), and C. Lindhagen (*The Servant Motif in the Old Testament*, 1950, p. 117) hold that Isaiah was a member of the Temple personnel (on the cultic associations of the account of Isaiah's call, cf. I. Engnell, *The Call of Isaiah*, 1949, pp. 25ff); Mowinckel (*Acta Orientalia*, xiii, 1934-5, p. 267; *J.B.L.* liii, 1934, p. 210) and Haldar (op. cit., pp. 112, 121) see in Jeremiah such a member; Haldar (loc. cit.) would add Ezekiel. Lindhagen (loc. cit.), in addition to holding Joel, Nahum, and Habakkuk to be cultic prophets, would add Haggai and Zechariah.

[3] Cf. G. von Rad, *Old Testament Theology*, E. Tr., ii, 1965, p. 189: "Nahum is the only prophet who may possibly have had a function within the framework of the cult." He allows (p. 189 n) that Hab. 1.2—2.4 may be the prophetic imitation of a cultic form.

[4] Isa. 5.1ff.

the cultic prophets. Here Mowinckel advanced the view that in the Second Temple they were incorporated in the ranks of the Levites and called the singers.[1] In this he is followed by Johnson,[2] who calls attention to the association of the prophets Haggai and Zechariah with the priests in the restoration of the Temple and holds that they were members of a definite company of the prophets who had an official connection with the cultus.[3] In the book of Nehemiah we read that Sanballat sent to Nehemiah saying: "Thou hast also appointed prophets to preach of thee at Jerusalem, saying, There is a king in Judah."[4] From this Johnson concludes that the prophet continued to enjoy official status in close association with the Jerusalem Temple down to the time of Nehemiah.[5] I am not persuaded that these must have been cultic prophets in the sense we have been considering, or indeed that the report of Sanballat was a true one. Johnson then argues that the Exile had brought the average type of professional prophet into disrepute, and that the final fall of Jerusalem had proved Jeremiah right in condemning the prophets who prophesied peace when there was no peace.[6] This seems to me to come much too close to the identification of the cultic prophets with the false prophets, and I am doubtful if the reasons Johnson suggests would have first begun to operate more than a century after the fall of Jerusalem to which he traces them.

I think it much more probable that the process whereby the cultic prophet was turned into a Levitical singer was more closely related to the reorganization of the Temple personnel to which I referred earlier.[7] Ezekiel had advocated the reduction of the priests of the country shrines to a subordinate status under the Zadokite priests, with the dismissal of all alien Temple servants.[8] That had not settled the issue and the struggle clearly continued until the Priestly Code finally settled the issue by establishing an "Aaronite" priesthood, with all the lower Temple staff classed as

[1] Cf. *Psalmenstudien III*, 1923, pp. 17ff. Cf. also G. von Rad, *Das Geschichtsbild des chronistischen Werkes*, 1930, pp. 113f; A. Jepsen, *Nabi*, 1934, pp. 236ff.

[2] Cf. *E.T.* xlvii, 1935–6, pp. 316ff; *The Cultic Prophet in Ancient Israel*, 2nd edn, pp. 69ff.

[3] Cf. *E.T.*, loc. cit., p. 316b; *The Cultic Prophet*, p. 65.   [4] Neh. 6.7.

[5] Cf. *The Cultic Prophet*, p. 66.   [6] Ibid., pp. 66ff.

[7] Cf. above, pp. 100f.   [8] Ezek. 44.9ff.

Levites.[1] It seems to me more likely that it was this struggle which lay behind the new status of the cultic prophets. This would mean that henceforth these prophets would be an hereditary order. In earlier days the prophets had been men who were called to their task, and the call could come to anyone; the priests had become an hereditary order confined to certain families, and while some fictions had to be accepted in tracing all the priests to Aaron and all the Levites to a single tribe, once they were accepted both orders became hereditary.

More important is the *fact* of the changed status of the cultic prophets, and the evidence for this presented by Mowinckel and Johnson seems to me to be quite convincing.

The Chronicler, who is generally agreed to be a better authority for the Temple arrangements of his own day than for those of the pre-exilic period, in describing David's arrangements for the musical service of the shrine, says that the musical guilds "prophesied" with their instruments.[2] Of the leaders of the musical bands he names Asaph, Heman, and Jeduthun.[3] In another passage Ethan takes the place of Jeduthun[4] and he may be the same person.[5] In different passages Heman, Asaph, and Jeduthun are all described by the Chronicler as seers.[6] Moreover, accord-

---

[1] Num. 18.1ff. Though the Levites lost status they gained in emoluments. G. B. Gray (*Numbers*, 1903, p. 236) says: "The dues here assigned to the tribe of Levi are immensely more valuable than those which are assigned, by direct statement or implication, to the Levites in Deuteronomy or any pre-exilic literature; and considerably more valuable than those required, for the priests, by Ezekiel. They are less valuable than those required in the Mishnah, and, in one respect, than those required in Lev. 27³⁰⁻³³." Cf. W. E. Addis, *The Documents of the Hexateuch*, ii, 1898, pp. 370f n, where Lev. 27.30–3 are assigned to a secondary stratum of P.

[2] 1 Chron. 25.1. This verse is sufficient to disprove the statement of A. González Núñez (*Profetas, Sacerdotes y Reyes en el Antiguo Israel*, 1962, p. 79) that "prophesy" is not translatable by poetic-musical activity, or any other cultic function.

[3] 1 Chron. 25.1. On 1 Chron. 25.1–6 cf. A. C. Welch, *Prophet and Priest in Old Israel*, 1936, pp. 130f n.

[4] 1 Chron. 15.19.

[5] Cf. *E.B.* ii, 1901, col. 2346. J. A. Selbie (in Hastings' *D.B.* ii, 1899, p. 555b) is less sure of this. It is improbable that the one name is a textual corruption of the other, or we should not expect to find it in several places.

[6] 1 Chron. 25.5; 2 Chron. 29.30; 2 Chron. 35.15.

ing to the Chronicler, David acted according to the advice of Gad the seer and Nathan the prophet in making his arrangements.[1]

Further, whereas in the account of Josiah's reform in 2 Kings we read that the priests and the prophets went up to the house of the Lord,[2] the Chronicler alters this to read "the priests and the Levites".[3] He therefore changes the "prophets" into the "Levites" to conform the terminology to that of his own day. He also calls the Temple musicians "Levites" in his account of the reign of Hezekiah.[4] Again, in his account of the reign of Jehoshaphat, the Chronicler records how a Levite, of the sons of Asaph, prophesied in the Temple.[5] All of this indicates how the Chronicler converts prophecy of an earlier day into song to modernize the language. In the account of David's bringing the Ark into Jerusalem he imports Levites[6] who were unmentioned in the earlier account of 2 Samuel.[7] This was partly because according to the Priestly Code, which laid down the procedure which the Chronicler felt ought to have been followed on that occasion, none but Levites should have borne the Ark,[8] and partly because in the earlier account there was mention of musicians who accompanied the Ark,[9] and these had to be turned into Levites.

Relevant to our subject here, it should be recalled that in the Psalter there are psalms ascribed to Asaph,[10] Jeduthun,[11] and Heman,[12] though in the case of Heman he is described as an Ezrahite and the psalm is ascribed also to the Korahites. Curiously

---

[1] 2 Chron. 29.25.   [2] 2 Kings 23.2.
[3] 2 Chron. 35.18.   [4] 2 Chron. 31.2.
[5] 2 Chron. 20.14ff. Note that the narrative continues by saying (verse 19) that the Levites stood up to praise the Lord.
[6] 1 Chron. 15.16.   [7] 2 Sam. 6.1ff.
[8] Num. 3.31; 4.15. Cf. 1 Chron. 15.2.
[9] 2 Sam. 6.5. Here the reference is to the first unsuccessful attempt to bring the Ark into Jerusalem. The Chronicler repeats this in 1 Chron. 13.8 in his account of the unsuccessful attempt, without mention of the Levites in this verse, though he has already imported them into verse 2, and matched it, with specific mention of the Levitical singers, in his account of the successful attempt.
[10] Pss. 50, 73—83.
[11] Pss. 39, 62, 77. Note that the last of these is ascribed to both Asaph and Jeduthun.
[12] Ps. 88.

enough there is also a psalm ascribed to Ethan,[1] who is also called an Ezrahite.[2] There are other psalms attributed to the Korahites,[3] who ended up as doorkeepers in the Second Temple.[4] Thirty years ago N. H. Snaith propounded the view that in the fifth century b.c. there was a struggle between the Korahites and the Asaphites, as the result of which the Korahites were excluded for a time from the service of the Temple.[5] He assigned Psalms 42 and 43, which together form a single psalm, to this period.[6] He believed that there was finally a concordat which allowed the Korahites back to the Temple service, but reduced them to the rank of doorkeeper, and thereafter they had the humiliation of having to hear the Asaphites sing the psalms which they had composed.[7] I am doubtful if we can date the Korahite psalms so closely as this theory proposed, but it is interesting that it assigns the struggle to the age in which I should put the reduction of the status of the Temple prophets to the rank of Levitical singers. I am also doubtful if the conflict of the Korahites was really with the Asaphites. In the Pentateuch, in a passage[8] which is assigned to the Priestly Code and which is therefore of post-exilic origin, we read of the claim of Korah and his company to share in the priestly privileges. This would suggest that they aimed to be incorporated in the priestly ranks rather than to share the rank of the Asaphite singers, but that they ended up in a more humble position than the singers.

I may sum up what I have said on the place of the cultic prophets in the ritual in the words of H. F. Hahn: "With this altered perspective on the prophetic function, it was possible to see priest and prophet, each in his own sphere, working for the furtherance of religion without being continually at cross-purposes. The priest had the help of the cult-prophet in teaching the significance of ritual actions; the canonical prophet added yet more by infusing

---

[1] Ps. 89.

[2] In 1 Kings 4.31 Ethan is again called an Ezrahite. The meaning of this term is obscure, but it would seem that there was some connection between Ethan and Heman.

[3] Pss. 42; 44-9; 84; 85; 87.   [4] 1 Chron. 26.1, 19.

[5] *Studies in the Psalter*, 1934, pp. 1ff.

[6] Ibid., pp. 19ff.   [7] Ibid., pp. 39ff.

[8] Num. 16.1ff. This is combined with a JE narrative about Dathan and Abiram (cf. G. B. Gray, *Numbers*, 1903, pp. 187f).

religious worship with an ethical content."[1] I would only modify this by saying that I would not deny to the cultic prophet the honour of desiring to infuse religious worship with an ethical content, but his instrument for doing this was less challenging and forthright than that of the great prophets of the eighth and seventh centuries, whose works are preserved for us in the Bible.

[1] Cf. *Old Testament in Modern Research*, 1954, p. 141. While the present work has been in the press two articles on the "office" of the prophet have appeared: H. Gross, *E.Th.L.* xli, 1965, pp. 5ff; J. Muilenburg, in *The Bible in Modern Scholarship*, ed. by J. P. Hyatt, 1965, pp. 74ff.

6

Psalmody and Music

There was a time when the Psalter was commonly referred to as the "Hymn Book of the Second Temple", and most of the individual psalms were believed to have been composed in the postexilic age. Wellhausen wrote: "It is not a question whether there be any post-exilic psalms, but rather, whether the psalms contain any poems written before the exile."[1] Duhm denied that any psalm was pre-exilic, and thought that two might come from the Persian period while the rest were composed in the Greek period and not a few of them in the Maccabaean age or even later.[2] Sellin allowed the possibility that there might be some Maccabaean psalms, but held that their presence had not been proved.[3] So far as the royal psalms are concerned, he thought it was undeniable that these must be pre-exilic.[4] Many years earlier G. B. Gray had argued that these royal psalms were post-exilic but contained no

[1] Cf. F. Bleek, *Einleitung in das Alte Testament*, 4th edn, ed. by J. Wellhausen, 1878, p. 507 n.

[2] Cf. *Die Psalmen*, 1899, pp. xixff. Cf. R. H. Kennett, *Old Testament Essays*, 1928, pp. 119ff, where it is argued that "the Psalter as a whole was composed during the period 168–141 B.C." (p. 145). R. H. Pfeiffer (*Introduction to the Old Testament*, 1941, pp. 619ff) does not go so far as this but holds that the Psalms are post-exilic and most of the individual poems come from the period 400–200 B.C. (p. 632). He allows only two psalms to be pre-exilic (p. 631).

[3] Cf. *Einleitung in das Alte Testament*, 7th edn, 1935, p. 133 (cf. *Introduction to the Old Testament*, E. Tr. by W. Montgomery of 3rd German edn, 1923, p. 205). Cf. also P. R. Ackroyd, *V.T.* iii, 1953, pp. 113ff; S. Mowinckel, *The Psalms in Israel's Worship*, E. Tr. by D. R. Ap-Thomas, ii, 1962, pp. 260f. T. C. Vriezen (*De literatuur van Oud-Israël*, 1961, p. 187) holds it improbable that there were any Maccabaean psalms.

[4] Cf. *Einleitung*, 7th edn, pp. 130ff (E. Tr., pp. 200f).

reference to a contemporary individual,[1] but such a view would find little support to-day, when all the tendency is to find pre-exilic elements in the Psalter.[2] There is also a greater reluctance to speak of the Psalter as a Hymn Book, since that term evokes wrong ideas.[3] In earlier chapters I have said that it is now increasingly believed that the psalms were used to accompany ritual acts, and that they may have been composed or sung by cultic prophets who shared with the priests in the official conduct of the worship of the Temple. This complete revolution in our approach to the Psalter is due in outstanding measure to two men, Gunkel and Mowinckel. Some of Mowinckel's views have already been referred to, but others will fall to be considered in this chapter. But first we must briefly refer to the views of Gunkel,[4] who preceded him and on whose work Mowinckel built. Gunkel recognized the cultic origin

[1] Cf. A Critical Introduction to the Old Testament, 1913, pp. 136f; also J.Q.R. vii, 1894–5, pp. 658ff. R. H. Pfeiffer (Introduction to the Old Testament, 1941, pp. 630f) held that Pss. 20, 21, 72 may have referred to a Persian king or to Alexander the Great, and that others of the Royal Psalms may have been composed in honour of the Hasmonaean rulers. In Preussische Jahrbücher, clviii, 1914, pp. 43f, Gunkel had already argued against the view that foreign kings were referred to in the Royal Psalms on the ground that in Ps. 45.7 (M.T. 8) we read "God thy God hath anointed thee", where the Elohistic Psalter has probably changed an original "Yahweh thy God", an expression which could hardly have been used of a foreign king, and similarly Ps. 72.1 probably originally read "Give the king thy judgements, O Yahweh".

[2] Cf. T. H. Robinson (in The Psalmists, ed. by D. C. Simpson, 1926, p. 27): "We are growing more reconciled to the idea that there may be a good deal more pre-exilic material in the Psalter than was commonly held by the generation now passing away." H. Gressmann (ibid., p. 15) denied that there are any Maccabaean psalms in the Psalter, though he held it to be probable that most of the psalms were post-exilic.

[3] Cf. A. J. Wensinck (Theologisch Tijdschrift, liii, 1919, p. 101; Semietische Studiën, 1941, p. 57): "This view does not express the intrinsic relation between the Psalms and the cult."

[4] For a fine survey of the work of Gunkel and other writers on the Psalms, cf. A. R. Johnson, in O.T.M.S., pp. 162ff. Cf. also the richly documented survey of J. J. Stamm, Th.R., N.F. xxiii, 1955, pp. 1ff, and J. Coppens, Les Études récentes sur le Psautier, 1962. Cf. also Mowinckel, V.T. v, 1955, pp. 13ff. Gunkel's work is criticized by G. W. Ahlström (Psalm 89, 1959, pp. 9ff), for which Ahlström is in turn criticized by S. Mowinckel (J.S.S. v, 1960, pp. 291ff). A. S. Kapelrud reviews Scandinavian contributions to the study of the Psalms in A.S.T.I. iv, 1965, pp. 74ff, and in Verkundigung und Forschung (Beiheft zu Evangelische Theologie), 1966, pp. 62ff.

of many of the psalms, though he did not press this so far as Mowinckel, but believed that most of the psalms in the Psalter were private compositions expressing the feelings of individuals in the face of their experiences and that they were more spiritual than cultic poems in their outlook. It may be observed in passing that, as Aubert observes, cultic religion is not necessarily devoid of piety.[1] Mowinckel sought to relate the whole Psalter to the cult, though he recognized that a few psalms, including Psalms 1, 112, and 127, may never have been ritually used.[2]

What Gunkel sought to do—and this is his most important contribution to the study of the Psalter—was to classify the psalms,[3] so that they could be considered not as a number of isolated units, but in groups in terms of the situations out of which they arose and the needs they might be thought to have served. His earliest work along these lines appeared in 1904,[4] and he developed it in a number of publications[5] and most fully in his commentary on the Psalms,[6] and especially in the important volume of Introduction which was completed after his death by J. Begrich.[7] In a paper read to the British Society for Old Testament Study in 1927 he drew attention to what he described as the four main classes in the psalms.[8] These were Hymns of Praise,[9] Private Hymns of Thanksgiving,[10] National Hymns of Lament,[11] and Private Hymns of Lament.[12] He believed that psalms of

---

[1] Cf. *R.Th.Ph.*, N.S. xv, 1927, p. 218: "Une religion cultuelle n'est pas nécessairement une religion de cérémonies extérieures auxquelles manquent les impulsions d'une vraie piété."

[2] Cf. *Psalmenstudien VI*, 1924, p. 26; *The Psalms in Israel's Worship*, ii, pp. 52, 116. G. Quell (*Das kultische Problem der Psalmen*, 1926, pp. 143ff) finds thirteen psalms not to have been used in the cult.

[3] H. J. Kraus (*Geschichte der historisch-kritischen Forschung des Alten Testaments*, 1956, pp. 166f) notes that de Wette anticipated Gunkel in *Gattungs-forschung*. J. H. Kroeze (in *Studies on the Psalms*, 1963, pp. 40ff) rejects Gunkel's *Gattungen*, together with any idea of a cultic setting for the Psalms.

[4] *Ausgewählte Psalmen*, 1904; 4th edn, 1917.

[5] *Reden und Aufsätze*, 1913, pp. 92ff; *R.G.G.* iv, 1913, cols. 1927ff; 2nd edn, iv, 1930, cols. 1609ff. Cf. also his essays translated by A. K. Dallas in *What Remains of the Old Testament*, 1928, pp. 57ff, 69ff.

[6] *Die Psalmen*, 1926.   [7] *Einleitung in die Psalmen*, 1933.

[8] Cf. *Old Testament Essays* (Foreword by D. C. Simpson), 1927, pp. 118ff.

[9] Ibid., pp. 125f.   [10] Ibid., p. 126.   [11] Ibid.

[12] Ibid., pp. 126f. On the relation of these psalms to prophetic laments, and the priority of this category of psalms to the prophets, cf. W. Baumgartner, *Die Klagegedichte des Jeremia*, 1913.

thanksgiving are older than psalms of lament, and national psalms older than individual. The Hymns of Praise he believed to have been sung by trained singers to exhilarating music on holy days, extolling the greatness of Yahweh and his power and grace, but held that in course of time similar hymns were privately composed as expressions of adoration and devotion. The Private Hymns of Thanksgiving he believed to have been sung to accompany thank-offerings, when men came to offer thanks to God for deliverance from illness, danger, or misfortune. The National Hymns of Lament he believed to have been used to accompany expiatory ritual on occasions of public distress, and he thought the Private Hymns of Lament were similarly used by individual worshippers to accompany their expiatory sacrifices in their individual misfortunes.[1]

In his introduction to the Psalter Gunkel added other classes, including Enthronement Songs,[2] Royal Psalms,[3] and a number of minor categories such as Pilgrimage Songs,[4] National Hymns of Thanksgiving,[5] Wisdom Psalms,[6] and Liturgies.[7] He held that the Enthronement Psalms were used to celebrate the enthronement of Yahweh as the universal Lord, while the Royal Psalms were those which had commonly been interpreted as messianic or related to the Hasmonaean rulers, but which were now related to the pre-exilic kings and believed to have been sung to celebrate special events in their life, such as their accession (Pss. 2; 101; 110), or wedding (Ps. 45), or some anniversary (Pss. 21; 72), especially the anniversary of the founding of the dynasty (Ps. 132), or the

[1] A. J. Wensinck (*Theologisch Tijdschrift*, liii, 1919, p. 100; *Semietische Studiën*, 1941, p. 55) maintained that prayer was the accompaniment of sacrifice. Cf. also A. C. Welch, *The Psalter*, 1926, p. 67: "Sacrifice was accompanied by a liturgical hymn, of which we have many examples in the Psalter"; A. Maillot, in *Vocabulary of the Bible*, ed. by J. J. von Allmen, E. Tr., 1958, p. 331b: "Prayer was often accompanied by a sacrifice, so that one may wonder whether prayer was the oral part of sacrifice."

[2] Op. cit., pp. 94ff. On the Enthronement psalms cf. W. Harrelson, *Interpreting the Old Testament*, 1964, pp. 419ff.

[3] Op. cit., pp. 140ff. Though he did not list these among his four categories of Psalms in the above-mentioned paper, he dealt with the Royal Psalms briefly at the end; cf. *Old Testament Essays*, pp. 138ff. Cf. *What Remains of the Old Testament*, E. Tr. by A. K. Dallas, 1928, p. 90.

[4] Cf. *Einleitung*, pp. 309ff.   [5] Ibid., pp. 314ff.
[6] Ibid., pp. 381ff.   [7] Ibid., pp. 407ff.

undertaking of a military campaign (Ps. 20), or the victorious return from such a campaign (Ps. 18). Gunkel recognized some mixed forms that did not fit neatly into his categories, and also found what he called Prophetic Liturgies, which owed something to the influence of the prophets and in turn influenced later prophets.[1] In the Individual Laments and in the Liturgies he found examples of what he called The Certainty of a Hearing,[2] when the worshipper was encouraged by the assurance that his plea would be heard and answered. He further found some Entrance Liturgies, or Torah Liturgies, in which the worshipper on entering the shrine was reminded of the qualities which were required of those who came into the Temple.[3] Examples of these are Psalm 15 ("Lord, who shall sojourn in thy tabernacle? Who shall dwell in thy holy hill?") and Psalm 24 ("Who shall ascend into the hill of the Lord? And who shall stand in his holy place?"), a psalm which was used when the Ark was carried in sacred procession. Older writers had thought of the psalms as related to worship in the sense that they were sung in the worship of the Second Temple, but this new approach directed attention to the possibility that the psalms arose out of cultic situations and accompanied ritual acts.[4]

This general approach was followed by J. P. Peters,[5] who, however, developed it along his own lines. He held that the psalms were composed for liturgical use in connection with the

[1] Cf. *Z.A.W.* xlii, 1924, pp. 191ff.   [2] Cf. *Einleitung*, pp. 243ff.

[3] Ibid., p. 408. On these Entrance liturgies cf. Mowinckel, *Psalmenstudien V*, 1923, pp. 57ff, 107ff, *Le Décalogue*, 1927, pp. 141ff, and *The Psalms in Israel's Worship*, i, pp. 177ff; K. Galling, *Z.A.W.* xlvii, 1929, pp. 125ff; K. Koch, in *Studien zur Theologie der alttestamentlichen Überlieferungen* (von Rad Festschrift), 1961, pp. 45ff; J. L. Koole, *O.T.S.* xiii, 1963, pp. 98ff (arguing that Ps. 15 was used in the royal accession rites); A. S. Kapelrud, *Nor.T.T.* lxvi, 1965, pp. 39ff (holding that Ps.15 was a Covenant renewal psalm). In *Le Décalogue*, pp. 141ff, Mowinckel argued that the Entrance liturgies were the origin of the Decalogue (cf. L. Aubert, *R.Th.Ph.*, N.S. xv, 1927, pp. 238f), but this view was modified in *The Psalms in Israel's Worship*, i, p. 180 n.

[4] G. Quell (*Das kultische Problem der Psalmen*, 1926) found three main groups of Psalms: Cultic, Cultic-religious, and Religious, with various types of Psalm in each group. Of these he found the third group to be non-cultic.

[5] Cf. *The Psalms as Liturgies*, 1922. Already in 1916 Peters had argued that the Psalms were ritual texts intended to be used to accompany sacrifice; cf. *J.B.L.* xxxv, pp. 143ff.

sanctuaries of the land, but argued that the Yahwistic psalms were used in the Jerusalem Temple, the Elohistic psalms in the northern shrines. The Korahite psalms he associated with the sanctuary at Dan and the Asaphite psalms with Bethel, though he believed that the psalms originally composed for the northern shrines were later revised for use in Jerusalem. J. M. Powis Smith[1] also followed Gunkel in holding that the psalms were composed for cultic use and he held that they accompanied the sacrificial ritual. Similarly A. C. Welch,[2] who maintained that the psalms were written directly for the public and private ritual acts of the Temple and that they are only to be understood in terms of the cult. The correct liturgy, he argued, was as important as the correct ritual. While there were still some scholars who continued to follow the older lines, the influence of Gunkel's approach was very widely felt[3] and it has continued to mark most of the work that has been done on the Psalter.[4]

[1] *The Religion of the Psalms*, 1922. Cf. also J. Paterson, *T.G.U.O.S.* xiv, 1953, pp. 42ff.

[2] Cf. *The Psalter in Life, Worship and History*, 1926, pp. 63ff.

[3] Cf. W. Staerk, *Lyrik*, 2nd edn, 1920; R. Kittel, *Die Psalmen*, 5th edn, 1929; J. Hempel, *Die althebräische Literatur*, 1930, pp. 30ff; H. Schmidt, *Die Psalmen*, 1934; W. O. E. Oesterley, *A Fresh Approach to the Psalms*, 1937; F. James, *Thirty Psalmists*, 1938; A. Lods, Introduction to Psalms in *La Bible du Centenaire*, iii, 1947, pp. iiiff; E. A. Leslie, *The Psalms translated and interpreted*, 1949; A. Weiser, *Die Psalmen*, 2 vols., 1950, 5th edn, 1959, E. Tr. by H. Hartwell, 1962; J. Paterson, *The Praises of Israel*, 1950; S. Terrien, *The Psalms and their Meaning for Today*, 1952; A. Bentzen, *Introduction to the Old Testament*, 2nd edn, i, 1952, pp. 146ff; R. T. Daniel, *How to Study the Psalms*, 1953; W. S. McCullough, *I.B.*, iv, 1955, pp. 3ff; F. Nötscher, *Echt.B.*, *Altes Testament*, iv, 1959, pp. 13ff; H. J. Kraus, *Psalmen*, 1960; G. W. Anderson, in Peake's *Commentary on the Bible*, 2nd edn, 1962, pp. 409ff; O. Eissfeldt, *The Old Testament: an Introduction*, E. Tr. by P. R. Ackroyd, 1965, pp. 102ff. For a different attempt to classify the Psalms cf. A. Descamps, in *Mélanges Bibliques* (Robert Festschrift), 1957, pp. 187ff. A. Robert (in *Miscellanea Biblica B. Ubach*, 1953, pp. 211ff), while recognizing the debt of scholarship to Gunkel, is critical of the *Formgeschichteschule*. On the other hand, J. W. Wevers (*V.T.* vi, 1956, p. 80) says: "The basic literary types discovered by Gunkel are now the *sine qua non* for all Old Testament scholars."

[4] Gunkel's influence was less visible in W. E. Barnes, *The Psalms*, 1931; H. Herkenne, *Das Buch der Psalmen*, 1936; J. Calès, *Le Livre des Psaumes*, 2 vols., 1936; B. D. Eerdmans, *The Hebrew Book of Psalms*, 1947. The older approach to the Psalter was continued and pressed to its extreme limit by M. Buttenwieser (*The Psalms chronologically treated*, 1938), who

This approach was taken up by Mowinckel and pressed much further than Gunkel had pressed it, and as we have already noted he sought to relate all the psalms to cultic acts and brought them into closer relation with the prophets than Gunkel had done. Here I think Mowinckel has made a valuable contribution.[1] It seems to me improbable that the Hymns of Praise were sung by choirs while the psalms that accompanied the private offerings were sung by the individuals who brought the offerings, as Gunkel suggested. It is far more likely that persons skilled in liturgical singing sang on these occasions also, and that the purpose of their singing was to awaken in the worshipper some sense of the meaning of that whereon he was engaged.

Not all of Mowinckel's ideas have been generally accepted. In many of the laments the sufferer complains that the "workers of iniquity" have been responsible for his troubles. Here Mowinckel holds that the trouble is traced to spells that were believed to have been cast on the suppliant by sorcerers and that it was believed that by the performance of the right ritual act accompanied by the right liturgical text the breaking of the spells was to be achieved.[2] The "workers of iniquity" are thus interpreted as sorcerers, and the texts are understood in the light of Babylonian and Egyptian texts. Adolphe Lods claims[3] that he anticipated[4] Mowinckel in this view, though Mowinckel developed it further.

That there were many in Israel who believed in sorcery is beyond question. We should not have had the condemnations of sorcery in the Old Testament[5] had it not been so. I have already in the previous chapter noted the condemnations of some prophets

tried to date every psalm exactly, and in many cases to determine their authors. He held Ps. 81 B to come from the time of Joshua, Ps. 68 B to be from the same hand as the Song of Deborah, three psalms to be from the author of the book of Job, and 115 psalms to be post-exilic.

[1] A. Causse (Les plus vieux chants de la Bible, 1926, p. 4) says: "C'est l'apparition des Psalmenstudien de Mowinckel qui a définitivement orienté l'exégèse du Psautier vers les voies nouvelles."

[2] Cf. Psalmenstudien I, 1922, pp. 29ff; Z.A.W. xliii, 1925, pp. 260ff. For a modification of his views cf. The Psalms in Israel's Worship, ii, p. 250.

[3] Cf. Histoire de la littérature hébraïque et juive, 1950, p. 738.

[4] Cf. R.H.R. lxxviii, 1918, pp. 276f. Cf. also Lods, in Vom Alten Testament (Marti Festschrift), 1925, pp. 181ff; R.H.P.R. vii, 1927, pp. 1ff. It should be noted, however, that Lods raises doubts against some of Mowinckel's positions; Cf. R.H.R. xci, 1925, pp. 33f.

[5] Lev. 19.26; Deut. 18.10; 1 Sam. 15.23; 28.3; 2 Kings 17.17; 21.6.

who are said to have dealt in spells.[1] But it is very doubtful whether the official cultus of Jerusalem provided counter-action against spells, since that could only have fostered the belief in witchcraft.[2] It is true that Mowinckel does not regard the ritual acts and the liturgical texts in the nature of counter-spells, but thinks of them as pleas to God to free the sufferers from the effects of the spells, but it is doubtful if men who believed in sorcery would think of them other than as counter-spells.[3]

Moreover, there is no need to limit the "iniquity" to this one special kind. As Johnson observes: "Mowinckel offers no convincing evidence to support his view that the term *'āwen*, as used of a power which was abused for anti-social ends and therefore issued in evil, was at any time restricted to forms of magic, however widely one may choose to understand this term. In short, there is no sufficient reason for abandoning the view that *pô'alê 'āwen* were "evil-doers" in a quite general sense."[4]

Humbert argues that Mowinckel has to do violence to some passages of the Old Testament in the interests of his theory,[5] while Aubert complains that he forces on his Biblical material ideas which he finds in Babylon and Egypt which are not convincing to

[1] Cf. above, p. 155.

[2] N. Nicolsky (*Spuren magischer Formeln in den Psalmen*, 1927) also found traces of magic in the Psalter.

[3] The most extensive reply to Mowinckel is in N. H. Ridderbos, *De "Werkers der Ongerechtigheid" in de individuelle Psalmen*, 1939. Other criticisms may be found in A. Causse, *R.H.P.R.* ii, 1922, pp. 283ff; E. Podechard, *R.B.* xxxii, 1923, pp. 141ff; P. Humbert, *R.Th.Ph.*, N.S. xi, 1923, pp. 73ff; L. Aubert, *R.Th.Ph.*, N.S. xv, 1927, pp. 211ff, esp. pp. 220ff; A. R. Johnson, in *O.T.M.S.*, pp. 197ff. On the enemies envisaged by the Psalmists cf. also H. Birkeland, *Die Feinde des Individuums in der israelitischen Psalmenliteratur*, 1933, and *The Evildoers in the Book of Psalms*, 1955; H. Schmidt, *Das Gebet der Angeklagten im Alten Testament*, 1928. In *Les "pauvres" d'Israël*, 1922, pp. 81ff, Causse had argued that the enemies of the psalmists were the oppressors among their own people. H. Ringgren (*The Faith of the Psalmists*, 1963, pp. 43f) defines the enmity between righteous and wicked as "between Israel as God's holy people . . . and those who stand outside the covenant". The latter could be "national enemies . . . or worshippers of foreign gods, or performers of magical practices". Cf. also G. W. Anderson, *B.J.R.L.* xlviii, 1965–6, pp. 18ff.

[4] *O.T.M.S.*, pp. 199f.

[5] *R.Th.Ph.*, N.S. xi, 1923, pp. 76ff. Humbert also notes (p. 75) the extreme rarity in the Psalms of the words which denote magic and magicians elsewhere in the Old Testament.

those who recognize an individual character in Israelite religion.[1] It is undeniable that Israel borrowed much from her neighbours. But it is unnecessary to make her a mere sponge that soaked up whatever came from her neighbours. Israel could never have exercised that enduring influence on the world which she has exercised if that had been so. There was that in her own heritage from the time of Moses which she did not derive from others, and it enabled her to borrow and to convert into the vehicle of her own faith that which she borrowed. To see Israel as wholly unique and to be set over against her neighbours is wrong; but it is equally wrong to read into the life and faith of Israel what we find only in her neighbours and what is without clear trace in the Old Testament. Moreover, if we read into the Old Testament from Babylonia the idea of magic as being the supposed cause of the misfortunes, it is not clear why we should not equally read into Israel the idea of the ritual and its accompanying texts as magical counter-spells, as was the case in Babylonia.

A second major theory of Mowinckel's has encountered much criticism. This is his view that there was an autumn New Year festival in Israel,[2] comparable with the Babylonian New Year

---

[1] *R.Th.Ph.*, N.S. xv, 1927, p. 225. In *The Psalmists*, ed. by D.C. Simpson, 1926, H. Gressmann (pp. 1ff) pressed the links between the Psalms and Babylonian and Egyptian literature, and A. M. Blackman (pp. 177ff) pressed the Egyptian links. G. R. Driver (pp. 109ff) was much more cautious in dealing with Babylonian parallels, which he drew on for illustration rather than for proof of any direct connection. R. G. Castellino (*Le lamentazioni individuali e gli inni in Babilonia e in Israele*, 1939) is similarly cautious, but less so are C. G. Cumming (*The Assyrian and Hebrew Hymns of Praise*, 1934) and G. Widengren (*The Accadian and Hebrew Psalms of Lamentation*, 1937).

[2] Cf. *Psalmenstudien II*, 1922; also in *R.G.G.*, 2nd edn, i, 1927, col. 2003; *Zum israelitischen Neujahr und zur Deutung der Thronbesteigungspsalmen*, 1952; *He that Cometh*, E. Tr. by G. W. Anderson, 1956, pp. 21ff. Cf. also P. Volz, *Das Neujahrsfest Jahwes*, 1912; G. Quell, *Das kultische Problem der Psalmen*, 1926, pp. 48ff; H. Schmidt, *Die Thronfahrt Jahves am Fest der Jahreswende*, 1927; G. Östborn, *Tōrā in the Old Testament*, 1945, pp. 76ff; F. M. Th. de Liagre Böhl, *Opera Minora*, 1953, pp. 262ff; J. Gray, *V.T.* xi, 1961, pp. 1ff. H. J. Kraus (*Die Königsherrschaft Gottes im Alten Testament*, 1951) criticizes the view of Mowinckel and proposes a post-exilic ritual association of the enthronement psalms. On this cf. J. R. Porter, *J.T.S.*, N.S. v, 1954, pp. 161ff, and H. Ringgren, *The Faith of the Psalmists*, 1963, pp. xviif. Cf. also V. Maag, *Oxford Congress Volume* (S.V.T. vii), 1960, pp. 129ff. Mowinckel traces to the ritual of this

festival.[1] In Babylon at this festival the king went to the temple of Marduk and renewed his sovereignty by taking the hands of the god. There was a sacred procession, referred to in Isaiah 46, in which the god Nabu was borne to the temple of Marduk, and Marduk was borne part of the way back. In the ritual of the festival[2] there was a representation of the death and resurrection of the god and also of the Creation myth in which Marduk vanquished Tiamat, a dramatization of the god's fight with his

autumn festival the roots of Old Testament eschatology. Cf. I. Engnell, in *S.B.U.* ii, 1952, cols. 245ff; also J. Morgenstern, *Amos Studies*, i, 1941, pp. 408f: "The roots of the concept of the Day of Yahweh were not new in any sense. They were embedded in the observance of the day of the fall equinox as the New Year's Day and its ritual in Solomon's new Temple in Jerusalem." J. Bright (*Interpretation*, v, 1951, p. 10) objects: "To seek its origins in the putative Enthronement Festival of the Hebrew monarchy aside from the question of the existence of such a thing in Israel, raises the question why Babylon, which certainly did have it, did not produce an eschatology." Cf. G. Pidoux, *Le Dieu qui vient*, 1947, pp. 49ff; G. W. Anderson, in *O.T.M.S.*, 1951, pp. 304ff; W. Eichrodt, *Theology of the Old Testament*, E. Tr., 1961, pp. 497f; also S. B. Frost, *Old Testament Apocalyptic*, 1952, pp. 32ff. W. S. McCullough (in *I.B.* iv, 1955, p. 7) objects to Mowinckel's view that "the idea that the Hebrew God could in any real sense be enthroned annually was poor theology, and could hardly have been seriously held by the nation's religious leaders". To this H. Ringgren (*The Faith of the Psalmists*, 1963, p. xv) effectively replies: "This objection reveals a certain misunderstanding of the nature of cultic celebration. The Jews are aware of the Exodus from Egypt as an historical fact, and yet they are asked to consider themselves as delivered from Egypt at every Passover. Roman Catholics know that Jesus died on Calvary, and yet they believe that His vicarious sacrifice is repeated in every Mass. Orthodox Christians know very well that the Resurrection took place long ago and that Jesus lives, and yet they repeat the response every Easter night, 'Christ is risen indeed'." R. Davidson (*The Old Testament*, 1964, pp. 128f) is sceptical of the New Year festival, while J. H. Kroeze (in *Studies on the Psalms*, 1963, pp. 43f) rejects it. J. D. W. Watts (*Th.Z.* xxi, 1965, pp. 341ff) finds varieties of classification within the psalms held to be associated with the festival.

[1] On the Babylonian festival cf. S. A. Pallis, *The Babylonian Akîtu Festival*, 1926, esp. pp. 249ff. H. Ringgren (*Biblical Research*, 1962, p. 2) observes that any reconstruction of the Israelite festival on the basis of the late Babylonian *akîtu* festival is hazardous.

[2] On the ritual background of the Decalogue in this festival in Mowinckel's view, cf. *Le Décalogue*, 1927, pp. 114ff. Cf. also A. Weiser, *The Psalms*, E. Tr., 1962, pp. 30ff. J. Morgenstern (*H.U.C.A.* xxxv, 1964, pp. 14ff) interprets much of the account of the revolt of Absalom in terms of the New Year ritual.

enemies in a ritual combat. There was also a sacred marriage in which the god was represented by the king, and by which the springs of fertility for the nation were believed to be released.

Some eleven years after Mowinckel propounded his view the British "Myth and Ritual" group advanced the view that there was a common pattern throughout the whole of the ancient Near East, including Israel, and in close agreement with Mowinckel maintained that the Israelite New Year festival shared all these features with the Babylonian.[1] Professor Hooke, who was the leader of the "Myth and Ritual" group, has since stated that the British group were unaware of the work of Mowinckel until they had begun their work and that they were entirely independent of Mowinckel and his work in their origin.[2] The features of the Babylonian festival to which they drew attention were the ones which Mowinckel had noted.

To read all this into the Old Testament has seemed to many scholars to go far beyond the evidence, and C. R. North criticized it on the ground that it read into the Old Testament what it found elsewhere, instead of basing itself on what it found in the Old Testament and working outwards.[3] So far as divine kingship is concerned, Mowinckel found in Psalm 45 clear evidence of this, since there in addressing the king we find the words: "Thy throne, O God, is for ever and ever".[4] To this North replied by justifying

[1] Cf. *Myth and Ritual*, ed. by S. H. Hooke, 1933, p. 8. Cf. also *In the Beginning*, 1947, pp. 17f. "Patternism" was taken up with enthusiasm by a number of Scandinavian, and especially Swedish, scholars. Against "patternism" cf. H. Frankfort, *The Problem of Similarity in Ancient Near Eastern Religions*, 1951; also M. Noth, *Z.Th.K.* xlvii, 1950, pp. 157ff. Cf. also H. Frankfort, *Kingship and the Gods*, 1948; J. de Fraine, *L'Aspect religieux de la royauté israélite*, 1954; K. H. Bernhardt, *Das Problem der altorientalischen Königsideologie im Alten Testament*, 1961 (on which cf. A. R. Johnson, *B.L.*, 1962, p. 42).

[2] Cf. *Myth, Ritual and Kingship*, ed. by S. H. Hooke, 1958, pp. 1f. S. G. F. Brandon, though critical of the "Myth and Ritual" school, says (ibid., p. 290): "He [i.e. Professor Brandon] sees the 'Myth and Ritual' thesis as one of the major developments in the comparative study of religion, and he believes that, despite all the opposition which it has encountered, when the final adjustments are made it will be found that its contribution has been of the highest importance and that its value is abiding."

[3] Cf. *Z.A.W.* l, 1932, p. 35; also *A.J.S.L.* xlviii, 1931–2, pp. 1ff. Cf., too, A. Lauha, *S.E.Å.* xii, 1947, pp. 183ff.

[4] Cf. *Psalmenstudien III*, 1923, pp. 96ff. So, earlier, H. Gunkel, *Preussische Jahrbücher*, clviii, 1914, p. 54.

the translation: "Thy throne is like God's for ever and ever".[1]
A. R. Johnson has noted[2] that whereas Mowinckel earlier wrote of
the king as "an incarnation of the national god",[3] he has more
recently avoided this expression. He now speaks of the king representing Yahweh in the cult, though not equated with him.[4] On
the other hand I. Engnell[5] and G. Widengren[6] have argued for
the belief in divine kingship in Israel. While recognizing that the
Old Testament prophets rejected the idea of divine kingship,
Hooke contented himself with noting that they were familiar with
the idea.[7] Johnson prefers to avoid the use of the expression, and
instead to speak of "sacral kingship",[8] as Widengren[9] and Bentzen[10]

[1] Cf. Z.A.W. loc. cit., pp. 29ff. Here North based himself on G. R.
Driver, in The Psalmists (ed. D. C. Simpson), 1926, p. 124. Cf. also A. R.
Johnson, Sacral Kingship in Ancient Israel, 1955, p. 27 n. H. Ringgren
(The Faith of the Psalmists, 1963, p. 113) renders "Your divine throne
endures for ever and ever", with R.S.V. M. Dahood (Psalms (Anchor
Bible), i, 1966, p. 269) renders "The eternal and everlasting God has
enthroned you".
[2] Cf. Myth, Ritual and Kingship, ed. by S. H. Hooke, 1958, pp. 233f.
[3] Cf. Psalmenstudien II, 1922, p. 301.
[4] Cf. The Psalms in Israel's Worship, i, p. 59. Cf. also J.S.S. v, 1960,
p. 294, where Mowinckel rejects the view that in the Israelite liturgy the
king as the incarnation of the god suffered and died and rose again.
[5] Cf. Studies in Divine Kingship in the Ancient Near East, 1943, pp. 174ff.
Cf. also E. Hammershaimb, Some Aspects of Old Testament Prophecy,
1966, p. 11.
[6] Cf. R.o.B. ii, 1943, pp. 49ff; Psalm 110 och det sakrala kungadömet
i Israel, 1941; Sakrales Königtum im Alten Testament und im Judentum,
1955. G. Cooke (Z.A.W. lxxiii, 1961, pp. 202ff) argues that the Israelite
king was Yahweh's son only in a metaphorical and adoptional sense, and
observes that "no Old Testament evidence shows that prophetic Yahwism
attacked Hebrew kings and kingship because of claims for the king's
divinity" (p. 225). Cf. G. Hölscher, Geschichte der israelitischen und
jüdischen Religion, 1922, p. 31.
[7] Cf. Myth and Ritual, pp. 10f.
[8] Cf. E.T. lxii, 1950-1, p. 41b. Cf. also his Sacral Kingship in Ancient
Israel, 1955; and his essays in The Labyrinth, ed. by S. H. Hooke, 1935,
pp. 71ff, and in Myth, Ritual and Kingship, ed. by Hooke, 1958, pp.
204ff, and the whole article in E.T., loc. cit., pp. 36ff. So also H. Ringgren,
Israelitische Religion, 1963, p. 213. W. S. McCullough criticized the work
of Johnson in E.T. lxviii, 1956-7, pp. 144ff, and Professor Johnson
replied, ibid., pp. 178ff.
[9] Cf. Psalm 110 och det sakrala kungadömet i Israel, 1941.
[10] Cf. Det sakrale kongedømme, 1945.

had already done.[1] This is much wiser and it prejudices fewer issues. So far as the sacred marriage is concerned, T. H. Robinson ventures to suggest that in the Temple of Jerusalem the goddess Anath stood beside Yahweh, and that at the festival they were removed to a hut in a vineyard, where the sacred marriage took place, and that this was succeeded by the death of Yahweh.[2] Others have claimed to find evidences of the sacred marriage in Israel,[3] and it has been held that the story of David and Abishag rests on this rite. It is believed that in this sacred marriage the king was required to represent the god and to marry a virgin and beget a child, and that if he failed in this he could no longer

[1] Johnson had earlier spoken of "divine kingship" (cf. *The Labyrinth*, 1935, p. 79).
[2] Cf. *Myth and Ritual*, pp. 185, 188ff.
[3] So S. H. Hooke, ibid., p. 12; W. O. E. Oesterley, ibid., pp. 139f; G. Widengren, *R.o.B.* vii, 1948, pp. 17ff, and *Sakrales Königtum im Alten Testament und im Judentum*, 1955, pp. 76ff. J. R. Porter (*Moses and Monarchy*, 1963, p. 11) interprets Ex. 4.22ff in terms of sacred marriage. In 1922 T. J. Meek brought the Song of Songs into association with the fertility cult and the sacred marriage. Cf. *A.J.S.L.* xxxix, 1922–3, pp. 1ff; also *The Song of Songs: a Symposium*, ed. by W. H. Schoff, 1924, pp. 48ff, and *I.B.* v, 1956, pp. 91ff. Many writers have subscribed to this view; cf. W. H. Schoff, op. cit., pp. 80ff; S. Minocchi, *Le Perle della Bibbia*, 1924, pp. 22f; L. Waterman, *J.B.L.* xliv, 1925, pp. 171ff (but cf. *The Song of Songs interpreted as a Dramatic Poem*, 1948, p. 2); W. Wittekindt, *Das Hohe Lied und seine Beziehung zum Istarkult*, 1926, pp. 179ff; Graham and May, *Culture and Conscience*, 1936, pp. 122f; F. Dornseiff, *Z.D.M.G.* xc, 1936, pp. 589ff; M. Haller, *Die fünf Megilloth*, 1940, pp. 21f; I. Engnell, in *S.B.U.* i, 1948, cols. 905ff; H. Schmökel, *Z.A.W.* lxiv, 1952, pp. 148ff, and *Heilige Hochzeit und Hohes Lied*, 1956; H. Ringgren, *Das Hohe Lied*, 1958, pp. 3f, and *R.o.B.* xviii, 1959, pp. 23ff; J. W. Wevers, in Hastings' one volume *D.B.*, rev. edn, 1963, pp. 930f. For a criticism of the view, cf. H. H. Rowley, *J.R.A.S.*, 1938, pp. 251ff, and *S.L.*, 2nd edn, 1965, pp. 223ff; also U. Cassuto, *G.S.A.I.*, N.S. i, 1925–8, pp. 166ff; N. Schmidt, *J.A.O.S.* xlvi, 1926, pp. 154ff; G. Ricciotti, *Il Cantico dei Cantici*, 1928, pp. 117ff; L. Dürr, *O.L.Z.* xxxi, 1928, cols. 113ff; R. Gordis, *The Song of Songs*, 1954, pp. 4ff. J. N. Schofield (*J.M.U.E.O.S.* xxii, 1938, pp. 42f) hazards the suggestion that the child born of the sacred marriage that took place at the autumn festival would be born in the month of Tammuz and was then vicariously slain so that the king might live. On this cf. below, p. 189, n. 6. Against the common equation of Tammuz with Adonis, found, for example, in the writers who see a cultic liturgy in the Song of Songs, cf. E. M. Yamauchi, *J.B.L.* lxxxiv, 1965, pp. 283ff, where this equation is denied and where the view of Tammuz as a dying and rising god is declared to be without evidence.

remain on the throne, and it is supposed that David failed to beget a child from Abishag.[1] The story of David and Abishag stands in the Succession History,[2] which is commonly dated in the reign of Solomon, and therefore within a few years of the events it describes. It seems to me quite incredible that within so few years the significance could be so completely misunderstood as this theory supposes. For we are specifically told that David had no sexual relations with Abishag,[3] but that she was introduced into his bed because he "gat no heat".[4] Here it is supposed that sexual heat is meant. But if so, it is curious that more bedclothes were tried first before Abishag was thought of.[5] If the supposed custom was one that continued through the monarchical period, it would be incredible for a writer in the reign of Solomon either to misunderstand it so completely or to try to conceal it from readers who would be familiar with it. I find it impossible to accept the view that the sacred marriage figured in the Jerusalem autumn festival.[6]

[1] Cf. N. H. Snaith, in *I.B.* iii, 1954, pp. 19f; J. Mauchline, in Peake's *Commentary on the Bible*, 2nd edn, 1962, p. 339b; J. Gray, *I and II Kings*, 1964, p. 76.

[2] Cf. L. Rost, *Die Überlieferung von der Thronnachfolge Davids*, 1926; G. von Rad, *Gesammelte Studien zum Alten Testament*, 1958, pp. 159ff.

[3] 1 Kings 1.4. Snaith (loc. cit., p. 20) accepts this as decisive evidence of the King's impotence, but Gray (loc. cit.) thinks Abishag was the regular concubine of David, while J. N. Schofield (*The Religious Background of the Bible*, 1944, p. 91) calls her David's last bride. It is true that Solomon chose to interpret Adonijah's request for Abishag as tantamount to a claim to the kingdom (1 Kings 2.22), as it would have been if Abishag had been the concubine of David (cf. 2 Sam. 16.21ff). But the fact that Bathsheba sponsored Adonijah's request (1 Kings 2.19ff) is decisively against this (cf. J. A. Montgomery, *The Books of Kings*, 1951, p. 72: "certainly that experienced woman would not have been caught unawares"). It would seem to be clear that Solomon merely seized on this as a pretext to get rid of Adonijah.

[4] 1 Kings 1.1.

[5] Ibid. Snaith (loc. cit., p. 20) thinks the bedclothes were used to induce sexual heat. While he links the incident to the idea that the king's virility was held to be vital for the well-being of the community, he rejects the idea that the incident is connected with the sacred marriage.

[6] Cf. Johnson, in *Myth, Ritual and Kingship*, p. 227: "The actual evidence offered in support of this theory was throughout very slight and indeed quite fragmentary." Of its relevance to the Song of Songs T. H. Gaster (*Thespis*, 1950, p. 233 n) says: "This theory is far from proved." J. Pedersen (*Israel III–IV*, 1940, p. 471) says: "Was the sacred marriage, too, celebrated by the Israelite king as part of his cult? If this was the case, every trace of it has disappeared."

As little can I accept the view that Yahweh was a dying and rising god, to which T. H. Robinson announced his adhesion in the passage above quoted. Here Haldar follows this view[1] though Hvidberg dismissed it,[2] and Mowinckel says it is quite out of the question that Yahweh was ever regarded in Israelite religion as a dying and rising god.[3]

While much in the view propounded by Mowinckel seems to be open to serious objection, this does not mean that his view is to be wholly rejected. It is true that we do not find in the Old Testament any account of a New Year festival such as Mowinckel describes, or of any part played by the king in the ritual of this kind, and this has been underlined by L. Pap in an examination of Mowinckel's work.[4] But there is Old Testament evidence of a part played by kings in the ritual, and there are passages in the Psalms which can be quite naturally interpreted in terms of a ritual combat in which the king played a part. These suggest that there were royal rites in some Israelite festivals, and are most probably to be associated with a New Year festival.[5] N. H. Snaith,

---

[1] Cf. *Studies in the Book of Nahum*, 1947, p. 154, where this view is surprisingly and erroneously attributed to A. R. Johnson. W. E. Staples (*A.J.S.L.* liii, 1936–7, pp. 145ff) regards the book of Ruth as a cultic text moving in the same world of ideas, and finds Elimelech to be the dying god and Ruth to be his devotee. It is necessary to read this into the text before it can be found there, and eisegesis is always a poor substitute for exegesis. Several writers have connected the Suffering Servant of Deutero-Isaiah with the myth of the dying and rising god; so H. Gressmann, *Der Ursprung der israelitisch-jüdischen Eschatologie*, 1905, pp. 328ff; H. Gunkel, in *R.G.G.* iii, 1912, cols. 1542f; S. Mowinckel, *De senere profeter*, 1944, p. 197; I. Engnell, *B.J.R.L.* xxxi, 1948, pp. 56ff.

[2] Cf. *Weeping and Laughter in the Old Testament*, E. Tr. by N. Haislund, 1962, p. 136: "In the Old Testament Yahweh nowhere appears as a dying and rising deity."

[3] Cf. *The Psalms in Israel's Worship*, i, p. 243. Cf. Johnson, *E.T.* lxii, 1950–1, p. 40: "There is nothing whatsoever in the writer's argument to suggest that Yahweh was regarded as a dying and rising god and that the king played His part or in fact that of any god in the ritual described."

[4] Cf. *Das israelitische Neujahrsfest*, 1933. Cf. also L. Aubert, *R.Th.Ph.*, N.S. xv, 1927, pp. 232ff; O. Eissfeldt, *Z.A.W.* xlvi, 1928, pp. 81ff (= *Kleine Schriften*, i, 1962, pp. 172ff); E. J. Young, *The Book of Isaiah*, i, 1965, pp. 494ff.

[5] Johnson (in *Myth, Ritual and Kingship*, p. 235) notes that the following features seem to be present in the Jerusalem autumn festival: (a) the celebration of Yahweh's original triumph over the forces of darkness and his enthronement as King in the assembly of the gods, and the

who contested many of Mowinckel's views and who ascribed the royal psalms to a quite late date, nevertheless held that in Israel there was an autumn New Year festival.[1] Of evidences that the king did in fact play a part in the ritual we may note the conduct of David when the Ark was brought into Jerusalem.[2] He wore a linen ephod and took part in a religious dance before the Ark, he offered sacrifice, and he pronounced the blessing on the people.[3] Similarly at the Dedication of the Temple Solomon is said to have offered prayer for himself and the nation and to have blessed the people.[4] These were special occasions and prove nothing for annual occasions. On the other hand, there are so many psalms which appear to have to do with the king that it is probable that he was present when they were used and that they were used on recurrent occasions, since there is nothing in them to indicate a single historic occasion. Psalm 24 is apparently a processional psalm for an occasion or occasions when the Ark was carried into the Temple. This was not the historic occasion on which David brought the Ark into Jerusalem, since it is implied that the Temple was already standing.[5] It could possibly have been first used when Solomon brought the Ark into the newly built Temple,[6] but its place in the Psalter suggests that it was used recurrently.

I cannot here review critically all of the Biblical material which is examined. Of British scholars Professor Johnson has given

demonstration of his might on the plane of history; (b) a dramatic representation of the dawn of the great eschatological "Day"; (c) the dramatic representation of the descent of the true Messiah to the Underworld and his deliverance by Yahweh; and (d) a triumphal procession in which the Ark and the king proceed to the Temple for the final act of enthronement. On the question of an Israelite New Year festival cf. the important critical survey by H. Cazelles, in S.D.B. vi, 1960, cols. 620ff.

[1] Cf. The Jewish New Year Festival, 1947. For Mowinckel's replies to the views of Snaith, cf. Zum israelitischen Neujahr und zur Deutung der Thronbesteigungspsalmen, 1952, pp. 39ff. Snaith argued (pp. 195ff, 205ff (cf. Studies in the Psalter, 1934, pp. 88ff); cf. H. J. Kraus, Die Königsherrschaft Gottes im Alten Testament, 1951, pp. 99ff) that Deutero-Isaiah preceded the composition of the Enthronement psalms and that they borrowed from him. Against this cf. also Mowinckel, He that Cometh, 1956, pp. 139ff; The Psalms in Israel's Worship, i, pp. 189ff.

[2] On this passage and the historification of myth in the Israelite cult, cf. A. Bentzen, J.B.L. lxvii, 1948, pp. 36ff.

[3] 2 Sam. 6.14, 17f. [4] 1 Kings 8.22ff, 54f. [5] Ps. 24.7. [6] 1 Kings 8.1ff.

more attention to this subject than any other scholar,[1] and while he would be the first to admit his debt to Mowinckel he is in no sense a mere purveyor of Mowinckel's ideas,[2] and I must be content here to summarize some of his conclusions. He has argued for an Israelite autumn festival, modelled on the old Jebusite festival of Jerusalem,[3] but related to the worship of Yahweh and given a character of its own, and he has interpreted a number of the psalms as ritual texts to be used at this festival.

In the late passage in the final chapter of the book of Zechariah the gift of rain is said to be dependent on the due celebration of the feast of Tabernacles at which the kingship of Yahweh was acknowledged.[4] While this evidence is late, it is unlikely that it was something newly invented. Professor Johnson brings into relation with this the psalms which Gunkel had described as

[1] Cf. above, p. 187, n. 8.

[2] For his acknowledgement of his debt as well as his criticisms of some of Mowinckel's views, cf. especially E.T. lxii, 1950–1, pp. 36ff, and Myth, Ritual and Kingship, pp. 204ff.

[3] So already in The Labyrinth, 1935, p. 81. Cf. J. R. Porter, J.T.S., N.S. v, 1954, p. 173: "It may therefore be suggested that our study points to David's having introduced a festival of the Canaanite New Year type into the Israelite cultus on the occasion of his accession in Jerusalem, and that this festival was thereafter celebrated annually and re-enacted both the enthronement of Yahweh and of the contemporary Davidic King." H. Ringgren (Biblical Research, 1962, pp. 1ff) notes that whereas Mowinckel calls the New Year festival an Enthronement festival, A. Weiser (cf. The Psalms, E.Tr., 1962, pp. 26ff, 35ff) and G. von Rad (cf. The Problem of the Hexateuch and Other Essays, E. Tr., pp. 36ff) call it a Covenant festival, the latter basing himself on Shechem traditions. He further observes that E. Nielsen (Shechem, 1955, pp. 237f) connects the Enthronement festival with Canaanite ideas, and then suggests that the Enthronement complex is of Jerusalemite origin and the Covenant renewal of Shechemite origin, but that the Covenant motif, which is the less marked in the Psalms, found its way into the kingship complex. Cf. also H. Ringgren, Israelitische Religion, 1963, p. 183, where he says that in pre-exilic times Israel celebrated Yahweh as Creator and King at the autumn festival and renewed the Covenant with him. Mowinckel also now emphasizes the Covenant element in the Israelite festival (The Psalms in Israel's Worship, i, p. 155). Cf. also W. Harrelson, Interpreting the Old Testament, 1964, pp. 421ff; R. E. Clements, Prophecy and Covenant, 1965, pp. 119f, and God and Temple, 1965, p. 69. For a valuable critical article on modern work on the Feast of Tabernacles, cf. G. W. MacRae, C.B.Q. xxii, 1960, pp. 251ff.

[4] Zech. 14.16f.

Enthronement psalms.[1] Those were the psalms such as those which declare that the Lord reigneth,[2] or Psalm 47,[3] which begins: "O clap your hands, all ye peoples; shout unto God with the voice of triumph. For the Lord Most High is terrible; he is a great king over all the earth." Aubert thinks that the universalism of these psalms marks them as much later than the period of the monarchy.[4] This does not seem to me cogent. What we have here is not comparable with the thought of Deutero-Isaiah, that Israel is called to share her faith with others, but rather the sense of the exaltation of Israel's God as supreme in the universe. In a familiar passage ascribed in the Bible to both Isaiah[5] and Micah[6] we have the thought of the day when men of all nations will acknowledge Yahweh and seek to understand and to do his will. Many scholars to-day would date that oracle in the eighth century,[7] and I regard it as significant that the two different ascriptions of the oracle both locate it in the same age. We have no reason to date this kind of universalism in the same age as the very different universalism of Deutero-Isaiah. But more than this. I have noted that Professor Johnson postulates an Israelite festival which is a modified version

[1] Cf. *Sacral Kingship*, pp. 51ff. C. Westermann (*Das Loben Gottes in den Psalmen*, 1953, p. 107) denies that there is any category of Enthronement psalms. On the Enthronement psalms cf. also J. Morgenstern, *H.U.C.A.* xxxv, 1964, pp. 1ff; J. Coppens, *E.Th.L.* xlii, 1966, pp. 225ff.
[2] On the expression rendered "the Lord reigneth" cf. L. Koehler, *V.T.* iii, 1953, pp. 188ff; J. Ridderbos, *V.T.* iv, 1954, pp. 87ff; D. Michel, *V.T.* vi, 1956, pp. 40ff; W. S. McCullough, in *A Stubborn Faith* (Irwin Festschrift), 1956, pp. 53ff; E. Lipiński, *La Royauté de Yahwé dans la poésie et le culte de l'ancien Israël*, 1965, pp. 336ff; J. D. Watts, *Th.Z.* xxi, 1965, pp. 341ff.
[3] On Ps. 47 cf. J. Muilenburg, *J.B.L.* lxiii, 1944, pp. 235ff; A. Caquot, *R.H.P.R.* xxxix, 1959, pp. 311ff. J. Morgenstern (*H.U.C.A.* xxxv, 1964, p. 42) dates this Psalm *circa* 490 B.C. and ascribes it to a Nationalist author.
[4] Cf. *R.Th.Ph.*, N.S. xv, 1927, p. 236.
[5] Isa. 2.2ff.   [6] Mic. 4.1ff.
[7] The following scholars have attributed this oracle to Isaiah or to Micah or to a prophet earlier than either: B. Duhm, *Das Buch Jesaia*, 2nd edn, 1902, p. 14; C. Cornill, *Introduction to the Canonical Books of the Old Testament*, E. Tr. by G. H. Box, 1907, pp. 269f; A. van Hoonacker, *Les douzes Petits Prophètes*, 1908, p. 381; G. H. Box, *The Book of Isaiah*, 1916, p. 31; E. Sellin, *Introduction to the Old Testament*, E. Tr. by W. Montgomery, 1923, p. 132; H. Schmidt, *Die grossen Propheten*, 2nd edn, 1923, p. 112 n; J. Fischer, *Das Buch Isaias*, i, 1937, p. 36; J. Lippl and J. Theis, *Die zwölf kleinen Propheten*, i, 1937, p. 200; E. J. Kissane, *The*

of the old Jebusite festival.¹ In the passage I have just quoted God is called Yahweh 'Elyon, the Lord Most High.² 'Elyon or El 'Elyon was the God whose priest Melchizedek was according to Genesis 14.³ That passage is no longer regarded as late,⁴ and I have argued that in its present form it comes from the time of David.⁵ Along different lines others have argued for a similar

Book of Isaiah, i, 1941, p. 22; A. H. Edelkoort, De Christusverwachting in het Oude Testament, 1941, pp. 194ff; L. Dennefeld, Les grands Prophètes, 1946, p. 28a; J. Steinmann, Le Prophète Isaïe, 1950, pp. 128f; H. Wildberger, V.T. vii, 1957, pp. 62ff; J. Ziegler, in Echt. B., Altes Testament, iv, 1958, p. 22; F. Nötscher, ibid., p. 761; G. von Rad, The Problem of the Hexateuch and Other Essays, p. 233; R. E. Clements, God and Temple, 1965, p. 81 n. Many other scholars have assigned the passage to a post-exilic date, when its double ascription would not seem so easy to explain.

¹ Cf. in The Labyrinth, 1935, pp. 81ff; Sacral Kingship, pp. 29ff, 42ff; cf. also H. Schmid, Z.A.W. lxvii, 1955, pp. 168ff. On the syncretism between Yahwism and Jebusite religion cf. R. E. Clements, God and Temple, p. 49 n.

² To this Johnson calls attention, Sacral Kingship, pp. 65f.

³ Gen. 14.18. R. E. Clements (Prophecy and Covenant, 1965, p. 59) speaks of "the adoption by Israel of some of the earlier cult-traditions belonging to El-'Elyon, who had been the chief deity worshipped by the Jebusites in Jerusalem before David's capture of the city". On El 'Elyon cf. H. Schmid, loc. cit., pp. 178ff.

⁴ It was for long the view that this chapter was a late midrash, of no historical worth. Cf. J. Wellhausen, Die Composition des Hexateuchs, 3rd edn, 1899, pp. 311ff; H. P. Smith, Old Testament History, 1911, p. 37; J. Meinhold, 1 Mose 14, 1911; J. Morgenstern, A Jewish Interpretation of the Book of Genesis, 1919, p. 119 (new edn, 1965, p. 113; cf. also Studies in Jewish Literature (Kohler Festschrift), 1913, pp. 223f.); H. Gunkel, Genesis, 5th edn, 1922, p. 289; K. Budde, Z.A.W. lii, 1934, p. 43; R. Dussaud, L'Art phénicien du IIᵉ millénaire, 1949, p. 32 n; R. H. Pfeiffer, Introduction to the Old Testament, 1941, p. 161; C. A. Simpson, The Early Traditions of Israel, 1948, p. 72; O. Eissfeldt, The Old Testament: an Introduction, E. Tr. by P. R. Ackroyd, 1965, pp. 211f. The view of W. F. Albright has ranged from holding it to be a political pamphlet of the time of Zerubbabel (cf. J.B.L. xxxvii, 1918, p. 136) to finding it to be a genuine historical document (cf. J.P.O.S. vi, 1926, p. 227), and he now affirms the "absolute antiquity of its contents" (B.A.S.O.R., No. 163, October 1961, p. 49). An elaborate monograph on the chapter, in which a great number of opinions are recorded and examined is by J. H. Kroeze, Genesis Veertien, 1937.

⁵ Cf. J.B.L. lviii, 1939, pp. 125ff; Festschrift für Alfred Bertholet, 1950, pp. 461ff.

date.[1] It is significant that Genesis 14 describes El 'Elyon as
"creator[2] of heaven and earth".[3] There is no reason to come down
to a late date for this kind of universalism.
To return to the view of Professor Johnson. Like others he sees
in some psalms evidence that the Ark was borne in procession on
festal occasions.[4] Here he adduces not only Psalm 24, but also
Psalm 132,[5] which Gunkel believed to have been composed for
the celebration of the anniversary of the Davidic dynasty,[6] and
which Mowinckel says "may be looked upon as the libretto of a
holy drama, in which at the annual festival the people present
and 'call to mind' the first time that Yahweh entered Zion, led by
David".[7] The psalm clearly recalls that occasion, and Johnson

[1] Cf. R. Kittel, *G.V.I.* i, 6th edn, 1923, p. 283; H. S. Nyberg, *A.R.W.*
xxxv, 1938, pp. 363f; T. C. Vriezen, *Vox Theologica*, xv, 1944, pp. 83f;
S. H. Hooke, *In the Beginning*, 1947, p. 76; A. R. Johnson, *Sacral Kingship*, p. 43; G. von Rad, *Genesis*, E. Tr. by J. H. Marks, 1961, pp. 175f.
E. Sellin (*Introduction to the Old Testament*, E. Tr. by W. Montgomery,
1923, p. 50) thinks it was a Canaanite record deposited in the archives at
Jerusalem and found by David when he captured Jerusalem. Cf. I.
Engnell (*Kyrkohistorisk Årsskrift*, liii, 1953, pp. 201f): "its import being to
legitimate Abraham as a fully authorized Canaanite by means of his
transition to the worship of the Jerusalem high god El 'Elyon. But quite
as significant is it to realize that Abraham at the same time covers the
figure of King David. David's syncretistic policy, forming the basis of the
entire later religious history of Israel, here gets its legitimation and
authorization."
[2] A.V. "possessor". The word may have either meaning; cf. J. A.
Montgomery, *J.A.O.S.* liii, 1933, p. 116; H. S. Nyberg, *A.R.W.* xxxv,
1938, p. 352; P. Humbert, in *Festschrift für Alfred Bertholet*, 1950,
pp. 258ff; G. Levi della Vida, *J.B.L.* lxiii, 1944, pp. 1ff; H. Ringgren,
Word and Wisdom, 1947, pp. 100f; H. Schmid, *Z.A.W.* lxvii, 1955, pp.
181f; M. H. Pope, *El in the Ugaritic Texts* (S.V.T. ii), 1955, pp. 51f;
A. R. Johnson, *Sacral Kingship*, pp. 42f n; J. Barr, *T.G.U.O.S.* xvii,
1959, pp. 58f; L. R. Fisher, *J.B.L.* lxxxi, 1962, pp. 266f. J. Gray (*The
Legacy of Canaan* (S.V.T. v), 1957, p. 194) says it "obviously" means
"creator" here. W. A. Irwin (*J.B.L.* lxxx, 1961, p. 138) maintains that
the meaning is "parent of heavens and earth".
[3] Gen. 14.19, 22. [4] Cf. *Sacral Kingship*, pp. 64, 66, 74.
[5] Ibid., pp. 17ff. On this psalm and 2 Sam. 6 cf. H. J. Kraus, *Die
Königsherrschaft Gottes im Alten Testament*, 1951, pp. 40ff, 51ff, and J. R.
Porter, *J.T.S.* N.S. v, 1954, pp. 161ff. In *Worship in Israel*, E. Tr., 1966,
p. 184, Kraus says that Ps. 132 "provides the decisive evidence for a
royal festival on Mount Zion".
[6] Cf. *Einleitung in die Psalmen*, p. 142.
[7] Cf. *The Psalms in Israel's Worship*, ii, p. 76.

says it "appears to have as its original *Sitz im Leben* a dramatic commemoration or liturgical re-enactment of the bringing of the Ark to Jerusalem and the consequent foundation of the Jerusalem cultus in close association with the Davidic dynasty".[1] He adds that it falls into two parts, a hymn beseeching Yahweh's continued favour on the house of David, and an oracular response in which the worshippers are assured that Yahweh will be faithful to his covenant with the Davidic house.[2] The pattern is the same as that of which the Chronicler tells us in his record of the reign of Jehoshaphat, when prior to leading his forces out to battle he proclaimed a national fast day and assembled the people in the Temple where he prayed on behalf of the nation and a Levite belonging to the Temple choir uttered a prophetic oracle assuring king and people of divine aid.[3] This would appear to be a regular ritual pattern, which could as naturally be followed in a recurring appeal for divine favour as in a particular appeal. Professor Johnson finds in the account of Jeroboam's making the Bethel shrine a royal sanctuary evidence[4] that a pilgrim festival was observed there in imitation of the Jerusalem autumn festival, and that this festival was designed to bind the people to the national God and to the reigning house.[5] This is exactly what Psalm 132[6] and its associated ritual might be expected to seek.

A number of the psalms represent the speaker as hard pressed by enemies, and then there follows a triumphant song of victory. These are believed by Johnson[7] to be written to accompany a

---

[1] Cf. *Sacral Kingship*, pp. 17f. On the historical motif in this and other psalms, cf. A. Lauha, *Die Geschichtsmotive in den alttestamentlichen Psalmen*, 1945; also H. J. Kraus, *Psalmen*, i, 1960, pp. lviff.

[2] *Sacral Kingship*, p. 18.

[3] 2 Chron. 20.3ff.   [4] 1 Kings 12.29ff.

[5] Cf. *Sacral Kingship*, p. 47. W. Harrelson (*Interpreting the Old Testament*, 1964, p. 424) emphasizes the Israelite character of the ritual as reflected in the psalms. He says: "These psalms associated with the ratification of the covenant between Yahweh and Israel give great prominence to Israel's obedience to the covenant law."

[6] On this Psalm cf. Johnson, *Sacral Kingship*, pp. 17ff; J. R. Porter, *J.T.S.* N.S. v, 1954, pp. 161ff (against H. J. Kraus, *Die Königsherrschaft Gottes im Alten Testament*, 1951); F. Asensio, *Gregorianum*, xxxviii, 1957, pp. 310ff; O. Eissfeldt, *W.O.* ii, 1954–9, pp. 480ff; in addition to the commentaries.

[7] *Sacral Kingship*, pp. 102ff, 107ff; cf. *The Labyrinth*, 1935, pp. 93ff. For a criticism of Johnson's positions by Mowinckel cf. *The Psalms in Israel's Worship*, E. Tr., ii, pp. 253ff.

ritual combat in which the king was hard pressed by his enemies and was then delivered by God. On this view there was a sacred mime, in which what the text announced was dramatically represented, and Johnson says that in principle this was not unlike the ritual humiliation of the king in Babylon.[1] Against Mowinckel's presentation of this view Aubert objected that the sacred mime was believed to produce what it represented.[2] There is thus something approaching a magical element here. But when Zedekiah the son of Chenaanah made horns and assured the king of Israel that with these he should gore the Syrians we find an undeniably similar element in Israel.[3] In all prophetic symbolism there was what could easily become a magical element.[4] But so also there was in the prophetic word.[5] Both were thought to release power to achieve what they declared.[6] But whereas magic is the belief that man by his volition can release power and constrain gods or spirits and thus achieve his will, the prophetic word and prophetic symbolism were thought to have power, not because the prophet constrained God, but because the prophet himself was constrained

[1] Cf. *The Labyrinth*, p. 100; *Sacral Kingship*, p. 104.

[2] Cf. *R.Th.Ph.*, N.S. xv, 1927, p. 234.

[3] 1 Kings 22.11. Cf. A. Lods, "Le Rôle des Idées magiques dans la mentalité israélite", in *Old Testament Essays* (Foreword by D. C. Simpson), 1927, pp. 55ff.

[4] On prophetic symbolism cf. H. W. Robinson, in *Old Testament Essays*, 1927, pp. 1ff, and *J.T.S.* xlii, 1942, pp. 129ff; D. Buzy, *Les Symboles de l'Ancien Testament*, 1923; A. Regnier, *R.B.* xxxii, 1923, pp. 383ff; W. F. Lofthouse, *A.J.S.L.* xl, 1923–4, pp. 239ff; A. Lods, *R.H.P.R.* ix, 1929, pp. 170ff; A. van den Born, *Profetie Metterdaad*, 1947; G. Fohrer, *Z.A.W.* lxiv, 1952, pp. 101f, and *Die symbolischen Handlungen der Propheten*, 1953. Lods says (loc. cit., p. 173): "Plusieurs des actes 'symboliques' accomplis par les hommes de Dieu israélites ou attribués à tel d'entre eux, ont une affinité évidente avec les rites de magie imitative pratiqués chez les non-civilisés ou dans l'antiquité pour agir, non pas sur les esprits des assistants, mais *sur les événements* eux-mêmes, sur l'avenir; ces actes sont tenus pour 'efficaces', non parce qu'ils sont 'impressionants', mais dans un sens bien autrement réel, *parce qu'ils produisent eux-mêmes ce qu'ils figurent.*" Cf. G. Fohrer, *Z.A.W.* lxxviii, 1966, pp. 25ff.

[5] Cf. A. R. Johnson, *The One and the Many in the Israelite Conception of God*, 2nd edn, 1961, p. 17; *The Cultic Prophet in Ancient Israel*, 2nd edn, pp. 37f. Cf. also O. Grether, *Name und Wort Gottes im Alten Testament*, 1934, pp. 103ff; J. Lindblom, *Prophecy in Ancient Israel*, 1962, pp. 53ff.

[6] Cf. Isa. 45.23; 55.10f.

of God to utter the word or perform the act.[1] When the word or act of the prophet was the expression of his own wish and not of true divine constraint, it became magic. As so often, *corruptio optimi pessimum*. Where the ritual mime was believed to be divinely instituted, and where it was designed to call men to renewed loyalty to God and remembrance of his mercies and renewed trust in him, the potentially magical element is transformed by the reminder that loyalty to God is the condition of the effectiveness of the ritual. We are therefore back at what I have said earlier, that the ritual act of sacrifice was valid only when it was accompanied by the spirit which made it indeed the act of the worshipper and that the prophetic condemnation of sacrifice in their day was that it was not the organ of the spirit and was therefore empty. That this is not just supposition is made clear in Psalm 132, to which I have just referred. There the response which brought the assurance that Yahweh could be true to his ancient covenant with David says: "If thy children will keep my covenant and my testimony that I shall teach them, their children also shall sit upon thy throne for evermore."[2] Here is no magic, but religion.

I can give but one example of the psalms which are held to accompany the ritual combat. Psalm 89[3] opens by recalling the mercies of God and his covenant with David and proceeds to sing of his power and his mighty acts in creation and then of the moral qualities which are inherent in his rule of the world, after which it returns to the thought of his covenant with David and the assurance of his continued loyalty to it. Here again it is made clear that there can be no magical constraining of God. For we read: "If his children forsake my law, and walk not in my judgements; if they break my statutes, and keep not my commandments; then will I visit their transgression with the rod, and their iniquity with stripes."[4] Then the psalm turns to lament at the humiliation of the

---

[1] Cf. H. W. Robinson, in *Old Testament Essays*, 1927, p. 14, *Redemption and Revelation*, 1942, p. 250; *J.T.S.* xliii, 1942, pp. 132f.

[2] Ps. 132.12.

[3] For Johnson's discussion of this psalm cf. *Sacral Kingship*, pp. 97ff. G. W. Ahlström has a monograph on this Psalm (*Psalm 89: Eine Liturgie aus dem Rituel des leidenden Königs*, 1959), interpreting it in terms of "patternism" as a cultic text of the royal cult, in which the king as the incarnation of the god suffered and died and rose again (cf. S. Mowinckel's criticism in *J.S.S.* v, 1960, pp. 291ff).

[4] Ps. 89.30f (M.T. 31f).

king. Professor Johnson says it is "reasonable to infer that the defeat and humiliation of the Davidic king, which is indicated in these lines, is not any specific historical event, for indeed there is none that can be made to fit this scene, but is an important element in the ritual drama".[1] Here the psalm does not close with an oracle of promise, but with a plea from the king that he may be delivered.[2]

In many of the psalms instead of God's work in creation being recalled as the ground of confidence in him, it is his saving power manifested in the history of Israel, and especially in his deliverance of his people from Egypt.[3] Here we have a transformation of the motif of the Creation Epic into the terms of Israel's experience, and an example of what Professor Bentzen called the "historification of myth".[4]

The royal Psalms, which have been traditionally given a messianic interpretation, are now brought into association with the reigning king,[5] and held to set before him for his example the

[1] Op. cit., p. 103.   [2] Ps. 89.49ff (M.T. 50ff).

[3] A. Weiser (in *Festschrift für Alfred Bertholet*, 1950, pp. 513ff) argued for the reactualizing of the Sinai Theophany in the ritual of the autumn festival. Cf. W. Beyerlin, *Origins and History of the Oldest Sinaitic Traditions*, E. Tr., pp. 133ff. J. R. Porter (*Moses and Monarchy*, 1963, p. 9) relates Ex. 19—24 to the ritual of the autumn festival. J. Pedersen (*Z.A.W.* lii, 1934, pp. 161ff; cf. *Israel III–IV*, 1940, pp. 728ff) held that Ex. 1—15 was used as a ritual text with no historical relation in the cult of the spring festival. This was rejected by Mowinckel (*St.Th.* v, 1952, pp. 66ff), who strongly insisted on its historical character. Cf. also H. Haag, in *S.D.B.* vi, 1960, cols. 1126ff; R. de Vaux, *Studies in Old Testament Sacrifice*, 1964, p. 21.

[4] Cf. *J.B.L.* lxvii, 1948, p. 39. Cf. E. Hammershaimb, *Some Aspects of Old Testament Prophecy*, 1966, p. 45: "The specifically Israelite contribution to the rites of the kingly feast in Jerusalem lay in the introduction of historically motivated features."

[5] Gunkel dealt with these Royal Psalms in 1914 in "Die Königspsalmen", *Preussische Jahrbücher*, clviii, 1914, pp. 42ff, where he found the following Royal Psalms: 2, 18, 20, 21, 45, 72, 97, 102, 110, 132 (pp. 64f). In R.G.G. iv, 1913, cols. 1939f the following Royal Psalms were distinguished: 2, 18, 20, 21, 45, 72, 101, 110, 132, and perhaps 60. In *What Remains of the Old Testament*, E. Tr. by A. K. Dallas, 1928, p. 90, Gunkel gives the Royal Psalms as 2, 18, 20, 21, 45, 72, 97, 101, 110, 132. In Gunkel and Begrich, *Einleitung in die Psalmen*, 1933, p. 141, Ps. 60 was omitted from the list, but Ps. 144.1–11 was added, and the list is concluded with: cf. 89.47–52. Mowinckel had already (*Kongesalmerne*, 1916) included all the psalms in all these lists and in addition: 28, 44, 61, 63,

concept of the ideal king.[1] Thus in Psalm 72 we find the opening: "Give the king thy judgements,[2] O God, and thy righteousness unto the king's son. He shall judge thy people with righteousness, and thy poor with judgement."[3] The thought then reaches out to the universality of the sway of the king when the ideal is attained: "He shall have dominion also from sea to sea and from the River unto the ends of the earth."[4] These psalms, therefore, are given both a present and a future reference, a present reference as an example[5] and a future reference as a promise of the day when the ideal will be realized.[6]

66, 68, 84, 118. Mowinckel observes (*The Psalms in Israel's Worship*, i, p. 47 n) that neither Gunkel nor Begrich realized the extent of the Royal Psalms and their significance for the understanding of psalm problems.

[1] Cf. *Sacral Kingship*, pp. 127ff. It is in this renewing and transforming of the eschatological and messianic interpretation of the royal psalms that the most significant contribution of Professor Johnson to their understanding lies. Cf. *Myth, Ritual and Kingship*, p. 234: "While I continue to reject the historical interpretation of the psalms which celebrate the Kingship of Yahweh, I now hold that from the first they were not only cultic in origin but also, like the associated royal psalms, eschatological in their orientation. If I am right, this means that the theory of royal psalms does not preclude their sometimes being 'Messianic' in what is now the established eschatological sense of this term."

[2] Here Johnson (*Sacral Kingship*, p. 7) reads "thy justice" with LXX, Syr., and Jer.

[3] Ps. 72.1f. For Johnson's discussion of this psalm cf. *Sacral Kingship*, pp. 6ff. For the last word in verse 2, he again renders "justice".

[4] Ps. 72.8. The River is generally understood to mean the Euphrates, as it often undoubtedly does elsewhere. But Johnson maintains (ibid., pp. 8ff) that here it means the all-embracing cosmic sea.

[5] This does not mean that there was any lack of criticism, either at the time or in retrospect, of kings who did not live up to the ideal. Cf. C. R. North, *A.J.S.L.* xlviii, 1931–2, pp. 1ff.

[6] Johnson brings Ps. 110 into association with this group of Psalms (cf. in *The Labyrinth*, pp. 109f, and *Sacral Kingship*, pp. 120ff) and finds in it traces of the ritual combat (cf. also A. S. Kapelrud, *Joel Studies*, 1948, p. 160), while Mowinckel (*The Psalms in Israel's Worship*, i, p. 63) thinks it was used in the rites at the king's accession. I am not persuaded that it was used in the annual rites, or in the regular accession rites, since we should expect to hear more of Melchizedek in the Old Testament if he figured in the living tradition as the ideal priest (cf. *Festschrift für Alfred Bertholet*, 1950, p. 467). Bentzen (*Studier over det Zadokidiske præsterkabs historie*, 1931, p. 13, and *Fortolkning til de gammeltestamentlige Salmer*, 1940, p. 564; cf. T. C. Vriezen, *Vox Theologica*, xv, 1944, p. 85) thought

"In this great act of worship", says Johnson, "the eschatological hope, which centres in the House of David, finds vivid expression in the contemporary scene, and that which is really yet to be occurs dramatically before one's eyes as a challenge and a means of

the psalm was written to celebrate the enthronement of David, and this seems to be most probable. This view was held by Ḳimḥi in his Commentary on this psalm. Gen. 14 was probably intended to legitimate the Jebusite priesthood (cf. above, p. 73) and this psalm appears to me to belong to the same time and to express the acknowledgement of David as king and Zadok as priest. Johnson (*Sacral Kingship*, p. 121) thinks it recognizes David and his successors as both kings and priests after the order of Melchizedek (cf. E. Podechard, *Le Psautier*, ii, 1954, pp. 171ff), but there is no evidence that the Davidic kings ever claimed a priesthood of a non-Israelite pattern. At the time of his conquest of Jerusalem, David appears to have confirmed Zadok in his priesthood, and to have brought the Israelite priest, Abiathar, into Jerusalem alongside him. When Abiathar was dismissed by Solomon, Zadok became the sole priestly head and the heir of both traditions, and it is not surprising that from that time the Melchizedek tradition should fall into the background, as it could not have done if it was annually commemorated in the ritual. G. von Rad (*Old Testament Theology*, E. Tr., i, 1962, p. 249 n) says that I hold that Zadok was the priest-king of Jerusalem, whom David conquered. This is a view which I explicitly rejected (loc. cit., p. 471): "Melchizedek exercises no kingly function in the story of Gen. xiv but only a priestly, and in Ps. cx it is only in connexion with the priestly, and not with the kingly, function that his name occurs", adding in a footnote: "It is very doubtful if David would have allowed the defeated king to occupy the position of priest in his own capital." Cf. also ibid., p. 472: "A Zadok who was priest but not king and a David who was, *ex hypothesi*, a priest-king could not both derive their office from a Melchizedek who was a priest-king. But if the priesthood in Ps. cx is the priesthood of Zadok, the pre-Davidic priest in Jerusalem, then the two passages are linked not alone by the name of Melchizedek but by a common use." David's title rested on conquest and needed no other legitimation. For other discussions of Ps. 110 cf. T. H. Gaster, *J.M.U.E.O.S.* xxi, 1937, pp. 37ff; G. Widengren, *Psalm 110 och det sakrala kungadömet i Israel*, 1941; M. A. Beek, *Vox Theologica*, xv, 1944, pp. 94ff; J. de Savignac, *O.T.S.* ix, 1951, pp. 107ff; H. Ringgren, *Z.A.W.* lxiv, 1952, pp. 124f; E. Nielsen, *Shechem*, 1955, p. 343; J. Coppens, in *The Sacral Kingship* (Supplements to *Numen*, iv), 1959, pp. 333ff; G. R. Driver, in *Sepher Segal*, 1965, pp. 17*ff. I. Engnell (*Kyrkohistorisk Årsskrift*, liii, 1953, pp. 202f) says: "Speaking concisely we might say that Ps. cx offers the 'rite' belonging to the 'myth' in Gen. xiv [cf. above, p. 160], i.e. the royal oracular saying—or part of it—by means of which the pre-Israelite Jerusalemite sacral kingship . . . is transferred to David, the remaining and returning Messianic king of Israel." The older view that Ps. 110 dates from the second century B.C. (so Duhm, *Psalmen*, 1899,

inspiration for all who are prepared to take it seriously."[1] And
again: "This great act of worship looks forward to the day when
. . . the true Messiah of the House of David . . . will have justified
the decisive intervention of Yahweh."[2] Of all this there can be
no absolute proof in the nature of the case, but it fills these psalms
with new meaning, and sees them as related to the ritual of Israel
in a similar way to that we have found in the case of other psalms.
It means that just as other psalms are believed to have been used
to interpret the ritual acts of other occasions, so the great autumn
festival by ritual drama and by interpreting text was designed to
evoke in the people a sense of what God had done for them, and
in the king, as the representative of the people with whom the
well-being of the nation was bound up, a sense of what God
expected of him, so that king and people alike might be challenged
to a new pledge of faithfulness to God and his demands.

For this construction the material of the Old Testament itself
is used, and all is related to the faith of Israel in a way that I find
impressive. As Johnson says, this is no cultic act of a magico-
religious kind, but worship which reveals a quite lofty spiritual
aim.[3] It means that just as Passover was given a new meaning in
the context of the deliverance which was associated with it, so this
autumn festival was transformed from a mere agricultural festival
when men rejoiced in the gifts of nature—though that was also
involved in it—into something that was charged with a spiritual
message to king and people. If it be objected that the Old Testament provides evidence that through long periods neither kings
nor people nor priests took any of this seriously, it can be replied
that many people to-day can attend a service without truly entering
into it or receiving its message into their hearts.

pp. 254ff) is still maintained by R. H. Pfeiffer (*History of New Testament
Times*, 1949, p. 48) and by M. Treves (*V.T.* xv, 1965, pp. 85ff), though
A. Bentzen (*Det sakrale kongedømme*, 1945, p. 64) observed that this view
"kan efter Gunkels tid næppe mere fastholdes". It has been assigned to a
pre-exilic date by Gunkel (*Psalmen*, 1926, pp. 484f), and recently by
E. R. Hardy, (*J.B.L.* lxiv, 1945, p. 384) and H. G. Jefferson (*J.B.L.*
lxxiii, 1954, pp. 152ff). W. E. Barnes (*The Psalms*, ii, 1931, p. 534)
thought the Psalmist was either Nathan or Gad, and the occasion the
Ammonite war, 2 Sam. 10.6–14; 6.1.

[1] Cf. *Sacral Kingship*, p. 133.
[2] Ibid., p. 134. On the messianism of Ps. 72 cf. P. Veugelers, *E.Th.L.*
xli, 1965, pp. 317ff.
[3] Cf. *Myth, Ritual and Kingship*, p. 235.

What seems to me particularly valuable about the whole approach to the Israelite cultus that I am presenting in this book is that it relates the parts of the Old Testament together and offers some explanation of their being gathered together into a single corpus. The once prevalent view, that the prophets were preachers of righteousness who had no interest in the cultus, and that they were followed by the priests who were only interested in mechanical ritual acts, and that finally pious people somehow appeared in a late age to compose spiritual songs, offered little explanation of the gathering together of the Old Testament. The relating of the parts together and the filling of the festivals with a meaning which is relevant to the character of the Old Testament as a whole, and so filling it with a meaning which is not brought to it from outside but found within the Old Testament itself, seems to me a very great gain.

I have left little space to speak of music in worship, but there is very little that can profitably be said. That there was music in Israel is clear from the Old Testament, and that there was music in the worship of the Temple is also specifically stated. But little is known of its character, save what may be surmised from the variety of musical instruments referred to and what the Chronicler tells us.

Secular music is referred to a number of times in the Old Testament. One of the descendants of Cain is said to have been the "father" of all who handle pipe and harp.[1] Laban reproaches Jacob for having left him without giving the opportunity to have a farewell party with songs and instrumental music,[2] and Isaiah refers to music at the drunken orgies of his day,[3] while later in the book of Isaiah we have a reference to the songs of harlots.[4] In the so-called Isaiah-Apocalypse there is a further reference to drinking songs,[5] and Isaiah's Song of the Vine is probably modelled on a drinking song of the time.[6] In the second century of our era Rabbi Akiba cursed those who sang passages from the Song of Songs as common ditties over their cups.[7]

---

[1] Gen. 4.21. [2] Gen. 31.27. [3] Isa. 5.11f.
[4] Isa. 23.15. [5] Isa. 24.9. [6] Isa. 5.1ff.
[7] Cf. Tosephta, *Sanhedrin* xii.10 (ed. by M. S. Zuckermandel, 2nd edn, 1937, p. 433); also Bab. Talmud, *Sanhedrin* 101a (ed. by L. Goldschmidt, *Der Babylonische Talmud mit Einschluss der vollständigen Mišnah*, vii, 1903, p. 442).

When David returned to Jerusalem after the revolt of Absalom was quelled, he invited Barzillai to accompany him, only to receive the answer: "Can I any more hear the voice of singing men and singing women?",[1] and in Eccles. 2.8 we read: "I gat me men singers and women singers, and the delights of the sons of men, concubines very many."[2] In Lamentations the poet mourns that the young men's music is silenced.[3] All of these seem to be examples of joyous music. But music could match the mood of sadness. David, who is called the sweet singer of Israel, sang laments over Saul and Jonathan[4] and over Abner.[5] Neither was a religious song. Jeremiah called for the professional mourning women to come to sing the song of Death the Reaper,[6] and the Chronicler tells us that in his day the singing men and singing women still sang a lament over Josiah.[7] Victors were hailed with songs of triumph. Thus Jephthah was greeted on his return from battle by his daughter, who was accompanied by music and dance,[8] and David was greeted with the song that stirred Saul's jealousy.[9]

Of a more definitely religious character was the Song of Miriam accompanied by her timbrel, after the deliverance at the Sea,[10] and we read that when Jehoshaphat returned victorious, he was accompanied to the house of the Lord with instruments of music.[11] The prophets whom Saul met below Gibeah were prophesying to the accompaniment of music,[12] and when Elisha was asked to advise Jehoshaphat before the battle against Moab, he called for a minstrel to stir his spirit to prophesy.[13] Isaiah refers to song in the night at sacred festivals and the instrumental music that accompanied processions to the house of the Lord.[14] Moreover, the references to dancing in connection with worship imply some musical accompaniment.[15]

The frequent mention of musical instruments in the Psalms sufficiently indicates that music had an important part in the

---

[1] 2 Sam. 19.35.
[2] In his account of his campaign against Hezekiah, Sennacherib says he took male and female musicians from Jerusalem (cf. *A.N.E.T.*, p. 288a).
[3] Lam. 5.14.   [4] 2 Sam. 1.19ff.   [5] 2 Sam. 3.33f.   [6] Jer. 9.17ff.
[7] 2 Chron. 35.25.   [8] Judges 11.34.   [9] 1 Sam. 18.6f.
[10] Ex. 15.20f.   [11] 2 Chron. 20.28.   [12] 1 Sam. 10.5f, 10.
[13] 2 Kings 3.15.   [14] Isa. 30.29.
[15] Cf. Ex. 32.19; 2 Sam. 6.14; Pss. 87.7; 149.3; 150.4. On dancing in worship cf. W. O. E. Oesterley, *The Sacred Dance*, 1923.

worship of the Temple, and Amos, in condemning the worship of the northern shrines, says: "Take thou away from me the noise of thy songs; for I will not hear the melody of thy viols."[1] Psalms which begin "Sing unto the Lord a new song"[2] clearly show that they were intended to be sung, as does such a psalm as that beginning: "Make a joyful noise unto the Lord, all ye lands. Serve the Lord with gladness: come before his presence with singing."[3]

All of this tells us little of the nature of the singing or of the character of the accompaniment. The Chronicler gives us an account of the singing guilds of his day, with the type of instrument which each guild used,[4] but though it is ascribed to David's time we cannot rely on this for the pre-exilic arrangements. In an earlier chapter I have said that it is believed that these singing guilds may go back to the cultic prophets of pre-exilic days,[5] but we cannot be certain that the only change that had been made was the enrolling of these singers in Levite guilds. That the musical arrangements had not continued unchanged from the time of David the Chronicler himself recognizes, for he tells us that Jehoiada restored them,[6] and again later he tells us that Hezekiah restored them.[7]

It may well be that the musical arrangements of the Temple go back in their beginnings to David. For we know from the story of his introduction to the court of Saul that he was a skilled player on the harp and that he was able to soothe Saul when he was disordered in spirit.[8] We cannot uncritically ascribe to him all the psalms that have "To David" at their head, though there is every reason to believe that he was no mean poet, and he may have written religious songs as well as secular. Some of the psalms which have "To David" in their heading seem to presuppose the existence of the Temple.[9] The headings of the Psalms provide an unsolved problem, and while it is undoubted that the ascription to David was understood of authorship, as is clear from some of the statements about the particular point in his life when they are said to have been composed, it is well known that there was a tendency to ascribe more and more psalms to him. Moreover, some of the psalms have a double ascription, and it is difficult to

---

[1] Amos 5.23. [2] Pss. 96.1; 98.1; 149.1. [3] Ps. 100.1f.

[4] 1 Chron. 15.16ff. [5] Cf. above, p. 161. [6] 2 Chron. 23.18.

[7] 2 Chron. 29.25ff. [8] 1 Sam. 16.17ff. [9] So Pss. 24; 27.

suppose that the *Lāmedh* is always the *Lāmedh* of authorship. A common theory has been that these headings indicate various Hymn Books, or collections of psalms, so that a double ascription means that a psalm was found in more than one collection.[1] This is very hard to accept, for one psalm is ascribed to Moses,[2] and if this came from a whole collection which bore his name, it is highly improbable that only a single psalm would have been taken from it. Engnell supposed that the title "To David" should be translated "For the king", and that it indicates that the psalms which have this heading were used in connection with the royal rites associated with divine kingship.[3] I have already said that I do not accept Engnell's views on divine kingship, and I am therefore unable to accept this view of the psalm heading.

Nevertheless, it may well be, as I have said, that the beginnings of Israelite Temple music go back to David. A recent article has offered a new line of support for this view by arguing that David had Kenite as well as Israelite blood in his veins, and so tracing him back to Cain.[4] This would bring little light for our subject, since it would throw no light on the part that music played in the worship of Israel.

As I have said, we know little of its character. It has been conjectured that the music was loud and piercing, and that it was always in unison.[5] That the worship was noisy is indicated by the fact that the word which is used for the battle cry,[6] which by its

---

[1] Cf. C. A. Briggs, *Psalms*, i, 1907, pp. lxff.   [2] Ps. 90.

[3] Cf. *Studies in Divine Kingship in the Ancient Near East*, 1943, p. 176. Engnell says that Dwd is a priestly-royal denomination taken over by David, and that it derived from the name of a vegetation deity corporalized in the king. This thesis is developed by G. W. Ahlström (*Psalm 89*, 1959, pp. 163ff), who sees in Dwd the son of El 'Elyon. On the argument cf. W. L. Moran, *Biblica*, xl, 1961, p. 239. Mowinckel (*J.S.S.* v, 1960, p. 297) is more sympathetic, though he finds "a strong inclination towards uncertain hypotheses and combinations".

[4] Cf. R. North, *J.B.L.* lxxxiii, 1964, pp. 373ff.

[5] Cf. A. W. Streane, in Hastings' one volume *D.B.*, 1909, p. 637a; cf. J. Millar in Hastings' *D.B.* iii, 1900, p. 457b: "It was evidently of a strident and noisy character"; J. Parisot, in Vigouroux' *D.B.* iv, 1908, col. 1355: "Les Orientaux aiment les instruments bruyants et les notes hautes." E. Werner (in *I.D.B.* iii, 1962, p. 457b) says: "Often the music barely exceeded the level of organized noisemaking."

[6] On this term cf. P. Humbert, *La "Terou'a": Analyse d'un rite biblique*, 1946.

nature would be loud and intended to fill the enemy with terror, is also used for the cry of the worshippers in the worship. But this does not mean that all the singing of the Temple would be of the same volume, or it is improbable that some of the instruments would have been heard. In the sacred processions, to which I have already referred, which were probably accompanied by dancing, the music would be joyous and loud. In Psalm 68 there is an allusion to the music that accompanied the procession of God to the Temple,[1] which probably means when the Ark was carried in sacred procession.[2] Here we read that the singers went first, followed by the minstrels and accompanied by maidens playing timbrels. All the music that accompanied the ritual acts of Temple worship would not be of this character. That some of the singing was antiphonal is rendered probable by the nature of some of the psalms, in which there is a manifest change of speaker, and to this I have already referred.[3]

It is both unnecessary and impossible for me here to discuss the variety of musical instruments referred to in the Old Testament. They include stringed instruments, such as the lyre and the harp, sometimes specified as having ten strings, wind instruments, such as the flute and the trumpet and the horn, and percussion instruments, such as the timbrel, the cymbal, and the castanet.[4] It is probable that over the years there was development in the use

---

[1] Ps. 68.24ff (M.T. 25ff). On this psalm cf. Johnson, *Sacral Kingship*, pp. 68ff. W. F. Albright (*H.U.C.A.* xxiii, 1950–1, pp. 1ff) maintained that this psalm was not a continuous composition, but a series of "incipits", a view which Johnson regards (p. 69 n) as a counsel of despair. Against Albright's view cf. Mowinckel, *Der achtundsechzigste Psalm*, 1953.

[2] So Johnson, op. cit., p. 74.   [3] Cf. above, p. 163.

[4] On the musical instruments of the Old Testament cf. E. Gerson-Kiwi, in *S.D.B.* v, 1957, cols. 1411ff; also J. Wellhausen, *The Book of Psalms*, 1898, pp. 217ff; J. Millar, in Hastings' *D.B.* iii, 1900, pp. 457ff; J. D. Prince, in *E.B.* iii, 1902, cols. 3225ff; H. Gressmann, *Musik und Musikinstrumente im Alten Testament*, 1903; I. Benzinger, in *P.R.E.*, 3rd edn, xiii, 1903, pp. 585ff (cf. *The New Schaff-Herzog Encyclopedia of Religious Knowledge*, x, 1911, pp. 148ff); J. Parisot, in Vigouroux' *D.B.* iv, 1908, cols. 1347ff; S. B. Finesinger, *H.U.C.A.* iii, 1926, pp. 21ff; A. Lods, *Journal de Psychologie*, xxiii, 1926, pp. 239ff; O. R. Sellers, *B.A.* iv, 1941, pp. 33ff; E. Kolari, *Musikinstrumente und ihre Verwendung im Alten Testament*, 1947; E. Werner, in *I.D.B.* iii, 1962, pp. 469ff; D. G. Stradling, in *N.D.B.*, 1962, pp. 852ff; A. W. Streane and R. A. Barclay, in Hastings' one volume *D.B.*, rev. edn, 1963, pp. 681f. On music in the Ancient Near East cf. M. Wegner, *Die Musikinstrumente des Alten Orients*, 1950.

and variety of the instruments employed in the worship, but it is impossible to trace the history of Temple music. The character of the music must have varied to match the mood of the songs it accompanied, and presumably where there was a change of mood within a particular psalm the music would change from grave to gay or from gay to grave to agree with the change.

If we knew more about the psalm headings we might be able to attain a greater certainty as to the uses of many of the psalms. Kennett held that the headings were all of musical significance and that they were intended to indicate the accompaniment of the psalms.[1] A common view has been that *'Al ʿalāmôth*[2] means that the psalm that bears this title was sung by trebles, while psalms headed *'Al sheminîth*,[3] understood to mean "on the octave", were sung by bass singers.[4] A number of psalms, with intriguing titles, have been supposed to carry the opening words of well-known songs to indicate the tunes to which they were to be sung. *'Ayyeleth hash-shahar*,[5] or "Hind of the morning", *Shôshannîm*, or "Lilies",[6] *Shûshan 'ēdhûth*, or "Lily of testimony",[7] *Yônath 'elem reḥōkîm*, variously rendered "The Silent dove of them that are afar off" or "The dove of the distant terebinths",[8] and *'Al tashḥēth*, or "Destroy not",[9] are examples of these headings. But these explanations are not convincing. We should expect more than the few psalms which bear these titles to be supplied with indications of the requisite tunes.

Mowinckel has endeavoured to give a cultic significance to very many of the titles, and has argued that they indicate the character of the ritual which the particular psalm was to accompany.[10] To a

---

[1] Cf. *Old Testament Essays*, 1928, pp. 121ff.

[2] Ps. 46. Cf. also 1 Chron. 15.20.   [3] Pss. 6; 12.

[4] E. Werner (in *I.D.B.* iii, 1962, p. 459b) dismisses this as untenable, since the division of the octave into eight tones was unknown to the ancient Hebrews. Cf. C. Sachs, *The History of Musical Instruments*, 1942, p. 117, where it is declared unproved and unprovable that the ancient Jews had the conception of the octave (cf. p. 107, where it is conjectured that the Hebrew *kinnôr* was a ten-stringed instrument tuned pentatonically without semitones through two octaves).

[5] Ps. 22.   [6] Pss. 45; 69.

[7] Ps. 60. Also *Shôshannîm 'ēdhûth*, or "Lilies, a testimony" in Ps. 80.

[8] Ps. 56.   [9] Pss. 57; 58; 59; 75.

[10] Cf. *Psalmenstudien IV*, 1923, and *The Psalms in Israel's Worship*, ii, pp. 207ff.

few titles he allows musical significance. Thus *N^ehîlôth*[1] indicates that the psalm was to be accompanied by flutes,[2] and so[3] where the heading has *Mah^alath*,[4] while *Bin^eghînôth*[5] shows that it was to be sung to the accompaniment of stringed instruments.[6] Some of the titles clearly indicate the character of the psalm and therefore its use in the ritual. The heading "A psalm of praise" well fits the first line of the psalm it heads: "I will extol thee, my God, O King; and I will bless thy name for ever and ever."[7] Similarly, the psalm which contains the verse: "Enter into his gates with thanksgiving, and into his courts with praise"[8] is appropriately headed "A psalm of thanksgiving".[9] Several psalms are headed "A prayer", where this is, as we should expect, appropriate to their contents.[10] The "Songs of Ascents"[11] are commonly held to be pilgrim psalms, but Mowinckel thinks they were used in the Temple itself at festivals.[12]

More specifically cultic significance he gives to other titles. The term *Lam^enasseah*, which stands at the head of fifty-five psalms,[13] and which R.V. renders "For the chief musician", Mowinckel believes to indicate that the psalm so headed was used in a ritual

---

[1] Ps. 5.

[2] Cf. *The Psalms in Israel's Worship*, ii, p. 210, where this interpretation is given with some reserve. In *Psalmenstudien IV*, p. 35, a different view was advanced.

[3] Cf. *The Psalms in Israel's Worship*, ii, p. 210. Again this view differs from Mowinckel's earlier view (*Psalmenstudien IV*, pp. 33ff).

[4] Ps. 53; cf. *Mah^alath l^e'annôth*, Ps. 88.

[5] Pss. 4; 6; 54; 55; 67; 76; also in Hab. 3.19. Cf. *'Al n^eghînath*, Ps. 61.

[6] Cf. *The Psalms in Israel's Worship*, ii, p. 210; cf. *Psalmenstudien IV*, p. 8.

[7] Ps. 145.   [8] Pss. 100.4.

[9] Here Mowinckel thinks the psalm was accompanied by a thank-offering, though not a private offering, at the Feast of Tabernacles; cf. *The Psalms in Israel's Worship*, ii, pp. 211f.

[10] Pss. 17; 86; 90; 102; 142.   [11] Pss. 120–34.

[12] Cf. *The Psalms in Israel's Worship*, ii, pp. 208f.

[13] Also in Hab. 3.19. On this psalm and its possible use in the cultus cf. J. H. Eaton, *Z.A.W.* lxxvi, 1964, pp. 144ff. On this psalm cf. also H. Bévenot, *R.B.* xlii, 1933, pp. 499ff; P. Humbert, *Problèmes du livre d'Habacuc*, 1944; W. F. Albright, in *Studies in Old Testament Prophecy* (T. H. Robinson Festschrift), 1950, pp. 1ff; S. Mowinckel, *Th.Z.* ix, 1953, pp. 1ff; W. A. Irwin, *J.N.E.S.* xv, 1956, pp. 47ff. Already in *J.T.S.* xvi, 1914–15, pp. 62ff, F. C. Burkitt had maintained that this psalm was composed for the liturgy of the Feast of Weeks.

designed to mollify God,[1] and he compares the priestly blessing
"The Lord make his face to shine upon thee"[2]—where, however,
the same root is not used. The term *Mikhtām*, found at the head
of six psalms,[3] he explains as marking a psalm of atonement,[4] and
Maśkîl, which stands at the head of twelve psalms,[5] he holds to
mark a cultic poem which is the outcome of supra-normal wisdom.[6] *Shiggāyôn*[7] he connects with the Akkadian *šegu* and defines
as a psalm of lamentation,[8] and *Higgāyôn*[9] as a psalm which should
be accompanied by a special flourish of the music.[10] The heading
le'annôth[11] he believes to designate a penitential psalm,[12] and
lehazkîr[13] a psalm to accompany the *'azkārāh*.[14] This is mentioned
in the Priestly Law,[15] where the priest is bidden to burn on the
altar a handful of a meal offering, as a memorial. G. R. Driver

[1] Cf. *Psalmenstudien IV*, pp. 17ff; *The Psalms in Israel's Worship*, ii,
pp. 212f. On this term cf. G. A. Danell, *Psalm 139*, 1951, pp. 3ff, where
Mowinckel's view is criticized, and where the view is expressed that the
term indicates some cultic official connected with the music. Danell
quotes (pp. 6f) the orally communicated view of Engnell, that it indicates
the king in his cultic function, and that it was perhaps originally the
North-Israelite equivalent of the Jerusalem *ledhāwîdh* (cf. *S.B.U.* ii,
1952, cols. 801f).

[2] Num. 6.25.   [3] Pss. 16; 56–60.

[4] Cf. *Psalmenstudien IV*, pp. 4f; *The Psalms in Israel's Worship*, ii,
p. 209.

[5] Pss. 32; 42; 44; 45; 52–5; 74; 78; 89; 142; also in 47.7 (M.T. 8).

[6] Cf. *The Psalms in Israel's Worship*, ii, p. 209; *Psalmenstudien IV*,
pp. 5ff. This term is discussed at length by G. W. Ahlström (*Psalm 89*,
1959, pp. 21ff), who holds that it denoted a psalm used in the renewal
rites. Mowinckel comments (*J.S.S.* v, 1960, pp. 295f) that on the
negative side Ahlström's treatment is good, but "on the positive it is an
archetype of a series of short circuits".

[7] Ps. 7. The plural, *Shighyônôth*, is found in Hab. 3.1.

[8] Cf. *The Psalms in Israel's Worship*, ii, p. 209; *Psalmenstudien IV*, p. 7.

[9] Ps. 9.16 (M.T. 17). The same word is translated in Ps. 19.14 (M.T.
15) "meditation", and in Ps. 92.3 "solemn sound" in R.V. and "melody"
in R.S.V.

[10] Cf. *The Psalms in Israel's Worship*, ii, p. 211; *Psalmenstudien IV*, p. 9.

[11] Ps. 88 (combined with *Maḥalath*, see above, p. 209, n. 4).

[12] Cf. *The Psalms in Israel's Worship*, ii, p. 212; *Psalmenstudien IV*,
p. 15.

[13] Pss. 38; 70. R.V. renders "to bring to remembrance", and R.S.V.
"for the memorial offering".

[14] Cf. *The Psalms in Israel's Worship*, ii, p. 212; *Psalmenstudien IV*,
pp. 15f.

[15] Lev. 2.2; 5.12; Num. 5.18.

suggests that the rendering should be "as a token".[1] The heading
Lîdhûthûn[2] or *'Al Y^edhûthûn*[3] Mowinckel renders "For confession", and thinks it refers to a particular part of the liturgy in
which the worshipper is led to humble confession.[4] My difficulty
with many of these interpretations is that we should expect other
psalms which have the same character to carry the same headings.
More ingenious are Mowinckel's suggestions for the headings
that have been held to indicate well-known tunes. For "The dove
of the distant terebinths"[5] he proposes the rendering "Over the
dove to the distant gods", and thinks it indicates that the psalm
was to accompany a ritual act similar to one described in Leviticus,[6]
but in which a dove was dipped in water mingled with the blood
of sacrifice and then let loose into the open field.[7] "The hind of
the morning"[8] he believes to indicate that the psalm was to be
sung to accompany the sacrifice of a hind at dawn.[9] "The Lilies"
or "The Lily of testimony"[10] he explains as accompanying a rite
in which omens were studied, and in Psalm 45 he thinks the
omens that were sought were omens of fertility.[11]

These examples must suffice.[12] They are given here because this

[1] Cf. *J.S.S.* i, 1956, pp. 99f. De Vaux (*Studies in Old Testament
Sacrifice*, 1964, p. 30) says the *'azkārāh* is either a "memorial" which
recalls the offerer to the mind of God, or a "pledge" which recalls that the
offering is to be considered as a whole, of which God accepts this part as
representative.

[2] Ps. 39.   [3] Pss. 62; 77.

[4] Cf. *The Psalms in Israel's Worship*, ii, p. 213; *Psalmenstudien IV*,
pp. 16f.

[5] Cf. above, p. 208.   [6] Lev. 1.14ff; 5.6–10.

[7] Cf. *The Psalms in Israel's Worship*, ii, pp. 213f; *Psalmenstudien IV*,
pp. 22ff.

[8] Cf. above, p. 208.

[9] Cf. *The Psalms in Israel's Worship*, ii, p. 214; *Psalmenstudien IV*,
pp. 19ff.

[10] Cf. above, p. 208.

[11] Cf. *The Psalms in Israel's Worship*, ii, p. 214; *Psalmenstudien IV*,
pp. 29ff.

[12] For other efforts to explain the Psalm headings cf. J. W. Thirtle, *The
Titles of the Psalms*, 1904; A. Bentzen, *Forelæsninger over Indledning til de
gammeltestamentlige Salmer*, 1932, pp. 65ff; W. O. E. Oesterley, *The
Psalms*, i, 1939, pp. 9ff; B. D. Eerdmans, *The Hebrew Book of Psalms*,
1947, pp. 51ff; I. Engnell, in *S.B.U.* ii, 1952, cols. 794ff; H. J. Kraus,
Psalmen, i, 1960, pp. xviii ff; E. Werner, in *I.D.B.* iii, 1962, pp. 459f;
J. J. Glueck, in *Studies on the Psalms*, 1963, pp. 30ff. R. H. Kennett (*Old*

approach is germane to our subject of the cultus, since they relate these titles to the particular ritual acts which the psalms are held to have accompanied. I am not persuaded, but neither am I persuaded by any alternative interpretation; and I have none to offer. We have no evidence on which to base our conjectures, and it seems profitless to speculate. Far more important than to speculate on the ritual accompaniments of the psalms on the basis of these cryptic headings is it to study the character of the psalms themselves and to ask what kind of ritual acts they might be supposed to fill with meaning for the worshipper. That is the approach followed by the scholars with whom I have aligned myself in this book, and it has brought altogether new life to the study of the Psalter and illumination for the wider understanding of the Old Testament as a whole.

Of the spiritual penetration of the psalms I shall have more to say later. In the previous chapter and in this I have been more occupied with studying the psalms as liturgical texts for the accompaniment of ritual acts in the ordinary or royal rites of the Temple. I may, however, conclude this chapter with some words of Sellin's, with which I would associate myself: "The literatures of Ancient Egypt and of Babylon show us that in respect of religious lyric, as of prophecy, the people of the revelation reached a height absolutely unique among the nations of the Ancient East. In spite of all the formal affinities of style, imagery, etc., it is here alone that the ethical is set free from the bondage of the natural; it is here alone that a consciousness of salvation is attained which in places already bears an almost New Testament character; it is here alone that the keynote is the hope of a Kingdom of God which is to embrace all nations, along with the heavens and the earth, a kingdom where 'mercy and truth are met together, righteousness and peace have kissed one another'."[1]

Testament Essays, 1927, pp. 121ff) interpreted the headings musically, while J. Begrich (*Einleitung in die Psalmen*, 1933, pp. 455ff) found ethnic significance in many of them.

[1] Cf. *Introduction to the Old Testament*, E. Tr., pp. 205f.

7

The Synagogue

In the previous chapters I have said much about altars and shrines and about the Temple and its ritual, but nothing about another centre of Jewish worship to which we find a number of references in the New Testament, the Synagogue. No account of Israelite and Jewish worship could be complete without some discussion of this very remarkable institution, which came into being at some time during the Old Testament period and which set the pattern for Christian and Muslim worship, as well as the worship which survived the destruction of the Temple for Judaism. Bamberger calls it a revolutionary departure[1] and such indeed it was. What makes it the more remarkable is that it is almost, if not quite, unmentioned in the Old Testament and that we have no account of its origin.

Jewish tradition traced the origin of the Synagogue back to the time of Moses or even the patriarchs. Josephus says that Moses ordained that men should leave their other occupations once a week to listen to the Law,[2] and this is generally understood to be a reference to the Synagogue. Philo similarly ascribed the beginnings of the Synagogue to Moses.[3] The Targum of Onkelos makes Jacob a synagogue minister,[4] while the Jerusalem Targum (Pseudo-Jonathan) says that Jethro advised Moses to teach the people the prayers they should offer in their synagogues,[5] and the Targum of Chronicles turns the high place of Gibeon into a synagogue.[6] The Targum of Jonathan imports a reference to the

---

[1] *U.J.E.* x, 1943, p. 120b. [2] *Contra Ap.* ii.17 (175).

[3] *De Vita Mosis*, ii.39 (215f). This reference follows F. H. Colson's arrangement in the Loeb edition. In other arrangements it is given as iii.27.

[4] Gen. 25.27. [5] Ex. 18.20. [6] 1 Chron. 16.39.

Synagogue into the Song of Deborah.[1] It is sometimes said[2] that in his speech at the Council of Jerusalem James reflected this tradition when he said that from generations of old Moses had been read every sabbath in the synagoguges.[3] But this in no sense implies that this custom had been observed from the time of Moses, but only that it was a long-established custom at the time of the Council; and of that there can be no doubt.

Rashi identifies "the house of the people" mentioned in Jer. 39.8 with a synagogue,[4] but that is due to the fact that one of the names for the synagogue was "house of the people",[5] as we learn from the Talmud, where we read that Rabbi Ishmael ben Eleazar condemned the common people who called the synagogue a house of the people.[6] It is more likely, however, that the true meaning of the expression in the Jeremiah text was the Temple, and that Rabbi Ishmael regarded the term as too holy to be used for the synagogue.[7]

None of this is of any real authority for determining the antiquity of the Synagogue, and there is only one passage in the Old Testament where any considerable body of scholars has found any reference to the Synagogue. This is Ps. 74.8, where A.V. and R.V. have "synagogues" and R.S.V. "meeting places". To this we shall return later. But first we must note that Jewish tradition was long followed by Christian, and in the seventeenth century, after the

---

[1] Judges 5.9. Cf. also Targum on Isa. 1.13. H. L. Strack observes (*New Schaff-Herzog Encyclopedia of Religious Knowledge*, xi, 1911, p. 213b) that these are examples of the habit of the Targums to attribute unhistorically to earlier times what belonged only to later.

[2] So W. Bacher, in *J.E.* xi, 1909, p. 619b (cf. Hastings' *D.B.* iv, 1902, p. 636b, where Bacher says this is perhaps the case). Cf. also E. Jacquier who says (*Les Actes des Apôtres*, 2nd edn, 1926, p. 777) that James perhaps alludes to the Mosaic origin of the Synagogue.

[3] Acts 15.21.

[4] Ad loc. Kimḥi (ad loc.) cites, but himself favours the view that the expression is a collective one, signifying the houses of the people.

[5] On this expression cf. F. Landsberger, *H.U.C.A.* xxii, 1949, pp. 149ff.

[6] T.B. *Shabb.* 32a. An alternative reading attributes this to Simeon ben Eleazar.

[7] So Landsberger (loc. cit., pp. 157ff), who adduces Mandaean evidence in support of this view. He thinks the transfer of the title to the Synagogue may have been due to the use of the term *Proseuchē* (see below, p. 230) for the Synagogue and Isa. 56.7 where, in a reference to the Temple, we read: "My house shall be called a house of prayer" (p. 154).

tradition had been challenged,[1] Grotius still accepted it.[2] In the nineteenth century, in a work of which only twenty copies are said to have been published and to which I have not had access, J. H. R. Biesenthal equated the term Bethel with synagogue,[3] and claimed that it was in continuous use from the time of Jacob. Within the present century so eminent a scholar as L. Finkelstein has maintained that Rebecca must have gone to a synagogue for a prophetic oracle[4] and that the Midrash of Iddo the seer, referred to by the Chronicler,[5] was not a literary composition but a synagogue,[6] while a doctoral dissertation presented to the University of Denver and published in abstract in 1915,[7] claims that the Synagogue "originated on the Jewish soil and in the earliest Biblical times, antedating even the Temple of Solomon".[8] The argument is not convincing, since the author holds the references to "the gate" as a meeting place in the Bible to reflect the beginnings of the Synagogue.[9] No real support is given to this view by the fact that in Amos 5.12, 15 the Targum of Jonathan renders "gate" by "synagogue".[10] The dissertation referred to argues that when the Temple was destroyed this new name was given and there was a development in use.[11] The author finds significance in the fact that the Septuagint very commonly has the word *sunagōgē*,[12] where, however, it never has the sense of synagogue, but renders

[1] See below, p. 225.

[2] Cf. *Annotata ad Vetus Testamentum*, i, 1644, p. 173, where in commenting on Deut. 31.12 he says: "Haec est institutio synagogarum." Cf. also J. C. G. Bodenschatz, *Kirchliche Verfassung der heutigen Juden*, ii, 1748, pp. 14ff, where the Synagogue is held to be pre-Davidic.

[3] *Theologisch-historische Studien*, 1847 (according to M. Silber, *The Origin of the Synagogue*, 1915, p. 7).

[4] *P.A.A.J.R.* i, 1930, pp. 49ff.

[5] 2 Chron. 13.22.   [6] Loc. cit.   [7] M. Silber, op. cit.

[8] Ibid., p. 22. G. L. Bauer already at the beginning of the nineteenth century (*Beschreibung der gottesdienstlichen Verfassung der alten Habräer*, ii, 1806, p. 125) rightly observed: "Diejenigen, welche ihnen [i.e. the synagogues] des höchste Alterthum zuschreiben, und ihren Ursprung schon in den Zeiten der Patriarchen suchen, oder sie von Mosis herleiten, oder wenigstens vorgeben, dass sie schon erbaut worden seyen, sobald die Israeliten im Lande Kanaan sich niedergelassen haben, können gar keinen historischen Grund für ihre leere Muthmassungen anführen." Cf. M. Leydekker, *De republica Hebraeorum*, 1704, p. 527, where the Synagogue is dated back to the earliest post-Settlement times.

[9] M. Silber, op. cit., pp. 17ff.   [10] Ibid., p. 19.

[11] Ibid., p. 18.   [12] Ibid., pp. 15ff.

a variety of terms, usually in the meaning of "assembly".[1] In
1 Kings 12.21, where Rehoboam is said to have assembled all the
house of Judah and Benjamin in Jerusalem, the Septuagint has
the *sunagōgē* of Judah, and in Gen. 1.9 it says God ordered the
primeval waters to be gathered in one *sunagōgē*. This could
scarcely be cited as evidence for the antiquity of the Synagogue!
In the article in Hastings' *Dictionary of Christ and the Gospels*
devoted to the Synagogue, R. W. Moss maintains that the Synagogue must have been in existence centuries before the exile.[2] He
maintains that it was a school and a court of local government
before it became pre-eminently a place of worship, and that from
the period of the exile dated the important modification of its
function whereby its religious use became its most important one.[3]
Solomon Zeitlin took a similar view of the Synagogue as first a
secular meeting place and later a religious centre, but he ascribed

[1] Silber notes that it is used 130 times for *'ēdhāh* and 25 times for
ḳāhāl, always in the sense of "meeting" or "assembly" (cf. E. H. Plumptre, in Smith's *D.B.* iii, 1863, p 1396b: "It appears in the LXX as the
translation of not less than twenty-one Hebrew words in which the idea
of a gathering is implied"). How this can supply the "proof" of the
antiquity of the Synagogue, as Silber claims, the reader is not told.

[2] In *D.C.G.* ii, 1908, p. 690a. Cf. J. J. S. Perowne (*Psalms*, 7th edn, ii,
1890, p. 28) where it is said that there must have been places for religious
worship in addition to the Temple in pre-exilic days. There were, of
course, the "high places", which are unlikely to be referred to in Ps. 74,
on which he is commenting, but it is gratituitous to assume that there
were also other places of worship scattered through the land. F. Nötscher
(*Echt. B.*, *Altes Testament*, iv, 1959, p. 162) thinks the reference in the
psalm is either to the "high places" or to synagogues outside Jerusalem
soon after the exile. W. S. McCullough (*I.B.* iv, 1955, p. 395) thinks the
reference is to "any sacred spot sanctified by ancient theophany or
former sacrificial practice". B. D. Eerdmans (*Psalms*, 1947, pp. 358f)
suggests that the reference is to private meetings through the country in
the period between Isaiah and Jeremiah, and denies that any foreign foes
are thought of, or any burning of the Temple, but thinks noisy young
people who broke up the meetings of the Hasidim are meant. E. J.
Janssen (*Juda in der Exilszeit*, 1956, pp. 105ff) attributes the beginnings
of the synagogues to the meetings of groups of the disciples of the
prophets in pre-exilic days.

[3] In *D.C.G.* ii, 1908, p. 690a. T. Witton Davies (*Psalms*, ii, p. 48) makes
the remarkable statement that "down to the destruction of the temple
in A.D. 71 the synagogue was merely a place of instruction". The use of
the term *proseuchē* for the synagogue long before this date (see below,
p. 230) sufficiently disproves this.

its beginnings to the period after the return from the exile.[1] Long before either of these writers, Leopold Löw had advanced a similar view of the development of the Synagogue.[2] Writing towards the end of the nineteenth century he argued that the Synagogue was a municipal centre before it became a place of worship, and traced it back to pre-exilic times, when he supposed it was used for the utterance of prophetic oracles and became gradually transformed into a meeting place for worship.[3]

Some writers have reacted against the traditional early dating of the Synagogue in an extreme way. In the nineteenth century at least three writers dated it no earlier than the Maccabaean age,[4] and others after the Maccabaean persecution.[5] Since there is now

[1] *P.A.A.J.R.* ii, 1931, pp. 69ff.

[2] *M.G.W.J.* xxxiii, 1884, pp. 97ff, 305ff, 458ff, especially pp. 98ff. This view is contested by F. Landsberger (*H.U.C.A.* xxii, 1949, pp. 149ff).

[3] A. Calmet (*Commentaire littéral sur tous les livres de l'Ancien et du Nouveau Testament*, vii, 1726, p. 32) maintains that the Synagogue was pre-exilic on the grounds that the Shunammite's visit to Elisha on the Sabbath day implies a synagogue, that Ps. 74.9 shows that there were synagogues in the time of Nebuchadrezzar, and that Judith must have gone to the synagogue to spend the night in prayer in the time of Manasseh. Little cogency attaches to any of these grounds. They are largely repeated in a recent work by I. Levy, *The Synagogue: its History and Function*, 1963, where it is held that early prayer meetings called by the prophets formed the beginnings of the Synagogue (p. 12), and that it was for such a prayer meeting that the Shunammite went to Elisha. Here also the view that Ps. 74 gives evidence of the existence of synagogues in the time of Nebuchadrezzar is repeated (p. 13). Cornelius à Lapide, *Commentaria in Josua, Judicum*, etc., 1740, p. 150) curiously held that Judges 20.1 refers to a synagogue at Mizpah.

[4] G. L. Bauer, *Beschreibung der gottesdienstlichen Verfassung der alten Hebräer*, ii, 1806, pp. 125f; L. Zunz, *Die Gottesdienstlichen Vorträge der Juden*, 1832, p. 3. J. Lawson and J. M. Wilson (*A Cyclopaedia of Biblical . . . Knowledge*, ii, 1866, p. 751b) held that "stated synagogues" did not begin to be erected in Palestine until Maccabaean times, though they may have existed in the Diaspora earlier, and held that the "synagogues" of Ps. 74 were places used occasionally for religious purposes.

[5] Cf. J. M. Jost, *Geschichte der Israeliten*, iii, 1822, p. 136, and *Anhang*, pp. 152f; A. T. Hartmann, *Die enge Verbindung des Alten Testament mit dem Neuen*, 1831, p. 233. F. W. Schultz (*Psalmen*, 1888, p. 167) thinks it uncertain whether there were any synagogues until after the Maccabaean period. *E.Brit.*, 11th edn, xxvi, 1911, p. 291b, observes: "The fact that the Books of the Maccabees never refer to synagogues is not evidence that synagogues were unknown in Judaea in the Maccabaean period" (unsigned).

archaeological evidence of the existence of synagogues before these dates, they are definitely ruled out.[1] Without going so far as this, Bousset and Gressmann placed the rise of the Synagogue in the Hellenistic age in the Diaspora,[2] and held that in the time of the Chronicler, which they placed in the third century B.C., the institution was unknown in Palestine. They therefore throw doubt on the commonly accepted reference to synagogues in Ps. 74.8.

Friedländer also denied that there is any reference to synagogues in this psalm,[3] and noted that in the books of Maccabees there is no mention of any destruction of synagogues, such as we might have expected if this psalm referred to their destruction in the persecution of Antiochus. To this M. Silber replies that the books of Maccabees concentrated their attention on the Temple, and moreover in 1 Enoch 46.8 there is evidence for attacks on synagogues in that age.[4] He does not note that in the psalm there is a reference to the setting of the Temple on fire,[5] and this, too, is unmentioned in the books of Maccabees.[6] So far as the reference in 1 Enoch is concerned Sjöberg has shown that it is improbable

---

[1] See below, p. 222.

[2] *Die Religion des Judentums in späthellenistichen Zeitalter*, 3rd edn, 1926, p. 172 (cf. Gunkel, *Psalmen*, 1926, p. 324). So also M. Friedländer, *Synagoge und Kirche in ihren Anfängen*, 1908, pp. 53ff, where it is maintained that there were no synagogues in Judaea before the time of Antiochus Epiphanes. Friedländer ascribed the beginnings of the Synagogue to the Greek Diaspora in the pre-Maccabaean period (pp. 31, 53). Cf. Oesterley and Box, *The Religion and Worship of the Synagague*, 1911, p. 337. In *A Fresh Approach to the Psalms*, 1937, pp. 153ff, Oesterley argues that the Synagogue was unknown in Palestine in the Maccabaean age, but that it was found in the Diaspora for a considerable time before this. Against this view I. Abrahams (*Studies in Pharisaism and the Gospels*, i, 1917, p. 1) holds that the Synagogue was a Palestinian institution of the Persian period.

[3] Op. cit., pp. 54f n. So also C. F. Keil, *Manual of Biblical Archaeology*, E. Tr. by P. Christie, i, 1887, p. 203.

[4] Op. cit., pp. 13f. Cf. L. Rabinowitz, in *Companion to the Bible*, ed. by T. W. Manson, 1939, p. 454.

[5] Ps. 74.7.

[6] In 1 Macc. 4.38; 2 Macc. 1.8; 8.33, we read of the burning of the gates of the Temple, but Ps. 74.7 appears to refer to a complete burning of the Temple.

that this is really a reference to synagogues.[1] Briggs[2] and Kraus[3] deny that the Hebrew in Ps. 74.8 can mean "synagogues", and it is significant that neither the Septuagint nor the Targum understood it in that sense,[4] though the later Greek versions of Aquila and Symmachus so understood it.[5] It is therefore uncertain, and indeed improbable, that any reference to synagogues is to be found in this verse or anywhere in the Old Testament.[6] It is equally

[1] *Der Menschensohn im äthiopischen Henochbuch*, 1946, p. 107 n. Cf. F. Martin, *Le Livre d'Hénoch*, 1906, p. 96, where the passage is rendered: "Et ils persécutent ses assemblées". Cf. also C. P. van Andel, *De Structuur van de Henoch-traditie en het Nieuwe Testament*, 1955, p. 31 n; W. Schrage, *Th.W.B.* vii, 1964, p. 811. But G. Beer (*Apokryphen und Pseudepigraphen des Alten Testaments*, ed. E. Kautzsch, ii, 1900. p. 273) thinks synagogues are referred to (so also K. Galling, *Z.D.P.V.* lxxii, 1956, p. 164).

[2] *Psalms*, ii, 1909, pp. 151, 154, 159.　　　[3] *Psalmen*, i, 1960, p. 516.

[4] LXX has "Let us cause the festivals of the Lord to cease from the land", and so Vulg. The Targ. and Syr. also rendered by "festivals", which is the normal meaning of the Hebrew word. Schleusner (*Lexicon Veteris Testamenti*, 2nd edn, ii, 1822, p. 202a) conjectured that the Hebrew *śāraph* meant "cause to cease" as well as "burn". Briggs (loc. cit., p. 159) preferred to emend the Hebrew verb, and so H. Pérennès (*Les Psaumes*, 1922, p. 163); G. R. Berry (*Psalms*, 1934, p. 146); M. Buttenwieser (*Psalms*, 1938, p. 607); W. O. E. Oesterley (*Psalms*, ii, 1939, p. 347); E. J. Kissane (*Psalms*, ii, 1954, p. 12). Theodotion rendered the Hebrew verb, but rendered "festivals" (cf. F. Field, *Origenis Hexaplorum quae supersunt*, ii, 1875, p. 217), though how festivals could be burned is not clear. Similarly Jerome in *Psalterium iuxta Hebraeos* rendered the Hebrew verb by *incenderunt*, but for the noun has *sollemnitates* (cf. the edition of J. M. Harden, 1922, p. 90, or the edition of H. de Sainte-Marie, 1954, p. 105). Pannier and Renard (*Les Psaumes*, 1950, p. 409) think the reference is to sacred sites associated with patriarchal traditions, such as Bethel, but this is very improbable, while Herkenne (*Psalmen*, 1936, p. 251) emends to secure the meaning "Sabbath and feasts have come to an end". The weight of ancient evidence is therefore strongly against any reference to synagogues or buildings of any kind. W. E. Barnes (*Psalms*, ii, 1931, p. 358) renders the noun by "assemblies" as in Lam. 1.15, and for the expression "burn up the assemblies" he compares 1 Macc. 3.5, where we find "he burned up those who troubled his people".

[5] Cf. F. Field, loc. cit.

[6] The following, among others, accept a reference to "synagogues" here: J. Olshausen (*Psalmen*, 1853, p. 317); F. Hitzig (*Psalmen*, ii, 1865, pp. 130ff); F. Baethgen (*Psalmen*, 1897, p. 229); B. Duhm (*Psalmen*, 1899, p. 195); T. Witton Davies (*Psalms*, ii, p. 49); W. F. Cobb (*Psalms*, 1905, p. 200); A. Bertholet (in *H.S.A.T.*, 4th edn, ii, 1923, p. 200); L. Randon (in *La Bible du Centenaire*, iii, 1947, p. 76).

uncertain or improbable that this psalm should be dated in the Maccabaean age.[1]

From the time of Rosenmüller[2] and de Wette[3] a long line of scholars have dated the psalm in that age[4] and accepted the reference to synagogues, and so have found here a *terminus ante quem* for their origin. Some have argued for earlier dates, however. Gunkel dated the psalm between the time of Nehemiah and that of Alexander the Great,[5] but we have no knowledge of any event in that period for which the psalm would be relevant. The same holds for the view of Strack which would locate it within that period in the reign of Artaxerxes III,[6] or Ewald's which would ascribe it to the time of Artaxerxes II.[7] At none of these times have we any evidence of the Temple being burned. As little is to be said for the view of Calès that the psalm was first written some years after the destruction of Jerusalem in 586 B.C.,

---

[1] The following, among others, date the psalm in the Maccabaean age: J. Olshausen (op. cit., p. 315); F. Hitzig (loc. cit.); J. J. S. Perowne (op. cit., p. 24); F. Baethgen (op. cit., pp. 227f); J. Wellhausen (*Psalms*, 1898, pp. 194f); B. Duhm (op. cit., p. 196, where he says that this is "so deutlich, dass eine nochmalige Aufzählung der Grunde überflüssig ist"); T. Witton Davies (op. cit., p. 46); W. F. Cobb (loc. cit.); A. Bertholet (loc. cit.); R. H. Kennett (*Old Testament Essays*, 1928, pp. 178ff); R. Kittel (*Die Psalmen*, 1929, p. 250); M. J. Lagrange (*Le Judaïsme avant Jésus-Christ*, 1931, p. 287); L. Randon (loc. cit.).

[2] *Scholia in Vetus Testamentum*, Pars IV, iii, 1904, pp. 2125f.

[3] *Die Psalmen*, 1811, p. 400. In the 4th edn, however (1836, p. 439), de Wette retracted this in favour of the view that the psalm referred to the destruction of the Temple by Nebuchadrezzar.

[4] The Targum appears to have interpreted Ps. 74.22 in terms of the Maccabaean age, since it rendered "the foolish man" by "the mad king". This is thought to be a reference to Antiochus Epiphanes, who was called Epimanes or madman (so Polybius, xxvi, 1a, 1, ed. W. R. Paton, v, 1926, p. 480). Cf. Calès, *Le Livre des Psaumes*, ii, 1936, p. 17.

[5] *Die Psalmen*, 1926, p. 322. R. Kittel (*Psalmen*, 5th edn, 1929, p. 250) while favouring the Maccabaean date, does not rule out the little-known period between Ezra and the Maccabees.

[6] In *New Schaff-Herzog Encyclopedia*, loc. cit., p. 213b. Cf. A. R. S. Kennedy, in Hastings' one volume *D.B.*, 1909, p. 882b; M. Buttenwieser, *Psalms*, 1938, p. 609.

[7] *Die Poetischen Bücher des Alten Bundes*, 2nd edn, ii, 1840, p. 355. Ewald later modified this view (cf. *Commentary on the Psalms*, E. Tr. by E. Johnson, ii, 1881, p. 227, and *G.V.I.* iv, 3rd edn, 1864, pp. 555ff) and located the psalm at the end of the sixth century B.C. or the beginning of the fifth.

and later worked over in the time of the Maccabees.[1] The most probable allusion in the psalm is to the destruction of the Temple by Nebuchadrezzar, and a number of scholars, including Kirkpatrick[2] and Briggs,[3] have followed this view.[4] This leaves us with no tangible evidence in the Bible for the origin of the Synagogue, and so far as the Old Testament is concerned we have no *terminus ante quem*, and the absence of any allusion to the Synagogue is very difficult to explain. The earliest

[1] *Les Psaumes*, ii, 1936, p. 18; cf. T. H. Robinson in W. O. E. Oesterley, *Psalms*, ii, 1939, p. 346.

[2] *Psalms*, 1902, pp. 439ff.

[3] *Psalms*, ii, 1909, p. 152. So also, among others, H. Hupfeld (*Die Psalmen*, iii, 1860, pp. 303, 309); F. W. Schultz (*Psalmen*, 1888, p. 167); J. Knabenbauer (*Psalmi*, 1912, p. 274); H. Pérennès (op. cit., p. 164); H. Schmidt (*Psalmen*, 1934, pp. 141f); H. Herkenne (*Psalmen*, 1936, pp. 250ff); C. Lattey (*The Psalter*, 1944, p. 139); E. Podechard (*Le Psautier*, i (Traduction et explication), 1949, pp. 325f); Pannier and Renard (*Psaumes*, 1950, pp. 405ff); E. J. Kissane (*Psalms*, ii, 1954, pp. 9f); G. Castellino (*Libro dei Salmi*, 1955, p. 306); R. Tournay and R. Schwab (*Psaumes*, 2nd edn, 1955, p. 288); F. Nötscher (loc. cit., p. 161); K. Galling (*Z.D.P.V.* lxxii, 1956, pp. 164f). Cf. A. Bentzen, *Fortolkning til de gammaltestamentlige Salmer*, 1940, p. 435. G. R. Berry (*Psalms*, 1934, p. 115) thinks this is the most probable time, but allows the possibility that the psalm might be dated between the time of Nehemiah and the Maccabaean period. W. S. McCullough (*I.B.* iv, 1955, pp. 393f) thinks the sixth century is the most probable date for the composition of the psalm. H. J. Kraus (*Psalmen*, i, 1960, p. 515) holds the reference to be to the destruction of the Temple by Nebuchadrezzar, but assigns the date to nearer 520 B.C. than the destruction itself. A. Weiser (*Psalms*, E. Tr. by H. Hartwell, 1962, p. 518) leaves the date entirely open, while S. Mowinckel (*The Psalms in Israel's Worship*, E. Tr. by D. R. Ap-Thomas, i, 1962, p. 118) says the Maccabaean age is out of the question, but leaves open the possibility that the psalm may refer to some calamity of the later monarchy, to 598 or 587, or to an unknown post-exilic spoliation of the Temple. J. Morgenstern (*H.U.C.A.* xix, 1945–6, p. 494, xxiv, 1953–3, p. 63 n, xxviii, 1957, p. 47, and *Studi Orientalistici* (Levi della Vida Festschrift), ii, 1956, p. 195) believes this psalm to refer to a calamity suffered by Jerusalem in 485 B.C. (on this cf. *M.B.*, 1963, pp. 238ff).

[4] F. Willesen (*V.T.* ii, 1952, pp. 289ff) holds that the psalm does not refer to any historical occasion, but is completely cultic (cf. J. A. Emerton, *J.T.S.*, N.S. ix, 1958, p. 234). On this cf. A. Weiser, *Psalms*, p. 518 n., and S. Mowinckel, *The Psalms in Israel's Worship*, i, 1962, p. 197 n. F. C. Cook (*Speaker's Bible*, iv, 1873, p. 338) dates the psalm in the time of Rehoboam in connection with Shishak's invasion, and identifies the 'meeting houses' of v. 8 with Gibeon and other sanctuaries other than the Jerusalem Temple.

synagogue which is mentioned by Josephus is one in Antioch, to which he says the successors of Antiochus Epiphanes gave the Temple vessels which that monarch plundered from the Temple.[1] There is, however, older archaeological evidence. Sukenik cites a synagogue inscription from Egypt dated in the reign of Ptolemy III, in the second half of the third century B.C.,[2] but gives the date of the oldest known Palestinian synagogue as the first century of our era.[3] We have therefore a secure *terminus ante quem*, which is consistent with the view that the Synagogue began in the Diaspora, though it does not require this and does not get us very far. An earlier but less secure *terminus ante quem* has been suggested on the basis of an ostracon from Elath,[4] which Albright would date at the end of the sixth century B.C.,[5] on which Torrey would read *bêth kᵉnîshāh*, or synagogue.[6] But here neither the date nor the reading can be regarded as certain.

Julian Morgenstern has argued that the Synagogue arose in Palestine out of the reform of Josiah, and that when the altars of the high places were broken down as the result of the Deuteronomic reform the country shrines continued to be used as religious meeting-places on sabbaths and festivals.[7] The statement in 2 Kings 23.8 that Josiah defiled all the high places does not seem to support this view. More recently J. Weingreen[8] has presented

[1] *B.J.* VII.iii.3 (44).

[2] *Ancient Synagogues in Palestine and Greece*, 1934, p. 1. On Palestinian synagogues cf. also H. G. May, *B.A.* vii, 1944, pp. 1ff. In the course of a valuable study of the rise and significance of the Synagogue (*N.T.T.* viii, 1919, pp. 43ff, 137ff) A. W. Groenman presents evidence for the Synagogue from Egyptian papyri (pp. 65ff).

[3] Op. cit., p. 69. More recently it has been claimed that the oldest synagogue in Palestine so far excavated is at Masada (cf. Yigael Yadin, *Observer*, 31 January, 1965).

[4] Cf. N. Glueck, *B.A.S.O.R.*, No. 82, April 1941, pp. 7ff.

[5] Cf. ibid., p. 11.

[6] Cf. *B.A.S.O.R.*, No. 84, December 1941, pp. 4f. J. Weingreen (*Hermathena*, xcviii, 1964, p. 69) observes that little attention has been paid to this article. The present writer noted it in *B.D.E.* 1950, p. 86 n., and *The Faith of Israel*, 1956, p. 140.

[7] *Studi Orientalistici* (Levi della Vida Festschrift), ii, 1956, pp. 192ff. N. H. Snaith (in Manson's *Companion to the Bible*, 2nd edn, 1963, p. 544) holds this to be a possibility. Further, R. H. Kennett (*Old Testament Essays*, 1928, p. 139) says the germ of the Synagogue may go back to pre-exilic days.

[8] *Hermathena*, xcviii, 1964, pp. 68ff.

a view somewhat similar to Morgenstern's, though recognizing that profaned shrines could not have continued to be used for public worship. But he says that it is natural to suppose that when Josiah profaned the country shrines he created other centres where prayers unaccompanied by sacrifice, the reading of Scripture, and the delivery of the sermon could be continued.[1] He therefore assumes that all these things had been going on in the Temple and in the country shrines before the time of Josiah. These are all very large conclusions to draw from the slenderest evidence. The law-book of Josiah is generally agreed to have been the book of Deuteronomy.[2] This law-book can scarcely be presumed to have contemplated the creation of new centres of worship without so much as mentioning them. Nor is it natural to suppose that Josiah built new places of worship throughout the land when the record of his reform does not hint at it. If the Synagogue had begun in a deliberate way in a great historical moment, it would be quite astonishing for its beginning not to be recorded. Moreover, Professor Weingreen bases his argument for services of prayer unaccompanied by sacrifice on such things as Hannah's prayer[3] and Solomon's dedicatory prayer at the consecration of the Temple.[4] But Hannah's prayer was not part of a public service, but a private prayer, while Solomon's was on a special occasion and is without evidence for regular non-sacrificial services. For the reading of the Scripture Professor Weingreen bases himself on Ezra's reading of the Law.[5] Since Ezra was sent specifically to put into force the law which he brought in his hand,[6] it was natural that its provisions should be publicly read, and this offers no evidence for regular reading, and since this was a post-exilic occasion it can

[1] Ibid., p. 72; cf. p. 78.
[2] Cf. *M.G.*, 1963, pp. 187ff, where this question is examined, and the common view is defended.
[3] Loc. cit., p. 76.   [4] Ibid.
[5] Ibid., p. 81. Professor Weingreen states, but without evidence, that Ezra "merely put into practice or, possibly, reintroduced, what had been normal procedure in pre-exilic times". What Ezra did in Jerusalem cannot of itself offer evidence of what went on throughout the land in pre-exilic times. Professor Weingreen further adduces (ibid., pp. 79f) Ps. 136 as evidence of congregational responses in the worship. But he produces no evidence that this psalm was used in the high places or in pre-exilic synagogues, so that this argument appears to me to be a complete *non-sequitur.*
[6] Ezra 7.14.

offer no evidence for pre-exilic practice. What is needed, but what is not provided, is evidence that there were regular services throughout the land in the "high places" comparable with the synagogue services. As for the sermon, Professor Weingreen adduces[1] the expansion of the commandment "Honour thy father and thy mother" in Deut. 5.16, where we read: "that thy days may be prolonged and that it may go well with thee". This is heavy overworking of the verse. It is not evidence that this verse was ever a sermon—one of the shortest on record[2]—and still less that it was ever delivered as a sermon in the Temple or in one of the country shrines which Deuteronomy abominated, or that there were regular sermons delivered in services of worship in the Temple or shrines.

It seems to me that the view which has long been widely accepted is more likely to be right. This is that the Synagogue arose among the exiles in Babylon, who began, perhaps first in one another's homes, to meet to keep their faith alive.[3] They were

[1] Loc. cit., p. 80.

[2] Weingreen (ibid.) describes it as the nucleus of a sermon. Even if this were allowed, it offers no evidence that it was delivered in a synagogue. In *Promise and Fulfilment* (S. H. Hooke Festschrift), 1963, pp. 187ff, Professor Weingreen argued that observations of this kind were evidence of the insertion of glosses or commentary in the text of the Bible. This is indeed probable. But literary commentary is not evidence of oral sermon delivered in a synagogue.

[3] Cf. Humphrey Prideaux, *The Old and New Testament Connected*, 1845, edn, i, p. 357: "That they had no synagogues before the Babylonish captivity is plain"; J. J. Kneucker, in Schenkel's *Bibel-Lexikon*, v, 1875, p. 443: "Ohne Zweifel verdanken sie ihnen Ursprung einer Zeit, da die Israeliten im Auslande lebten und ihr Tempeldienst stillstand"; A. Edersheim, *The Life and Times of Jesus the Messiah*, 11th impression, i, 1901, p.431; "That Synagogues originated during, or in consequence of, the Babylonish captivity, is admitted by all"; K. Kohler, in *D.A.C.*, ii, 1918, p. 541b: "The synagogue is a new creation for which the Exile alone offered the conditions"; S. M. Zarb, *Angelicum*, v, 1928, p. 272: "Probabilius est ergo synagogas, deficiente Templo, in exsilio ortas, et post reditum, reaedificato Templo, conservatas, cum ipsis Iudaeis in provincias Diasporae propagatas esse"; N. Drazin, *History of Jewish Education*, 1940, p. 5: "While all the Jews were still in Babylonia and mourning the loss of their sacred Temple, they began to construct synagogues in which the people might gather for divine worship and prayer. Similar synagogues were later established in the country towns of Palestine." Prideaux (loc. cit.) argues that since the main service of the Synagogue was

far from the Temple, and it is improbable that they erected shrines where sacrifice could continue to be made, though Torrey thought there might have been Jewish temples in Babylonia,[1] and L. E. Browne thought that Ezra 8.17 referred to such a temple, where Ezra's brother was priest.[2] This seems very hazardous, and it is more likely that the exiles sought to preserve their religion by meeting for prayer and meditation in a simple and informal way, and the very humbleness of the beginnings of the Synagogue would explain why its origin is unrecorded. That somehow the exiles did preserve their faith is beyond question. For the prophecies of Deutero-Isaiah give ample evidence of this.[3] Moreover, more than a century later Ezra went from Babylon to put into effect in Jerusalem the book of the law which he carried with him.[4] The Targum of Ezek. 11.16 expresses the view that the Synagogue arose out of the exile. That verse says: "Thus saith the Lord God: Whereas I have removed them far off among the nations, and whereas I have scattered them among the countries, yet will I be to them a sanctuary for a little while in the countries where they are come." Here the Targum has "synagogues for my sanctuary" instead of "a sanctuary". While this rendering carries no evidential value, it is of interest as an anticipation of the view which is so widely held among scholars.

The earliest modern writer to suggest this date and the Babylonian scene for the origin of the Synagogue was C. Sigonio,[5] who in the sixteenth century wrote: "I . . . would surmise that they (i.e. synagogues) were first erected in the Babylonian exile, so that those who were deprived of the Temple, where they were used to

the reading of the law, there could not have been a pre-exilic synagogue. For when Jehoshaphat sent teachers through the land to instruct the people in the law (2 Chron. 17.9) they carried a book of the law with them, and hence there could not have been copies in the cities to which they went.

[1] *Ezra Studies*, 1910, p. 317.

[2] *J.T.S.* xvi, 1916, pp. 400f, and *Early Judaism*, 1920, p. 53.

[3] That many succumbed to the pressure of the influences around them is doubtless true, but it is equally certain that many did not. Cf. J. Morgenstern, *Studi Orientalistici* (Levi della Vida Festschrift), ii, 1956, p. 194.

[4] Ezra 7.

[5] *De republica Hebraeorum*, 1582, pp. 63f (reprinted in B. Ugolino, *Thesaurus antiquitatum sacrarum*, iv, 1745, p. ccxci).

pray or teach, might have a place similar to the Temple, where they could meet and observe the same kind of service, and that the other Jews of the Diaspora, whether in Asia, Egypt, or Europe, did the same." This view has been followed by Winer,[1] Kuenen,[2] Wellhausen,[3] Schürer,[4] Moore,[5] and many others,[6] and though it can in no sense be said to be proved it can claim much probability. As Rabinowitz observes,[7] this period presents the conditions under which its birth can be most naturally explained. If it is true, it means that from the disaster of the Exile there was born a new and profoundly spiritual centre of worship which has been an incalculable blessing to three great religions. This would suggest that not all the religion of the pre-exilic days was as dead as the prophetic denunciations would seem to imply, and would

---

[1] *Biblisches Realwörterbuch*, 3rd edn, ii, 1847, p. 548.

[2] *The Religion of Israel*, iii, 1883, p. 17.

[3] *Israelitische und Jüdische Geschichte*, 5th edn, 1904, pp. 198f.

[4] *G.J.V.*, 4th edn, ii, 1907, pp. 500f, where Schürer assigns the origin to the time of Ezra or to the period of the Exile. In *H.J.P.*, E. Tr. by S. Taylor and P. Christie, II.ii, 1890, p. 54 (translated from the second German edition) he had said the Synagogue perhaps went back to the time of Ezra. Strack and Billerbeck (*Kommentar zum Neuen Testament aus Talmud und Midrasch*, iv, Part 1, 1928, p. 115) and W. Schrage (*Th.W.B.* vii, 1964, p. 810) assign the beginnings of the Synagogue to the time of Ezra or to the period of the Exile.

[5] *Judaism*, i, 1927, p. 283.

[6] Cf. I. J. Peritz, in *E.B.* iv, 1907, col. 4833; A. R. S. Kennedy, in Hastings' one volume *D.B.*, 1909, p. 882b; E. Jacquier, *Les Actes des Apôtres*, 2nd edn, 1926, p. 777; A. Menes, *Z.A.W.* l, 1932, pp. 268ff; M. Simon, in Manson's *Companion to the Bible*, 2nd edn, 1963, p. 391; W. Förster, *Palestinian Judaism in New Testament Times*, E. Tr. by G. E. Harris, 1964, p. 8. F. Nötscher (*Biblische Altertumskunde*, 1940, pp. 300f) places the origin of the Synagogue in the Diaspora in the period following the Exile.

[7] In *Companion to the Bible*, ed. T. W. Manson, 1939, p. 453; cf. W. Bacher, in Hastings' *D.B.* iv, 1902, p. 636b. P. Volz (*Z.S.T.* xiv, 1937, pp. 79f) dated the Synagogue from the Exile, but with great improbability thought it was designed to express prophetic religion as against priestly religion. But Synagogue worship was in no sense opposed to Temple worship, and Jesus, whose custom it was to attend the Synagogue when he was not in Jerusalem (Luke 4.16), attended the Temple when he was there, and charged the cleansed lepers to present themselves to the priests (Luke 17.14). Similarly Paul went to the Synagogues when he was on his missionary journeys, but went to the Temple when he was in Jerusalem (Acts 21.26).

be more consistent with the view of worship which I have presented than the view that the pre-exilic worship was scarcely distinguishable from Canaanite worship and was devoid of any spiritual quality. The rise of the Synagogue is sometimes attributed to Ezra.[1] If there had been any formal institution of the Synagogue as part of the work of Ezra, we should have expected this to be recorded, and certainly to be associated with his name in tradition. It therefore seems to me more likely that its beginnings in Palestine, as in the Diaspora, were more humble. It could conceivably have begun in Palestine in the same way as in Babylon, though there seems to have been less spiritual vitality in the Palestinian community than in the exiled community. Whether any sacrifices continued to be offered on the site of the ruined Temple cannot be known. In the book of Jeremiah we read of some northerners from Shechem and Shiloh and Samaria who were journeying to Jerusalem after the destruction of the Temple, bringing offerings to the Temple.[2] Kennett argued[3] for the view that the Bethel priests migrated to Jerusalem after the exiles had been carried to Babylon and served the altar there until the return, when the concordat between them and the returning Zadokites combined both groups into the Aaronites of the Priestly Code. We must therefore reckon with the possibility that despite the ruined state of the Temple, the conditions of worship in Palestine were not so radically changed as they were for the exiles, and the need for what became the Synagogue would not be so acutely felt. But the returning exiles long before the time of Ezra could have established in Judaea meeting places like those which had come to have so much meaning for them in Babylon, where non-sacrificial worship could be shared in the intervals between visits to the Temple. That the Synagogue had been established long before the

---

[1] Cf. C. Vitringa, *De synagoga vetere*, 1696, pp. 413ff; J. Jost, *Geschichte des Judenthums und seiner Sekten*, i, 1857, pp. 38f. W. Bacher (in Hastings' *D.B.* loc. cit., pp. 636f) thinks the activity of Ezra led to the rise of synagogues throughout the country, and says "we may confidently place the origin of the synagogue in Palestine at the period of the Persian domination". Cf. H. Lesêtre, in Vigouroux' *D.B.* v, 1912, col. 1900; *E.Brit.*, 11th edn, xxvi, 1911, p. 291a (unsigned). B. J. Bamberger (in *U.J.E.* x, 1943, p. 120a) contents himself with ascribing the development of the Synagogue to the early post-exilic period.

[2] Jer. 41.5.   [3] *Old Testament Essays*, 1928, pp. 82ff.

beginning of the Christian era is beyond question.[1] This is clear
from the fact that in New Testament times synagogues were found
not merely throughout Palestine[2] but wherever Jewish communities were to be found.[3] Wherever Paul went he found worshipping Jewish communities and his first preaching was always
to them. It is improbable that an institution would have become
so widespread except over a long period. Moreover, the already
quoted words of James[4] imply that the Synagogue was believed to
be very ancient. The fact of the Maccabaean rebellion would seem
to be evidence that the Synagogue had existed in Palestine for
some time before that rising. Clearly something had kept alive a
passionate devotion to the Jewish faith, which was widespread
through the nation, and this could hardly be thought to have been
achieved by such visits to Jerusalem as were possible for ordinary
people throughout the land. Moreover, copies of the Law were
confiscated and burned during the persecution,[5] and apparently
they were found widely among the people. This bespeaks not
merely an interest in the Law, but the ability to read and study
it, and would imply that schools were common in the land. The
Synagogue was not merely the house of worship, but the house of
study, as we shall see, and it is more likely that this developed out
of its function in worship than the other way round, since the

[1] M. Rosenmann (*Der Ursprung der Synagoge*, 1907, pp. 22ff) propounded the view that the Synagogue arose from the ma'amadoth. These
were divisions of representatives of the people in twenty-four groups, who
attended the daily services of the Temple in rotation, corresponding to
the divisions of the priests and Levites (cf. Schürer, *G.J.V.*, 4th edn, ii,
1907, pp. 337f; *H.J.P.* II. i, p. 275). Rosenmann advanced the theory
that from these representatives the institution of the Synagogue spread
among those they represented. Against this I. Sonne (in *I.D.B.* iv, 1962,
p. 479b) raises the objection that the institution of the ma'amadoth is
probably much younger than the establishment of the Synagogue. Cf. also
E. Schürer, *Th.L.Z.* xxxii, 1907, col. 663.

[2] The synagogues of Nazareth (Matt. 13.54; Mark 6.2; Luke 4.16) and
Capernaum (Mark 1.21; Luke 7.5; John 6.59) are mentioned in the
Gospels, and frequently Jesus is said to have taught or wrought a miracle
in a synagogue, where the place is unnamed, while Mark 1.39 says he
preached in all the synagogues throughout Galilee.

[3] Of synagogues outside Palestine mentioned in Acts we may note
Damascus (9.20), Salamis (13.5), Antioch in Pisidia (13.14), Iconium
(14.1), Philippi (16.13), Thessalonica (17.1), Beroea (17.10), Athens
(17.17), Corinth (18.4), Ephesus (18.19; 19.8).

[4] Acts 15.21.   [5] 1 Macc. 1.56f.

study was exclusively religious. Moreover, the third-century synagogue of Egypt cannot be presumed to be the first to be built. All of these indications support the probability that the origins of the Synagogue must lie much farther back, at least in the fourth or fifth century B.C. It may well be that Ezra's public reading of the Law[1] stimulated the regular reading of it, even though it is unlikely that he first created the Synagogue in Palestine. George Foot Moore, who believes that the Synagogue had its antecedents in spontaneous gatherings of Jews in Babylonia and other lands of their exile, suggests that the development of its form may owe much to the Pharisees in the second century B.C.[2]

Schürer observes[3] that the primary object of the Synagogue was not devotion but instruction in the written Law. Philo calls the Synagogue a school,[4] and Josephus says: "He [i.e. Moses] appointed the Law to be the most excellent and necessary form of instruction, ordaining, not that it should be heard once for all or twice or on several occasions, but that every week men should desert their other occupations and assemble to listen to the Law and to obtain a thorough and accurate knowledge of it."[5] W. Schrage says the Synagogue is before all the place of the Torah,[6] and cites a synagogue inscription which states the purpose of the building as "for the reading of the Law and for the teaching of the commandments".[7] This purpose was fulfilled, not merely through the public services, but through the use of the Synagogue as a place of education, where the Bible was the chief or the sole subject

---

[1] Neh. 8.   [2] *Judaism*, i, 1927, p. 286.
[3] *H.J.P.*, E. Tr. by S. Taylor and P. Christie, II.ii, 1890, p. 54. Cf. I. J. Peritz, in *E.B.* iv, 1907, col. 4836; R. W. Moss, in *D.C.G.* ii, 1908, p. 691b. H. Lesêtre (in Vigouroux' *D.B.* v, 1912, cols. 1899f) says "La synagogue n'était pas, comme le Temple, la 'maison de la prière'. Sans doute, la prière n'en était pas bannie; mais la synagogue était avant tout consacrée à l'enseignement de la Loi."
[4] *Didaskaleion*; cf. *Vita Mosis*, ii.39 (216). In the alternative arrangement this is numbered iii.27.
[5] *Contra Ap.* ii.17 (175), H. St J. Thackeray's rendering.
[6] In *Th.W.B.* vii, 1964, p. 820.
[7] Ibid. J. Juster (*Les Juifs dans l'empire romain*, i, 1914, pp. 457f) well observes: "C'est dans le synagogue que se concentre la vie juive: c'est elle son foyer." M. Friedländer (*Synagoge und Kirche in ihren Anfängen*, 1908, pp. 64, 215) distinguishes between Diaspora synagogues, which were schools, and Pharisaic synagogues, which were houses of prayer, but it is doubtful if this distinction is justified.

studied. Elementary education and more advanced studies belonged to its function,[1] and it was doubtless in the Synagogue that Jesus had acquired his intimate knowledge of the Old Testament and that his hearers had acquired the knowledge of it which he so often took for granted.

Most of the Palestinian synagogues were built on the highest sites in towns,[2] in agreement with what later became the accepted rule.[3] The account of our Lord's visit to the synagogue in Nazareth indicates that it was so sited.[4] In Hellenistic countries, however, the custom of building synagogues near water was common.[5] It will be recalled that at Philippi Paul and Silas sought a "place of prayer" by the river side,[6] and Josephus records a decree of the people of Halicarnassus that Jews should be allowed to build "places of prayer" near the sea.[7] Here we note that the term *proseuchē* or "place of prayer" indicates that worship rather than education is the primary purpose of these centres, and this is the term found in inscriptions from Egypt of the third to the first century B.C.[8]

A distinction is sometimes drawn between a *proseuchē* and a synagogue.[9] Thus Vernon Bartlet says this term points to the

[1] Cf. W. Bacher, in Hastings' *D.B.* iv, 1902, p. 642; I. Sonne, in *I.D.B.* iv, 1962, p. 487.

[2] So I. Sonne, in *I.D.B.* iv, 1962, p. 485a. R. W. Moss (in *D.C.G.* ii, 1908, p. 690b) says the Galilaean ruins show that this rule was not followed in the first century in Palestine, since the ruins do not occupy prominent positions, but E. L. Sukenik (*Ancient Synagogues in Palestine and Greece*, 1934, p. 49) says Palestinian synagogues mostly satisfy this specification.

[3] Tosephta, *Megillah* iv, 22f (ed. by M. S. Zuckermandel, 2nd edn, 1937, p. 227). A. R. S. Kennedy (in *D.A.C.* ii, 1918, p. 542a) thinks this custom is to be traced back to the location of the "high places", while I. Levy (*The Synagogue: its history and function*, 1963, p. 30) thinks it was in imitation of the location of the Temple.

[4] Luke 4.29.

[5] Cf. I. Sonne, *I.D.B.* iv, 1962, p. 485a. E. Jacquier (*Les Actes des Apôtres*, 2nd edn, 1926, p. 777) thinks Ps. 137.1 refers to a religious assembly by a river.

[6] Acts 16.13.   [7] *Ant.* XIV. x. 23. (258).

[8] Cf. I. Sonne, in *I.D.B.* iv, 1962, p. 477b.

[9] Cf. E. H. Plumptre, in Smith's *D.B.* iii, 1863, p. 1398a; C. F. Keil, *Manual of Biblical Archaeology*, E. Tr. by P. Christie, i, 1887, p. 202. Humphrey Prideaux had earlier (*The Old and New Testament Connected*, 1845 edn, i, pp. 372ff) drawn a sharp distinction between the synagogue and the *proseuchē* on the ground that the former was a covered building

fewness of the Jews in Philippi.[1] It is improbable, however, that any distinction should be seen.[2] For Josephus writes of a *proseuchē* in Tiberias that it was a huge building, capable of holding a large crowd, in which a general assembly of the town was held.[3] While it is quite likely that the Jewish community of Philippi was small, this cannot rightly be deduced from the term *proseuchē*.[4]

Josephus cites an edict of Augustus in which the synagogue is referred to as *sabbateion*,[5] which is presumably derived from the resort to the synagogue on the sabbath, and Sonne says that at the beginning of the Christian era Valerius Maximus appears to have confused the Jews with the worshippers of Sabazius.[6] The cult of Sabazius was a syncretistic worship current in Asia Minor.[7] Tcherikover cites an inscription from Thyatira dating from the time of Hadrian in which a building is called *sambatheion*,[8] and he thinks this was a Jewish synagogue.[9]

The orientation of the synagogue appears to have been towards Jerusalem.[10] When Daniel prayed he looked towards Jerusalem,[11] so that this usage seems to have been at least as ancient as the composition of the book of Daniel. F. Landsberger says: "If we may infer backward from the Galilean synagogues of the second and third Christian centuries—these being the oldest which have

while the latter was an open court. Cf. also J. V. Bartlet, *The Acts*, p. 289; F. F. Bruce, *The Book of the Acts*, 1954, p. 331. On the *sunagōgē* and the *proseuchē*, cf. A. W. Groenman, *N.T.T.* viii, 1919, pp. 65ff.

[1] *Acts*, p. 289.
[2] Cf. E. Schürer, *H.J.P.*, E. Tr., II.ii, 1890, p. 73 (*G.J.V.* 4th edn, ii, 1907, pp. 517f); Strack-Billerbeck, *Kommentar zum Neuen Testament aus Talmud und Midrasch*, ii, 1924, p. 742; W. Bacher, in Hastings' *D.B.* iv, 1902, p. 636a; R. J. Knowling, in *E.G.T.* ii, p. 345; Lake and Cadbury, in *B.C.* iv, 1933, p. 191.
[3] *Vita*, 54 (277).
[4] Cf. F. F. Bruce (*The Acts of the Apostles*, 1951, p. 314), who says there is no thought of a synagogue here, as only women are mentioned (cf. also *The Book of the Acts*, 1954, p. 331).
[5] *Ant.* XVI. vi. 2 (164).   [6] In *I.D.B.* iv, 1963, p. 478a.
[7] On the cult of Sabazius cf. W. O. E. Oesterley, in *The Labyrinth*, ed. by S. H. Hooke, 1935, pp. 113ff.
[8] *Corpus Papyrorum Judaicarum*, iii, 1964, p. 46 (cf. E. Schürer, *G.J.V.* 4th edn, iii, 1909, p. 562).
[9] Objections to this view are discussed by Tcherikover (loc. cit.).
[10] Cf. E. L. Sukenik, *Ancient Synagogues in Palestine and Greece*, 1934, p. 50.
[11] Dan. 6.10 (M.T. 6.11).

survived at least in ruins—the synagogue had already recognized a prayer direction resembling that of Daniel in his chamber, namely, through open spaces between the worshipper and Jerusalem."[1] He suggests that the location of synagogues on high ground may have been so that the outlook towards Jerusalem could the more readily be effected.[2]

The officers of the Synagogue were few and they are referred to in the New Testament. In Luke 7.3 we read that the centurion sent the "elders of the Jews" to Jesus, and from the sequel it would appear that they belonged to a particular synagogue, where they probably formed a body responsible for the management of the synagogue. Jairus, who is called *archōn tēs sunagōgēs*,[3] may have been a member of such a body, though Sonne is more probably right in equating this title with the *archisunagōgos* of whom we read elsewhere.[4] When Jesus healed the woman with a spirit of infirmity in a synagogue, the *archisunagōgos*, or ruler of the synagogue, was moved with indignation.[5] Here he appears to be the officer responsible for the conduct of worship and the maintenance of order, and Peritz defines his duties as "related to the care and order of the synagogue and its assemblies and the supervision of the service".[6] Some have thought the *archisunagōgos* might have been the chief of the elders or *archontes*,[7] but Schürer says his office was quite distinct from theirs, and that he was charged with the supervision of the public worship.[8] Against this, however, Strack and Billerbeck point out that whereas in Luke 8.41 Jairus is called *archōn tēs sunagōgēs*, in verse 49 he is called *archisunagōgos*.[9] In the synagogue of Antioch in Pisidia

---

[1] *H.U.C.A.* xxviii, 1957, p. 183.   [2] Ibid., p. 184.   [3] Luke 8.41.

[4] In *I.D.B.* iv, 1962, p. 489a. On the *archisunagōgos* cf. Schrage, in *Th.W.B.* vii, 1964, pp. 842ff.

[5] Luke 13.14.

[6] In *E.B.* iv, 1907, col. 4837. Cf. I. Sonne, in *I.D.B.* iv, 1962, p. 489a.

[7] Cf. E. H. Plumptre, in Smith's *D.B.* iii, 1863, p. 1399a. L. Rabinowitz (in *Companion to the Bible*, ed. by T. W. Manson, 1939, p. 460) says the *archisunagōgos* was chosen from the *archontes*, but a few lines below he says the office of *archisunagōgos* was hereditary. H. L. Strack (in *The New Schaff-Herzog Encyclopedia*, xi, 1911, p. 214a) says he was probably chosen from the elders (so G. F. Moore, *Judaism*, i, 1927, p. 289).

[8] *H.J.P.*, E. Tr., II. ii, 1890, pp. 63ff.

[9] *Kommentar zum Neuen Testament aus Talmud und Midrasch*, iv, Part 1, 1928, p. 145. I. J. Peritz (in *E.B.* iv, 1907, col. 4837) says the two offices were quite distinct, though the same person might hold both.

the *archisunagōgoi* invited Paul and Silas to give an address.[1] Another officer of the Synagogue was the *ḥazzān*, who in Luke 4.20 is called the "attendant". There we read that Jesus handed the scroll back to him after reading from Isaiah.[2] One of his functions was thus the care of the synagogue scrolls. He was a paid official and he had the care of the building and its furnishing. He announced from the synagogue roof the advent of the sabbath and of festival days, and often acted as schoolmaster, though this was no necessary part of his duties. He sometimes dwelt on the premises. He also served as the officer of the synagogue court for the administration of punishment.[3]

Another person not mentioned in the New Testament was the *sheʾliaḥ ṣibbûr*, or "messenger of the community".[4] He was frequently been thought of as the prototype of the "angel of the Church" of the book of Revelation,[5] but Lesêtre thinks the "angel" was more comparable with the "ruler of the synagogue".[6] The duty of the "messenger" was to act as the representative of the community and to recite the prayers in the service.[7] Plumptre says the conditions laid down for this office remind us of Paul's rule for the selection of a bishop: he must be active, of full age, the father of a family, not rich or engaged in business, possessing a good voice, apt to teach.[8] It is, however, doubtful if we should think of him as originally an official, but as a person who is called upon for this duty.[9] Frequently, especially in small communities, the *ḥazzān* would act as the messenger, and in the course of time

[1] Acts 13.15. The term stands here in the plural, though normally there was only one *archisunagōgos* in a synagogue.

[2] Luke 4.20.

[3] Cf. W. Bacher, in Hastings' *D.B.* iv, 1902, pp. 640f; I. J. Peritz, in *E.B.* iv, 1907, col. 4834; R. W. Moss, in *D.C.G.* ii, 1908, p. 691a; G. F. Moore, *Judaism*, i, 1927, pp. 289f; Strack and Billerbeck, *Kommentar zum Neuen Testament aus Talmud und Midrasch*, iv Part 1, 1928, pp. 147ff; I. Sonne, in *I.D.B.* iv, 1962, pp. 489f.

[4] Cf. Bacher, in *D.B.* loc. cit., p. 641a; Strack and Billerbeck, op. cit., pp. 149ff.

[5] Cf. E. H. Plumptre, in Smith's *D.B.* iii, 1863, p. 1400a.

[6] In Vigouroux' *D.B.* v, 1912, col. 1904.

[7] Cf. I. Sonne, in *I.D.B.* iv, 1962, p. 490a.

[8] In Smith's *D.B.* iii, 1863, p. 1399b.

[9] Cf. E. Schürer, *H.J.P.*, E. Tr., II.ii, 1890, p. 67; I. J. Peritz, in *E.B.* iv, 1907, col. 4837; H. L. Strack, in *The New Schaff-Herzog Encyclopedia*, xi, 1911, p. 214b.

the two offices became merged and the two titles became synonymous.[1]

The service of the Synagogue consisted of the Shema', prayer, the reading of the Law and the Prophets, and the Blessing.[2] The Shema' consisted of Deut. 6.4–9; 11.13–21; Num. 15.37–41.[3] Our Lord cited the opening words when asked which was the greatest commandment of the Law,[4] but with no reference to its liturgical use. It has been conjectured that the Shema' was read from a scroll which contained also the Decalogue, but that the reading from a scroll was discontinued when the Decalogue ceased to be used.[5] Schürer says the Shema' was regarded as a confession of faith rather than as a prayer,[6] but Peritz says this belongs to later times and that its earlier purpose was to inculcate the sacredness and importance of the Law.[7]

The Prayer is known as the Sh^{e}mōneh 'eśrēh, or Eighteen Benedictions.[8] The present form of the prayer is attributed to Simeon hap-Pakôlî around A.D. 110.[9] Some of the petitions did

[1] Cf. I. Sonne, in I.D.B. iv, 1962, p. 490a.

[2] Cf. Mishnah, Megillah iv.3 (see the notes on the passage in J. Rabbinowitz, Mishnah Megillah, 1931, pp. 114ff).

[3] C. W. Dugmore (The Influence of the Synagogue upon the Divine Office, 1944, pp. 18, 20) notes that the Shema' consisted originally of Deut. 6.4 only, and that Deut. 11.13–21 was added perhaps half a century before the reign of Antiochus Epiphanes, and Num. 15.37–41 in the Roman period.

[4] Mark 12.28ff; Matt. 22.35ff.

[5] Cf. I. Sonne, in I.D.B. iv, 1962, p. 490b. L. Finkelstein (The Pharisees, i, 1938, p. 65) says the excision of the Decalogue occurred in the middle of the first century A.D. Cf. G. F. Moore, Judaism, iii, 1930, pp. 95f. C. W. Dugmore (op. cit., p. 21) observes that the Decalogue continued to be used at Fusṭaṭ long after it ceased to be in use in Palestine. The account of its omission is given in the Babylonian Talmud, Berachoth 12a (cf. E. Tr. by A. Cohen, 1921, pp. 73f). On the Shema' cf. Strack and Billerbeck, op. cit., pp. 189ff.

[6] H.J.P., E. Tr., II.ii, 1890, p. 77. Cf. A. R. S. Kennedy, in D.A.C. ii, 1918, p. 543b; C. W. Dugmore, op. cit., p. 16.

[7] In E.B. iv, 1907, col. 4838.

[8] On this prayer cf. Strack and Billerbeck, Kommentar zum Neuen Testament aus Talmud und Midrasch, iv, Part 1, 1928, pp. 208ff; also E. G. Hirsch, in J.E. xi, 1909, pp. 270ff; C. W. Dugmore, The Influence of the Synagogue upon the Divine Office, 1944, pp. 114ff.

[9] Cf. I. J. Peritz, in E.B. iv, 1907, col. 4838; G. Dalman, in The New Schaff-Herzog Encyclopedia, xi, 1911, col. 214b.

not antedate the Fall of Jerusalem in A.D. 70,[1] and Schürer says it must have attained virtually its present form between A.D. 70 and 100, but that its groundwork must be considerably older.[2] The congregation stood for the prayer and at the end responded with Amen, thus making the prayer their own.[3] To this the Christian use of Amen is to be traced. Plumptre cites[4] a custom of the Alexandrian Church recorded by Clement of Alexandria, who tells how the worshippers stretched out their necks and raised their hands and leapt into the air, and traces this back to a custom of the synagogue when the Trisagion of Isaiah 6 was recited by the assembly accompanied by a threefold leaping in the air.

The reading from the Law followed a triennial cycle which completed the Pentateuch once every three years, and this system is believed to go back to the first century B.C.[5] In a later age it was divided into fifty-four sections.[6] The reading of the Prophets in New Testament times was probably not according to any fixed rule, and it may have been left to the choice of the reader or to that of the ruler of the Synagogue or the ḥazzān.[7] We cannot therefore be sure whether our Lord himself selected the passage from Isaiah which he read in the synagogue of Nazareth. In the account of Paul's visit to Antioch in Pisidia we find a reference to the reading of the Prophets,[8] but without indication of the passage. Any member of the congregation might be called upon

---

[1] G. F. Moore (*Judaism*, i, 1927, p. 293) says: "There are, as we should expect, expressions which imply the destruction of Jerusalem and the cessation of the sacrificial cultus, but these seem to be engrafted on older petitions or to be modifications of them, rather than the substance of new ones."

[2] *H.J.P.*, E. Tr., II.ii, 1890, pp. 87f. Cf. A. Marmorstein, "The Oldest Form of the Eighteen Benedictions", *J.Q.R.* xxxiv, 1943–4, pp. 137ff.

[3] Cf. G. Dalman, in *The New Schaff-Herzog Encyclopedia*, xi, 1911, p. 214b.

[4] In Smith's *D.B.* iii, 1863, p. 140lb.

[5] So I. Sonne, in *I.D.B.* iv, 1962, p. 490b. G. F. Moore is more doubtful. He says (*Judaism*, i, 1927, p. 300): "It may be inferred that it was not authoritatively established before the third century, though it may have earlier become customary." Aileen Guilding (*The Fourth Gospel and Jewish Worship*, 1960, p. 44) has maintained that "the triennial cycle is as old as or older than the Pentateuch in its final form". On this cf. J. R. Porter, in *Promise and Fulfilment* (S. H. Hooke Festschrift), 1963, pp. 163ff.

[6] Cf. Moore, *Judaism*, i, 1927, pp. 299f.

[7] Cf. I. J. Peritz, in *E.B.* iv, 1907, col. 4840.   [8] Acts 13.15.

to read the Scripture, though in practice it must often have fallen upon the *ḥazzān*.[1] The reading of the Scripture was followed in Palestine and Babylonia by its translation into Aramaic.[2] This was done by any competent person who might be present and who was called upon to do it. Even minors might be asked to do this if they had the necessary ability.[3] The translator might prepare his version beforehand, but was not supposed to have any written translation before him.[4] The translation was not expected to be widely different in substance from the original, and we read that anyone who violated this rule was silenced and sharply rebuked.[5] Elsewhere[6] we read that one of the rabbis laid down what Moore describes[7] as a difficult standard for the translator when he said: "He who translates a passage word for word [i.e. in a woodenly literal way] is a falsifier, while he who adds to the meaning is a blasphemer." In later times written Aramaic translations or Targums were prepared, and these differ considerably in their closeness to the original.

The reading of the Scripture might be followed by an exposition, though this was not an invariable element in the service.[8] Apparently the address was more often based on the prophetic reading than on the Law.[9] It was at the invitation of the ruler of the synagogue, perhaps conveyed by the *ḥazzān*, that the address was given. So Jesus gave an address at Nazareth[10] and Paul and Silas at Antioch in Pisidia.[11] We read that Jesus frequently taught in synagogues,[12] though sometimes the authorities disapproved of what he said or did there. Similarly Paul again and again addressed the congregations in synagogues when he came to a fresh place, and continued to teach there so long as he was able. The address in the synagogue was given by the speaker seated,

[1] Cf. R. W. Moss, in *D.C.G.* ii, 1911, p. 690a.
[2] Cf. Mishnah, *Megillah*, iv. 4.   [3] Cf. Mishnah, *Megillah*, iv.6.
[4] Cf. Moore, *Judaism*, i, 1927, pp. 303f.   [5] Mishnah, *Megillah*, iv.9.
[6] T.B. *Kiddushin*, 49a.   [7] *Judaism*, i, 1927, p. 304.
[8] Cf. I. J. Peritz, in *E.B.* iv, 1907, col. 4840: "The Scripture exposition was not a required part of the service; neither was it the prerogative of an ordained class; any one able to instruct might be invited to speak, though ordinarily it fell to the rabbis of the community."
[9] Cf. G. Dalman, in *The New Schaff-Herzog Encyclopedia*, xi, 1911, p. 215b.
[10] Luke 4.21ff.   [11] Acts 13.15ff.
[12] Cf. Matt. 4.23; 13.34; John 6.59; 18.29. Miracles performed in synagogues are recorded in Mark 1.23ff; Matt. 12.9ff; Luke 13.10ff.

as we learn from the account of the address of Jesus at Nazareth.[1] The service was closed by the priestly blessing pronounced by a priest at a sign from the *ḥazzān*.[2] Since only a priest could pronounce this, when no priest was present it could not be pronounced, as Dalman notes.[3] Peritz thinks that this custom could only have been taken over from the Temple after the destruction of the Temple.[4] The priest faced the congregation for the blessing, while the congregation stood with hands raised as high as their shoulders, repeating the formula word by word after the priest and responding with Amen after each of the three parts of the blessing.[5] N. H. Snaith has maintained that in Palestinian circles by New Testament times there was a triennial cycle for the Psalter, so that during a three-year period all of the psalms were read in the synagogues.[6] While not going so far as this Oesterley says: "The liturgical use of psalms in the Jewish Church in pre-Christian times is too well known to need many words. The adaptation of the Temple Liturgy by the Synagogue took place while the Temple was still standing. The place of the psalms in the synagogal liturgy has undergone variation; the number in use is larger now than was originally the case; though even now only about half the psalms of the Psalter are used."[7] But Moore does not go so far as this. He says: "Whether the use of select Psalms had established itself in the service of the synagogue at as early a time as that with which we are here occupied is not entirely certain, though it would seem natural that with other features of the temple worship the songs of the levites at the morning and evening sacrifices should be imitated in the synagogue. The first group of Psalms to be so employed was Psalms 145–150; but it appears that in the middle of the second century the daily repetition of these Psalms was a pious practice of individuals rather than a regular observance of the congregation."[8]

---

[1] Luke 4.20.   [2] Cf. G. F. Moore, *Judaism*, i, 1927, p. 289.
[3] In *The New Schaff-Herzog Encyclopedia*, xi, 1911, p. 215a. Cf. L. Rabinowitz, in *Companion to the Bible*, ed. by T. W. Manson, 1939, p. 458. A. R. S. Kennedy (in Hastings' one volume *D.B.*, 1909, p. 883b) says that when no priest was present, a layman gave the blessing in the form of a prayer. But this was a later practice.
[4] In *E.B.* iv, 1907, col. 4839.   [5] Cf. I. J. Peritz, ibid.
[6] *Z.A.W.* li, 1933, pp. 302ff.
[7] *The Jewish Background of the Christian Liturgy*, 1925, p. 73.
[8] *Judaism*, i, 1927, p. 296.

The reading of the lessons and the recital of the prayers was done from a raised platform,[1] which may have begun from the platform which Ezra used for the reading of the Law.[2] The platform was probably made of wood, and this would explain the non-survival in the excavated ruins of Palestinian synagogues. One in stone, dating most probably from the sixth century of our era, has survived.[3] The platform is unmentioned in the New Testament, but the passage in which Jesus refers to the scribes and Pharisees as sitting on Moses' seat[4] has been connected with this.[5] That passage used to be interpreted metaphorically, but excavations of synagogues have brought to light examples of stone seats which are believed to have been "seats of Moses",[6] and attention has been drawn to a rabbinical reference to the throne of Solomon as "like the seat of Moses",[7] Opinions are divided as to the use of the "seats of Moses". Renov holds[8] that they were seats of honour reserved for the noted Jewish scholars, and that they were placed at the head of the synagogue, facing the congregation. But Cecil Roth thinks[9] it very unlikely that Jews would have given the name "seat of Moses" to a seat set aside for a contemporary teacher, however eminent. He therefore argues that it was used by the reader of the Scripture.[10]

[1] Cf. W. Bacher, in Hastings' *D.B.* iv, 1902, p. 639b; I. Sonne, in *I.D.B.* iv, 1962, p. 488b.

[2] Neh. 8.4 (where M.T. has *mighdāl* = "tower", and LXX has *bēma* = "tribune"). G. Widengren (*J.S.S.* ii, 1957, pp. 5ff) brings this into association with the pillar by (or on) which Josiah stood (2 Kings 23.3), with which the pillar by (or on) which Joash stood (2 Kings 11.14) is to be compared (here Josephus, *Ant.* X. iv. 3 (63), has *bēma*), and the 'brazen scaffold" (R.S.V. "bronze platform") which the Chronicler says (2 Chron. 6.13) Solomon used at the dedication of the Temple.

[3] Cf. E. L. Sukenik, *Ancient Synagogues in Palestine and Greece*, 1934, p. 57.

[4] Matt. 23.2.   [5] Cf. I. Sonne, in *I.D.B.* iv, 1962, p. 488b.

[6] Cf. E. L. Sukenik, op. cit., pp. 57ff.

[7] Cf. Sukenik, op. cit., p. 59. Cf. also C. Roth, *P.E.Q.* lxxxi, 1949, pp. 100ff; I. Renov, *I.E.J.* v, 1955, pp. 262ff.

[8] Loc. cit., p. 262, where it is said to have been "a symbol of Jewish legal authority conferred upon teachers of Jewish law. It expressed itself in the form of special seats for them in a conspicuous place at the head of congregation in the synagogue." W. Bacher (*R.E.J.* xxxiv, 1897, pp. 299ff) held that it was the chair reserved for the President of the Council.

[9] *P.E.Q.* lxxxi, 1949, pp. 103ff.

[10] Cf. A. R. S. Kennedy, in *D.A.C.* ii, 1918, p. 543a.

The synagogue was not only used for worship and education. It was also used as a court for the administration of justice.[1] In Luke 12.11 we read: "When they bring you before the synagogues . . . be not anxious how or what ye shall answer",[2] while in Matt. 10.17 Jesus says: "In their synagogues they will scourge you."[3] In his speech before Agrippa Paul says: "Punishing them oftentimes in all the synagogues, I strove to make them blaspheme."[4] The infliction of the punishment was done by the *ḥazzān*.[5] Public meetings were held in the synagogues. I have already referred to the gathering in the synagogue of Tiberias, to which Josephus refers.[6] That was called to discuss a political question. As our concern is but with worship, these other uses need not be pursued here. Nor need we linger over the question whether the women were originally separated from the men. Kohler affirms categorically[7] that the women were always separated from the men, while others believe this was a later custom.[8] That women could have an honourable place in the life and worship of the Synagogue seems to be implied in the references to Lydia at Philippi.[9]

It is impossible to exaggerate the significance of the institution of the Synagogue. Here worship was wholly spiritual. I may repeat some words I wrote many years ago: "It [i.e. the Synagogue] was other than the Greek schools, where men gathered to study and to discuss philosophy and religion. In the Synagogue religion was not only discussed, but practised, and it fostered not merely an

---

[1] Cf. E. H. Plumptre, in Smith's *D.B.* iii, 1863, p. 1401b; R. W. Moss, in *D.C.G.* ii, 1908, p. 692a.

[2] Cf. Luke 21.12.   [3] Cf. Matt. 23.34; Mark 13.9.   [4] Acts 26.11.

[5] Cf. W. Bacher, in Hastings' *D.B.* iv, 1902, p. 642b; R. W. Moss, in *D.C.G.* ii, 1908, p. 692a.

[6] *Vita* 54 (277ff).

[7] In *D.A.C.* ii, 1918, p. 544b. Cf. E. Schürer, *H.J.P.*, E. Tr., II.ii, 1890, p. 75.

[8] Cf. H. L. Strack, in *The New Schaff-Herzog Encyclopedia*, xi, 1911, p. 213a. So R. W. Moss, in *D.C.G.* ii, 1908, p. 690b. I. Sonne (in *I.D.B.* iv, 1962, p. 486f) says that according to one school the silence of the earlier rabbinic authorities on women's galleries implies that in those circles no provisions at all were made for women in the synagogue, because they were excluded from active participation in worship. Sonne thinks that provisions for the separation of the sexes began in synagogues with a Hellenistic tinge. Cf. H. Rosenau, *P.E.Q.* lxix, 1937, pp. 196ff.

[9] Acts 16.14.

intellectual understanding of the faith of Judaism, but the spirit
of humble obedience to the demands of the faith. For it was
essentially and fundamentally the organ of spiritual worship, the
united outpouring of the spirit before God in prayer, the united
attention to the Word of God, and the united acceptance of the
claims of the faith."[1] Marcel Simon observes[2] that the life of the
Synagogue tended to shape itself on the life of the Temple, but
there was a completely different emphasis. Here attention was
directed to no ritual act of sacrifice which might be supposed to
have validity in itself, but to the lifting of men's thought to God
and his Word and the prostrating of the soul before him in adoration and prayer, and Moore rightly says that it was a wholly
unique institution.[3] It was the Synagogue and not the Temple
which fostered the study of the sacred literature of the Jews and
elevated the Bible to the position it has continued to have in
Judaism. Before the destruction of the Temple this great instrument of worship had been fashioned, and it was the only instrument for large numbers of Jews in the Diaspora.[4] For Jews in
Palestine visits to the Temple must in most cases have been infrequent, and for the Jews of the Diaspora they must have been
exceedingly rare, and it is hard to see how they could have maintained any strong religious life without it. It is happily possible
to worship God in private, as Jeremiah was able to when he was
excluded from the Temple.[5] But religion is not easily communicated in that way, and for most people it is nourished best by
corporate worship as the spring and inspiration of private worship.
The cardinal mistake of the Deuteronomists was to ignore this.
Their centralization of worship was designed to suppress all the
abuses of the country shrines, but they made no provision for
worship anywhere but in the single permitted shrine, which could
not be the resort of the whole nation for regular worship.

The institution of the sabbath, which has been of incalculable
blessing to men, however little it may be valued to-day, was pre-

[1] *I.M.W.*, 1939, pp. 123f.

[2] In Manson's *Companion to the Bible*, 2nd edn, 1963, p. 393.

[3] *Judaism*, i, 1927, p. 284.

[4] Cf. F. J. Foakes Jackson and K. Lake, *B.C.* I.i, 1942 edn, p. 160:
"The synagogue worship, it may be said without exaggeration, proved to
be the salvation of Judaism."

[5] Jer. 36.5.

served by the Synagogue.[1] In pre-exilic days, when shrines abounded in the land, men could repair to the local shrine on that day, though many found it irksome and spent it in eager desire to resume the business of the following day, as the prophets tell us.[2] In post-exilic days, if there had been no synagogues, it is difficult to see how it could have survived, and it is significant that in our day impatience with the sabbath as a day of rest is the accompaniment of the widespread abandonment of the sabbath as a day of worship. When the Temple was destroyed in A.D. 70 and its sacrificial ritual was no longer possible for the Jews on the only site which Judaism accepted as legitimate, the Synagogue provided the means for the continuation of worship and saved Judaism from the irreparable disaster which the destruction of the Temple might otherwise have been.[3] Marcel Simon observes: "The historian must notice that the destruction of the Temple in A.D. 70, though resented by the Jews as a national and religious catastrophe, did not alter fundamentally the conditions under which they practised their religion, precisely because the synagogal system was there already, omnipresent, and could assume the rôle until then played by the Temple. To the vast majority of the Jews, living far from Jerusalem, the Temple never had been much more than a symbol. It is the synagogal system which ensured the survival of Judaism until to-day."[4]

To the Christian Church, too, the Synagogue has been of the greatest importance. In the New Testament the church is perhaps

---

[1] That the sabbath was from the beginning intended to be a religious institution is clear from its inclusion in the Decalogue (see above, p. 41), though there it would appear that its holiness lay in abstinence from work. It had become in the pre-exilic period a day for attendance at the Temple or other shrines or for resort to a prophet, and in the synagogues the sabbath was a day for resort for worship and prayer and the study of Scripture.

[2] Cf. Amos 8.4f.

[3] Cf. G. H. Box, in *E.R.E.* xii, 1921, p. 794b: "The disappearance of the old sacrificial cultus was felt by pious Jews at the time as a real catastrophe. But the way had already been prepared ... for a spiritualizing of the sacrificial idea; and this tendency received a strong impulse from the exigencies of the situation which left the synagogue as the sole religious institution in which the Jewish religious consciousness could express itself."

[4] In Manson's *Companion to the Bible*, 2nd edn, 1963, p. 391.

once called a synagogue,[1] and the Church continued to use the same type of worship as had been found in the Synagogue. It is true that the Church used a different name, apart from that one passage. Instead of *sunagōgē* we have *ekklēsia*, and some have traced the one name back to the Hebrew '*ēdhāh* and the other to the Hebrew *ḳāhāl*.[2] But Moore dismisses this as unnecessary and thinks the choice of *ekklēsia* was but to distinguish the Christian community from the Jewish.[3] But the Church continued to use the same pattern of worship, including prayer, the reading of Scripture, and exposition. There have, of course, been variations of the pattern, but variations within a limited design. To the Scriptures of the Old Testament those of the New have been added, and the emphasis of the exposition has been accordingly modified. The *Shemōneh 'eśrēh* has been replaced by other prayers. The Jewish sabbath has been replaced by the Lord's Day as a day of rest and worship. But this does not diminish the significance of the Church's debt to the Synagogue. After a careful discussion of the influence of the Synagogue upon the Christian Divine Office C. W. Dugmore concludes: "We are forced to conclude that the influence of the Synagogue upon the worship of the Church is to be seen in the type of worship and the times at which public prayer was held. Such early Christian prayers as have survived do not suggest any wholesale borrowing from the liturgy of the Synagogue. . . . The Christians' debt to the past is revealed rather in the subjects of their prayers and the general framework of their services than in the phraseology employed in their petitions."[4]

Another aspect of the significance of the Synagogue is its part in the spread of the faith. As the New Testament sufficiently

---

[1] James 2.2, where, however, it may equally well be rendered by "assembly" (so R.S.V.). Cf. J. B. Mayor, *The Epistle of St. James*, 2nd edn, 1897, pp. 79f; I. J. Peritz, in *E.B.* iv, 1907, col. 4833; G. F. Moore, *Judaism*, iii, 1930, p. 89.

[2] Cf. I. Sonne, in *I.D.B.* iv, 1962, p. 478a. Cf. E. Schürer, *H.J.P.*, E. Tr., II.ii, pp. 58f n. In the LXX *ḳāhāl* is rendered by *sunagōgē* thirty-five times and by *ekklēsia* sixty-eight times.

[3] Cf. *Judaism*, iii, 1930, p. 89. Cf. also I. J. Peritz, in *E.B.* iv, 1907, col. 4833. I. Sonne (in *I.D.B.* ii, 1962, p. 478b) thinks the assonance of Sinai may have helped to bring about the Jewish preference for the name synagogue.

[4] *The Influence of the Synagogue upon the Divine Office*, 1944, p. 113.

informs us, proselytes to Judaism had been made almost everywhere where there were Jews. Not all who became attached to Judaism became proselytes, but that was due to the severity of the conditions of their reception. While our information about the conditions imposed on proselytes is very much later than New Testament times,[1] it is probable that it reflects the conditions of those times. Every male proselyte had to be circumcised and both males and females had to undergo a ritual bath and to present a sacrifice at Jerusalem.[2] It is not agreed by all scholars that the ritual bath antedated the fall of Jerusalem, though probability seems to be in favour of this.[3] But so far as sacrifice is concerned, the requirement must go back to the time when the Temple was still standing. And this condition alone must have discouraged many who might otherwise have become proselytes. They did become what were called "God fearers",[4] sharing in the worship of the Synagogue and conforming to the principles of the Jewish faith.[5]

Our Lord refers to the proselytizing zeal of the Pharisees.[6] Some scholars have contested this,[7] and A. Jellinek even maintained

[1] Especially in the Tractate *Gerim* (ed. by R. Kirchheim, in *Septem libri Talmudici parvi Hierosolymitani*, 1851, and by M. Higger, in *Seven Minor Treatises*, 1930).

[2] This is stated in T.B. *Kerithoth*, 9a; *Sifre* on Numbers, § 108 (on Num. 15.14); *Mekilta de R. Simeon ben Yohai*, on Ex. 12.48; *Gerim*, ii.4. This is accepted as trustworthy by Schürer (*H.J.P.* II.ii, 1890, pp. 319f), Moore (*Judaism*, i, 1927, pp. 331f, 334), and J. Bonsirven (*Le Judaïsme palestinien*, i, 1934, pp. 29f).

[3] I have discussed this in *M.Q.*, 1963, pp. 211ff, with references to many authorities on both sides.

[4] *Phoboumenoi ton Theon*, Acts 10.2, 22; 13.16, 26; *sebomenoi ton Theon*, Acts 16.14; 18.7; or simply *sebomenoi*, Acts 13.50; 17.4, 17.

[5] Moore (*Judaism*, i, 1927, p. 325) says: "Such converts were called religious persons, and although in a strict sense outside the pale of Judaism, undoubtedly expected to share with Jews by birth the favour of the God they had adopted, and were encouraged in this hope by their Jewish teachers."

[6] Matt. 23.15.

[7] Cf. C. G. Montefiore, *The Synoptic Gospels*, ii, 1909, p. 728: "The charge is exaggerated and unhistorical. The Palestinian Rabbis were, on the whole, not particularly favourable to proselytes." Cf. also J. Derenbourg, *Essai sur l'histoire et la géographie de la Palestine*, i, 1867, pp. 227f; H. Graetz, *M.G.W.J.* xviii, 1869, pp. 169f; E. G. Hirsch, *J.E.* x, 1905, p. 221; M. Friedländer, *Die religiösen Bewegungen innerhalb des Judentums im Zeitalter Jesu*, 1905, pp. 31ff.

that only a single proselyte was made in each year,[1] while I. Lévi recognizes that there were always two attitudes in Judaism on this question,[2] but recognizes that outside Palestine the tendency favourable to proselytes was always stronger than inside.[3] B. J. Bamberger examined this question,[4] starting from the conviction that Judaism was always opposed to the making of proselytes[5] but reaching the conclusion that the Gospel text accurately reflects the attitude of contemporary Judaism.[6] Certainly there is no evidence that the Palestine Jews ever sent out missionaries charged with the task of winning converts; but the evidence of the New Testament references makes it plain that proselytes were numerous.[7] They were made partly by the austerity and nobility of the lives of the Jews. In the corrupt pagan society around them they preserved a loftiness of life which interested serious men and women around them, and led them to inquire what was the secret of that life, and brought them to the synagogues where they were instructed in the faith of the Jews. It is hard to see how proselytes could have been made without any centre of worship, and in any case the religious life of Jew and proselyte would have been infinitely poorer without any such centre.

From the Synagogue the Church adopted, but with a new zeal, the task of winning proselytes. The Church believed itself to be the new Israel and the heir of the task of sharing the worship of Israel's God with the world. Paul found his first converts among the Jews and proselytes whom he found in the synagogues, and

---

[1] *Beth ha-Midrasch*, 2nd edn, v, 1938, pp. xlvif.
[2] Cf. L. Finkelstein, *The Pharisees*, ii, 1938, p. 516; also G. Kuhn, in *Th.W.B.* vi, 1959, pp. 737f.
[3] *R.E.J.* li, 1906, p. 28.
[4] *Proselytism in the Talmudic Period*, 1939.   [5] Ibid., p. 297.
[6] Ibid., pp. 267ff (cf. also pp. 21ff, 149ff). Cf. also Strack-Billerbeck, *Kommentar zum Neuen Testament aus Talmud und Midrasch*, i, 1922, pp. 924ff. H. G. May (*J.B.R.* xvi, 1948, p. 103a) observes that "the emphasis on proselytes in the post-exilic period was something more than mere tolerance of them".
[7] Cf. G. F. Moore, *Judaism*, i, 1927, pp. 323ff; J. Bonsirven, *Le Judaïsme palestinien*, i, 1934, pp. 22ff; Bousset and Gressmann, *Die Religion des Judentums im späthellenistichen Zeitalter*, 1926, pp. 76ff; A. Causse, *Israël et la vision de l'humanité*, 1924, pp. 129ff; B. J. Bamberger, in *U.J.E.* ix, 1943, pp. 1ff; J. Morgenstern, *H.U.C.A.* xvi, 1941, pp. 42ff, in *U.J.E.* x, 1943, p. 356a, and *J.B.L.* lxiv, 1945, pp. 27ff; G. Kuhn, in *Th.W.B.* vi, 1959, pp. 727ff.

other Christian missionaries must have done the same where they found synagogues.[1]

In the earlier chapters I have maintained that the pre-exilic worship was not as empty as the pressing of certain passages in the prophets might suggest, though without diminishing the importance of the prophetic protest against the hollowness of so much of the worship of their times or the importance of their emphasis on the spirit and the life as against the merely ritual act. I have also argued that the post-exilic age was not marked by the spiritual deadness and formalism that has often been supposed. Many may have been dead and formal then, as in pre-exilic days, and unquestionably the emphasis on unwitting and involuntary ritual sins brought great inherent dangers. But post-exilic Judaism could never have provided the matrix out of which Christianity came if that were all that was to be said, and if post-exilic Judaism created and shaped the Synagogue then it must have included large numbers of men and women of real spiritual penetration. The New Testament denunciations of Pharisees do not justify the condemnation of Pharisaism. That there were bad Pharisees, as there had been bad priests and bad prophets and bad citizens in previous ages, does not mean that all Pharisees were bad, and still less that Judaism was bad. Judaism itself could speak of the plague of the Pharisees when thinking of bad Pharisees,[2] yet owed so much to the good Pharisees. Worship that had sunk so low in the post-Settlement period and that often had periods of declension had risen in the Synagogue to heights which have been an inestimable blessing to the world, and the Church which has received so much from Judaism should always recognize with gratitude the greatness of her heritage. Islam too has received much from Judaism, and as Moore says: "Judaism gave to the world not only the fundamental ideas of these great monotheistic religions, but the institutional forms in which they have perpetuated and propagated themselves."[3]

[1] A. R. S. Kennedy (in Hastings' one volume *D.B.*, 1909, p. 883b) observes that the synagogues became the seed-plots of Christianity.

[2] Cf. J. Klausner, *Jesus of Nazareth*, E. Tr., by H. Danby, 1925, pp. 215ff.

[3] *Judaism*, i, 1927, p. 285.

8

The Forms and the Spirit

"The basic meaning of Israelite worship", says W. J. Harrelson, "is to be found in the quality of the relationship which it both affirmed and established between God and man."[1] In this chapter I wish to examine some aspects of that basic meaning. In the previous chapters we have considered ritual acts of worship and liturgical texts which accompanied them to interpret their meaning. The interpretation was always more important than the act—though this was not always perceived—and it has survived the act. The more discerning religious leaders of Israel were always aware that it was the spirit that gave meaning to the act and that the spirit was more important than the act. For heinous sins, such as murder and adultery, no sacrifice could atone and none was prescribed by the Law.[2] Yet there could be forgiveness and reconciliation with God even after heinous sins where there was true penitence. The prophet Nathan who confronted David with his sin stirred the king to humble penitence[3] and was then the mouthpiece of God's word of forgiveness: "The Lord hath put away thy sin."[4] So early in Israel was it perceived that the spirit without the ritual act could suffice. Yet where the ritual act was prescribed, sincerity of penitence could not dispense with it. Neither could the act dispense with the spirit, and the prophets therefore insisted that the act must be infused with the spirit.

When sacrifice could no longer be offered, the texts which were designed to evoke the spirit that gave meaning to the acts could continue to be used and could continue to evoke the same spirit. They have been so used in Synagogue and Church. The psalmist

---

[1] In Hastings' one volume *D.B.*, rev. edn, 1963, p. 1044a.
[2] Cf. E. König, *Theologie des Alten Testaments*, 3rd edn, 1923, pp. 294ff.
[3] 2 Sam. 12.1ff.   [4] 2 Sam. 12.13.

could say: "The sacrifices of God[1] are a broken spirit",[2] and the broken spirit has continued to be offered to him. For the Christian animal sacrifice has ceased, not because the Temple has been destroyed, but because it has been superseded in a sacrifice anticipated in the Old Testament, a sacrifice that gathered into itself the meaning of sacrifice at its highest point, the sacrifice of a morally unblemished Man who freely yielded himself to be sacrificed that thereby men might be stirred to penitence and find in him the organ of their redemption.[3] Yet to this sacrifice they must bring their spirit of penitence and surrender before it becomes effective for them, and they must continue to bring to God the sacrifices of the spirit. In the New Testament we read: "Through him then let us offer up a sacrifice of praise to God continually, that is, the fruit of lips which make confession to his name."[4] "A sacrifice of praise"—in Judaism and in Christianity the spirit is now regarded as a sacrifice without the accompanying Temple act, and in our worship we sing:

> Father, unto thee we raise
> This our sacrifice of praise.[5]

That the service of the Temple could not have been so wholly unspiritual as is sometimes thought is clear when we remember Simeon, who was righteous and devout and looking for the consolation of Israel and who frequented the Temple,[6] and Anna, the prophetess, who departed not from the Temple, worshipping with fastings and supplications night and day.[7] The prophet had said: "My house shall be called a house of prayer for all nations."[8] Not all had made it a place of merchandise,[9] and the spiritual worship which had been offered here could be transferred to the Synagogue, and the Psalms which had moved men's spirit here could nourish their spiritual life through the centuries to our own day.[10]

---

[1] We should probably read "My sacrifice, O God" (so many editors). This involves the change of one vowel only, and it avoids the awkward change from the plural to the singular, and maintains the "I–Thou" relationship of verses 3–18 (so E. R. Dalglish, *Psalm Fifty-one*, 1962, p. 194).

[2] Ps. 51.17 (M.T. 19).   [3] Cf. *U.B.*, 1956, pp. 104ff.   [4] Heb. 13.15.

[5] In F. S. Pierpoint's hymn, "For the beauty of the earth".

[6] Luke 2.25ff.   [7] Luke 2.36ff.   [8] Isa. 56.7.   [9] John 2.16.

[10] On the religious significance of the Psalter cf. H. Ringgren, *The Faith of the Psalmists*, 1963.

Many of the psalms are spoken in the first person singular. Smend argued that these psalms were really collective and that the "I" was the corporate body of the nation or the community.[1] This view was dismissed contemptuously by Gunkel,[2] and many scholars have preferred the view that these psalms were intended for individual use or arose out of some individual experience.[3] To-day it is common to treat both of these approaches as inappropriate and to view these psalms from the point of view of what Wheeler Robinson called "corporate personality".[4] The community could be thought of as an individual and could be individualized in its members. "The whole group", said Wheeler Robinson, "including its past, present and future members might function as a single individual through any one of those members conceived as representative of it."[5] In the royal rites the king represented the nation, and when he said "I" it could mean both himself and the nation he represented, or either. Thought could move back and forth between the community and the individual who represented it or whose experience was typical of that of the community.[6] In some psalms we find rapid transitions from the

[1] Cf. Z.A.W. viii, 1888, pp. 49ff.
[2] Einleitung in die Psalmen, 1933, p. 173.
[3] Cf. E. Balla, Das Ich der Psalmen, 1912.
[4] Cf. in Werden und Wesen des Alten Testaments, ed. by J. Hempel, 1936, pp. 49ff. Cf. also The Psalmists, ed. by D. C. Simpson, 1926, pp. 82ff, The People and the Book, ed. by A. S. Peake, 1925, pp. 375ff, and The Cross of the Servant, 1926, pp. 32ff. Cf. also J. Pedersen, Israel I–II, 1926, pp. 275ff; S. A. Cook, in C.A.H. iii, 1925, p. 493 (cf. The Old Testament: a Reinterpretation, 1936, pp. 164f); T. Worden, The Psalms are Christian Prayer, 1961, pp. 29ff; S. Mowinckel, The Psalms in Israel's Worship, E. Tr., i, 1962, pp. 42ff; J. Hempel, Das Ethos des Alten Testaments, 2nd edn, 1964, pp. 41ff; and J. de Fraine, Adam et son Lignage, 1959, pp. 178ff.
[5] Werden und Wesen des Alten Testaments, p. 49.
[6] Cf. H. W. Robinson, in The Psalmists, ed. by D. C. Simpson, 1926, p. 83: "One result of this corporate personality is that a speaker can pass much more readily from the consciousness of an individual experience to its representative character, and so to the experience of the group with which he identifies himself"; The Old Testament: its Making and Meaning, 1937, p. 138: "The speaker in many of the psalms . . . may seem to us to be neither an individual nor the representative of a group nor the whole nation, but all three at once, a voice which expands or contracts the scope of its reference from verse to verse"; The Cross of the Servant, pp. 33f: "There is a fluidity of conception, a possibility of swift transition from the one to the many, and vice versa, to which our thought and language have

plural to the singular and *vice versa*. Here the individual worshipper may have been making his own the confession or the prayer in which all were sharing. The Psalms expressed the worship of all, but they also expressed the worship of each, just as individuals and congregations to-day make these ancient psalms the vehicle of their individual and corporate approach to God. That many read or chant them in a detached way, without entering into them, but brings us back to what we have already seen, that no forms of worship can constrain the spirit to worship, and that without the spirit the forms are no real worship. Worship without animal sacrifice may be as dead as it could be with it. But the glory of the Psalter is that texts which were written to fill with meaning ancient rites are still capable of filling our worship with meaning. We do not have to bring that meaning to them, but to find it in them, because men of rich spiritual penetration put it there.

There is much that binds the Old Testament psalms to Egyptian[1] and Babylonian[2] and Ugaritic[3] sacred literature. The poetic technique has much similarity, and there are innumerable links of phrase. The uses of the psalms have much in common with the liturgies of these peoples. All this has been frequently insisted on and is not to be denied. Sometimes excessive conclusions have been drawn from the evidence, and Israelite psalmody has been presented as a mere imitation of that of her neighbours.[4] Forty years ago G. R. Driver contested this view and emphasized the no real parallel"; in *The Psalmists*, ed. by D. C. Simpson, 1926, p. 47: "The Psalms always give us the point of view of an individual poet; but in that point of view he often becomes so conscious of his identity with either Israel, or the worthier elements of it, that without warning he will generalize from his own experience, and speak also in the name of the larger or smaller group, without any sense of inconsistency."

[1] Cf. A. M. Blackman, in *The Psalmists*, pp. 177ff.

[2] Cf. G. R. Driver, in *The Psalmists*, pp. 109ff; also G. Widengren, *Accadian and Hebrew Psalms of Lamentation*, 1937; R. G. Castellino, *Le Lamentazioni individuali e gli inni in Babilonia e in Israele*, 1939.

[3] Cf. J. H. Patton, *Canaanite Parallels in the Book of Psalms*, 1944; J. Coppens, *Les Parallèles du Psautier et les textes de Ras Shamra-Ougarit*, 1946. Cf. also works cited above, p. 11, n. 2. M. Dahood, *Psalms* (Anchor Bible), i, 1966, draws heavily on Ugaritic for the interpretation of the Psalms.

[4] Thus, for example, H. Gressmann (in *The Psalmists*, pp. 1ff) maintained that some of the Psalms were directly inspired by Babylonian and Assyrian psalms. He held that the first part of Ps. 19 was inspired by an Akkadian psalm, whose existence is merely his assumption (pp. 16f).

moral and spiritual gulf that separated Biblical from Babylonian psalmody. "The similarities between these two literatures", he said, "are significant as showing how alike was the diction and, superficially, the thought of these two great peoples; but how much more significant are the differences, both moral and spiritual! The same seed, indeed, was sown in the hearts of both races, but along what different lines did it grow to maturity and what different fruit did it bear!"[1] I would repeat what I wrote in 1940: "The genius of Israel is not to be wholly divided amongst her neighbours, and the unique quality which has made the Psalter the enduring vehicle of spiritual worship cannot be credited to a literature that none would dream of substituting for it to-day. . . . That quality in Hebrew psalmody which makes it unique is something that Israel learned, not from her neighbours, but from her own experience of God, and it is something vastly greater and more significant than all there is in common between the Psalter and Accadian psalmody."[2]

In previous chapters I have directed attention to the ritual acts of Temple worship and to the psalms as designed to lead the worshipper to make those acts truly his own. In this chapter I wish to examine the various elements of spiritual worship which have survived in the Psalms. Many of the individual psalms are prayers, though only five are called Prayers in their headings.[3] Outside the Psalter there are many prayers in the Old Testament. Koehler says: "If one does not apply too strict a standard one can count about 85 original prayers in the Old Testament. In addition there are about 60 whole Psalms and 14 parts of Psalms which may be called prayers, though it is often very hard to determine whether they are or not."[4] Prayer is a very important element in worship,[5] though it is not the whole of worship, and in prayer many elements may be combined. There is nothing necessarily spiritual in prayer. It may be thought of as a technique for imposing one's will on God, or for extracting something from him. It may be merely

[1] *The Psalmists*, p. 172.
[2] *The Bible and Modern Religious Thought*, No. 18, January 1940, pp. 9f.
[3] Pss. 17; 86; 90; 102; 142; also Hab. 3.
[4] *Old Testament Theology*, E. Tr., 1957, p. 251.
[5] On the Old Testament attitude to prayer cf. D. R. Ap-Thomas, *S.J.T.* ix, 1956, pp. 422ff, and on postures in prayer cf. Ap-Thomas, *V.T.* vi, 1956, pp. 225ff, and A. Maillot, in *Vocabulary of the Bible*, ed. by J. J. von Allmen, E. Tr., 1958, p. 332a.

the expression of one's selfish desires. There is nothing very exalted in this, and if the prayers of the Psalter were no more than this, there would be nothing rewarding in the effort to understand the spirit with which they sought to infuse worship. Happily there is much more, much that is of enduring worth.

The real meaning of worship derives in the first place from the God to whom it is directed.[1] The God of the Old Testament is supremely great and supremely good. That many of the Israelite people entertained less worthy ideas of God is recognized in the Bible, but that does not alter the richness of the idea of God set before them in their faith. Here I can do no more than mention a few of the passages in the Psalms where God's character is set forth. That he is a personal God is everywhere taken for granted. There are passages which might suggest that he is but one of many gods, and it is undoubted that behind the religion of Israel lies polytheism. Psalm 82 begins: "God standeth in the congregation of God; he judgeth among the gods."[2] Here there is a recognition of other gods as existing, though the psalm goes on to tell how sentence of death was pronounced on them for their misrule. Though they were allowed to have once been real, they were so no longer. It is doubtful if the psalmists believed in the current reality of other gods.[3] If they existed, they were not merely not for Israel, but they were negligible, and when the psalmist hails God as "a great king above all gods",[4] this does not imply a belief in the existence of other gods any more than it would imply that I believed in the reality of the gods of Greece and Rome if I said that the God of the Old Testament is immeasurably greater than those gods.

The God of the Psalms is the Creator of all things and the

[1] Cf. T. H. Robinson's essay on "The God of the Psalmists" in *The Psalmists*, ed. by D. C. Simpson, 1926, pp. 23ff; also J. M. P. Smith, *The Religion of the Psalms*, 1922, pp. 129ff; H. Ringgren, *The Faith of the Psalmists*, 1963, pp. 47ff.

[2] A. R. Johnson (*Sacral Kingship*, p. 89) renders: "God taketh His stand in the divine assembly; Amidst the gods He pronounceth judgement".

[3] T. H. Robinson (in *The Psalmists*, p. 26) thinks otherwise. He says: "He [i.e. the Psalmist] admits, perhaps even glories in, the existence of other deities besides Him whom he is directly addressing, because to him his own God, Jahveh, is supreme over all." J. M. P. Smith (*The Religion of the Psalms*, 1922, pp. 135f) holds that the reference is to the kings of the ancient world, who had exercised sway over Israel, and who were acclaimed as divine and given the title and worship belonging to gods.

[4] Ps. 95.3.

controller of all the forces of Nature: "By the word of the Lord
were the heavens made; and all the host of them by the breath
of his mouth";[1] "The heavens declare the glory of God; and the
firmament sheweth his handiwork";[2] "My help cometh from the
Lord, which made heaven and earth";[3] "He watereth the mountains from his chambers: the earth is satisfied with the fruit of thy
works";[4] "O Lord, how manifold are thy works! In wisdom hast
thou made them all: the earth is full of thy riches".[5] His years are
unending and his power is subject to no decay: "The Lord sitteth
as king for ever";[6] "The Lord shall reign for ever";[7] "For this
God is our God for ever and ever".[8]

He rules over the universe and to the righteous King-Messiah
he promises dominion over all the earth: "The Lord reigneth;
he is apparelled with majesty";[9] "Be still and know that I am
God; I will be exalted among the nations, I will be exalted in
the earth";[10] "He shall have dominion also from sea to sea, and
from the River unto the ends of the earth".[11] He is depicted as
exalted on high, and this is psychologically true, as it means that
men look to him as One who is immeasurably superior to them in
majesty and dignity: "Unto thee do I lift up mine eyes, O thou

---

[1] Ps. 33.6.   [2] Ps. 19.1 (M.T. 2).   [3] Ps. 121.2.
[4] Ps. 104.13. Many commentators are dissatisfied with this sense and
emend the text. W. O. E. Oesterley (*The Psalms*, ii, 1939, pp. 441f),
following Hans Schmidt (*Die Psalmen*, 1934, pp. 187f) proposed "from
the moisture of thy heavens"; A. Weiser (*The Psalms*, E. Tr. by H.
Hartwell, 1962, pp. 664f) "from the gift of thy heaven"; L. Randon (in
La Bible du Centenaire, iii, 1947, p. 108) "from thy heavens"; H. Gunkel
(*Die Psalmen*, 1926, pp. 446, 455) and H. J. Kraus (*Psalmen*, ii, 1960,
pp. 706, 708) "from the moisture of thy treasures"; B. Duhm (*Die
Psalmen*, 1899, p. 243) "from the flasks of heaven"; R. Tournay and R.
Schwab (*Les Psaumes*, 2nd edn, 1955, p. 379) "from the fruit of thy
heaven"; R. Kittel (*Die Psalmen*, 1929, pp. 335f) "from thy clouds"; G.
Castellino (*Libro dei Salmi*, 1955, p. 496) "from the drippings of thy
heavens". The meaning, as the parallel shows, is in any case the rain.
[5] Ps. 104.24. R.S.V. renders "full of thy creatures", and so many
editors.
[6] Ps. 29.10.   [7] Ps. 146.10.   [8] Ps. 48.14 (M.T. 15).
[9] Ps. 93.1.   [10] Ps. 46.10 (M.T. 11).
[11] Ps. 72.8; cf. Zech. 9.10. A. R. Johnson (*Sacral Kingship*, pp. 8ff) holds
that the reference in "from sea to sea" is to the all-embracing cosmic sea,
and in "the River" to the current of the cosmic sea which nourishes the
holy city. For a review of other interpretations cf. H. Gross, *Weltherr-
schaft als religiöse Idee im Alten Testament*, 1953, pp. 11ff.

that sittest in the heaven";[1] "Who is like unto the Lord our God, that hath his seat on high".[2] Nevertheless, he is not remote and unaware of what is happening among men. He is omnipresent and omniscient, perceiving men's deeds and penetrating to the very thoughts of their hearts: "If I ascend up into heaven, thou art there: if I make my bed in Sheol, behold, thou art there. If I take the wings of the morning, and dwell in the uttermost parts of the sea; even there shall thy hand lead[3] me, and thy right hand shall hold me";[4] "O Lord, thou hast searched me and known me. Thou knowest my downsitting and mine uprising, thou understandest my thought afar off. Thou searchest out my path and my lying down, and art acquainted with all my ways";[5] "He knoweth the secrets of the heart".[6]

Even more important for religion than the conception of the greatness and power of God is the conception of his character. The psalmists conceived of that character in terms which are found throughout the Old Testament. He is first and foremost holy and righteous: "All that is within me, bless his holy name";[7] "But thou art holy, O thou that inhabitest the praises of Israel";[8] "Exalt ye the Lord our God, and worship at his holy hill; for the Lord our God is holy";[9] "The Lord is righteous in all his ways";[10] "The judgements of the Lord are true, and righteous altogether";[11] "Good and upright is the Lord";[12] "Thy righteousness, O God, is very high";[13] "His righteousness endureth for ever".[14] He is the judge of all, and to his judgement they who love him gladly submit themselves: "He cometh to judge the earth";[15] "He shall judge the world in righteousness, he shall minister judgement to the peoples in uprightness";[16] "Examine me, O Lord, and prove me; try my reins and my heart".[17]

---

[1] Ps. 123.1.   [2] Ps. 113.5.
[3] Many editors read "shall take me", claiming that this is the reading of LXX and Syr. Actually LXX agrees with M.T. and Syr. transposes the verbs in the two parallel lines. Neither offers any support for a different reading.
[4] Ps. 139.8ff.   [5] Ps. 139.1ff.   [6] Ps. 44.21 (M.T. 22).   [7] Ps. 103.1.
[8] Ps. 22.3 (M.T. 4). Some editors follow LXX in reading "Thou dwellest in the sanctuary, the praise of Israel". M. Dahood (*Psalms*, i, p. 136) renders "While you sit upon the holy throne, the Glory of Irsael."
[9] Ps. 99.9; cf. verse 5.   [10] Ps. 145.17.   [11] Ps. 19.9 (M.T. 10).
[12] Ps. 25.8.   [13] Ps. 71.19.   [14] Pss. 111.3; 112.3.
[15] Pss. 96.13; 98.9.   [16] Ps. 9.8 (M.T. 9).   [17] Ps. 26.2.

The psalmists no less than the Deuteronomist cherish the thought that God has chosen Israel to be his people and set his love upon her: "The Lord hath chosen Jacob unto himself, and Israel for his peculiar treasure";[1] "We are his people, and the sheep of his pasture";[2] "The Lord taketh pleasure in his people";[3] "He hath remembered his lovingkindness and his faithfulness toward the house of Israel";[4] "The Lord loveth the righteous";[5] "The mercy [i.e. ḥesedh,[6] which R.S.V. renders "the steadfast love"] of the Lord is from everlasting to everlasting upon them that fear him, and his righteousness unto children's children".[7]

The memory of God's saving acts in the deliverance from Egypt became the ground of assurance that he was still a saving God, as many had found in their own experience: "He led forth his own people like sheep, and guided them in the wilderness like a flock";[8] "He brought forth his people with joy, and his chosen with singing";[9] "Surely his salvation is nigh unto them that fear

[1] Ps. 135.4. [2] Ps. 100.3. [3] Ps. 149.4.
[4] Ps. 98.3. [5] Ps. 146.8.

[6] This word is variously rendered "lovingkindness", "mercy", "kindness", in A.V. and R.V. It has no exact equivalent in English. G. A. Smith (*Jeremiah*, 3rd edn, 1924, p. 104) maintains that "troth" is the nearest English word, while A.R. Johnson (*Interpretationes ad Vetus Testamentum pertinentes* (Mowinckel Festschrift), 1955, pp. 100ff) argues that the best English word is "devotion" (cf. the rendering of J. Moffatt in Jer. 2.2: "I remember your early devotion"). N. H. Snaith (*Distinctive Ideas of the Old Testament*, 1944, p. 95) calls it "covenant-love", and says that without the prior existence of a covenant there could be no ḥesedh (cf. G. E. Wright, *The Challenge of Israel's Faith*, 1944, pp. 73f; J. Bright, *The Kingdom of God*, 1953, p. 28 n). According to A. Lods (*The Prophets and the Rise of Judaism*, E. Tr. by S. H. Hooke, 1937, p. 89) it is fairly close to *pietas* in meaning. M. Burrows (*An Outline of Biblical Theology*, 1946, p. 252) best expresses the meaning: "The Hebrew word commonly rendered 'kindness' or 'loving-kindness' means primarily 'loyalty', but it often implies also a beneficence which exceeds anything the recipient has a right to expect". It expresses the Divine initiative in grace towards men and the response which man *ought* to make to that grace; it also expresses the quality which men ought to show to one another, both in grace and response, in reflection of the Divine quality. W. F. Lofthouse (*Z.A.W.* li, 1933, p. 33) notes that ḥesedh is only used where there is some recognized tie. Cf. T. H. Robinson, in *The Psalmists*, ed. by D. C. Simpson, 1926, pp. 36f; A. Neher, *L'Essence du prophétisme*, 1955, pp. 264ff, and the monograph of N. Glueck, *Das Wort Ḥesed im alttestamentlichen Sprachgebrauche*, 1927.

[7] Ps. 103.17. [8] Ps. 78.52. [9] Ps. 105.43.

him";[1] "Thou hast delivered my soul from death".[2] The compassion he had shown unto their fathers was recognized to be still
of the essence of his character: "The Lord is full of compassion
and gracious. . . . Like as a father pitieth his children, so the Lord
pitieth them that fear him".[3] For God is ever faithful and to be
counted on, mindful of his covenant and loyal to it: "Thy faithfulness reacheth unto the skies";[4] "Thy faithfulness is unto all
generations";[5] "He hath remembered his covenant for ever";[6]
"My mercy [i.e. ḥesedh again] will I keep for him for evermore,
and my covenant shall stand fast with him. . . . My covenant will
I not break, nor alter the thing that is gone out of my lips";[7]
"He will ever be mindful of his covenant".[8]

God comes to men with the demand for obedience to his will,
and obedience consists in the reflection of his own holiness and
purity and love, in so far as these can be reflected within human
conditions: "Who shall ascend into the hill of the Lord? And
who shall stand in his holy place? He that hath clean hands and a
pure heart";[9] "Lord, who shall sojourn in thy tabernacle? Who
shall dwell in thy holy hill? He that walketh uprightly, and worketh
righteousness, and speaketh truth in his heart";[10] "Let the words
of my mouth and the meditation of my heart be acceptable in thy
sight, O Lord, my rock, and my redeemer";[11] "For the Lord is
righteous; he loveth righteousness: the upright shall behold his
face".[12] And finally, when men have fallen into sin and return to
him in true penitence, he is a forgiving God: "Who forgiveth all
thine iniquities";[13] "But there is forgiveness with thee";[14] "For
thou, Lord, art good, and ready to forgive, and plenteous in
mercy [ḥesedh once more] unto all them that call upon thee';[15]
"According to the multitude of thy tender mercies blot out my
transgressions".[16]

All of these qualities of God's character are found elsewhere in
the Old Testament, but the Old Testament was not to be found
in every Israelite home. Much of it was not collected in pre-exilic

---

[1] Ps. 85.9 (M.T. 10).   [2] Pss. 56.13 (M.T. 14); 116.8.
[3] Ps. 103.8, 13.   [4] Ps. 36.5 (M.T. 6).   [5] Ps. 119.90; cf. 100.5.
[6] Ps. 105.8.   [7] Ps. 89.28, 34 (M.T. 29, 35)   [8] Ps. 111.5.
[9] Ps. 24.3f.   [10] Ps. 15.1f.   [11] Ps. 19.14 (M.T. 15).
[12] Ps. 11.7. Dahood (*Psalms*, i, p. 68) renders the last line "Our face
shall gaze upon the Upright One", and finds here "a statement of belief
in the beatific vision of the afterlife" (p. 71).
[13] Ps. 103.3.   [14] Ps. 130.4.   [15] Ps. 86.5.   [16] Ps. 51.1 (M.T. 3).

times and such parts as were then collected were not familiar to all the people. It is of no little significance that in the liturgy of the Temple men should be acquainted with this conception of God.[1] We may now turn to ask what kind of worship Israel brought to this God,[2] and what elements of worship we can discover in the liturgical texts that have come down to us in the Psalter.[3] Men came with eager joy to the Temple because it was the house of God: "Lord, I love the habitation of thy house, and the place where thy glory dwelleth";[4] "I was glad when they said unto me, Let us go unto the house of the Lord";[5] "One thing have I asked of the Lord, that will I seek after; that I may dwell in the house of the Lord all the days of my life, to behold the beauty of the Lord, and to inquire in his temple";[6] "Beautiful in elevation, the joy of the whole earth, is mount Zion, on the sides of the north,[7]

---

[1] H. Ringgren (*The Faith of the Psalmists*, 1963, p. 27) says: "An important feature of the religion of the Psalms is its theocratic . . . character. It is God and not man who is the focus of the psalmist's interest."

[2] Cf. H. W. Robinson's essay on "The Inner Life of the Psalmists", in *The Psalmists*, ed. by D. C. Simpson, 1926, pp. 45ff; also A. C. Welch, *The Psalter*, 1926, pp. 89ff; H. Gunkel, "The Religion of the Psalmists", in *What Remains of the Old Testament*, E. Tr. by A. K. Dallas, 1928, pp. 69ff.

[3] N. K. Gottwald (*A Light to the Nations*, 1959, p. 514,) says: "The prime contribution of the Psalms to the student of the faith of Israel is the manner in which these poems vividly illustrate the amazing range of Israel's piety and its living developmental character."

[4] Ps. 26.8.   [5] Ps. 122.1.

[6] Ps. 27.4. Dahood (*Psalms*, i, p. 165) emends (cf. p. 167) to secure for the first words "One thing I have asked a hundred times."

[7] The Hebrew word here is *ṣāphôn*, and we have the identification of Zion with Mount Zaphon, the abode of Baal in Canaanite mythology, in order to transfer to Zion the significance of Mount Zaphon. On the identification of Zaphon with the Mons Casius of classical sources, cf. O. Eissfeldt, *Baal Zaphon, Zeus Kasios und der Durchzug der Israeliten durchs Meer*, 1932 (cf. also W. F. Albright in *Festschrift für Alfred Bertholet*, 1950, pp. 1ff), and R. de Langhe, *Les textes de Ras Shamra-Ugarit et leurs rapports avec le milieu biblique de l'Ancien Testament*, ii, 1945, pp. 217ff, where the Ras Shamra evidence is presented. Cf. also the monograph of A. Lauha, *Zaphon: der Norden und die Nordvölker im Alten Testament*, 1943, esp. pp. 36ff; J. Morgenstern, *H.U.C.A.* xvi, 1941, pp. 47ff (where Mount Zaphon is located in the mountains of Armenia); B. Alfrink, *Biblica*, xiv, 1933, pp. 52ff. On the thought of the Psalmist here, cf. R. de Langhe, op. cit., p. 242: "Le poète ne veut

the city of the great King";[1] "Walk about Zion, and go round about her: tell the towers thereof";[2] "The Lord hath chosen Zion; he hath desired it for his habitation".[3] This might be nothing more than aesthetic delight in the splendour of the building, or a superstitious regard for the Temple such as Jeremiah rebuked in his contemporaries, who believed that because they had the Temple in Jerusalem no harm could befall them.[4] That there was more to it than this, at least on the part of the creators of the Psalms and those who entered into their spirit, becomes clear when we look further into the worship of the psalmists.

The first element in worship is adoration. The Hebrews expressed this by their posture and not alone by their word. For they prostrated themselves before God. "O come, let us worship and bow down; let us kneel before the Lord our Maker";[5] "Exalt ye the Lord our God, and worship at his footstool".[6] They did not come with an easy familiarity into the presence of God, but were aware of his greatness and majesty, and came with a sense of privilege to his house. Alexander Stewart says: "Adoration is, in the first place, the attitude of the soul which is called forth by the loftiest thoughts and realizations of God. Before His perfections the soul abases itself; it seeks to get beyond earth and earthly things and to enter into His nearer presence."[7] In adoration humility is expressed. In a passage found outside the Psalter we read: "Let not the wise man glory in his wisdom, neither let the mighty man glory in his might, let not the rich man glory in his riches: but let him that glorieth glory in this, that he understandeth and knoweth me, that I am the Lord which exercise

évidemment pas dire que la montagne sainte de Sion se trouve dans le Nord le plus reculé, ou le plus élevé. Il fait plutôt allusion, pense-t-on, à la croyance d'après laquelle on plaçait dans les profondeurs du Septentrion une montagne très sainte qui, pour certains peuples païens, servait de lieu du séjour et de réunion pour les dieux, une sorte d'Olympe sémitique. . . . Le psalmist ne croit donc pas pouvoir mieux louer le mont Sion qu'en le présentant comme la vraie montagne du Nord, disons, par analogie, comme le véritable Olympe" (cf. E. Podechard, *Le Psautier* (Traduction et explication), i, 1949, p. 214; M. Dahood, *Psalms*, i, 1966, p. 289). Cf. further A. R. Johnson, *Sacral Kingship*, pp. 77ff; R. E. Clements, *God and Temple*, 1965, pp. 4ff; H. J. Kraus, *Worship in Israel*, E. Tr., pp. 199f.

[1] Ps. 48.2 (M.T. 3). [2] Ps. 48.12 (M.T. 13). [3] Ps. 132.13.
[4] Jer. 7.4. [5] Ps. 95.6. [6] Ps. 99.5; cf. 132.7.
[7] In Hastings' *D.B.* i, 1898, p. 42b.

lovingkindness, judgement, and righteousness, in the earth: for in these things I delight, saith the Lord."[1] The psalmists would have found no fault with that; for adoration leaves no place for self-glory. "O Lord, our Lord, how excellent is thy name in all the earth! Who hast set thy glory upon the heavens. . . . When I consider thy heavens, the work of thy fingers, the moon and the stars, which thou hast ordained; what is man that thou art mindful of him? And the son of man, that thou visitest him?"[2]

Closely associated with adoration is reverence and awe. This, too, could be symbolized in action, as in Moses' removal of his shoes at the Burning Bush.[3] Often in our English versions the word "fear" stands, where "reverence" or "awe" would be more appropriate, and in some of these cases the Revised Standard Version has substituted the more appropriate word. The Hebrew commonly uses the same word, whether it implies cowering dread or reverence. Sometimes it quite certainly means the former: "Thou, even thou, art to be feared: and who may stand in thy sight when once thou art angry?";[4] "Who knoweth the power of thine anger, and thy wrath according to the fear that is due unto thee?"[5] At other times the thought is clearly of reverence rather than of terror: "Let all the earth fear the Lord: let all the inhabitants of the world stand in awe of him";[6] "Ye that fear the Lord, praise him; all ye the seed of Jacob, glorify him; and stand in awe of him, all ye the seed of Israel";[7] "As for me, in the multi-

---

[1] Jer. 9.23f. [2] Ps. 8.1, 3f (M.T. 2, 4f). [3] Ex. 3.5. [4] Ps. 76.7 (M.T. 8).

[5] Ps. 90.11. For "and thy wrath according to the fear that is due unto thee" LXX has "and from the fear of thy wrath" and Syr. "and the terror of thy wrath". Editors read "who sees the depth [lit. midst] of thy wrath?" (so Gunkel, *Die Psalmen*, 1926, pp. 397, 401; H. Schmidt, *Die Psalmen*, 1934, p. 169; E. Dhorme, *La Bible de la Pléiade*, Ancien Testament, ii, 1959, p. 1101; H. J. Kraus, *Psalmen*, 1960, pp. 627f), or "who sees thy wrath?" (so B. Duhm, *Die Psalmen*, 1899, p. 226), or "who fears the violence of thy wrath?" (so Oesterley, *The Psalms*, ii, 1939, pp. 404f; E. Podechard, *Le Psautier*, ii, 1954, pp. 125, 131; R. Tournay and R. Schwab, *Les Psaumes*, 2nd edn, 1955, p. 344), or "who is afraid of thy wrath?" (so R. Kittel, *Die Psalmen*, 5th edn, 1929, pp. 298ff; A. Weiser, *The Psalms*, E. Tr., 1962, pp. 594f), or "who (knows) the dread of thy wrath?" (so G. Castellino, *Libro dei Salmi*, 1955, p. 346), or "who understands the length of thy wrath?" (so E. J. Kissane, *Psalms*, ii, 1954, pp. 101f), or "how terrible is thy wrath!" (so J. Calès, *Le Livre des Psaumes*, ii, 1936, p. 152). Of these Gunkel's or Calès' seems to yield the most appropriate sense.

[6] Ps. 33.8. [7] Ps. 22.23 (M.T. 24).

tude of thy lovingkindness will I come into thy house: in thy fear will I worship toward thy holy temple";[1] "The secret[2] of the Lord is with them that fear him; and he will shew them his covenant";[3] "Ye that fear the Lord, trust in him: he is their help and their shield".[4] The words of the Shema‘, which were recited at the beginning of the Synagogue service, were designed to evoke the sense of awed privilege at the approach to God: "Hear, O Israel: the Lord our God is one Lord; and thou shalt love the Lord thy God with all thine heart, and with all thy soul, and with all thy might."[5] The psalmists no less clearly recognized that humble reverence was the beginning of worship.

When the silence of adoration and reverence is broken by speech, it should be to praise and bless the name of God. Such speech abounds in the Psalter, which is called in Hebrew the book of Praises. The psalmists realized that the first purpose of worship is to glorify God: "I will bless the Lord at all times: his praise shall continually be in my mouth";[6] "I will praise thee, O Lord my God, with my whole heart; and I will glorify thy name for evermore";[7] "O magnify the Lord with me, and let us exalt his name for ever";[8] "My mouth shall speak the praise of the Lord";[9] "Praise God in his sanctuary. . . . Let everything that hath breath praise the Lord";[10] "I will sing, yea, I will sing praises unto the Lord";[11] "Bless the Lord, O my soul: and all that is within me, bless his holy name";[12] "Sing unto the Lord, bless his name":[13] "O sing unto the Lord a new song: sing unto the Lord all the earth";[14] "O sing unto the Lord a new song; for he hath done marvellous things";[15] "Sing forth the glory of his name: make his praise glorious".[16] Examples could be multiplied, for this is one of the dominant notes of the Psalter. It is scarcely necessary to observe that when the Bible talks of praising and glorifying and blessing God, it does not mean that we confer anything on God, but that we recognize his glory and goodness. No element of patronage can enter into our worship when it begins with adoration and reverence, for, like Isaiah at his call, we recognize that it is but of his goodness that we are not consumed in his holy presence.[17]

---

[1] Ps. 5.7 (M.T. 8).   [2] R.S.V. "friendship".   [3] Ps. 25.14.
[4] Ps. 115.11.   [5] Deut. 6.4f.   [6] Ps. 34.1 (M.T. 2).   [7] Ps. 86.12.
[8] Ps. 34.3 (M.T. 4).   [9] Ps. 145.21.   [10] Ps. 150.1, 6.   [11] Ps. 27.6.
[12] Ps. 103.1.   [13] Ps. 96.2.   [14] Ps. 96.1.   [15] Ps. 98.1.
[16] Ps. 66.2. R.S.V. "give to him glorious praise".   [17] Isa. 6.5.

Another great element of worship must ever be thanksgiving, and this again abounds in the Psalms: "Bless the Lord, O my soul, and forget not all his benefits";[1] "Oh that men would praise the Lord for his goodness, and for his wonderful works to the children of men!";[2] "Let us come before his presence with thanksgiving";[3] "Enter into his gates with thanksgiving, and into his courts with praise";[4] "We will give thanks unto thy name for ever";[5] "Oh give thanks unto the Lord; for he is good; for his mercy endureth for ever";[6] "I will give thanks unto the Lord with my whole heart; I will shew forth all thy marvellous works".[7] The psalmists remember with gratitude the mercies of God to their fathers: "Our fathers trusted in thee: they trusted and thou didst deliver them".[8] They also remember God's mercies to themselves: "I sought the Lord, and he answered me, and delivered me from all my fears";[9] "What shall I render unto the Lord for all his benefits toward me?"[10] Sometimes the thanksgiving is for some great public deliverance, as was the case with the Song of Moses in Exodus 15 and the Song of Deborah,[11] or as when the psalmist sang: "The Lord hath done great things for us; whereof we are glad".[12] Sometimes it was for deliverance from illness or misfortune: "He brought me up also out of an horrible pit,[13] out of the miry clay; and he set my feet upon a rock, and established my goings";[14] "The cords of death compassed me, and the pains of Sheol gat hold upon me: I found trouble and sorrow. Then called I upon the name of the Lord . . . I was brought low and he saved me".[15] The Koran speaks with scorn of those who make vows when buffeted by a tempest at sea, but who forget their vows when the tempest is past.[16] The psalmists call

---

[1] Ps. 103.2.   [2] Ps. 107.8, 15, 21, 31.   [3] Ps. 95.2.   [4] Ps. 100.4.
[5] Ps. 44.8 (M.T. 9).   [6] Ps. 107.1.   [7] Ps. 9.1 (M.T. 2).
[8] Ps. 22.4 (M.T. 5).   [9] Ps. 34.4 (M.T. 5).   [10] Ps. 116.12.
[11] Judges 5.1ff.   [12] Ps. 126.3.
[13] R.S.V. "from the desolate pit" (with a slight change of the text). Gressmann (apud Gunkel, Psalmen, 1929, p. 170) suggested changing one letter to yield "from the pit of Sheol", and so Oesterley, Psalms, i, 1939, p. 233. Dahood (Psalms, i, 1966, p. 243) renders "from the pit of Destruction".
[14] Ps. 40.2 (M.T. 3).   [15] Ps. 116.3f, 6.
[16] Sura x.23f: "If a tempestuous gale overtake them, and the billows come on them from every side, and they think that they are encompassed therewith, they call on God, professing sincere religion: 'Wouldst thou

for the fulfilment of vows in the spirit of thanksgiving to God for his mercies: "Offer unto God the sacrifice of thanksgiving; and pay thy vows unto the Most High";[1] "Vow, and pay unto the Lord your God";[2] "I will come into thy house with burnt offerings, I will pay thee my vows, which my lips have uttered, and my mouth hath spoken, when I was in distress";[3] "I will pay my vows unto the Lord, yea, in the presence of all his people".[4] We may further note that the psalmists could thank God for spiritual blessing, as well as for physical and material gifts: "He guideth me in the paths of righteousness";[5] "Thou forgavest the iniquity of my sin".[6] This and so much more that was designed to express the gratitude of the ancient Israelite when he came to the Temple, or to move his heart to realize all the bounty and the mercy of God, can still continue its timeless service to worshippers to-day. Its words can be reinterpreted in terms of men's experience to-day, that its spirit may infuse the worship they bring.

Yet none can stand in the presence of the holy God without being conscious of the gulf that separates him from God. When Isaiah beheld the glory of God and heard the seraphim cry: "Holy, holy, holy is the Lord of hosts",[7] his first thought was of his own unholiness. In that presence nothing that was unholy could survive, and he cried: "Woe is me! for I am undone; because I am a man of unclean lips, and I dwell in the midst of a people of unclean lips".[8] Either he must perish with his sin, or his sin must perish that he might live. For God is "of purer eyes than to behold evil".[9] Psalmists, too, knew the same experience: "If thou, Lord, shouldest mark iniquities, O Lord, who shall stand?"[10] They came into God's presence with confession on their lips: "For thy name's sake, O Lord, pardon mine iniquity, for it is great";[11] "I will declare mine iniquity; I will be sorry for my sin".[12] Of all the Psalms the one which most deeply enters into the consciousness of sin and most profoundly moves the heart of the worshipper to penitence is Psalm 51: "Have mercy upon me, O God, according to thy lovingkindness: according to the multitude of thy tender

but rescue us from this, then will we indeed be of the thankful.' But when we have rescued them, lo! they commit unrighteous excesses on the earth!" (Rodwell's translation).

[1] Ps. 50.14. [2] Ps. 76.11 (M.T. 12). [3] Ps. 66.13f. [4] Ps. 116.14.
[5] Ps. 23.3. [6] Ps. 32.5. [7] Isa. 6.3. [8] Isa. 6.5. [9] Hab. 1.13.
[10] Ps. 130.3. [11] Ps. 25.11. [12] Ps. 38.18 (M.T. 19).

mercies, blot out my transgressions. Wash me throughly from mine iniquity, and cleanse me from my sin. For I acknowledge my transgressions: and my sin is ever before me. Against thee, thee only, have I sinned, and done this evil in thy sight. . . . Purge me with hyssop, and I shall be clean: wash me, and I shall be whiter than snow. . . . Create in me a clean heart, O God; and renew a right spirit within me."[1] Psalmists, too, knew something of the experience of Isaiah, and the sense of cleansing: "I acknowledged my sin unto thee, and mine iniquity have I not hid: I said, I will confess my transgressions unto the Lord; and thou forgavest the iniquity of my sin";[2] "Blessed is he whose transgression is forgiven, whose sin is covered".[3] True worship is ever a cleansing and a renewing experience.

Of course petition was an element of worship, and the psalmists freely brought their needs to God. This does not mean that they regarded their prayer, even though accompanied by sacrifice, as a means of imposing man's will upon God—though it is probable that some of the worshippers so thought of it, as many still do to-day. For they used the language of beseeching. Some years ago a well-known Biblical scholar invited me to join him in a campaign to make the language of prayer scientific, and amongst other things he wished to eliminate the language of beseeching from prayer. God does not need to be besought to hear us, he said, since of course he hears. To this I replied that the language of beseeching is psychologically justified, since it means that we come into the presence of God, not as men who know they are bound to be heard, but as men who realize that it is of God's mercy that we are heard. We have no claim on him to the fulfilment of our desires, but present our petitions humbly before him. Our prayers may express our agonized desires, but we trust the wisdom of God to grant them or not. Too often the element of agony is less found in our prayers for others than in those for ourselves. The psalmists did not shrink from asking God for the supply of their needs. Often these were for deliverance from sickness or from their enemies or for success in individual or national enterprises: "The cords of death compassed me, and the

---

[1] Ps. 51.1–4, 7, 10 (M.T. 3–6, 9, 12). On this psalm cf. E. R. Dalglish, *Psalm Fifty-One*, 1962, and N. H. Snaith, *The Seven Psalms*, 1964, pp. 47ff.

[2] Ps. 32.5.   [3] Ps. 32.1.

pains of Sheol gat hold upon me: I found trouble and sorrow. Then called I upon the name of the Lord; O Lord, I beseech thee, deliver my soul";[1] "Save me, O God; for the waters are come in unto my soul. I sink in deep mire, where there is no standing";[2] "Pluck me out of the net that they have laid privily for me";[3] "Deliver me not over unto the will of mine adversaries; for false witnesses are risen up against me, and such as breathe out cruelty";[4] "Lord, how long wilt thou look on? Rescue my soul from their destructions";[5] "Hear my voice, O God, in my complaint: preserve my life from fear of the enemy";[6] "Save now, we beseech thee, O Lord: O Lord, we beseech thee, send now prosperity"[7]—or, as the R.S.V. has, "give us success". There is nothing wrong in bringing our petitions to God, so long as we submit them to him and do not demand them from him.

Intercession is not a prominent element in the prayers of the Psalter. Psalm 20 is a prayer of intercession for the king: "The Lord answer thee in the day of trouble; the name of the God of Jacob set thee up on high".[8] We find prayer for Jerusalem: "Pray for the peace of Jerusalem: they shall prosper that love thee. Peace be within thy walls, and prosperity within thy palaces".[9] But outside the Psalter there are many intercessory prayers in the Old Testament. Notable among them is the great intercessory prayer of Solomon at the dedication of the Temple.[10] We have in earlier chapters noted the intercessory prayers of Abraham[11] and Moses[12] and Samuel,[13] and have seen that intercession was one of the functions of the prophets. These intercessions were not uttered in any shrine as a part of the worship. For worship is not confined to the sanctuary, and especially prayer is not confined to its walls. Indeed, it may be said that he who prays only in the sanctuary does not really pray at all. For worship in the sanctuary is designed to elevate the soul to a relationship with God to be carried from the sanctuary into the whole of life. Paul could write: "Pray without ceasing."[14] Of all the Old Testament characters it was Jeremiah who most entered into the riches of the experience of prayer, which belonged to the warp and woof of his daily

[1] Ps. 116.3f. [2] Ps. 69.1f (M.T. 2f). [3] Ps. 31.4 (M.T. 5).
[4] Ps. 27.12. [5] Ps. 35.17. [6] Ps. 64.1 (M.T. 2). [7] Ps. 118.25.
[8] Ps. 20.1 (M.T. 2). [9] Ps. 122.6f. [10] 1 Kings 8.23ff.
[11] Gen. 18.23ff. [12] Ex. 32.31ff. [13] 1 Sam. 12.23.
[14] 1 Thess. 5.17.

experience.[1] For prayer, and indeed all true worship, is fundamentally communion with God.

The greatest gift of God is himself, and the supreme end of worship is to be lifted into the spirit of God, to share his life, his thought, his purpose. And this element of worship is not wanting in the Psalter:[2] "My soul longeth, yea, even fainteth for the courts of the Lord; my heart and my flesh cry out to[3] [or, as the Authorized Version has, "for"] the living God";[4] "How precious is thy lovingkindness, O God! And the children of men take refuge under the shadow of thy wings. They shall be abundantly satisfied with the fatness of thy house; and thou shalt make them drink of the river of thy pleasures. For with thee is the fountain of life: in thy light shall we see light";[5] "As the hart panteth after

---

[1] Cf. especially Jer. 11.18—12.6; 15.10–21; 17.9f, 14–18; 18.18–23, 20.7–12, 14–18. These passages are often referred to as the "Confessions of Jeremiah". Cf. W. Baumgartner, *Die Klagegedichte des Jeremia*, 1917; J. Skinner, *Prophecy and Religion*, 1922, pp. 301ff; G. A. Smith, *Jeremiah*, 1923, pp. 317ff; M. A. Beek, *Het Twistgesprek van de mens met zijn God*, 1946, pp. 16ff; E. A. Leslie, *The Intimate Papers of Jeremiah*, 1953, and *Jeremiah*, 1954, pp. 137ff; L. Leclercq, in *Études sur les Prophètes d'Israël*, 1954, pp. 111ff; P. A. H. de Boer, *Jeremia's Twijfel*, 1957; G. M. Behler, *Les Confessions de Jérémie*, 1959; G. von Rad, *Old Testament Theology*, E. Tr., ii, 1965, pp. 201ff. O. Eissfeldt (*Wissenschaftliche Zeitschrift der Martin-Luther-University Halle-Wittenberg*, xiv, 1965, pp. 181ff) studies these passages as indications of Jeremiah's involvement in situations which gave rise to some of his prophecies. J. Bright (*Jeremiah*, 1965, p. cxv) says: "That Jeremiah's own relationship to his God was intensely private and inward was no doubt due in good part to his unusually sensitive and introspective nature, as well as to the loneliness which the faithful discharge of his office enforced upon him." P. E. Bonnard has maintained that Jeremiah was the source of the inspiration of many of the Psalms, and has traced his influence in no fewer than thirty-three Psalms; cf. *Le Psautier selon Jérémie*, 1960. The argument is not convincing, however. It would be easier to understand Jeremiah's reflecting ideas and expressions used in the liturgy of the Temple than to understand many different psalmists' finding their inspiration in the words of Jeremiah, which could not have been collected in the present book of Jeremiah until post-exilic days, and embodying them in the later liturgy. Questions of literary dependence are notoriously difficult to settle, unless the evidence on the date is irrefutable for both of the literatures involved.

[2] Cf. H. Ringgren, *The Faith of the Psalmists*, 1963, pp. 20ff.
[3] R.S.V. "sing for joy to".   [4] Ps. 84.2 (M.T. 3).
[5] Ps. 36.7–9 (M.T. 8–10).

the water brooks, so panteth my soul after thee, O God. My soul thirsteth for God, for the living God".[1] It is this love of God for God himself and entering into the riches of fellowship with him which gives to men the peace and poise of spirit which enables them to face whatever life holds with quiet confidence: "I have set the Lord always before me: because he is at my right hand, I shall not be moved".[2] Here is no proud self-confidence,[3] but a calm trust in the sustaining presence of God. Just as the Lord was with Joseph in all his swift changes of fortune,[4] so he is with those who dwell in the secret place of the Most High and abide under the shadow of the Almighty.[5]

Yet other important elements of worship are represented in the Psalter. Just as Isaiah, when the live coal from the altar had touched his lips and cleansed his whole being by burning up his sin, responded in the consecration of himself to the service of God,[6] so the soul that has enjoyed enriching fellowship with God proceeds to holy resolve and the consecration of himself to the Divine service: "I delight to do thy will, O my God; yea, thy law is within my heart";[7] "With my whole heart have I sought thee: O let me not wander from thy commandments";[8] "Give me understanding, and I shall keep thy law; yea, I shall observe it with my whole heart";[9] "I am purposed[10] that my mouth shall not transgress';[11] "Shew me thy ways, O Lord; teach me thy paths. Guide me in thy truth, and teach me; for thou art the God of my salvation; on thee do I wait all the day".[12] The end of resolve is not merely integrity of life in obedience to the will of God in daily life, such as the great pre-exilic prophets had called for, but the glorifying of God before men and testifying for him: "Sing unto the Lord, bless his name; shew forth his salvation from day to day. Declare his glory among the nations, his marvellous works among all the peoples";[13] "I will give thanks unto

---

[1] Ps. 42.1f (M.T. 2f).   [2] Ps. 16.8.

[3] Such as we find referred to for condemnation in Ps. 10.6; 30.6 (M.T. 7).

[4] Gen. 39.3, 21.

[5] Ps. 91.1. For the text of this Psalm in a Qumran recension from Cave 11, cf. J. van der Ploeg, *R.B.* lxxii, 1965, pp. 210ff.

[6] Isa. 6.8.   [7] Ps. 40.8 (M.T. 9).   [8] Ps. 119.10.   [9] Ps. 119.34.

[10] R.S.V., in agreement with many editors, slightly changes the word rendered "I am purposed" to yield "wickedness in me" and attaches it to the preceding line; cf. R.V. marg.

[11] Ps. 17.3.   [12] Ps. 25.4f.   [13] Ps. 96.2f.

thee, O Lord, among the nations, and will sing praises unto thy name".[1]

It would be easily possible to go on citing passages from the Psalter to show how much of permanent value for worship we can find there.[2] Originally intended to accompany the ritual act, it has been divorced from the rite,[3] and has continued to minister to the spirit of men for more than two millennia.[4] It would be a curious circumstance if what has proved of such enduring spiritual worth to men were devoid of spiritual value in its creation. It is more reasonable to find in the riches of the Psalter the evidence of the potential worth of the worship of the Temple. I say potential, because the recitation or chanting of the Psalms could be perfunctory on the one side and received with indifference by the worshipper. The same could often be said of the reading of the Sermon on the Mount. The penetration of the Psalter is not to be judged by its reception by the spiritually dead, but by its capacity to minister to the spirit of men who make it the vehicle of their approach to God. If the Priestly Code is the priests' handbook and the Psalter the cultic prophets' or the Temple singers' handbook and both were intended to be used in association, then the one should not be judged without the other, and the worship of Israel was more meaningful than we often assume.

We must not leave unnoted, however, the elements in the

[1] Pss. 57.9 (M.T. 10); 108.3 (M.T. 4).

[2] H. W. Robinson (in *The Psalmists*, ed. by D. C. Simpson, 1926, p. 48) speaks of "the strong, simple faith of the Psalmists, the courage of their convictions, the persistency of their purpose, the true catholicity of their fundamental assumptions".

[3] Cf. A. C. Welch, *The Psalter*, 1926, p. 93: "The cult-practice could not of itself have supplied the motives and the themes for the hymns which gathered round it. The fact that they have been able to separate themselves from the cult and even to survive it is enough to make that suggestion more than difficult."

[4] Cf. Welch, ibid., p. 92: "It [i.e. the Psalter] sprang up on the soil of Palestine to guide worshippers at the Temple. Yet not only has it never been out of use since the day it was completed, but it has spread to the ends of the earth. And the most alien races can still recite its prayers and thanksgivings with profit. That is a phenomenon which is unique in the history of religion." Cf. also W. Harrelson, *Interpreting the Old Testament*, 1964, p. 407: "The book of Psalms is the treasure house of Israelite faith and piety. This collection of Israel's prayers and praises has provided spiritual life and direction for the community of Israel and for the Church throughout the centuries."

Psalter which raise problems for us.[1] The imprecatory psalms, the cries for vengeance, the harsh denunciations of enemies, whether personal or national, are unsuited to be the vehicle of our worship. We shudder when we read the closing verses of Psalm 137: "O daughter of Babylon, that art to be destroyed; happy shall he be that rewardeth thee as thou hast served us. Happy shall he be, that taketh and dasheth thy little ones against the rock."[2] The sustained malediction of Psalm 109 is little better: "Let his days be few; and let another take his office.[3] Let his children be fatherless, and his wife a widow. Let his children be vagabonds, and beg; and let them seek their bread out of desolate places (or, with R.S.V., "may they be driven out of the ruins they inhabit").[4] Let the extortioner catch all that he hath; and let strangers make spoil of his labour. Let there be none to extend mercy unto him; neither let there be any to have pity on his fatherless children".[5] Yet we should keep two things separate. Our condemnation of those who uttered such sentiments should be tempered by understanding

---

[1] Sometimes there is a note of self-complacency in the psalmists, akin to that aspect of Pharisaism which is condemned in the Parable of the Pharisee and the Publican (Luke 18.9f). Cf. Ps. 26.4ff: "I have not sat with vain persons; Neither will I go in with dissemblers. I hate the congregation of evil-doers, And I will not sit with the wicked. I will wash mine hands in innocency; So will I compass thine altar, O Lord". A similar note is struck in Job 31.6: "Let me be weighed in an even balance, That God may know mine integrity; If my step hath turned out of the way, And mine heart walked after mine eyes, And if any spot hath cleaved to mine hands". H. W. Robinson (loc. cit., p. 54) says: "They may be perfectly true in fact, and yet there is a wrong emphasis in the inner life of the man who utters them. On the other hand, historical exegesis must recognise that the Jew did stand high above his neighbours in moral character and conduct, and that his natural pride before men was accompanied in the Psalms by a genuine and deep humility before God."

[2] Ps. 137.8f. Cf. also Ps. 58.10 (M.T. 11): "The righteous shall rejoice when he seeth the vengeance: He shall wash his feet in the blood of the wicked".

[3] R.S.V., as many editors, has "seize his goods". This does not represent a different text, but a different interpretation. The Hebrew word rendered "office" can mean "office" or "charge" (cf. Num. 15.16), or "store" (cf. Isa. 15.7). The latter would seem to be the more appropriate meaning here, but LXX takes it in the former sense, and Acts 1.20 is evidence that it was so understood in the Early Church.

[4] The Hebrew does not mention "bread" which is supplied to make sense of M.T. The rendering of R.S.V. follows LXX.

[5] Ps. 109.8–12.

of what they had endured. We do not know what suffering provoked the curses of Psalm 109, but we do know something of what lay behind Psalm 137. Read with understanding the book of Lamentations and you may find it harder to condemn the wish for terrible sufferings for the Babylonians than to condemn the atrocities actually wrought in the streets of Jerusalem by the Babylonians. We ourselves are not always full of sweet thoughts of those by whom we have been wronged, or even slighted. Even Jeremiah, in many ways the gentlest of Old Testament characters, could cry for vengeance on his own kinsmen when they plotted against him: "O Lord of hosts . . . let me see thy vengeance on them."[1] But if we should be merciful in our condemnation of those who created and used the imprecatory psalms, we should be resolute in refusing to make them the vehicle of our spirit. Their use in worship is sometimes defended by regarding them as directed against evil rather than against evil persons. J. Mauchline says: "In estimating Psalms which express vindictive and imprecatory sentiments, we should note that they express abhorrence of evil, and are not the utterance of private malice. But even if that interpretation could not be given in some instances of this element in the Psalms, it could be regarded as an illustration of human desire breaking into the act of prayer and throwing into sharp relief the gospel temper and teaching."[2] The examples I have cited seem to be clearly directed against persons, and it seems to me wiser to regard these passages as calling for understanding of those who created and used them, but in liturgical use as warnings against sharing their temper. Much in the Old Testament that is not for our example is recorded for our instruction. Even those who recorded David's sin did not do so for its imitation, but for warning. While that was not the purpose of the imprecatory psalms, and we should in no sense disguise that fact, we can nevertheless use them for warning whenever we read or sing them, making them not the vehicle of our spirit but the

---

[1] Jer. 11.20; 20.12. Cf. also 12.3: "Pull them out like sheep for the slaughter, and prepare them for the slaughter".

[2] In Hastings' one volume *D.B.*, rev. edn, 1963, p. 788b. R. Sorg (*Hesed and Hasid in the Psalms*, 1953, pp. 35ff) goes far beyond this in justifying the imprecatory Psalms and their continued use in worship. He argues that they are mild in comparison with the New Testament, and adduces the ecclesiastical anathemas pronounced on heretics.

challenge to our spirit to rise above them. One who, in the hour of his crucifixion, prayed, "Father, forgive them; for they know not what they do",[1] taught us to love our enemies and to pray for those who despitefully use us,[2] and bade us pray: "Forgive us our trespasses, as we forgive them which trespass against us."[3] On these passages in the Psalms I have written elsewhere: "The less noble ideas that we find in the Psalter may therefore help us to develop a historical sense, to teach that revelation has a climax in Christ and to see that there are some things in the Old Testament which are not for ever valid as the standard for men, though they may always be instructive for men".[4] Above all, we should never see these passages out of proportion, or let them blind our eyes to all that is great and good in the Psalter[5] and in the worship of the Temple.

Worship is not all prayer, as I have said, though prayer is a most important element. In the worship of the Temple there was a ritual element which perished with the Temple and was not transferred to the Synagogue. But in the Synagogue there was a new element which had no place in the Temple. This was the reading of the Law and the Prophets. Outside the Psalter there are riches in the Old Testament which brought new meaning into the worship of the Synagogue and which have been taken over by the Christian Church. For if the Psalter can be the vehicle of man's approach to God, the Scripture as a whole is God's approach to man, through which he instructs and challenges our spirit. Its history is recorded not for history's sake, but that through it the character and will of God might be known. The prophetic words are recorded not so that we might sit in detached judgement on men in ancient situations in which we are not involved, but that we might enter into the heart of God and understand the enduring principles on which individual and corporate life should be based. Running through the Old Testament is the fundamental recognition that in the will of God is man's well-being to be found, and

---

[1] Luke 23.34. [2] Luke 6.27f.

[3] Matt. 6.12 (Tyndale's Version and Prayer Book Version); cf. Luke 11.4.

[4] *Religion in Education*, xii, 1945, p. 39b.

[5] Cf. H. W. Robinson, in *The Psalmists*, ed. by D. C. Simpson, 1926, p. 65: "By spending themselves the Psalmists have all unconsciously bought the gratitude of the world; by going out of their own hearts they have entered for ever those of all devout men."

that men belong to one another and all belong to God. Too often in our day the reading of the Scripture is the least meaningful part of worship, and we receive it with little sense of wonder and awe. We call it the "lively oracles of God",[1] but we do not hear God speaking in it. Yet if the purpose of prayer is to lift us into the spirit and purpose of God that we might do his will, it behoves us to listen to his word. We should also remember with humble gratitude that this great and enduring organ of worship was bequeathed to us and to Judaism by that ancient Israel we too often depreciate.

In the Temple we have found a prophetic element, though the cultic prophets do not seem often to have uttered words of rebuke and of summons to national policy comparable with those of the major prophets. Yet sometimes those other prophets spoke their word in the Temple courts, and we cannot know to what extent the prophetic word addressed directly to the situation of the hour and to the current behaviour of men was spoken there. In the Synagogue there was exposition of the Scripture. This followed the reading of the prophetic portion of Scripture and appears to have often been the exposition of that portion. When Jesus expounded the prophetic word at Nazareth it was to apply it to his own day and to his hearers.[2] The Synagogue gave the Church the sermon as an instrument of worship. It may be used to unfold the spiritual riches of the Bible of both Testaments, to awaken the hearer to the revelation of God of which we have the record in the Bible, and to re-apply the prophetic message to our day. For just as the Psalms could be divorced from the ritual and find a new mission in worship, so the prophetic message can be divested of ancient situations and invested with new meaning in our day.

Many years ago I read the book of Jeremiah with a class of theological students in China. They came reluctantly to the Old Testament as a book that had little meaning for China. Soon they were deeply interested and were finding in Jeremiah much that was relevant to their own country and their own time. I was careful not to apply the book in this way, lest I should be thought to be talking politics in a land in which I was a guest. I tried to study Jeremiah first in the setting of his times and then to see the enduring principles that lay behind his message. My class was able to see the meaning of those principles for their own time in

---

[1] Cf. Acts 7.38 (Geneva Version and A.V.).   [2] Luke 4.21.

their own country. The exposition of the prophets as relevant to our day need not mean a pulpit edition of the morning paper, for that has no prophetic quality. For the prophets were not primarily concerned with right national policies, but with a right attitude to God and with policies that derived from that attitude. They were sure that in a society that flouted the will of God the wisdom of God would not be found. The worship of the shrine must prove its reality by inspiring daily life, where the will of God had to be worked out in human relationships that reflected the character of God. The love that God had manifested to Israel must be reflected in man's love for man. The Covenant between God and Israel implied a covenant between man and man, and the loyalty to the Covenant that men looked for and found in God demanded a like loyalty to one another, as well as to him. For worship is more than ritual and liturgy; it is more than listening to Scripture and to exhortation. It consists in encounter with God and it has corollaries that touch every aspect of life. That is why worship, true worship, is the greatest service man can offer to God and the source of his finest service to his fellow man.

While not everything at which we have looked in this book is on the same level, and I would deprecate any effort to gloss over or idealize all the lower levels, I would assert my recognition of the greatness of Israel's achievement in worship. Many of the forms of her worship have passed away. But she invested the forms with a spirit which has survived them and which is still of immeasurable worth to men.

Index of Subjects

Aaron, 73, 99; and Golden Calf, 51ff
Aaronite priesthood, 50, 99, 100f, 227
Abel, 113
Abiathar, 67n, 72, 73, 78, 95, 201n
Abimelech (Genesis), 16, 163
Abimelech (Judges), 59n
Abinadab, 80n
Abishag, 188n
Abner, 204
Abraham, 3f; a local numen?, 5n;
a prophet?, 69n; altars of, 22f;
and Abimelech, 163; and dis-
honour of Sarah, 34f; and history,
5n; and local shrines, 22f; and
Lot, 7; and Melchizedek, 17ff,
75, 136, 195n; and Mesopotamia,
7; and sacred trees, 16, 23; and
sacrifice of Isaac, 25ff; and Sodom,
17, 34; and springs, 16; and stones,
16; and Ur, 29; character of, 35f;
covenant of, 23, 30f; election of,
38n; encounters of, with God, 29ff;
God of, 14; intercession of, 17,
34, 53, 69, 163; rescues Lot, 17;
Shield of, 14; superior to Jacob, 7,
34f, 36n
Absalom, 204
Accadian psalmody, and Psalter, 249f
Achan, 56
Adonijah, 189n
Adonis, 188n
Adoration, 257f
Ahab, 148
Ahaz, 94, 113, 121, 148
Ahijah (priest), 66, 150
Ahijah (prophet), 148
Ahimelech, 73n
Ahitub, 73n
Akiba, Rabbi, 203
akîtu, 185n
'Al (deity), 19n
'*Al* '*alāmôth*, 208
'*Al n*'*ghînôth*, 209n
'*Al sh*'*mînîth*, 208
'*Al tashḥēth*, 208
'*Al Y*'*dhûthûn*, 211
Alexander the Great, 220
Altar(s), and Egyptian Passover, 117;
at Shiloh, 59f; built for occasion,
23f, 51; east of Jordan, 57; law

of, 52, 60, 76; of Aaron, 51f; of
Ahaz, 94, 113; of burnt offerings in
Temple, 86; of Gideon, 60; of
Gilgal, 57; of incense in Temple,
84f; of Jethro, 51; of Moses, 51;
of patriarchs, 22ff; of Tabernacle,
57; on Carmel, 152; on Ebal, 57;
priests and, 120; site of Temple, 76
Amalekites, 55f
Amarna age, and monotheism, 14n
Amaziah, 158f
Amen, 235, 237
Ammonites, 59
Amos, a prophet?, 159n; and Bethel,
157ff; and ecstasy, 146; and
Jerusalem, 105; and music, 204f;
and sabbath, 90; and sacrifice, 41f,
115f; and the cultus, 1fn; cultic
prophet?, 157ff; liver diviner?, 158
Amphictyony, 48n, 58f
Anathoth, 95, 150
Angel of Church, 233
Animism, patriarchs and, 15ff
Anna, 247
Antioch (Syria), synagogue in, 222
Antioch in Pisidia, 228n, 232, 235f
Antiochus Epiphanes, 218, 220n, 234
Aphek, 55
apsû, 82
Aquila, 219
'*ārar*, 67n
Araunah, 26, 75n, 76f
archisunagōgos, 23f
archōn tēs sunagōgēs, 232
archontes, 232
Ark of Yahweh, 53ff, 66; and Bethel,
59; and Decalogue, 55; and Deuteronomy, 54, 106; and Moses, 53f,
72, 79; and Samuel, 55; and
Shiloh, 54n, 55, 80n; and Temple,
79f; and Tent, 54n; and war, 55;
brought to Jerusalem, 72ff, 77, 173,
191, 196; capture of, 64, 148;
David and, 72, 75, 95, 191; JE and,
54; Joshua and, 54; pledge of
Yahweh's presence, 55, 77, 105;
procession of, 180, 191, 195, 207;
return of, 127; Samuel and, 55;
Song of, 54f; throne of Yahweh?, 79n

Index of Authors

U

Index of Biblical References